Proc

Canadian Rules of Evidence

Fourth Edition

Paul Atkinson,
B.A., B. Ed., LL.B., LL.M.

with contributions from
Daniel Atkinson, LL.B., LL.M.

Proof: Canadian Rules of Evidence, Fourth Edition
© LexisNexis Canada Inc. 2018
August 2018

Library and Archives Canada Cataloguing in Publication

Atkinson, Paul, 1953-
    Proof: Canadian rules of evidence / Paul Atkinson.

Includes index.
ISBN 978-0-433-49570-3

    1. Evidence (Law)—Canada. I. Title.

KE8440.A85 2007   347.71'06   C2007-902424-6
KF8935.ZA2A85 2007

Published by LexisNexis Canada, a member of the LexisNexis Group
LexisNexis Canada Inc.
111 Gordon Baker Road , Suite 900
Toronto , Ontario
M2H 3R1

Customer Service
Telephone: (905) 479-2665 • Fax: (905) 479-2826
Toll-Free Phone: 1-800-668-6481 • Toll-Free Fax: 1-800-461-3275
Email: customerservice@lexisnexis.ca
Web Site: www.lexisnexis.ca

Printed and bound in Canada.

For Bev

Acknowledgments

I would like to thank LexisNexis and their fine editorial staff for supporting this new edition. Special thanks to all the students and professors who purchased the first three editions of the book, especially those who have provided feedback on possible improvements.

My teaching colleagues at Sir Sandford Fleming College have been helpful and I always value their insight. John Marsland and Amy Maycock have alerted me to important precedents that I may have missed otherwise. I sincerely hope all suggestions have been effectively incorporated into the new edition.

My students continue to inspire me, make me laugh and force me to explain potentially complex legal concepts more directly. Whatever clarity you find in this book I owe to them.

Since the last edition was published, the Supreme Court of Canada and provincial Courts of Appeal have been busy creating new precedents of significance to the law of evidence. I have found analyzing some of these decisions particularly challenging since some of the cases have caused splits in the court panels. In several instances, I have again found the dissenting opinions more compelling than those of the precedent-setting majority. My goal has been to present the law accurately where there seems to be some controversy.

My wish is that this text will help you to see the logic in the rules of evidence and stimulate your curiosity for an area of the law that is of fundamental importance for investigators, forensic analysts and advocates, yet is constantly evolving as courts create new precedents and governments tinker with statutory guidelines. I hope that you will forgive me for missing or omitting some of the principles of evidence that others may feel are more important, but trust that you will be captivated enough to continue your own path of discovery in this fascinating legal realm.

Paul Atkinson
March 2018

About the Author

Paul Atkinson has taught law courses in Canadian colleges and universities for over 30 years and worked as a lawyer in Halifax, Nova Scotia many years ago. Paul has law degrees from the University of Alberta and Osgoode Law School at York University and degrees in Economics and Education from Brock University. With this edition, Paul has been blessed with many useful contributions from his son, Daniel Atkinson. Dan is a graduate of the University of Leicester (LL.B.) and the University of Nottingham (LL.M.). He is currently a PhD. candidate at Osgoode Law School at York University and pursuing admission to the Law Society of Ontario.

Table of Contents

Dedication iii

Acknowledgments v

About the Author vii

INTRODUCTION 1

CHAPTER 1
THE CANADIAN JUSTICE SYSTEM AND THE MOST
BASIC EVIDENCE CONCEPTS 3

Three Categories in the Canadian Justice System 3

An Adversarial System 4

Criminal Trials are Skewed Contests 4

A Civil Trial is a Purer Form of Adversarial System 7

The Role of the Judge in an Adversarial System 7

Rules of Evidence 8

Relevance – The Starting Point 9

A Judge's Discretion to Exclude Relevant Evidence 10

Types of Evidence 11

Statutes Mentioned 13

Cases Mentioned 13

Test Yourself 13

CHAPTER 2
EVIDENCE STATUTES 15

Canada Evidence Act 15

Provincial and Territorial Evidence Acts 16

The Importance of Recognizing Whether Federal or
  Provincial or Territorial Statutes Apply 17

Canadian Charter of Rights and Freedoms 17

Criminal Code 18

Controlled Drugs and Substances Act 21

Identification of Criminals Act 21

Other Provincial and Territorial Statutes Containing Rules of
  Evidence 22

Statutes Mentioned 23

Cases Mentioned 23

Test Yourself 23

CHAPTER 3
COURT CASES YOU'LL NEED TO KNOW 25

The Concept of *Stare Decisis* and Court Hierarchies 25
Finding Case Reports 28
Reading Case Reports 29
Supreme Court of Canada Cases 32
Provincial and Territorial Appeal and Trial Court Cases 35
Cases from Other Common Law Jurisdictions 37
Test Yourself 39

CHAPTER 4
WITNESSES 41

The Key Component of Any Case 41
Basic Rules of Questioning 42
Competence to Testify 43
Oaths and Solemn Affirmations 45
Compellability 46
Privilege – When Witnesses Refuse to Divulge Confidential
     Information 48
Warning of the Risk of Relying on the Untrustworthy "Vetrovic"
     Witness 52
Special Treatment for Complainants in Sexual Assault Cases 54
Special Treatment for Children and Witnesses with Disabilities 55
Religious Facial Coverings 56
Test Yourself 58

CHAPTER 5
OPINION EVIDENCE AND EXPERTS 59

Opinion Evidence and the Non-Expert Witness 59
Expert Evidence 61
The Process for Getting Expert Evidence Admitted 62
New Areas of Expertise 64
The Rule against Oath-Helping 68
Limits on the Use of Expert Witnesses 68
Experts and Eyewitness Testimony 70
Gathering Evidence for Expert Analysis 72
Test Yourself 74

CHAPTER 6
CHARACTER AND SIMILAR FACT EVIDENCE 75

Prejudicial Effect versus Probative Value 75
Character Evidence and Previous Convictions 75
Similar Fact Evidence 79
Evidence of Gang Involvement 83
An Accused's Good Character Evidence 86
Attacking the Character of the Victim 86
Character Evidence in Civil Trials 87
Test Yourself 89

CHAPTER 7
HEARSAY 91

The Basic Hearsay Rule 91
The Rationale Behind the Exclusion of Hearsay 91
Exceptions to the Basic Rule of Exclusion 92
   1. The Purpose Exception 92
   2. Statements by a Party 94
   3. Original Declarant Unavailable 94
      (i)   Dying Declarations 94
      (ii) Statements of Mental State 96
      (iii) Business Records 96
      (iv) Testimony from a Prior Hearing 97
      (v) *Res Gestae* Statements 98
      (vi) Statements against Interest 98
      (vii) The Principled Approach 99
   4. Prior Inconsistent Statements 104
   5. Prior Consistent Statements 106
Test Yourself 109

CHAPTER 8
ADMISSIONS, CONFESSIONS AND CHARTER PROTECTIONS
AGAINST SELF-INCRIMINATION 111

Admissions and Confessions 111
Persons in Authority 112
Voluntariness 115
Voir Dire 117
The Effect of *Charter* Sections 7 and 10 118
Narrowing the Protections of *Charter* Sections 7 and 10 124
Clause 11(*c*) of the *Charter* 128
Section 13 of the *Charter* 128
Test Yourself 131

CHAPTER 9
SEARCH AND SEIZURE AND SECTION 8 OF THE
CHARTER.. 133

Balancing Privacy Expectations and Criminal Control 133
Reasonable Expectation of Privacy 134
What is a Search?.. 138
What is a Seizure?... 139
Agents of the State 140
Warrantless Searches.. 142
A Search "Incident to an Arrest"... 146
Other Justifications for Warrantless Searches.. 149
Use of Technology to Search 150
Use of Sniffer Dogs and Reasonable Suspicion 152
Use of Warrants to Conduct Searches... 155
Use of Force... 157
Test Yourself.. 160

CHAPTER 10
OTHER CHARTER RIGHTS AND REMEDIES............................ 161

Right to Disclosure 161
Section 9 of the *Charter*.. 162
Charter Subsection 24(1) Remedies.. 164
Charter Subsection 24(2) Remedy 168
R. v. Grant Rejects a Conscriptive or Non-Conscriptive
    Evidence Focus 169
Actions of the Investigators 171
Test Yourself.. 173

CHAPTER 11
GATHERING AND ORGANIZING EVIDENCE............................ 175

Judicial Notice 175
Certificates and Affidavits – Alternatives to Live Witnesses 176
Documents and Other Real Evidence 177
Photos and Videotape... 178
Demonstrative Evidence 179
Ensuring that Witnesses Attend 179
Test Yourself.. 181

CHAPTER 12
**SOME PARTING TIPS FOR INVESTIGATORS, ADVOCATES
AND WITNESSES**... 183

Investigators 183
Advocates 184
Witnesses 184
Reliance on Notes while Testifying 185
Go to Court 188
Challenge Yourself 189

APPENDIX 1
Key Portions of the *Canada Evidence Act*, R.S.C. 1985, c. C-5
(sections 1-24)... 191

APPENDIX 2
Excerpts from the *Canadian Charter of Rights and Freedoms* 201

APPENDIX 3
Case Report Sample – *R. v. Coté* 205

APPENDIX 4
Glossary of Terms 245

Index 253

Introduction

You probably understand the rationale behind the rules of evidence already. After all, most of us are exposed to the basic concept from an early age.

"Mom, Billie stole the chocolate bar I was saving in the fridge."

"I did not!"

"You did so!"

"Then, PROVE IT!"

Mom, when called upon to *judge* such a dispute, might take the easy way out and transfer *jurisdiction* over the matter to Dad. Whoever accepts the role of arbiter would set certain standards for the type of proof that they would need before anyone will be punished.

"Did you see Billie take the chocolate bar?"

"No, but I know Billie took it!"

"How do you know?"

Feelings, past conflicts, even past "crimes" by Billie of the same sort may not be enough to convince a parent to impose punishment in a situation like this one. In fact, parents, like judges in Canadian courts may refuse to take this sort of information, with its questionable *relevance* and the very real possibility that any and all these matters might be unfairly misleading, into account at all.

Even if a parent is suspicious that the allegation may be valid, it is unlikely that this will be enough to prompt the parent to pick sides in the dispute and start imposing terms of repayment, groundings or the suspension of an allowance. Faced with Billie's denial (if Billie has not exercised a *right to remain silent*), there may have to be a thorough investigation of when the chocolate bar was placed in the fridge, whom else had access to the fridge during the time frame, whether or not the wrapper wound up in the garbage basket in Billie's room, an analysis of the chocolate-coloured stains on Billie's clothing and any number of other bits of potentially *relevant evidence*.

If a parent is likely to be this demanding in requiring convincing proof of an allegation, is it any wonder that our justice system has developed a set of rules, principles and guidelines to assess the bits of information that could become *evidence* in court or other decision-making tribunals, where the consequences of the conclusions reached could result in jail sentences, orders for substantial financial payments, job loss, or other serious ramifications?

Some of the rules of evidence are set out in *statutes*, government-created laws enacted by the federal and provincial levels of government. For example, people working in the criminal justice system will find it useful to go on the Justice Canada website online: http://www.justice.gc.ca and look up the *Canada Evidence Act* (while it is great to get in the habit of finding relevant statutes online, significant portions of the Act can also be found in Appendix 1 at the back of this book). The *Canada Evidence Act* is a fine starting point for understanding some of the rules of evidence, but if you think that this will give you the full picture, you will soon learn otherwise. In fact, despite its hopeful name, this statute barely scratches the surface of what you are going to need to know. Statutes like the *Criminal Code, Youth Criminal Justice Act, Controlled Drugs and Substances Act* and, of course, the *Canadian Charter of Rights and Freedoms*, which is Part I of the *Constitution Act, 1982* (excerpts located in Appendix 2) all contain important rules of evidence in sections that seem to be buried among other laws that the statutes address. This text will point you to the key government-created rules of evidence.

Many other important rules of evidence and principles for dealing with questionable evidence have been developed in court by judges. In our *common law* approach to justice, judges will try to provide predictability by resolving similar or *common* issues in a *common*, consistent way. Each time a judge faces a tricky evidentiary issue, he or she will apply statutory rules of evidence if there are any, and if it is clear how the statute should be applied in a particular real life situation. If not, the judge will have to look to earlier, *precedent*-setting court decisions for guidance. If a thorough search of the case law fails to reveal a useful way for dealing with the issue, a judge may create a new *precedent* that others will follow by applying logic and principles of fairness to decide on the best way to handle the information. This text will discuss important, precedent-setting court cases dealing with evidence issues and the ramifications of these cases for people working in the justice system. These people must conduct investigations, gather evidence and hope to be able to present their proof to a judge, jury, or other decision maker for consideration in arriving at important decisions.

Of course, governments change laws regularly and courts can establish new precedents each time they are faced with a challenging issue. This text will offer practical tips for keeping up-to-date as the law evolves.

The laws and principles that affect the use of evidence in court and other decision-making forums can seem complex and confusing at first. As you read the text, keep in mind your early grounding in the fundamental concepts behind the rules of evidence and look for the logic in dealing with individual bits of information that are accepted or rejected as proof in a trial or other hearing that aims to achieve a *just* outcome. By taking this approach, you will be able to cut through a lot of the complexity. I suspect no one needs to tell you how fundamentally important a sound grasp of the rules of evidence will be for someone who hopes to work in the Canadian justice system.

Chapter 1

The Canadian Justice System and the Most Basic Evidence Concepts

THREE CATEGORIES IN THE CANADIAN JUSTICE SYSTEM

The *criminal* justice system, which is used when society alleges that a person has done something wrong and should be punished, and the *civil* justice system, applying when one person sues another to get financial compensation for harm that has been caused, both use Canadian courts as the ultimate decision-making forum. The processes, documents and *standards of proof* used in the criminal justice system differ from those used when civil justice matters are being settled. This is true even though crimes and lawsuits may be dealt with in the same court building and may even be resolved by the same judges.

The *administrative* category of justice applies to legal issues that are handled by specialty boards and other government-appointed decision makers like the Parole Board, the Human Rights Commission, Police Services Board and the people working for the Ministry of Transportation who decide whether or not you have the qualifications to get a driver's licence. These boards and government agents have their own distinct processes for arriving at fair decisions. Sometimes, the process used looks an awful lot like a trial held in court. Other times, decisions are based entirely on written documents that are submitted or on tests that are performed successfully.

Not surprisingly, the criminal justice system, where the outcome of a trial could easily impact on a person's freedom, uses the most stringent rules of evidence. Additionally, the *Canadian Charter of Rights and Freedoms* protects us all from overly intrusive or unfair interference from agents of the various levels of Canadian government. Since police officers, forensic scientists and prosecutors who gather and present evidence on behalf of Canadian society at a criminal trial are all agents of government, the "Legal Rights" guaranteed in ss. 7 through 14 of the *Charter* provide strict controls over criminal investigations and the use of evidence in criminal trials.

A person who acquires an understanding of the complexity of the rules and principles of evidence applying to criminal trials should be able to quickly grasp modifications that have been made in the civil justice system and by administrative decision makers. In both spheres, the rules of evidence are relatively relaxed. While agents of the government may be involved in some administrative hearings, like those of the Parole Board, the evidentiary issues addressed in the *Canadian Charter of Rights and Freedoms* are a far more prominent part of the criminal justice system and seldom have application in civil lawsuits.

AN ADVERSARIAL SYSTEM

The Canadian court system is known as an *adversarial system* of justice. At its simplest, this means that a trial is a contest between the *parties* (society and the defendant in a criminal case or the plaintiffs and defendants in civil cases). The trial, as a contest with a great deal at stake, involves some complicated rules, including, prominently, the *rules of evidence* that have developed over the years to ensure that the process is fair. Lawyers and paralegals are trained to understand these rules and are hired by the contestants to assist them throughout the contest and to act as *advocates*, promoting the client's position on the legal issue, within the bounds of the rules.

During the contest, the judge serves as a neutral referee who helps to ensure that both sides follow the rules and to settle disputes that may arise about how the rules should be applied. Generally, it is only when an advocate for one of the parties raises an *objection,* challenging the *admissibility* of the opponent's evidence (whether it should be used as part of the decision-making process) that the judge will enter the fray and say "yes" or "no".

At the end of the contest, either the judge alone or a jury will decide who has won, based on the totality of evidence presented through the witnesses called by the competing parties.

CRIMINAL TRIALS ARE SKEWED CONTESTS

In a criminal trial, of course, only the defendant's freedom and reputation are at stake. In addition, the defendant is up against a contestant that has the financial backing of Canadian taxpayers. Police investigators, crime investigation equipment and labs and forensic analysts are publicly funded, as are the *prosecutors*, the lawyers who represent society in a criminal trial. Not many criminal defendants can match those prosecutorial resources in gathering and presenting evidence that can assist in convincing a judge or jury that the individual has not committed the offence as alleged by society's agents.

Clearly a criminal trial is a skewed contest. That is why society must meet the onerous burden of proving the defendant's guilt *beyond a reasonable doubt*. If the prosecutors cannot produce enough evidence to meet the burden, or if the defence lawyers are able to raise a reasonable doubt in the minds of the judge or jury, the defendant will be found "not guilty". The defendant is not required to prove anything. It is never the defendant's responsibility to prove that he or she is innocent. As the Supreme Court of Canada said in *R. v. Boucher* (2005), and repeated in *R. v. Gibson* (2008), the burden of proof never shifts to the accused. Nevertheless, there will be many instances when the defence will choose to present available evidence to the judge or jury that could raise a doubt in their minds about the defendant's guilt.

In order to justify a criminal conviction, the concept of *proof beyond a reasonable doubt* requires a judge or jury to arrive at a decision, based on all the evidence presented during a trial, that the accused person's guilt is the "only reasonable conclusion available on the totality of the evidence". This is the way the concept was explained by the Ontario Court of Appeal in a case called *R. v. D.D.T.* (2009).

Consider a situation like this one: there is a break-in at an office building. The thief or thieves appeared to gain access through a window that was removed from the rear of the building. Computer equipment and a fridge were stolen. When a police investigator checked the window pane that had been removed, he noticed multiple fingerprints, seven of which were clear enough to take impressions. Almost a year later, a youth was fingerprinted and two of the prints lifted from the window were considered to be a "match" for the youth's fingerprints, according to the Forensic Identification Service used by the police. Based on this fingerprint match, the youth was charged with break and enter and theft. At his trial, police testified about taking the fingerprint impressions from the access window and the apparent "match" with the youth's fingerprints. There was no evidence presented of motive to commit the theft on the part of the youth and no evidence of his whereabouts, or opportunity to be involved at the time of the theft. The young person did not testify, nor was any defence evidence presented on his behalf. Do you think that the young person's guilt is the only reasonable conclusion based on this fingerprint evidence? While the fingerprint evidence might be convincing evidence that the youth touched the window at some time, should a judge make the additional inference that he did so in the course of a break-in on a particular date? In the case called *R. v. D.D.T.* (2009), Justice Epstein of the Ontario Court of Appeal said that the youth's guilt was not the only rational conclusion based on the fingerprint alone and a guilty verdict would therefore be unreasonable.

The same principle was applied with a different result in the recent Ontario Court of Appeal decision in *R. v. Youssef* (2018), though not without controversy. The case involved a bank robbery in London, Ontario. There were eyewitnesses and surveillance video, but they were of limited use in identifying the perpetrator, who wore sunglasses, a bandana, hat and gloves. Evidentiary links to the accused, Abdullah Youssef, were supplied through expert testimony that identified Mr. Youssef's DNA on a pocket knife that had been left in an area of the bank by the robber, and more of his DNA on a black t-shirt that had been found in a stolen getaway car that had been abandoned and set on fire. The trial judge was convinced that "there is no other reasonable innocent explanation for Mr. Youssef's DNA" on these articles. Youssef must be the robber. He was convicted.

When Mr. Youssef appealed his conviction, two of three judges at the Court of Appeal level agreed with the trial judge that, "the accused's guilt was the only reasonable conclusion available on the totality of the evidence" (at para. 4). The third appeal court judge was not convinced. As Justice Feldman pointed out, while the pocket knife contained Youssef's DNA, along with that of two other people, it could not have been deposited on the knife during the robbery because the robber was wearing gloves.

Similarly, while Mr. Youssef's DNA was found on a black T-shirt in the burning get-away car, the robber, as seen by eyewitnesses and captured on the video camera in the bank, was not dressed in a black T-shirt. In Justice Feldman's view, "because there is no evidence that indicates when the appellant's DNA came to be on those objects, they do not link him to the robbery". From his dissenting perspective, Justice Feldman was not convinced that Youssef being the robber was the only reasonable explanation for the presence of his DNA on the knife and the T-shirt, and would have been in favour of acquitting Youssef.

If three Court of Appeal judges cannot agree on the application of a fundamental evidentiary concept like proof beyond a reasonable doubt, you might begin to see that the study of evidence and its central role in the justice system creates challenges for people working in the system. While this particular challenge may ultimately be resolved at the Supreme Court of Canada level (a split decision at the Court of Appeal entitles the accused to appeal to the highest court without asking for *leave*, or permission from the Supreme Court judges), consider having to explain rules such as these to jurors, none of whom have had the benefit of the Court of Appeal Judges' advanced legal education or years of practice in our courts.

The issue recently arose in the trial of three railway employees charged with criminal negligence causing death after 47 people were killed when a runaway train exploded in Lac-Megantic, Quebec. Jury members, who had been sequestered at the end of the trial for the purpose of reaching a verdict, returned to the courtroom to ask the trial judge for further instruction on the concept of reasonable doubt.[1]

Justice Cromwell, of the Supreme Court of Canada, had outlined the sort of instruction generally given to jurors on the issue of reasonable doubt in a case called *R. v. Villaroman* (2016): "A reasonable doubt is a doubt based on reason and common sense; it is not imaginary or frivolous; it does not involve proof to an absolute certainty; and it is logically connected to the evidence or absence of evidence." (para. 28)

Clear as mud? It must have been clear enough for the jurors in the *Lac Megantic* case to have found a source of reasonable doubt in the evidence presented during that trial. They acquitted all three of the accused railway workers.

Of course, most members of Canadian society who seriously consider the issue would not really consider it a "win" if a criminal trial resulted in the wrong person being convicted. Because of this concern, the lawyers who represent society in a criminal trial have a moral and ethical obligation "to ensure that justice is done"; even if that means that the defendant is acquitted. As a result, a prosecutor should never really view an acquittal as a loss.

---

[1] Guiseppe Valiante, "Lac-Mégantic jurors fail to reach verdict on fifth day of deliberations" *The Globe and Mail* (January 16, 2018) at A4.

Another way of balancing the inequalities of a criminal trial is to ensure that the prosecutors *disclose* any information that is gathered during the society-funded investigation, prior to the accused person being put on trial. Not only must they disclose evidence that could be used *against* the defendant at trial, but they must also share any evidence collected that would tend to raise a doubt about the defendant's guilt. This allows the defendant to exercise a *Canadian Charter of Rights and Freedoms* protected right to "make full answer and defence" to the charges society is levelling against him or her. In most circumstances, the accused person is not required to make advance disclosure to prosecutors of evidence that he or she may be planning to use.

A CIVIL TRIAL IS A PURER FORM OF ADVERSARIAL SYSTEM

A civil trial is a contest between two or more individuals, all of whom may have hired lawyers or paralegals to help them deal with the complexities of the competition. In a civil case, one of the parties will win if he or she can produce evidence to show that it is more likely than not that his or her position is correct. In other words, the standard of proof is a simple *balance of probabilities.* It is a contest that can be resolved by a judge or jury by the narrowest of margins. In fact, a judge or jury could even decide to apportion responsibility at the end of a trial among any number of parties, so the result could look like a tie, or a pie divided irregularly among diners with varying appetites.

The plaintiffs and defendants in a civil trial are required to *disclose* to their opponents, well in advance of the trial, any evidence in their possession (or that they can access) that could be relevant to an issue that will have to be resolved during the trial. The primary reason for this is to encourage the parties to settle their differences without going to court if they can find some common ground. The secondary purpose is to ensure that neither party is taken by surprise if there is a trial and that the case will be decided on the relative merits of the parties' positions, rather than through trickery.

THE ROLE OF THE JUDGE IN AN ADVERSARIAL SYSTEM

In some parts of the world, courts employ an *inquisitorial system,* where judges play a very active role in directing the actions of investigators who will gather the pieces of information, or *evidence* that will be presented in court and on which the judge will base his or her decision. In the adversarial system of justice used in Canada, the role of the judge in relation to the gathering and presentation of evidence is very passive. The judge allows the *parties* to the dispute, through their lawyers and investigators, to gather the evidence that the parties feel is most important for the judge or jury to consider in arriving at a decision. It is expected that the bias of one party, in gathering evidence helpful to that party's position, will be balanced by the evidence gathered by the other party and by challenges made by the opponent to any attempt to use evidence unfairly.

The judge, as an independent arbiter and expert in the law and legal procedure becomes the *trier of law.* He or she will make decisions about the *admissibility* of evidence (whether or not it is actually used as part of the decision-making process), but usually only if one of the lawyers makes an *objection*, a challenge to the use of a particular piece of evidence his or her opponent attempts to bring before the judge or jury for consideration. It is in responding to objections that judges apply principles and rules of evidence that are laid out in government-created statutes or court-created precedents.

This system puts pressure on the advocates who appear in court representing clients at the centre of a dispute to be competent and have a firm grasp of the rules of evidence. As Justice Charron of the Supreme Court of Canada stated in *R. v. S.G.T.* (2010):

> In an adversarial system of criminal trials, trial judges must, barring exceptional circumstances, defer to the tactical decisions of counsel ... There is a 'strong presumption' that ... counsel are competent in advancing the interests of their clients ... Moreover, counsel will generally be in a better position to assess the wisdom, in light of their overall trial strategy, of a particular tactical decision than is the trial judge. By contrast, judges are expected to be impartial arbiters of the dispute before them; the more a trial judge second guesses or overrides the decisions of counsel, the greater is the risk that the trial judge will, in either appearance or reality, cease being a neutral arbiter and instead become an advocate for one party. For these reasons ... the burden to raise evidentiary issues properly rests on the shoulders of counsel.

If evidence is *admitted* for consideration by the judge acting as a *trier of law*, it is then up to the judge or jury, acting in the second important role as *trier of fact* to decide how much *weight*, or importance is going to be given to this evidence in arriving at the ultimate decision as to whether a crime has been committed, or an injured person should receive financial compensation for a loss.

RULES OF EVIDENCE

Most of the rules and principles of evidence are a set of factors a judge should consider in exercising his or her discretion as to whether or not to *admit* pieces of information as *evidence* during a trial. Some of the rules are set out in *statutes*; many more have been developed as common law, or court-created principles. Let's face it, whenever judges apply statutory rules to real-life situations, precedents are created that other judges will follow when faced with similar situations.

A good example involves s. 24(2) of the *Canadian Charter of Rights and Freedoms*. This very important statutory rule requires a judge to exclude evidence from a trial if it, "... was obtained in a manner that infringed or denied any rights or freedoms guaranteed by this *Charter* ... if it is established that, having regard to all the circumstances, the admission of it in the proceedings would bring the administration of justice into disrepute". An extremely long line of court cases that have wound their way all the way to the Supreme Court of Canada, including *R. v. Marakah* (2017), *R. v. Spencer* (2014), *R. v. Vu* (2013), *R. v. Cote* (2011), *R. v. Morelli* (2010), *R. v. Grant* (2009), *R. v. Collins* (1987) and *R. v. Stillman* (1997) discuss the elements of this statutory rule of exclusion and factors to be considered in applying it to a particular piece of challenged evidence. You cannot begin to understand the impact of this statutory rule without also acquiring a grasp of the court decisions. We will look at the rule and an array of court cases in Chapters 8, 9 and 10.

RELEVANCE – THE STARTING POINT

The first rule or principle is that the information a party is asking a court to consider should be *relevant*. To be relevant, evidence must have *probative value*. This means it must tend to prove a *material* (important) issue in the trial.

What are the material issues in a criminal trial? The identity of the person who is alleged to have committed the criminal act is always a material issue. Evidence that points a finger at the accused, or that might raise a reasonable doubt that the person on trial actually did the deed would be relevant.

The *actus reus*, or actions that constitute the crime as described in a section of the *Criminal Code* or other charging statute, represent another material issue. For example, clause 265(1)(*c*) of the *Criminal Code* states that, "[a] person commits an assault when while openly wearing or carrying a weapon or an imitation thereof, he accosts or impedes another person or begs." Evidence that an accused person was seen carrying a weapon, while stopping pedestrians and asking for money would all be relevant to proving the crime was committed.

If the statute requires the prosecutor to prove that the action was done *intentionally*, then *mens rea*, or evidence of a mental element also relates to a material issue. Clause 265(1)(*a*) of the *Criminal Code* states that, "[a] person commits an assault when without the consent of another person, he applies force *intentionally* to that other person, directly or indirectly" [emphasis added]. Proof of the uninvited application of force to another is not enough to get a conviction. The prosecutor also needs some evidence that demonstrates this action was intentional and not just accidental. Someone who has seen the accused take careful aim and punch the victim squarely in the nose, rather than just seeing someone thrashing their arms around would be helpful in a case like this one.

If there is a potential *defence* available to the accused person, then evidence that tends to prove circumstances which constitute this defence would be relevant. In relation to the clause 265(1)(*a*) description of assault, the application of force could be criminal if it is done "… without the consent of another …". Obviously, proof that the alleged victim consented to a fight with the accused or even invited an attack is relevant on this issue.

In civil trials, *liability*, or whether the actions of the person being sued amount to a legitimate legal reason to be held financially responsible, is always a material issue. Assault is not just a criminal charge. Common law has also established assault as a reason for the victim to sue his or her attacker. Proof of an uninvited application of force, or even of a threat of violence that causes a reasonable fear would establish the liability element for an assault lawsuit.

There are *defences* available to people who are being sued, in the same way that there are defences available to people facing criminal charges. For example, someone removing a trespasser who is reluctant to leave from his or her home may be justified in using a "reasonable" amount of force to accomplish this. Evidence relating to such a justification would be relevant.

The *damages* suffered, or the extent of the harm to the victim is also a material issue for a court that is trying to decide on appropriate compensation, one of the key components of a civil lawsuit. Evidence of time lost at work, or expensive medical care to treat injuries would be considered relevant.

In both criminal and civil trials, the *credibility*, or believability of the witnesses who will be testifying is also relevant for a judge or jurors who may have to choose between conflicting accounts of the events. Many principles and rules of evidence have developed around how an opposing lawyer might appropriately challenge the credibility of witnesses who are testifying on behalf of the other party. These will be discussed throughout the book.

A JUDGE'S DISCRETION TO EXCLUDE RELEVANT EVIDENCE

As Justice Karakatsanis of the Supreme Court of Canada said in *R. v. Grant* (2015), "The truth-seeking function of the trial creates a starting premise that all relevant evidence is admissible." (at para. 18) Yet, our court system has developed not only around strict rules of law, but also on principles of "equity" or fairness. This has a big impact on the rules and principles of evidence. Importantly, judges are given the discretion to exclude relevant evidence if the *prejudice* to one of the parties created by that evidence *outweighs the probative value.*

Consider the example of an accused person who is charged with one count of breaking and entering, where the evidence linking this person to the crime is a little tenuous. Let's say he was located in the general area of the break-in half an hour after the incident was reported. He was wearing a dark balaclava and gloves, but it was winter. Police found a screwdriver in his jacket pocket that could have been used in the break-in and a large quantity of cash in a pants' pocket. The victim reported cash stolen, but was uncertain how much was missing.

Would this amount to proof beyond a reasonable doubt that this accused committed the crime? Seems unlikely, but what if the judge or jury was also presented with evidence that this particular accused had a lengthy criminal record that included several convictions for break and enter? Is this evidence relevant? I suspect that most jury members would find it so. It does relate to the issue of identifying the accused as a person capable of committing a crime like this one. But does it have much value in proving that the accused committed this particular crime? Not so much. But, if the jury had access to this information, does the other evidence start to look more convincing? Have we created such a level of prejudice in the minds of the jury members against this accused that they can no longer fairly evaluate the evidence directly related to this charge?

A judge faced with the decision of admitting evidence of past convictions in this situation would probably decide to keep it out, because the prejudicial effect of this evidence on the jurors' attitude toward the accused would outweigh the probative value of the evidence in demonstrating that the accused had committed this offence. There is a useful example in the Ontario Court of Appeal decision in *R. v. Bomberry* (2010). In this case, an admitted prostitute and crack addict was charged with murdering one of her sex clients. After Ms. Bomberry was found guilty of second degree murder at trial, the appeal court judges ruled that it had been unfairly prejudicial for the trial court judge to admit evidence that Bomberry had been convicted of four previous assault charges. The appeal court judges quashed the conviction and ordered a new trial.

As we will discuss in Chapter 6, there have been cases where the balance between probative value and prejudicial effect has shifted in favour of admitting evidence of past crimes, where the probative value of that evidence in demonstrating that society is pointing an accusatory finger at the right person outweighs the prejudicial effect that is caused. This seems to occur more often when the past offences demonstrate a truly distinctive pattern of behaviour, or *modus operandi*, which has been repeated in the incident that is the subject of the new trial.

TYPES OF EVIDENCE

Evidence is categorized as being *direct* or *circumstantial*. Direct evidence is actually quite rare in a trial. It is evidence that, if the judge or jury believes it, resolves an important trial issue. For example, if an eyewitness were to say, "I heard Paul threaten to kill Zeke, then I saw him pull out a gun and do just that", this could be *direct* evidence at Paul's murder trial. So might a video of the incident. If the judge or jury believes the eyewitness, or is convinced that the video is an accurate depiction of what occurred and has not been altered or tampered with, they could reach a conclusion that a murder was committed by the accused.

Circumstantial evidence is far more common. This type of evidence requires the judge or jury to make *inferences* about the significance of the evidence in relating it to a material issue. For example, in a situation where no one but the deceased and the killer were present at a murder scene, the judge or jury is unlikely to hear any direct evidence (the victim will not be available to testify and the accused has a right to remain silent if he or she was, in fact, the other person on the scene). The jury is more likely to have to consider several individual pieces of *circumstantial* evidence, compiled and presented by the investigators and prosecutor to try to infer whether or not a murder was committed by the person on trial. For example, one witness may be able to testify that she heard the accused threaten the victim two days before the alleged killing. Another witness may be able to show the judge or jurors a gun that was found at the scene. Yet another witness may be able to testify that the gun was dusted for fingerprints and that these were compared with fingerprints provided by the accused. A ballistics expert may be able to conclude that this gun fired the bullet that entered the victim. A pathologist may offer a conclusion that the wound caused by the bullet killed the victim. A bystander may be able to say that he saw the accused running from the scene, shortly after he heard what sounded like a small explosion. Are any of these individual pieces of evidence *direct* evidence that a murder was committed by the accused? No, but if you compile enough of these *circumstantial* pieces of evidence and the inferences that can be drawn from their existence and relationships to one another, a judge or jury may be able to arrive at a conclusion on the issues that have to be decided at a murder trial.

If you watch a great deal of television, you may have been misled into believing that no one can be convicted of a criminal offence if there is "nothing but circumstantial evidence". That is nonsense. Circumstantial evidence that convinces a judge or jury beyond a reasonable doubt that the accused committed the alleged crime may well be better than direct evidence from an eyewitness whose credibility is questionable. People are regularly convicted on "nothing but circumstantial evidence". The truth of the matter is, if a prosecutor discloses to an accused and the accused's lawyer in advance of the trial that there is believable direct evidence that the crime occurred, there will often be no trial. The accused's lawyer may simply try to negotiate a favourable sentencing recommendation from the prosecutor in exchange for a "guilty" plea, rather than fruitlessly fighting the charge.

Physical objects that are used as evidence are often categorized as *real* evidence. In the scenario above, the gun and bullet fragments removed from the victim would be examples. *Real* evidence is also circumstantial evidence because inferences will have to be made to link these items to issues that have to be resolved in court, such as how the gun was used, or the significance of the bullet fragments in deciding how the victim died and/or who did the killing.

It is often handy for witnesses to be able to point to charts, diagrams, maps or photos to help them explain what they saw or the location of relevant items that were discovered during an investigation. This type of evidence is called *demonstrative* evidence, and not only must it be relevant and helpful to the judge or jury in understanding the testimony, it must also be prepared in such a way that it is a fair and accurate depiction of what is being demonstrated.

Unfair distortions would make any demonstrative evidence inadmissible if an opposing party were able to successfully challenge the accuracy of what was being depicted.

STATUTES MENTIONED

Canadian Charter of Rights and Freedoms, Part I of the *Constitution Act, 1982*, being Schedule B to the *Canada Act 1982* (U.K), 1982, c. 11.

Criminal Code, R.S.C. 1985, c. C-46, as am.

CASES MENTIONED

R. v. Bomberry, [2010] O.J. No. 3286, 258 C.C.C. (3d) 117 (C.A.)

R. v. Boucher, [2005] S.C.J. No. 73, [2005] 3 S.C.R. 499

R. v. Collins, [1987] S.C.J. No. 15, [1987] 1 S.C.R. 265

R. v. Cote, [2011] S.C.J. No. 46, 2011 SCC 46

R. v. D.D.T., [2009] O.J. No. 5486, 2009 ONCA 918

R. v. Gibson, [2008] S.C.J. No. 16, [2008] 1 S.C.R. 397

R. v. Grant, [2009] S.C.J. No. 32, [2009] 2 S.C.R. 353

R. v. Grant, [2015] S.C.J. No. 9, 2015 SCC 9

R. v. Marakah, [2017] S.J. No. 59, 2017 SCC 59

R. v. Morelli, [2010] S.C.J. No. 8, 2010 SCC 8

R. v. S.G.T., [2010] S.C.J. No. 20 at para. 36, [2010] 1 S.C.R. 688

R. v. Spencer, [2014] S.C.J. No. 43, 2014 SCC 43

R. v. Stillman, [1997] S.C.J. No. 34, [1997] 1 S.C.R. 607

R. v. Villaroman, [2016] S.C.J. No. 33, 2016 SCC 33

R. v. Vu, [2013] S.C.J. No. 60, 2013 SCC 60

R. v. Youssef, [2018] O.J. No. 140, 2018 ONCA 16

TEST YOURSELF

1. Lou punched Sal outside a local tavern. Sal suffered a broken jaw and several chipped teeth. The police charged Lou with *assault causing bodily harm*. Sal has also started a lawsuit, based on the assault and is claiming financial compensation for the injuries he has suffered.

   Assume that the criminal charge will come to court before the lawsuit. If Lou is acquitted of the criminal charge because the evidence that the prosecutor is able to produce is not enough to convince the judge *beyond a reasonable doubt* that Lou committed the crime, does this mean that Sal should give up on the lawsuit for financial compensation? Briefly explain why or why not.

2. Categorize *each* of these potential pieces of evidence that could be used in the criminal and/or civil trials as *direct* or *circumstantial*:

   (i)   Sal's testimony about what happened;

   (ii)   the loose pieces from Sal's chipped teeth;

   (iii) Sal's doctor's testimony about the nature of Sal's injuries;

   (iv)   photos of the injured Sal taken after the incident by a police investigator;

   (v)   the testimony of a tavern bartender, who overheard a loud argument between Lou and Sal, shortly before the incident;

   (vi)   grainy video of the incident from a security camera monitoring activity outside the front entrance to the tavern;

   (vii) Lou's roommate's testimony that Lou came home and complained that his knuckles were cut up from, "poundin' some smart ass at the tavern"; and

   (viii) Lou's testimony that Sal swung at him first and he simply defended himself.

3. Which, if *any* of these pieces of evidence would be categorized as *real* or *demonstrative*?

4. Using a computer, search for "Supreme Court of Canada – Decisions". When you get to the correct website, you will find that the Court's decisions are organized by the year in which they were decided, then the cases decided in a particular year are split up in several "volumes" of decisions. If you search in the cases listed for Volume 2 of the Court's decisions from 2005, you will be able to find a case called *R. v. Turcotte* (for those of you knowledgeable about *citations*, this case is cited as [2005] S.C.J. No. 51, [2005] 2 S.C.R. 519). As you read through the Court's decision, check to see if there was any *direct* evidence presented at Thomas Turcotte's murder trial. List the *circumstantial* evidence that was used at his trial. Did the jury find this evidence to amount to *proof beyond a reasonable doubt* of Mr. Turcotte's guilt, or was he acquitted at trial? What is your opinion of the jury's finding? Briefly explain.

Chapter 2

Evidence Statutes

CANADA EVIDENCE ACT

Law-making power is divided between the federal and provincial levels of government in the *Constitution Act, 1867*.

Enumerated power 27 in s. 91 of that part of our Constitution gives the federal government power over, "The Criminal Law ... including the Procedure in Criminal Matters." Laws related to evidence are considered procedural, so federal statutes, notably the *Canada Evidence Act* apply when the courts are dealing with criminal charges that arise under federal laws like the *Criminal Code* and the *Controlled Drugs and Substances Act*. As we will discuss later in this chapter and throughout the text, the *Code* and the *Controlled Drugs and Substances Act* contain both criminal charges and procedural rules, including specific rules of evidence that apply when charges under the respective statutes go to trial.

Consistently with the federal power granted in the *Constitution Act, 1867*, s. 2 of the *Canada Evidence Act* stipulates that it applies, "... to all criminal proceedings ...". The Act goes on to add, "... and to all civil proceedings and other matters whatever respecting which Parliament has jurisdiction". The constitutional statutes actually give Parliament (the federal government) jurisdiction over a relatively limited number of civil matters. These would include patent and copyright disputes, bankruptcy and navigational issues and lawsuits against federal government employees. Any of these matters can be dealt with in the Trial Division of the Federal Court.

Technically, the *Canada Evidence Act* also applies to federal administrative tribunals, like the National Parole Board and the Canadian Radio and Television Commission. In reality, the statutes that create the individual tribunals typically specify that the decision makers are not bound by the formal rules of evidence and can consider anything the board or tribunal members decide is relevant. In other words, rules and principles of evidence are not strictly applied in most administrative tribunal hearings. This also means that it can actually be more difficult to predict what will and will not be admitted for consideration when administrative boards and tribunals exercise discretion on individual items of evidence that might be specifically controlled by a statute or common law principles in a court setting.

The *Canada Evidence Act* establishes rules on the use of various types of documentary evidence and on the treatment of particular witnesses, notably husbands and wives of people charged with criminal offences and children and people with physical or mental disabilities. The use of *oaths* or *solemn affirmations* to emphasize the importance of being truthful when testifying and steps that can be taken to compel a reluctant witness to tell his or her story, or to challenge the credibility of a witness are also addressed.

Procedures are also provided to deal with refusals by government agents to disclose information on national security grounds.

Specific sections of the *Canada Evidence Act* will be discussed throughout this text. The first 24 sections of the Act have been included, as Appendix 1 at the end of the book. As with any federal government statute, it is useful to get in the habit of finding the law on the Justice Canada website, where any new amendments to the law will be included promptly after changes are made.

PROVINCIAL AND TERRITORIAL EVIDENCE ACTS

The vast majority of civil lawsuits are dealt with in the provincially and territorially organized trial courts. Enumerated power 14 in s. 92 of the *Constitution Act, 1867* gives provinces the power over, "The Administration of Justice in the Province, including the ... Organization of Provincial Courts ... and including Procedure in Civil Matters in those Courts". Federal statutes have provided the three territories with the same powers. The most common lawsuits, including those that arise from people failing to live up to contractual obligations and from negligence, assault, nuisance, false arrest and a variety of other *torts* (court-created justifications for suing someone) take place in these courts and are subject to provincial and territorial *Evidence Acts*.

Enumerated power 15 in s. 92 of the *Constitution Act, 1867* gives provinces the power to impose fines, imprisonment or other penalties on people who violate valid provincial laws. This would include highway traffic laws, environmental statutes, fishing and hunting controls, liquor laws and occupational health and safety Acts. These types of charges are often called "quasi-criminal", because, while they are not technically criminal offences, which can only be created by the federal government, they are similar and include many criminal law procedural requirements. Nevertheless, provincial or territorial *Evidence Acts* apply to these prosecutions. Consequently, knowledge of the provincial or territorial Acts is important for anyone involved in investigating and prosecuting provincial or territorial offences, or for lawyers or paralegals who act as advocates for people facing such charges.

The statutes of each of Canada's provinces and territories can be accessed online and any of the popular search engines will put you on the right track with a query as simple as "Statutes of Saskatchewan". Most of the pertinent websites will allow you to search for a particular statute alphabetically by title, while others also allow searches by subject matter or key word. While most of the provincial and territorial *Evidence Acts* are called just that, some have slightly longer names, like the *Alberta Evidence Act* and the *Manitoba Evidence Act*. In Quebec, evidence rules are found in *Book Seven* of the *Civil Code of Quebec*.

THE IMPORTANCE OF RECOGNIZING WHETHER FEDERAL OR PROVINCIAL OR TERRITORIAL STATUTES APPLY

While there are similarities between the provisions of the *Canada Evidence Act* and the various provincial or territorial *Evidence Acts*, there are also significant differences. The *Canada Evidence Act* is 54 sections long, while British Columbia's *Evidence Act* is 73 sections and the *Manitoba Evidence Act* is 96 sections in length. There are bound to be discrepancies, and people working in the justice system have to be mindful of which Act applies to a particular proceeding and check the correct statute to ensure that differences are not overlooked.

Even when the statutes address the same topic, different governments may treat the matter distinctly. For example, s. 7 of the *Canada Evidence Act* would require an advocate to ask a judge's permission if the advocate wished to use more than five *expert* witnesses during a hearing (the special treatment of *expert* witnesses will be discussed in greater detail in Chapter 5). Section 12 of Ontario's *Evidence Act* and s. 9 of Yukon's *Evidence Act* would require the advocate to ask for special permission if he or she wanted to use more than three experts. If an advocate overlooked these distinctions and had prepared a case that was dependent on using extra experts, a client's case might be seriously harmed if the judge denied the permission.

CANADIAN CHARTER OF RIGHTS AND FREEDOMS

The *Canadian Charter of Rights and Freedoms* is intended to protect us all from too much government interference. Section 32 of the *Charter* specifies that this part of our Constitution controls the actions of federal, provincial and territorial governments. The Supreme Court of Canada, in a 1997 case called *Godbout v. Longueuil (City)* made it clear that municipal governments, which get their powers from the provinces are also controlled by the *Charter*.

All agents of government, including police officers, prison personnel, customs officers, prosecutors and forensic analysts working in government-funded labs are affected by the *Charter* restraints against interference with personal rights and freedoms.

Subsection 24(2) of the *Charter* directs judges to exclude evidence from consideration in a trial if "... that evidence was obtained in a manner that infringed or denied any rights or freedoms guaranteed by this Charter ...". The subsection adds an important qualifier, "... if it is established that, having regard to all the circumstances, the admission of it ... would bring the administration of justice into disrepute".

The rights and freedoms that relate most directly to legal procedures are nicely grouped under the heading, "Legal Rights" in ss. 7 through 14. Taken individually, the key sections are not overly difficult to read (you can find them in Appendix 1, at the end of this book). For example, s. 8 of the *Charter* says that, "Everyone has the right to be secure against unreasonable search or seizure." Simple enough, right? Okay, assume for a moment that you are working as a police officer and you receive an anonymous tip that there is a meth lab operation in the basement of a house that is located on your regular beat. As you drive by the house, you notice the glow of bright lighting, shining from the basement windows, which appear to be uncovered. Can you get out of the car and walk up to the house to get a better look in the windows? If you do, have you conducted a "search"? If so, would your search be considered "unreasonable"? If this is a search and it is unreasonable, do you think that a judge would conclude that your actions, "… would bring the administration of justice into disrepute", according to the wording of subs. 24(2)? Would this result in any evidence that you discover through your actions being excluded from a potential trial of the homeowner?

Can you even answer these questions without reading the court cases that have analyzed the meaning of the words of these sections in the context of real investigations? Did you think you might need a *warrant* (a judge's formal authorization) before you started an investigation like this one? There is certainly no mention of a warrant in s. 8. As we will discuss in much greater detail in Chapter 9, there are Supreme Court of Canada cases that have analyzed each of these issues. Perhaps you would be surprised to learn that one important precedent has stated that when a homeowner has a "reasonable expectation of privacy", a *warrantless* search would be unreasonable unless "… exigent circumstances render obtaining a warrant impracticable" (Mr. Justice Sopinka in *R. v. Grant* (1993) at para. 29). There seem to be a few more variables that we need to understand!

Applying *Charter* principles to real life situations creates complex legal issues that cannot be ignored. As part of Canada's Constitution, the *Canadian Charter of Rights and Freedoms* is like a super law, capable of overriding any law created by the federal, provincial, territorial or municipal levels of government. For example, in the *R. v. Grant* case, police were relying on a federal statute that seemed to authorize warrantless searches around the outside of a house. The Supreme Court ruled that the federal law went too far in authorizing violations of *Charter* protections against unreasonable searches. That statute has since been replaced and wording in the replacement law is consistent with the legal parameters set by the Supreme Court. Even before the statute was changed, police officers had to alter their investigative procedures to comply with the court precedent that had been set, or risk losing the use of evidence they had gathered when similar cases went to trial. The *Charter* and *Charter*-related cases have had an enormous impact on the way investigations are conducted. People working in the justice system have to become experts in understanding both.

CRIMINAL CODE

A primary purpose of the *Criminal Code* is to specify the behaviours that society has decided are unacceptable and to attach appropriate penalty ranges for people convicted of engaging in these behaviours. The Code also contains a significant amount of procedural law that affects criminal prosecutions, including rules of evidence.

Some of the evidentiary rules are very narrow in application, at times applying to only one type of offence, like s. 133 of the *Criminal Code*. That section specifies that no one can be convicted of perjury (lying in court) on the evidence of only one witness. There would have to be other *corroborative* (supportive) evidence.

There is an interesting contrast in s. 274, which applies to a whole range of offences that involve sexually assaultive behaviour. Mindful of the fact that assaults often occur behind closed doors and that the assaults may not be reported for a variety of reasons until a significant period of time has lapsed, the federal government has specified in this section that "… no corroboration is required for a conviction and the judge shall not instruct the jury that it is unsafe to find the accused guilty in the absence of corroboration".

As Osgoode Hall law professor, Alan Young has noted, "Historically, the requirement of corroboration has been an effective tool for controlling unreliable evidence." Yet Professor Young goes on to quote his law school colleague, Lisa Dufraimont, who has concluded that with limited exceptions such as s. 133 of the *Criminal Code* mentioned above, "…such rules have fallen out of favour and are now essentially unknown to Canadian law".[1] Perhaps this was driven, in part, by an observation of Justice Dickson in *R. v. Vetrovec*, [1982] S.C.J. No. 40, [1982] 1 S.C.R. 811 at 829: "It is, I think, unfortunate that the word 'corroboration' ever became part of the legal lexicon. It is not a word of common parlance. When explained to juries it is given a technical definition, the exact content of which is still a matter giving rise to difference of opinion among jurists."

Sections 276 and 277 are rules of evidence aimed at protecting alleged victims of sexual assault from the use of evidence of their past sexual conduct or sexual reputation as a basis for challenging their credibility during a trial or for formulating a suggestion that they would be more likely to have consented to the sexual activity they are alleging occurred. Sections 278.1 through 278.9 provide a procedure for strictly limiting the use that could be made of confidential medical or counselling records of alleged victims of sexual assault.

Sections 715.1 and 715.2 allow for the use of videotaped evidence of allegations of sexual assault by purported victims under 18 years of age or those suffering from physical or mental disabilities that would make providing live testimony difficult. The witness whose taped testimony is admitted would still have to be in court to "adopt" the contents of the videotape and to be available for cross-examination by an advocate of the accused.

When a qualified analyst produces a certificate of a breath or blood sample analysis of evidence taken from an alleged impaired driver, s. 258 of the *Criminal Code* allows that certificate to be used in court without the need for the analyst to be in attendance. This, of course, is an exception to the way evidence must usually be presented, through a witness whose credibility can be assessed by the

---

[1] Alan Young, "False Confessions: The Attitude and Approach of Canadian Courts" in Berger, Cunliffe and Stribopoulos, eds., *To Ensure that Justice is Done: Essays in Memory of Marc Rosenberg* (Toronto: Thomson Reuters, 2017) 147 at 170.

judge or jury and whose testimony can be challenged through the cross-examination techniques of the accused's advocate. In order to take advantage of this evidentiary exception, prosecutors must provide the accused with a copy of the certificate they intend to use in advance of the trial. If the accused's advocate wants the analyst to be available for cross-examination purposes, he or she must make this request prior to the trial date.

With marijuana legalization, concerns about the need to detect driver impairment generated by drugs rather than alcohol have heightened. Section 254(3.1) of the *Criminal Code* and *Evaluation of Impaired Operation (Drugs and Alcohol) Regulations* address the issue by outlining a 12-step drug recognition test which can be administered by specially trained "drug recognition experts" (DRE). As we'll discuss in Chapter 5, expert witnesses normally have to go through a preliminary qualification process in each trial in which they are called to testify. But, as the Supreme Court of Canada ruled in *R. v. Bingley,* [2017] S.C.J. No. 12, [2017] 1 S.C.R. 170, this legislation overrides the need for such an assessment and a DRE can be called to testify without going through a *voir dire* to assess his or her expertise.

Various sections of the *Criminal Code* deal with search warrants and warrants authorizing the seizure of particular types of evidence. A warrant is an order from a judge or justice of the peace granting permission to a peace officer to take a particular action. The general requirements for getting a warrant are laid out in s. 487.

If time is of the essence and it would not be practical to appear in person before a judge or justice of the peace to get a warrant, s. 487.1 enables peace officers to contact a judge or justice of the peace by phone to secure a *telewarrant*.

Specific *Criminal Code* sections provide legal justifications for warrants aimed at seizing obscene materials (s. 164) and child pornography (s. 164.1) and for conducting raids on locations where illegal gambling is believed to be taking place (s. 199).

Section 487.05 justifies the issuing of warrants to obtain bodily substances from a suspect, so that DNA analysis and comparisons could be carried out, while s. 487.092 enables a judge or justice of the peace to issue a warrant authorizing a peace officer to take steps to get fingerprints, footprints or tooth impressions from a person of interest in an investigation.

Other sections of the *Criminal Code* specify circumstances in which searches can be conducted, or evidence seized without the prior authorization by a judge or justice of the peace. For example, s. 117.02 allows peace officers to search for and seize weapons or explosives if they have reasonable grounds to believe they were used in an offence and the situation is an urgent one, when it would not be practicable to get a warrant.

Subsection 269.1(4) renders evidence related to any criminal charge inadmissible if it was obtained through torture. This is not surprising, since, thankfully, subs. 269.1(1) makes torture itself a crime, punishable by up to 14 years in jail.

CONTROLLED DRUGS AND SUBSTANCES ACT

Section 11 of the *Controlled Drugs and Substances Act* is quite similar to s. 487 of the *Criminal Code*, setting out the requirements for obtaining a warrant to conduct a search and seizure for evidence of drug offences. Section 12 of the Act allows peace officers to "use as much force as is necessary in the circumstances" to carry out these searches.

Like s. 258 of the *Criminal Code*, s. 51 of the *Controlled Drugs and Substances Act* allows prosecutors to use a certificate of analysis to demonstrate the nature of an illegal drug that has been seized, without having to call the analyst to testify as a witness. The prosecutor must provide the accused's advocate with reasonable notice ahead of the trial of the intent to rely on the certificate. If the accused's lawyer wants the analyst to be at the trial for cross-examination purposes, he or she must make that request prior to the trial.

IDENTIFICATION OF CRIMINALS ACT

This very short statute authorizes investigative personnel to take fingerprints, palmprints and identification photographs of anyone who has been charged with an *indictable offence* and to make use of this information during the investigation and while testifying in court. There is nothing in the statute to prevent the use of the information gathered in relation to investigations of other charges.

In spite of the fact that the statute is entitled, the *Identification of Criminals Act*, a person does not have to have been convicted of anything to be required to provide the potential forms of evidence listed. The statute simply requires being charged with an indictable offence and the process is often carried out at the time of arrest. If an officer has chosen to compel the accused person's attendance in court through the use of an appearance notice or a summons, rather than through an arrest, a portion of that document will also require that the accused attend the police station in advance of his or her court date to enable the police to take the prints and photos. A person who fails to appear for this purpose can be charged with an offence under s. 145 of the *Criminal Code.*

Only the federal government has the power to label an offence as indictable, which they do for the more serious charges under the *Criminal Code, Controlled Drugs and Substances Act* and other statutes. If a person has been charged with a *hybrid* offence (one capable of being dealt with as an indictable or summary conviction offence at the discretion of the Crown prosecutor), the offence is considered indictable for the purposes of the *Identification of Criminals Act* requirements.

There is no legal authority to require a person to provide prints or photographs if he or she is facing a provincial, territorial or municipal by-law offence or for a federal offence that is labeled as a summary conviction matter only.

OTHER PROVINCIAL AND TERRITORIAL STATUTES CONTAINING RULES OF EVIDENCE

Provinces and territories have statutes that set out procedural rules for dealing with provincial and territorial offences. In Ontario, Newfoundland and Labrador and some other provinces, the statutes are called, *Provincial Offences Act.* Alberta's statute has a minor variation on the name; it is the *Provincial Offences Proce- dure Act.* British Columbia simply calls its statute, *Offence Act,* while in Yukon the statute is the *Summary Convictions Act.*

Each of these statutes contains rules of evidence. Commonly, subjects such as the type of evidence that can be used if someone challenges a parking ticket are addressed, as may be how the ownership of a vehicle involved in an offence can be proven. Many of the statutes also deal with issues related to the issuing of search warrants and telewarrants.

While many of the statutes cover similar ground, there are enough distinc- tions that a person who will be acting as an advocate, or appearing regularly as a witness in relation to provincial or territorial offences should locate the relevant statute and become familiar with its idiosyncrasies.

We have already discussed federal statutes, like the *Criminal Code* and the *Controlled Drugs and Substances Act,* the main purpose of which may be to control behaviour and define offences and related penalties, but which also contain rules of evidence that may have very specific applications. Similarly, provincial and territorial statutes aimed at controlling traffic on the highways, regulating fishing and hunting and the sale and distribution of liquor often contain rules of evidence. The charging statute should always be carefully exam- ined for these procedural provisions that could affect the way evidence will be presented and might be challenged.

STATUTES MENTIONED

Alberta Evidence Act, R.S.A. 2000, c. A-18, as am.

Canada Evidence Act, R.S.C. 1985, c. C-5, as am.

Canadian Charter of Rights and Freedoms, Part I of the *Constitution Act, 1982*, being Schedule B to the *Canada Act 1982* (U.K.), 1982, c. 11.

Civil Code of Quebec, CCQ-1991.

Constitution Act, 1867 (U.K.), 30 & 31 Vict., c. 3, reprinted in R.S.C. 1985, App. II, No. 5

Controlled Drugs and Substances Act, S.C. 1996, c. 19, as am.

Criminal Code, R.S.C. 1985, c. C-46, as am.

Evidence Act, R.S.B.C. 1996, c. 124, as am.

Evidence Act, R.S.O. 1990, c. E.23, as am.

Evidence Act, R.S.Y. 2002, c. 78, as am.

Identification of Criminals Act, R.S.C. 1985, c. I-1, as am.

Manitoba Evidence Act, R.S.M. 1987, c. E.150, as am.

Offence Act, R.S.B.C. 1996, c. 338, as am.

Provincial Offences Act, S.N.L. 1995, c. P-31.1, as am.

Provincial Offences Act, R.S.O. 1990, c. P.33, as am.

Provincial Offences Procedure Act, R.S.A. 2000, c. P-34, as am.

Summary Convictions Act, R.S.Y. 2002, c. 210

CASES MENTIONED

R. v. Bingley, [2017] S.C.J. No. 12, [2017] 1 S.C.R. 170

Godbout v. Longueuil (City), [1997] S.C.J. No. 95, [1997] 3 S.C.R. 844

R. v. Grant, [1993] S.C.J. No. 98, 84 C.C.C. (3d) 173

R. v. Vetrovec, [1982] S.C.J. No. 40, [1982] 1 S.C.R. 811

TEST YOURSELF

1. Simon was charged with breaking and entering a dwelling on the evening of February 22. At his trial, a friend of the accused, named Garfunkel, provided an alibi defence by testifying that he and Simon attended the opera together on the evening in question.

   Officer Maloney knows that Garfunkel has lied at Simon's trial, because she had Garfunkel under surveillance throughout the evening of February 22. Garfunkel was suspected of trafficking in cocaine and was in the Seahorse Tavern that whole night. Simon was nowhere in sight.

    (a)   Can Garfunkel be charged with *perjury* and convicted on the basis of Officer Maloney's testimony alone? Briefly explain.

    (b)   Provide an example of other evidence that could be used as *corroboration* for Officer Maloney's testimony if Garfunkel is put on trial for perjury.

2. Effram was charged under s. 155 of the *Criminal Code* after his 10-year-old daughter told her school teacher that her father forced her to have sexual intercourse with him.

    Can Effram be convicted of this offence if there is no evidence other than the testimony of the child to prove that the offence was committed? Why or why not?

3. Marta has been charged with sexually assaulting a 17-year-old young man. She is alleged to have fondled his genitals.

    Marta's lawyer wants to call a witness who can testify that the young man is a male prostitute. Marta's defence is that this boy made up the whole story just because Marta was not prepared to pay $200 for his sexual "services".

    Is the evidence of this witness admissible? Briefly explain your answer.

4. Officer Dewdney is working undercover in a local bar that has long been suspected as a hotbed of illegal drug distribution. The officer sees some money and a small glass tube change hands between two people at the edge of the dance floor. The male suspect who received the tube immediately heads toward the men's washroom. Officer Dewdney follows this suspect into the washroom.

    When Officer Dewdney enters the washroom, the only evidence of another occupant is a pair of feet he can see under the partition to a toilet cubicle. There also appears to be some white powder sprinkling to the floor by the feet.

    (a)   In these circumstances, should Officer Dewdney boost himself up on the partition and peer into the cubicle to further investigate his suspicions? Why or why not?

    (b)   Should the officer burst through the door of the toilet cubicle and seize the evidence he suspects he will find in there? Explain why you feel this is or is not a wise course of action.

Chapter 3

Court Cases You'll Need to Know

THE CONCEPT OF *STARE DECISIS* AND COURT HIERARCHIES

Canada uses a *common law* approach to justice. This simply means that judges try to resolve common disputes in a common way. Our courts want the justice system to be predictable and fair to each person that comes before the courts, looking for justice. If one judge rules that a certain type of evidence is admissible, other judges will make every effort to be consistent, admitting that type of evidence in trials that they are conducting as well. If a judge interprets the wording of a *statute* in a particular way, other judges will follow this lead. The first judge to deal with a legal issue sets a *precedent*, lighting a legal path for other judges that will pass that way in the future. Precedent-setting judges make law that other judges will follow. No one can gain an understanding of the law of evidence without acquiring a firm grasp of the important court decisions that have shaped this area of law. Legal scholars, judges and lawyers seem to agree that the law of evidence is actually affected more by court decisions or common law than by the various evidentiary statutes discussed in Chapter 2. This, of course, adds to the challenge of learning the law of evidence initially and then keeping up with the incremental changes that can be brought about by every court decision that addresses an evidentiary issue.

Sometimes, a judge will look at a *precedent* that has been set by another judge and will question the legal reasoning that went into the initial decision. Judges, with their background as lawyers, have been trained to be critical. In addition, lawyer advocates who appear in a judge's court, keen on promoting the best interests of clients, will often make convincing arguments to encourage a judge to deviate from the reasoning of a previous court decision. To what extent are our judges free to follow their instincts if they are confronted with *precedents* that they become convinced are wrong, or unjust? Does our common law system require a judge to follow a path that he or she might feel is leading the justice system astray?

To a great extent, the answer to these questions depends on the *level* of court that set the initial precedent. Not all judges are considered equal in terms of the precedent value of their rulings. There is a clear *hierarchy* of courts in each province or territory of Canada, with the decisions of higher levels of court being recognized as having higher precedent value. A very simple diagram of this court hierarchy would look like this:

Supreme Court

of Canada

∧

∧

Provincial or Territorial

Court of Appeal

∧

∧

Provincial or Territorial

Trial Courts

In our justice system, trial courts, where judges listen to witnesses and get to see and hear the evidence that is presented in order to convince the judge or jury that justice favours one of the parties involved in the dispute, make up the largest number of courts, by far. They are also the busiest courts. This is where all criminal and civil cases start out. While these courts handle the largest number of disputes and, consequently, render the largest number of judgments, they are at the bottom of the hierarchical pyramid of courts, and the precedents set in the trial courts are accorded the lowest precedent-setting value. Another trial court judge who is dealing with a similar legal issue in the future will try to follow the precedent for the sake of consistency in common law. In other words, he or she will be *influenced* by this decision, but will not be legally required, or *bound*, to follow it if he or she feels that the earlier judgment is based on faulty legal reasoning.

If people are unhappy with the outcome of a trial, to the extent that they feel that a legal error has been made, they will *appeal* the trial judge or jury's decision to a provincial or territorial court of appeal. These judges do not get to see or listen to witnesses presenting evidence. They are more likely to simply read what happened at the initial trial in the form of a *transcript*, a written record of the questions that were asked, the answers given and the rulings made by the trial judge. They will then listen to lawyers for the competing parties presenting arguments about what went wrong at the initial trial, or why the trial decision should be considered correct.

The judges at the court of appeal level will usually deal with an appeal as a panel of three. When two of the three, or all three render a judgment that either supports the trial outcome, overturns that outcome, or sends the case back to be re-tried in order to correct errors that may have been made at the initial trial, the appeal court judges set precedents that are of great value. A provincial or territorial appeal court is considered a higher level of court than the provincial or territorial trial courts. Trial court judges in that province or territory are legally *bound* to follow the precedents set in the court of appeal if they are facing a similar legal issue. Let's face it; if a trial judge were to deviate from a precedent set by a court of appeal, this would simply give the party that was negatively affected by this deviation from precedent a legitimate legal reason to appeal the trial judge's decision to the court of appeal anyway.

It is important to keep in mind that each province or territory in Canada is a separate legal jurisdiction. As a result, while trial judges in British Columbia are bound to follow precedents set by the British Columbia Court of Appeal, they are not bound to follow the court of appeal decisions that have been made in another province, say, by the Nova Scotia Court of Appeal. Nevertheless, it is recognized that out-of-province decisions also have value as common law precedents that are worthy of consideration if the local court of appeal has not directed their minds to a particular issue. Common law decisions from out of province or out of territory do provide a discussion of a legal issue and a ruling that will be *influential*, but not binding on a judge in a different province or territory.

In each Canadian province or territory, the Supreme Court of Canada serves as a possible final court of review for decisions that are made by provincial or territorial courts of appeal. People who are unhappy with decisions that have been made by a provincial or territorial court of appeal can ask the Supreme Court of Canada for *leave*, or permission to appeal the court of appeal decision to this last level of appeal in the country. Usually, judges in the Supreme Court of Canada will do a preliminary review of the legal issues involved in the appeal request and decide whether or not the legal issues are of sufficient national importance to merit the attention of this last rung in our precedent-setting ladder. If the Supreme Court of Canada justices refuse the request, the provincial or territorial court of appeal decision will be the end of the road for that particular case. Whatever precedent was set by the provincial or territorial court of appeal will establish the law on that issue for all the courts in that province or territory, and the influential value of that decision in other provinces and territories may be raised somewhat by the fact that the Supreme Court of Canada has refused to review the ruling that was made at the court of appeal level.

If the Supreme Court of Canada agrees to deal with an appeal from a provincial or territorial court of appeal, the decision that it will ultimately make will have the highest possible precedent value all across the country. Not only would provincial and territorial trial courts be legally *bound*, or required to follow a Supreme Court of Canada precedent if dealing with a similar issue, so would provincial or territorial courts of appeal. Again, if any of these lower levels of court chose to ignore a precedent set by the Supreme Court of Canada, this in itself would give the negatively affected party a legitimate legal reason to appeal.

The process of searching for potentially *influential* common law precedents does not end at our national borders. There are lots of other countries in the world where justice systems are also based on common law concepts. Britain and former British Empire countries like Australia, New Zealand, India, Jamaica, the Bahamas and many others follow common law principles. So do courts in the United States. If any of these common law courts have dealt with a legal issue that becomes relevant in a Canadian case, one of the lawyers representing the party that is most likely to benefit from the foreign ruling could bring the case report to the attention of the Canadian judge. The Canadian judge is <u>not</u> <u>bound</u> to follow the ruling from a foreign jurisdiction, but if he or she accepts the legal reasoning behind that judgment as sound, it may well *influence* the way the Canadian judge deals with the same legal issue.

The whole process that we have just discussed of dealing with the nuances of the hierarchy of courts and the reality that some precedents are binding on judges, while others are influential, is known in justice circles by the Latin expression, *stare decisis*. I think a rough translation of the words themselves would mean "to stand by a decision", which is probably a pretty good starting point for labelling a concept that relies on precedents. Of course, it has come to represent a system that is a little more complex in the way it is applied in our courts.

FINDING CASE REPORTS

You should feel fortunate that you live in the age of the computer. Finding *case reports* of important court decisions from Canadian courts has become a whole lot easier since many of those decisions are accessible using some fairly basic computer searching skills. With a little practice, you will be able to find all recent Supreme Court of Canada decisions, decisions made by provincial or territorial courts of appeal and some trial court decisions as well. Using any of the popular search engines and search words as direct as "Supreme Court of Canada decisions", you can get started.

Prior to computer accessibility to case reports, it was necessary to have access to a well equipped legal library. Historically, case reports were published, not by the courts themselves or any government agency, but by private book publishing companies. They would listen to recommendations from editorial boards made up of lawyers, judges and law professors from across the country who would recommend the publication of cases that these board members felt established important new legal precedents. Since learning about these precedents would be important for lawyers and their clients, the publishers knew they could sell their collections of case reports to law firms and legal libraries. These privately published collections of case reports are still available in law libraries and are still considered valuable research tools. Part of the reason for their continued value is that the publishers do a very good job of compiling their collections with excellent subject indexes that make legal research easier. For example, if you were interested in focusing on cases where judges had made decisions about dealing with *hearsay evidence*, you could use the index to quickly locate "evidence" as a general subject category, and then zero in on the subcategory of "hearsay". Relevant cases would be listed with the *citation* information that is used to quickly locate any particular case in the multi-volume set of case reports. *Citation* information tells you the exact page number in the correct book where the case would be found.

An additional benefit of the case report collections that are prepared by private publishing companies is that many of the collections are directed toward people conducting research on specific subject areas of the law. For example, lawyers who specialize in prosecuting or defending criminal cases find collections like that known as *Canadian Criminal Cases* very valuable for keeping up with the precedents from across Canada in their field. There are similar collections in other specialty areas, like the *Family Law Reports* and the *Insurance Law Reports*. Other case report collections focus on important case precedents from a particular jurisdiction, like *Alberta Reports*, while still others may compile all the decisions from a particularly important level of court, like *Supreme Court Reports*.

Today, people conducting computer-based research can gain access to these privately published collections of case reports and their valuable research indexes by paying for access through computer research services like the very extensive service offered in Canada by the publisher of this book, LexisNexis. You may find that your college or university subscribes to this service and the librarians may be able to assist you in conducting research in these valuable sources.

Recognizing the fundamental importance of court decisions in making new law, many of our courts now make their decisions available on their own websites, or that of the Canadian Legal Information Institute (CanLII), which allows public access. The decisions go on to the websites as soon as they are released to the parties that are being affected by the decision. If you were to hear in the media that the Supreme Court of Canada had made a newsworthy decision, you would probably be able to access the full text of that decision on your computer moments later.

READING CASE REPORTS

What exactly would you find when you located the *case report* of a recent Supreme Court of Canada decision? You would certainly not locate the *transcript* of all the questions that were asked and answers given when the evidence in that case was presented in the trial court. Instead, what you would find is a written summary of the case, prepared by one, or several of the judges that listened to the appeal of that case when it came before the Supreme Court of Canada. In the summary, judges provide the "facts" of the case that they think are most important in setting up the legal issues that have to be resolved in court. The judge or judges would then clarify which legal issues they intend to resolve.

At the Supreme Court of Canada level, this would be a brief outline of the issues that caused the appeal of a lower level of court's resolution of the case. Finally, the judge would express his or her *ruling*, or decision on how the legal issues must be resolved.

The Supreme Court of Canada and other appeal courts always hear the cases in odd numbered panels (*e.g.*, three, five, seven or nine judges) so that there will not be a tie among the judges in resolving the legal issues. If the judge who is writing the summary is in agreement with the *majority* of the judges on the panel for this case, his or her ruling will form a *precedent* that adds to our body of common law.

Sometimes, judges who are not in agreement with a majority of the judges that have dealt with the case will write to express their view of the way the law should have been applied in this particular case. Their reasoning would be considered a *dissenting* opinion. The dissenting opinion of a Supreme Court of Canada judge does not establish a *precedent* that other judges would be legally bound to follow. Nevertheless, the dissenting view may stir debate around the legal issue in government circles, or among groups that are interested in advocating for changes to government statutes that could impact on the issue. A dissenting opinion may also trigger lawyers to try a different approach to the issue if it comes up again in future court cases.

Dissenting opinions given by judges at the provincial or territorial court of appeal level may provide a sufficient justification for the Supreme Court of Canada to give permission to appeal that case to that ultimate level of appeal. If you find yourself reading a court of appeal case report that does include a dissenting opinion, it is wise to check whether or not this case was appealed to the next level. The case report you are reading may not be the last word on the state of the law related to that issue. There have been lots of cases where a majority of the Supreme Court of Canada justices have actually agreed with the reasoning of a dissenting judge from the court of appeal, rather than the majority of judges at that lower level.

A useful example is a case called *R. v. Kong*, [2006] S.C.J. No. 40, [2006] 2 S.C.R. 347, which was dealt with by the Supreme Court of Canada in September of 2006. The accused had been convicted of manslaughter in a jury trial. The evidence showed that he had stabbed the victim during a fight between two groups. The accused had testified that he acted in fear and self-defence. The trial judge refused to explain the defence of self-defence to the jury because the judge felt that the accused's claim lacked "an air of reality". The Alberta Court of Appeal had dismissed his appeal, but one judge at that level wrote a *dissenting* opinion, stating that the trial judge should have explained self-defence to the jury, so they could decide whether or not it applied. When the accused appealed the Alberta Court of Appeal decision to the Supreme Court of Canada, the five justices who heard the case agreed completely with the *dissenting* judge at the Alberta Court of Appeal level and sent the case back to the trial level for a new trial.

The Supreme Court of Canada's 2014 decision in *R. v. Sekhon*, [2014] S.C.J. No. 15, 2014 SCC 15, provides another example. The accused was charged with importing 50 kilograms of cocaine that was concealed in a pickup truck that he was driving into Canada from the U.S. Mr. Sekhon's defence was that he was driving the truck as a favour for an acquaintance and had no idea that it held cocaine in a hidden compartment. The Crown called a police officer to testify as an expert on the habits of drug couriers. During this expert's testimony, the Crown asked the officer if, during his 33-year career, involving thousands of drug importation investigations he had ever encountered a "blind courier" who didn't know about the drugs he was transporting. The officer's answers were to the effect that he had never encountered that situation.

When Sekhon was convicted, and the trial judge used this evidence as part of his justification for finding the accused guilty, Mr. Sekhon's lawyer appealed. The thrust of the lawyer's argument was that the officer's testimony about what other drug couriers he had encountered knew about their cargos was irrelevant and unfairly prejudicial in determining whether Mr. Sekhon knew what was in the truck. While the majority of the British Columbia Court of Appeal disagreed, Justice Newbury, in a dissenting opinion felt that this evidence was purely anecdotal, was not amenable to cross-examination and was not proper expert opinion evidence. Justice Newbury would have ordered a new trial.

When the case got to the Supreme Court of Canada, Justice Moldaver wrote the decision for the majority. The majority of the Supreme Court Justices were not prepared to order a new trial, finding that the trial judge had heard enough other evidence to justify Sekhon's conviction, but they did agree with Justice Newbury that this part of the police officer's evidence was anecdotal and should never have been admitted as part of an expert's opinion evidence. Three dissenting judges at the Supreme Court level not only agreed with Justice Newbury's categorization of the evidence as inadmissible, but also agreed with her that the accused should have been entitled to a new trial.

Suffice it to say, when reading case reports to acquire a better understanding of the law of evidence, it is important that you recognize whether you are reading judge's reasoning that formed part of the precedent-setting majority, or a dissenting opinion. It is also important to explore whether the case report you are reading represents the end of the appellate road for that particular case. The Supreme Court of Canada is, of course, the end of the road, but a decision by a provincial or territorial court of appeal may not be.

While case reports from the trial levels of court do not have as high a precedent-setting value as case reports from appeal courts, they are influential on other judges and may represent the only level of court that has dealt with a particular evidentiary issue. As a result, they are part of our common law and cannot be ignored, but again a careful check should be made to ensure that they represent the last word on the issues raised in that case and that the decision you are reading has not been appealed to the appropriate provincial or territorial court of appeal.

There is good news in relation to reading trial level case reports. You do not have to concern yourself with *dissenting* opinions. There is always only one judge responsible for a trial and his or her reasons for deciding the case in a particular way will establish the *precedent* for that case.

You will not find case reports of the trial level of cases that have been decided by juries. That is because jurors are not required to provide reasons for the decisions they make, only judges are. Juries decide issues collectively, behind closed doors and only announce the ultimate outcome of their deliberations — that the accused in a criminal trial is guilty or not guilty or that the plaintiff or defendant should win the lawsuit and receive a certain sum as compensation.

That is certainly not to say that jury trials do not become the subject of case reports at the appellate level. When there is a jury trial, judges are expected to make procedural decisions throughout the trial about the types of evidence that can be presented to the jury (*admissible*) and the evidence that parties would like to use that should not be available to jurors (*inadmissible*). In addition, judges are expected to explain to jurors the relevant law that should be applied to the evidence they have heard, prior to the jury going behind closed doors to start their decision-making deliberations. After the jury renders its decision, a lawyer for a party that has lost at the trial level will carefully consider each of the judge's rulings on the evidence and legal directions provided to the jurors. If the lawyer decides the judge may have made a legal error in these tasks, this will form the basis for an appeal. As a result, you will find yourself reading many cases related to the law of evidence that involve someone claiming that a trial judge either does not understand, or cannot explain the law of evidence very well. You may find it downright shocking when you find that appeal court judges will, occasionally, agree with this assessment of their brothers and sisters in the trial courts.

I think it is wise to keep judicial errors in mind if you start to feel hopelessly confused when you begin reading your first few case reports involving the law of evidence. The concepts can seem complex and even a little overwhelming. It will take you a while to get a handle on the legal terminology that the judges will use when they write these decisions. It may also require reading a fair number of case reports until you can confidently evaluate the clarity of the case report itself. There is no doubt that some judges write much more clearly than others. Do not give up. It does become easier to wade through the wording and understand the most important elements of the precedents that are being set as you acquire more experience in working with this important component of the law of evidence.

SUPREME COURT OF CANADA CASES

Throughout this text, we will deal with evidentiary issues like the use of expert evidence, similar fact evidence, hearsay and the exclusion of evidence due to violations of rights protected by the *Canadian Charter of Rights and Freedoms*.

For each of these topics, there will be key Supreme Court of Canada decisions establishing *common law* principles that apply.

Important precedents can start from humble beginnings. It would be difficult to find an evidence precedent that was relied on and referred to more often than Mr. Justice Lamer's judgment in *R. v. Collins*, [1987] S.C.J. No. 15, [1987] 1 S.C.R. 265. The case started one afternoon in a bar in Gibsons, British Columbia. An undercover drug squad officer grabbed Ruby Collins by the throat and pulled her to the floor of the bar, demanding that she release whatever it was she was holding in her hand. It turned out to be a green balloon, containing heroin. Ms. Collins was charged with possession of heroin for the purpose of trafficking. At her trial, the key issue became whether or not the evidence of the green balloon and its contents were admissible. Of course, without this evidence, it would be impossible to prove possession of an illegal substance and there could be no conviction on the charge.

Ms. Collins' lawyer argued that the officer's actions in securing the evidence amounted to an *unreasonable search and seizure* in violation of s. 8 of the *Canadian Charter of Rights and Freedoms*, which protects us all from such searches. If a *Charter* right is violated during a search, subs. 24(2) of the *Charter* provides for the exclusion of the evidence if letting it be used at trial, "... would bring the administration of justice into disrepute".

During the trial, the officer who had grabbed Ms. Collins explained that he was "suspicious" that she was involved in trafficking heroin in the bar. The trial judge concluded that suspicion is not the same as having "reasonable grounds" to conduct a search in this manner. As a result, the trial judge did believe that Ms. Collins' *Charter*-protected right to be free from an unreasonable search and seizure had, in fact, been violated. Nevertheless, the trial judge admitted the evidence anyway, concluding that to do so in these circumstances would not bring the administration of justice into disrepute, under subs. 24(2) of the *Charter*. The evidence found in the green balloon was ruled to be admissible and Ms. Collins was convicted of the possession for the purpose of trafficking charge.

Ms. Collins' lawyer appealed this result to the British Columbia Court of Appeal. The provincial appeal court judges unanimously agreed with the trial court judge and dismissed Ms. Collins' appeal. Still not satisfied, Ms. Collins' lawyer appealed this decision to the Supreme Court of Canada.

At the Supreme Court of Canada level, Mr. Justice Lamer wrote the majority decision. Justice Lamer concluded that admitting the evidence without having a more detailed justification for his actions from the officer who seized the drugs would bring the administration of justice into disrepute. The Court ordered that there should be a new trial. I am not sure if there ever was a new trial or not. Quite frankly, for people looking at this case as an important precedent, that is quite irrelevant. What is important about this case is that in arriving at a decision, Mr. Justice Lamer outlined and discussed a list of factors that had been developed by provincial courts of appeal for assessing whether or not a particular *Charter* violation would bring the administration of justice into disrepute. This is crucial for any court making a decision as to whether or not evidence should be excluded from a trial under subs. 24(2) of the *Charter*.

The case became a valuable, much relied upon precedent not because of what happened to Ruby Collins, but because Justice Lamer provided a useful analysis of the factors that a court should consider in deciding whether or not to exclude evidence that has been gathered in violation of a *Charter*-protected right. In fact, *R. v. Collins* created the gold standard for deciding upon the exclusion of evidence under subs. 24(2) of the *Charter* and was applied in thousands of cases between 1987 and 2009.

In 2009, the Supreme Court of Canada, being of course the only court that could override this precedent, decided that it was time to narrow the range of factors that should be considered most important in a subs. 24(2) analysis. You should not be surprised to find that the factual situation underlying the important new replacement precedent, *R. v. Grant*, [2009] S.C.J. No. 32, [2009] 2 S.C.R. 353, seems even less distinctive than Ruby Collins' rather violent encounter with the police. Donnohue Grant was a young black man, walking down a Toronto street in the middle of the day when he came to the attention of three police officers. The officers, two in plainclothes and one in uniform were just on a routine patrol in a school area. Young Mr. Grant supposedly drew their attention by staring at them and fidgeting with his coat and pants. An ensuing conversation led to Grant admitting that he had both a small bag of "weed" and a gun. The nature of this encounter triggered questions of whether ss. 9 and 10 of the *Charter* had been violated by the officers and, if so, whether evidence of firearms charges should be excluded from use at trial, pursuant to subs. 24(2). The precedent set in addressing these *Charter* issues has created a new foundation for evidence exclusion analysis and will be discussed in greater detail later in this book.

You will find as you work with case reports that the "facts" of cases that wind their way through the appeal courts to the Supreme Court of Canada often do little more than set the scene. The value of the precedent comes from the legal reasoning and analysis that goes into resolving the legal issues that have to be decided. In a very real sense, the people and the legal problems that got them into court in the first place fade into the background as the judges wrestle with the legal issues.

As someone planning a career in the justice system, it will be helpful for you if you can pinpoint the important rule of evidence, or other legal principle that forms the precedent from a case report. It will be even more helpful if you can imagine how this precedent will be applied in a real life situation you may encounter as an investigator, or an advocate for someone immersed in the trial processes. It is important to realize that the precedent will probably have a much broader application than the narrow parameters of the specific "fact" situation behind the case report itself.

PROVINCIAL AND TERRITORIAL APPEAL AND TRIAL COURT CASES

In evolving areas of the law, it is possible that an issue may not have been dealt with at the level of the Supreme Court of Canada, where a precedent could be set that would have application across the country. That does not mean that decisions from "lower" levels of court will not be helpful and influential for judges who will be dealing with similar issues and for people working in the justice system who require some guidance in preparing cases of their own.

Video and computer technology has made it possible to produce videotaped *re-enactments* and computer-generated *re-creations* of events that may involve crucial elements of a case that is before the courts. It is tempting for investigators and lawyers to make use of this technology to demonstrate their version of what transpired to help clarify the event for the judge or jurors who must base their decision on the evidence related to them of the past event.

The Ontario Court of Appeal decision in a case called *R. v. MacDonald*, [2000] O.J. No. 2606, 146 C.C.C. (3d) 525 (C.A.) dealt with a situation where police officers produced a videotaped "re-enactment" of a controversial incident that formed the basis for charges of aggravated assault and dangerous driving against one of the accused. The police had prepared the videotape without input from the accused, who testified that events transpired significantly differently. The so-called re-enactment was prepared months after the event at a different location, different time of day, using different vehicles and with events occurring much slower than during the actual incident. The trial judge had allowed the prosecutor to show the videotape with commentary from one of the police officers involved in the incident, ruling that it would help the jury by clarifying relative positions of the parties, fields of view and the testimony of the officer.

The Ontario Court of Appeal in a unanimous decision of three judges ruled that while any videotaped re-enactment would have to be assessed on a case-by-case basis, this one should not have been admitted. They found that because of the inaccuracies in the re-enactment, it had little or no probative value and that it was highly prejudicial to the accused. "The video permitted the prosecution to put before the jury its own version of what occurred, distilled into a neatly packaged, compressed, and easily assimilated sight and sound bite. The violent, visual and highly impressionistic imagery gave the Crown an unfair advantage in this trial". (Laskin J.A. at para. 48) The decision would provide someone considering the use of video re-enactment a useful guideline on what not to do in its production.

It seems that finding a provincial or territorial appeal court decision is tougher when the use of computer-generated re-enactments is the issue. There are some trial court decisions on point, however. *Green v. Winnipeg (City) Police Department*, [1996] M.J. No. 219, 109 Man. R. (2d) 168 (Q.B.), was a Manitoba Court of Queen's Bench trial that involved a lawsuit against the police. Mr. Green was paralyzed in an incident in which a police officer used some force to subdue him. The lawyers representing the police wanted to use a computer re-creation depicting their version of how the police officer would have subdued the plaintiff. Justice MacInnes of the Manitoba Court of Queen's Bench felt the depiction of the scenario was not sufficiently reliable and that it could be misleading and prejudicial.

In *R. v. Suzack*, [1995] O.J. No. 4237, 5 O.T.C. 12 (Gen. Div.), a murder case, an Ontario trial judge allowed a pathologist to use a computer-generated video to illustrate bullet wounds and injuries suffered by the victim. The pathologist was able to testify about the accuracy of the depiction and the judge felt that this computer-generated image would actually be less prejudicial to the accused than bloody photos taken of the corpse of the victim.

R. v. Hinkley, [2011] A.J. No. 1012, 2011 ABQB 567 is a trial level decision of Justice Marshall of the Alberta Court of Queen's Bench. It deals with the intriguingly worded s. 714.1 of the *Criminal Code* which states: "A court may order that a witness in Canada give evidence by means of technology that permits the witness to testify elsewhere in Canada in the virtual presence of the parties and the court ...". Justice Marshall was being asked by the Crown to use this section to allow a toxicology expert to testify in an impaired driving case being heard in Wetaskiwin, Alberta via video link from her office in Manitoba. The defence lawyer opposed this, believing it would limit his ability to effectively cross examine this expert if she wasn't physically in the courtroom.

Justice Marshall commented that, "Judicial commentary on this provision has been somewhat limited." (para. 5). In other words, there weren't many previous precedents on how this section should be applied and all the ones that were available seemed to be other trial level decisions. In spite of the fact that none of these would be binding on Justice Marshall, the judge found several of them useful, including a decision from out of province, *R. v. Young*, [2000] S.J. No. 590, 2000 SKQB 419, and one from an Alberta provincial court, a lower trial level court than Justice Marshall's own, *R. v. Denham*, [2010] A.J. No. 1435, 2010 ABPC 82.

Relying on the rationale from these cases, Justice Marshall ruled that it would be appropriate to allow for the remote testimony in this situation. Citing agreement with yet another provincial trial level case from Ontario, *R. v. Allen*, [2007] O.J. No. 1780, 2007 ONCJ 209, Justice Marshall commented that the "face-on view" of the witness that would be available through the video feed, "... is often superior to the traditional physical arrangements found in many courtrooms when the judge views witness demeanor and assesses credibility". (para. 17)

Judge Jackson of New Brunswick's Provincial Court followed the *Hinkley* rationale in *R. v. Burtt*, [2012] N.B.J. No. 43, 2012 NBPC 6. An alleged assault victim named Foster had moved to Ontario and the Crown sought to have her testify by video link from that province. The victim had limited financial resources. The trial judge noted that: "[e]Even though the travel expenses would eventually be reimbursed by the Province of New Brunswick, it appears that Foster does not have a credit card or the necessary financial capability to pay those costs 'up front'". (para. 8). Why the prosecutor couldn't make the travel arrangements wasn't really addressed, but the trial judge was inclined to grant the Crown's request for testimony via video link "I share the view expressed in *Hinkley*, that while effective communication is critical, technological advances have made it possible to view and assess a witness's demeanour as effectively through videoconferencing as is the case in personal attendance." (para. 13)

In *R. v. S.D.L.*, [2017] N.S.J. No. 247, 2017 NSCA 58, Chief Justice MacDonald of the Nova Scotia Court of Appeal had to consider the use of a video link that allowed a 15-year-old witness to testify from another province about sexually inappropriate touching that had allegedly been done to him when he was seven. The video link involved serious technical difficulties, with the screen freezing, disrupting the flow of both direct examination and cross-examination. In these circumstances, the Court of Appeal ruled that the accused's right to make full answer and defence was jeopardized, and ordered a new trial. In doing so, the Court of Appeal laid out eight guidelines for trial judges in assessing whether video evidence should be permitted under s. 714.1 of the *Criminal Code* (R.S.C. 1985, c. C-46). One was that when credibility of the witness is a key trial issue, as it was in this case, video evidence should only be allowed in exceptional circumstances.

Even though decisions like these may not be binding on another judge, their influential value and the utility for people trying to gain a better understanding about the way courts may deal with this type of evidence is evident.

CASES FROM OTHER COMMON LAW JURISDICTIONS

Court decisions from other countries that follow the common law approach to justice have been influential in formulating Canadian precedents in the past and will undoubtedly continue to do so in the future. Back in 2010, the Ontario Court of Appeal decision in *R. v. S. (N.)*, [2010] O.J. No. 4306, 102 O.R. (3d) 161 (C.A.) dealt with the interesting issue of whether or not a female Muslim witness should be entitled to wear a niqab, or veil, when testifying in a criminal case. Canada is not the only country that has grappled with this question. In analyzing the issue, Justice Doherty of the Ontario Court of Appeal discusses court decisions from both New Zealand, *Police v. Razamjoo*, [2005] D.C.R. 408 and a District Court in Western Australia, *R. v. Anwar Sayed* (19 August 2010), Perth 164/2010 (W.A.D.C.). When the Ontario Court of Appeal decision was further appealed to the Supreme Court of Canada, Chief Justice McLachlin again relied on comments made by the judge in the New Zealand case of *Razamjoo* in formulating the Supreme Court's majority decision (*R. v. S. (N.)*, [2012] S.C.J. No. 72, 2012 SCC 72).

A very useful illustration of the influence of foreign decisions on the Canadian law of evidence can be found in the development of the way our criminal courts have dealt with *similar fact* evidence, which will be discussed in greater detail in Chapter 6. *Similar fact* evidence is evidence that a person who is charged with a particular offence has been involved in similar types of activities in the past. This type of evidence is usually excluded from a trial because the prejudice that it creates to the accused person in the minds of a judge or jury is far greater than any value that evidence may have in proving that the accused person committed the specific crime for which he or she is now on trial. For example, if the prosecution is allowed to produce evidence that an accused has formerly been convicted of 10 robberies, are they going to focus on the evidence that demonstrates whether or not he committed a new robbery, or are they simply going to focus on the fact that he has been a robber in the past, and so he probably did this one too?

Nevertheless, there are common law exceptions to the general principle that similar fact evidence would be kept out of a trial. Sometimes Canadian judges will decide to let this type of evidence in. The exceptions actually started with a case that arose in Australia, called *Makin v. Attorney-General for New South Wales*, [1894] A.C. 57 (P.C.). At the time, cases from Australia (like those from Canada) could be appealed to the Privy Council in England. This "foreign" decision has been a foundation of the development of the law in Canada for over a hundred years, being discussed again by Justice Binnie of the Supreme Court of Canada in 2002 in a very important precedent called, *R. v. Handy*, [2002] S.C.J. No. 57, [2002] 2 S.C.R. 908. Additional English precedents, including *Director of Public Prosecutions v. Boardman*, [1975] A.C. 421 (H.L.) and *R. v. Straffen*, [1952] 2 Q.B. 911 (C.C.A.) have also been very influential, and often cited by Canadian judges as the common law has developed in this country. Interestingly, the British precedents have remained influential in Canada even after the government in the United Kingdom statutorily adopted a different approach to "bad character" evidence with the legislated "gateways" to admission stipulated in s. 98 of their *Criminal Justice Act 2003*.

In 2013, Justice Clark of Ontario's Superior Court of Justice was dealing with a Toronto murder case where the Crown alleged that the victim was killed because he was a member of a rival street gang who had encroached on the territory of the gang to which the alleged killers belonged. The Crown wanted the judge to admit YouTube videos in which the perpetrators had participated and rap song lyrics and other written materials that were purported to demonstrate the accuseds' gang membership, threats to kill and derogatory terms they had used for the rival gang to which the victim belonged. In ruling on the admissibility of this evidence, Justice Clark commented: "Given the paucity of Canadian cases concerning written material related to street gangs, as I did in the original ruling respecting the admissibility of YouTube videos, I have referred to a number of American authorities on point." (*R. v. Williams*, [2013] O.J. No. 2421, 2013 ONSC 3100 at para. 50). Justice Clark then cited 10 American cases, including *People v. Toluao*, 2012 Cal. App. Unpub. LEXIS 7209 (C.A.), in support of a decision to admit the evidence.

TEST YOURSELF

1. Kelly Marie Ellard was a teenager, who was charged with murdering another young teen in British Columbia in 1997. The Supreme Court of Canada dealt with her case in 2009. Use a computer to locate the case report (a small hint — you will find it in the second volume of the Supreme Court Reports of 2009). Why was this case still in the court system in 2009, 12 years after the event? What legal error did the lawyers representing Ms. Ellard claim was made by the judge at her most recent trial? How did the Supreme Court of Canada deal with this appeal? Did any of the Supreme Court of Canada judges dissent from the decision of the majority? Was a new trial for Ms. Ellard possible so long after the original incident?

2. The Ontario Court of Appeal released a decision in the case of *R. v. Ricketts*, [2010] O.J. No. 5196, 2010 ONCA 820 on December 2, 2010. Use a computer to locate the court decision. What charge was the accused facing? According to the Ontario Court of Appeal, what error did the trial judge make in deciding to convict the accused, Kevin Ricketts? Did the Ontario Court of Appeal overturn the trial judge's decision? Why or why not?

3. Use a computer to locate a trial level case report from your province or territory. If possible, try to locate a case that deals with an evidence issue.

4. Locate and read the Ontario Court of Appeal decision in *R. v. Atkinson*, [2012] O.J. No. 2520, 2012 ONCA 380 (No, the accused is NOT the author of this book!). What was the key piece of evidence involved in this case? What other legal issues came into play in arriving at the decision as to whether or not this evidence should have been admitted for consideration at trial? Is the Court of Appeal in agreement with the way the trial judge handled these issues?

Chapter 4

Witnesses

THE KEY COMPONENT OF ANY CASE

It does not matter if you literally have the smoking gun, a great diagram of the crime scene, fingerprints, photographs, video or audio tapes, saliva, semen or other great DNA to analyze — you need witnesses to get any of this evidence into court. One witness or several witnesses must bring the evidence to court and explain what it is, where it came from, how it was processed, how it relates to the issues that must be decided in the case. Each witness must also explain his or her involvement in the case and how he or she came to know the things that are being presented to the judge or jury for their consideration.

Our criminal and civil trials involve a form of storytelling, where one side will outline the version of the story that they hope the judge or jury believes, while the other side will attack the accuracy of that version and/or offer an alternative story. The story must be told through witnesses. Our system is based on the judge or jury being able to determine which story, or which portions of conflicting stories most closely represent a true account of an event, or series of events that have brought the matter to court.

The lawyer or agent who is acting as the prosecutor, advocate for a plaintiff in a civil case or a defendant in a criminal or civil case must take on the roles of producer and director for the storytelling on behalf of the client. Nothing these advocates might say in court is considered evidence on which a judge or jury can base a decision. Only information delivered by a witness with some helpful knowledge of the case is evidence worthy of inclusion in the decision-making process. The advocates must select the witnesses, organize the order in which they will testify and then develop a set of questions that will encourage these witnesses to tell the story as clearly and convincingly as possible. In a way, this job is much tougher than that of a movie director or producer. Advocates are not working with professional actors, nor do they get to write the lines for the witnesses. They must encourage these witnesses to tell the truth as they know it. Through pre-trial meetings and preparation, the advocate can help shape the way the evidence is expressed, but the advocate does not control the content of the knowledge of the case that the witness possesses. That is what the witness will be called upon to share with the judge or judge and jury.

BASIC RULES OF QUESTIONING

The lawyer or agent who calls upon a witness to testify cannot use *leading* questions to extract evidence from that witness on *material issues*. What is a leading question? A question that suggests a particular answer is a leading question. For example, "The car you saw was blue wasn't it?" is a question that clearly suggests a state of affairs to the person to whom the question is directed. If the colour of the car was an important (*material*) issue in identifying a particular car that was involved in an accident the witness had seen, it would be *objectionable* for the advocate who called upon that witness to ask the question in this way. I suspect you could think of a non-leading question or series of questions that a witness could be asked to ensure that the colour of the car was being provided by the witness, rather than by the advocate asking the questions.

You should realize that it is not being unnecessarily picky to restrict questioning in this way. It is simply done to ensure that key pieces of evidence are a reflection of what the witness actually saw, heard, experienced, or knows from investigative efforts that he or she has made, and not what an advocate wants that individual to say to best contribute to the position the advocate is trying to promote. Realize that there is nothing unethical or illegal about the advocate meeting in advance with a witness he or she intends to call, going over potential questions and the answers the witness would truthfully provide. In this way, a lawyer or agent should be able to ask open-ended (non-leading) questions and be confident about the answers he or she will hear from the properly prepared witness.

In order to speed up the process of testifying, lawyers and agents can ask their own witnesses leading questions on background, non-material issues. For example, a lawyer or agent might start with questions like this to ease a witness into her testimony:

"Your name is Martha Johnson?" or

"You work as a detective with the Peel Regional Police?"

You can usually recognize a leading question as one that will simply require a "yes" or "no" answer from the witness. With the examples given, this background information tells the judge or jurors something about the person who is going to provide the evidence, but the answers will not affect important (material) issues that have to be decided in the case. Once the lawyer or agent gets to that stage of the testimony, the leading questions will have to stop or the opposing lawyer or agent will object. A judge will sustain the objection and direct the advocate to ask questions that do not suggest preferred answers to the witness.

After a witness has provided the key evidence he or she is there to deliver in response to open-ended questions from the lawyer or agent that called this witness, the witness will be asked to remain in the witness box. The opposing lawyer or agent will be given an opportunity to *cross-examine* the witness. The purpose of *cross-examination* is to challenge the accuracy of the evidence that has been provided, or to suggest alternative views of the witness's evidence that the witness may not have considered but may be prepared to accept. The opposing lawyer may also wish to challenge the basic *credibility* of the witness. In other words, is the witness telling the truth? Should the judge or jury trust what this witness has to say?

Lawyers and agents who are cross-examining a witness are allowed to ask leading questions. In fact, that is the accepted technique that advocates will be trained to adopt when they work at formulating questions to challenge the evidence of an opponent's witness. It is pretty hard to challenge a witness, or to suggest alternative ways of viewing the witness's evidence without being allowed to ask questions that suggest a particular answer. Leading questions are definitely not *objectionable* during cross-examination.

COMPETENCE TO TESTIFY

Before an advocate calls upon any witness to provide evidence in court, it is necessary to give some thought to whether or not that person will be considered *competent* to testify. The Supreme Court of Canada dealt with the issue of competence in 1993 in a case called, *R. v. Marquard*, [1993] S.C.J. No. 119, [1993] 4 S.C.R. 223. The key to determining if a particular witness is competent to provide evidence is as simple as assessing whether or not that person has the *capacity* to perceive an event (observe and interpret what has happened), remember what he or she has experienced and be able to communicate this experience to the judge or jury. For the purposes of a court proceeding, it is also important that the potential witness promises to tell the truth. The *Marquard* case represents a common law expansion or explanation of the statutory tests for competence laid out in s. 16 of the *Canada Evidence Act* and similar provisions in provincial and territorial evidence statutes. The statutes allow a judge to conduct an inquiry into competence if a potential witness is young or a mentally challenged adult and one of the parties has made a motion asking the judge to assess the witness's competence.

Canadian judges will *presume* that a witness who is called upon to testify in court is *competent*. If one of the advocates wishes to challenge a potential witness's competence, the issue must be raised with the judge. If there is a reasonable basis for the challenge the judge will then conduct an inquiry to assess the witness's abilities to perceive, remember and communicate. This will occur before the witness begins his or her relevant testimony.

Testing of the witness's competence is done by asking the witness a series of questions, the answers to which could demonstrate a general capacity to perceive, remember and communicate. Since it has not yet been determined whether this witness will be allowed to provide evidence related to the trial issues, the questions will steer clear of specifically relevant events. For example, with a witness who has been called to describe the events surrounding an assault she witnessed two years ago, preliminary questions testing competence might ask the witness where she celebrated her birthday two years ago, what she did on that occasion and with whom. While the answers will do nothing to shed light on this particular court case, they may be a reasonable method of assessing the witness's competence to testify.

The evidence statutes, including s. 6 of the *Canada Evidence Act* aim to remove barriers created by a potential witness's physical limitations by providing that, "… the court may order that the witness be permitted to give evidence by any means that enables the evidence to be intelligible". A sign language interpreter could assist a mute person in testifying, or technological devices like laptop computers and projection screens could be used.

Section 14 of the *Canadian Charter of Rights and Freedoms* provides that a party or witness, "… who does not understand or speak the language in which the proceedings are conducted or who is deaf has the right to the assistance of an interpreter". Court cases have recognized that everyone who claims to need an interpreter may not be doing so legitimately. There can be practical problems in assessing the credibility of a witness who is testifying through an interpreter. Some lawyers will argue that the intervention of an interpreter can lessen the effectiveness of cross-examination. As a result, it is open to a lawyer to challenge a claim that a particular witness needs the assistance of an interpreter. If this happens, the judge will conduct an inquiry to ensure that the services of an interpreter really are required for the witness to understand what is going on and/or to communicate.

Section 3 of the *Canada Evidence Act* contains a strange double negative that would have driven my high school English teacher crazy, "[a] person is not incompetent to give evidence by reason of interest or crime." What the heck does this mean and why would a government feel the need to put it into an evidence statute? It means that people with a financial interest in the outcome of a case and people who have been convicted of or charged with criminal behaviour are entitled to testify. At one time, common law cases made it clear that courts were not prepared to listen to the testimony of witnesses like these. In other words, under the old precedents, an accused would not have been allowed to testify at his or her own trial, nor would someone who was alleged to have been an accomplice. In civil trials, anyone with a financial interest in the outcome would have been excluded. This, of course, would often have made it impossible for either the plaintiff or the defendant to give evidence. On a more positive note, if these precedents still represented the state of the law, some of the very questionable testimony of jailhouse "informants" that has contributed to a number of notorious wrongful convictions might never have been admitted. The rationale behind the old precedents was simply that this type of witness was too untrustworthy to even consider any evidence he or she might provide. Section 3 and its provincial and territorial equivalents (some provinces, like Manitoba use the same strange wording that is found in the federal statute, while others accomplish the same thing with better grammar) eliminated these common law barriers. Today, the competence of an accused, an accomplice or someone with a financial interest in the outcome of the case would be evaluated using the same criteria that would be applied to any other witness.

OATHS AND SOLEMN AFFIRMATIONS

Section 16 of the *Canada Evidence Act* and similar provincial and territorial provisions stipulate that an inquiry into competence should include an assessment of whether or not the witness understands, "... the nature of an *oath* or a *solemn affirmation*" [emphasis added]. Subsection 16(3) of the Act adds that a witness who is able to communicate but, "... does not understand the nature of an oath or a solemn affirmation ..." may testify, "... on promising to tell the truth". Section 16.1(2) of the *Canada Evidence Act* streamlines the process for child witnesses (under 14) by eliminating the use of an oath or solemn affirmation altogether.

These statutory provisions recognize an historical evolution in the justice system that reflects a trend in society away from nearly universal beliefs in a Supreme Being and the spiritual and religious consequences people would have expected if they were to lie in court. Canadian common law cases from the early 1900s show that people who did not believe in a Supreme Being, or who did not believe that lying would result in some sort of punishment from this Being were simply not considered competent to testify. The sentiment was that any testimony such a witness provided would be too untrustworthy for a court to consider.

An *oath* involves a potential witness swearing to tell the truth while holding or touching a religious document or symbol that has significance for the individual (*i.e.*, Bible, Qur'an, *etc.*). Over the years, Canadian judges have recognized that even people who are not particularly religiously oriented could accept the significance of an oath. As Justice MacKinnon of the Ontario Court of Appeal said back in 1982 in *R. v. F. (K.J.)*, [1982] O.J. No. 153 at para. 28, 1 C.C.C. (3d) 370 (C.A.): "Those adults to whom the sanctity of the oath has lost its religious meaning, nonetheless have a sense of moral obligation to tell the truth on taking the oath and feel their conscience bound by it."

A witness who objects to using any religious symbolism can simply give a *solemn affirmation*. The form of the affirmation is provided in subs. 14(1) of the *Canada Evidence Act*: "I solemnly affirm that the evidence to be given by me shall be the truth, the whole truth and nothing but the truth."

If it becomes clear that a witness does not understand the concepts behind an oath or solemn affirmation, the judge can still allow that witness to testify if he or she promises to tell the truth. In *R. v. I. (D.A.)*, [2012] S.C.J. No. 5, 2012 SCC 5, a case involving the alleged sexual assault of a 26-year-old complainant who had the mental capacity of very young child, a majority of the Supreme Court ruled that it was an error for the trial judge to engage the witness in an abstract inquiry into an understanding of a duty to speak the truth. While an inquiry into her capacity, or ability to communicate the evidence was required, her promise to tell the truth should not have been subject to additional probing during a pre-testimony *voir dire*.

Subsection 16.1(7) of the *Canada Evidence Act* specifically stipulates that: "No proposed witness under fourteen years of age shall be asked any questions regarding their understanding of the nature of the promise to tell the truth …". In *R. v. S. (J.Z.)*, [2008] B.C.J. No. 1915, 2008 BCCA 401, Madam Justice Smith of the British Columbia Court of Appeal rejected a challenge to the validity of this provision, stating: "Parliament, in enacting s. 16.1, has decided that a promise to tell the truth is sufficient to engage the child witness's moral obligation to tell the truth." (para. 52) Justice Smith went on to add that once the child is allowed to testify, he or she could still be cross-examined on his or her cognitive ability to answer questions about "truth" and "lies", noting that such challenges would properly go to the *weight* or importance to be placed on the child's evidence, rather than the issue of not admitting the child's evidence at all. This British Columbia Court of Appeal decision was affirmed by the Supreme Court of Canada (*R. v. S. (J.Z.)*, [2010] S.C.J. No. 1, 2010 SCC 1).

COMPELLABILITY

A *subpoena* is a court order, requiring a potential witness to come to court to provide whatever relevant information he or she might have. A witness is considered to be *compellable* if he or she could legally be forced to come to court to testify using a subpoena. If a witness were to ignore a subpoena and fail to show up in court, the judge would issue a *warrant* authorizing peace officers to arrest the witness to bring the person to court. If a compellable witness came to court and then refused to answer questions, or to provide other evidence in his or her possession, he or she could be found to be in *contempt of court*.

As Justice Hamilton of the Manitoba Court of Appeal said in *R. v. Abdullah*, [2010] M.J. No. 270, 2010 MBCA 79: "A person has a general duty to testify when called upon to do so, except in clearly defined cases…This duty is not owed just to the courts, but to society as a whole and is essential to the proper administration of justice." (para. 34)

In *R. v. Normore*, [2018] N.J. No. 43, 2018 NLCA 10, a trial judge warned a key Crown witness who had refused to answer a question that he was putting himself in jeopardy, but then took no further action to force the witness to answer. Justice White of the Newfoundland and Labrador Court of Appeal ruled that this was an error that justified quashing the accused's convictions for attempted murder and other charges and ordered a new trial. A two judge majority of the Newfoundland and Labrador Court of Appeal believed that after the trial judge was met with a persistent refusal to answer, "It was incumbent upon the judge to take all reasonable steps…to compel Mr. Thomas to answer the question put to him. By not doing so, the trial judge jeopardized the fairness of the trial process." (para. 27)

Madam Justice Hoegg did not agree that the trial judge was required to do more to force the witness to answer in the circumstance of the *Normore* case, pointing out that the Supreme Court of Canada had ruled in *Carey v. Laiken,* [2015] S.C.J. No. 17, [2015] 2 S.C.R. 79 at para. 36 that "A court's decision to cite for and find contempt is a discretionary one." (para. 68) In addition, in the Supreme Court decision in *Morasse v. Nadeau-Dubois,* [2016] S.C.J. No. 44, [2016] 2 S.C.R. 232 at para. 21, the Court cautioned: "In all cases of contempt, it is crucial that courts stay alert to the exceptional nature of their contempt powers, using it only as a measure of last resort. A conviction for contempt should only be entered where it is genuinely necessary to safeguard the administration of justice."

How far can judges go to "safeguard the administration of justice" when faced with a witness's contempt? Common law powers include the ability to send a witness in contempt of a court order to testify to jail *until the witness is prepared to cooperate!* At the time of the writing of the first edition of this book, an Ontario man by the name of Andrew Lech had been in jail for more than 29 months for refusing to reveal information in a civil lawsuit over missing investment money.

Most competent witnesses are also compellable, but there are some exceptions. Section 4(1) of the *Canada Evidence Act* makes it clear that an accused person in a criminal case, and the husband or wife of that person, is a competent witness for the defence, if he or she wants to testify. Section 4(6) makes it clear that the failure of the accused, or his or her wife, "...shall not be made the subject of comment by the judge or by counsel for the prosecution".

The accused is not competent or compellable to testify for the prosecution. This principle is supported by a couple of provisions in the *Canadian Charter of Rights and Freedoms.* An accused person's right to silence is protected as one of the principles of fundamental justice covered in s. 7. In addition, clause 11(*c*) of the *Charter* states that, "Any person charged with an offence has the right not to be compelled to be a witness in proceedings against that person in respect of the offence."

Section 4(2) of the *Canada Evidence Act* now provides that: "No person is incompetent, or uncompellable, to testify for the prosecution by reason only that they are married to the accused." This is a recent change in the statute that used to protect spouses from compellability, except in relation to a set of listed offences.

Most provinces and territories provide specific statutory protections from compellability for people facing provincial, territorial or municipal charges. Even in provinces like Prince Edward Island and Manitoba where there is no legislated protection, clause 11(*c*) of the *Charter* is likely to provide it anyway.

Obviously, if more than one person is being tried at a time, the co-accused can all exercise their right to remain silent and none of them can be compelled to testify. The situation becomes cloudier if several people are facing the same or related charges, but they are given separate trials. Section 5 of the *Canada Evidence Act* and s. 13 of the *Canadian Charter of Rights and Freedoms* provide a form of protection on the use that can be made of the evidence given if someone is compelled to testify at someone else's trial. Section 13 of the *Charter* provides: "A witness who testifies in any proceedings has the right not to have any incriminating evidence so given used to incriminate that witness in any other proceedings ...".

This would seem to eliminate any risk of testifying at someone else's trial, since the evidence you provided could not be used against you at your own trial. It also appears to remove a justification for refusing to testify. Those of you who watch a lot of crime-related programming originating in the United States will realize that this law is significantly different than the law in that country, which permits people to refuse to say anything at someone else's trial that could be self-incriminating. People in the U.S. have no protection from having anything they choose to say used against them in any future trial of their own, the reverse of the situation here in Canada.

The Supreme Court of Canada decision in *R. v. Nedelcu*, [2012] S.C.J. No. 59, 2012 SCC 59, makes it clear that the protection afforded by section 13 is limited by the wording of the section to the use of *incriminating* evidence from an earlier proceeding. Marius Nedelcu was charged with both dangerous and impaired driving causing bodily harm in relation to a motorcycle accident. When Nedelcu crashed a motorcycle he was driving into a curb, his passenger suffered permanent brain damage and Nedelcu spent the night in hospital.

In addition to the criminal charges, Nedelcu was also sued by his injured passenger. During an examination for discovery that was part of the preparatory process for the civil trial, Nedelcu had testified that he had no memory of what had happened on the day of the crash. Nevertheless, when Mr. Nedelcu testified at his criminal trial, he provided a very detailed account of the events leading up to the crash. Hearing this, the prosecutor asked the trial judge for permission to use Mr. Nedelcu's statement from the civil trial's examination for discovery to impeach his credibility. The trial judge granted the request and Nedelcu was convicted.

On appeal, Justice Moldaver, writing for the majority of the Supreme Court agreed with the trial judge's decision on the basis that the evidence Mr. Nedelcu had provided at the examination for discovery could not be considered *incriminating*. He hadn't testified that he was guilty of anything, or even involved in criminal behaviour of any kind, simply that he didn't remember the incident. As a result, Justice Moldaver ruled, "... I am satisfied that the use of Mr. Nedelcu's non-incriminating discovery evidence for impeachment purposes, and nothing else, could not and did not trigger the application of s. 13." (para. 25)

PRIVILEGE – WHEN WITNESSES REFUSE TO DIVULGE CONFIDENTIAL INFORMATION

Subsection 4(3) of the *Canada Evidence Act* states that no husband or wife can be compelled to disclose any communication with his or her spouse during the course of their marriage. In other words, even though that spouse may be compelled to testify about what he or she saw, the witness cannot be compelled to talk about any confession his or her accused spouse may have made. The witness spouse could disclose the information voluntarily, but cannot be forced to talk about any such communication in court. Historically, the legislation has recognized that the sanctity of marital communications is more important than forcing a reluctant spouse to rat out his or her significant other.

The protection from compellability about spousal communications is limited to people who are legally married. While arguments have been made that these provisions discriminate against spouses in "common law" relationships and violate s. 15 (1) of the Charter, courts have upheld this type of discrimination as a "reasonable limit" that is constitutionally justified under s. 1 of the Charter (see *R. v. Nguyen,* [2015] O.J. No. 2098, 2015 ONCA 278, leave to appeal refused [2015] S.C.C.A. No. 365 and *R. v. Nero,* [2016] O.J. No. 1027, 2016 ONCA 160. The protections also do not apply with respect to couples who have divorced, or are separated without a realistic possibility of reconciling (*R. v. Salituro,* [1991] S.C.J. No. 97).

This is the one statutory example of a scenario where a witness, who is otherwise compellable, could claim a *privilege* with respect to a specific type of information. Other types of *privilege* have developed through common law court decisions, in situations where society may recognize that it is more important to protect a confidential relationship than it is to force someone to provide information that could be helpful to a judge or jury.

The most consistently recognized common law form of privilege is *solicitor-client privilege.* Our courts realize that the justice system works better if members of the public get expert legal advice when they have a problem that could end up in court. People would be very reluctant to go to a lawyer and disclose the nature of their legal dilemmas if they thought that lawyers could be forced to disclose what they have been told. As a result, the courts protect communications between a lawyer and his or her client and between the client and the lawyer's secretaries and law clerks from any form of forced disclosure in court.

It is important to realize that this form of privilege is a right that belongs to the client. It is not up to a lawyer to decide to disclose confidential information received from a client; only the client can make that choice. Lawyers who do disclose confidential information without a client's permission could face disciplinary punishment from their professional organization, the provincial or territorial bar society.

The majority of the Supreme Court of Canada in a case called, *R. v. Fink,* [2002] S.C.J. No. 61, [2002] 3 S.C.R. 209, made it clear that solicitor-client privilege is a principle of fundamental justice and "a civil right of supreme importance in Canadian law". They struck down s. 488.1 of the *Criminal Code* which allowed for the seizing of client documents from a law office pursuant to a warrant, then set up a process for deciding whether or not privilege applied to those documents. The Supreme Court said that this was an unreasonable search and seizure, contrary to s. 8 of the *Canadian Charter of Rights and Freedoms*.

In *Alberta (Information and Privacy Commissioner) v. University of Calgary,* [2016] S.C.J. No. 53, 2016 SCC 53, Justice Cote of the Supreme Court stated, "This Court has repeatedly affirmed that...solicitor-client privilege must remain as close to absolute as possible and should not be interfered with unless absolutely necessary." (para. 43).

R. v. Douglas, [2017] M.J. No. 187, 2017 MBCA 63, leave to appeal refused [2017] S.C.C.A. No. 296 is a recent case in which the accused was charged with real estate fraud. Police got a warrant that authorized seizing a variety of documents, including "legal correspondence". Justice Cameron of the Manitoba Court of Appeal said that the judge who issued such a warrant, "...was without jurisdiction to issue warrants for legal correspondence...on the basis that such documents are presumptively privileged". He went on to add that "...the seized documents must remain sealed until such time as a determination can be made regarding the issue of privilege. That determination must be done by a trial judge, not the Crown prosecutor or any other lawyer involved in the case. When it was disclosed that some of the investigating RCMP officers may have viewed some of the documents, Justice Cameron ordered, "...that each of the RCMP officers, who may have viewed a document presumptively protected by solicitor-client privilege...not be allowed to disclose the documents or use their knowledge of the documents in furtherance of this investigation..." (para. 88)

Solicitor-client privilege works in relation to all communications made for the purpose of seeking legal advice, but would not protect communications that amounted to criminal behaviour or attempts to seek advice on how to commit a future crime. In other words, if a lawyer were involved in a conspiracy with his or her client, the communications would not be covered by a privilege claim. The recent British Columbia Supreme Court case of *R. v. Mastop,* [2012] B.C.J. No. 2903, 2012 BCSC 2085 at para. 68, provides an example of a situation where, "... the police knew the applicant was trusted by Mr. Manolakos and believed him to be a member of the Greeks criminal organization. They also believed he advised Greeks members on how to avoid apprehension and should have known that advice of this sort would not attract solicitor-client privilege."

Nor can a client hide physical evidence, such as the murder weapon, by giving it to his or her lawyer. Discussions about this evidence are privileged, but a lawyer would have to find some way to turn the actual item over to investigators, without necessarily assisting them in making a link to his or her client.

Police officers and other government investigators are usually granted a *privilege* from having to disclose the identities of their informants. This is a public policy issue aimed at preventing reprisals against the informants, and at encouraging others to come forward with relevant information that could assist criminal investigations. The Supreme Court of Canada explained the concept in *R. v. Basi,* [2009] S.C.J. No. 52 at para. 36, 2009 SCC 52:

The privilege arises where a police officer, in the course of an investigation, guarantees protection and confidentiality to a prospective informer in exchange for useful information that would otherwise be difficult or impossible to obtain. In appropriate circumstances, a bargain of this sort has long been accepted as an indispensable tool in the detection, prevention and prosecution of crime.

It is not an absolute protection, but pretty darn close. The one exception that courts have recognized is that a judge might decide to order disclosure if the accused's lawyer could convince the judge that disclosure is necessary to establish the innocence of the accused. As Justice Fish of the Supreme Court of Canada stated in the *R. v. Basi* case, even the *Charter*-protected right of an accused person "to make full answer and defence", which normally requires full disclosure of evidence collected by the prosecution is not enough to override informer privilege: "... the right to make full answer and defence does not alone trigger an exception to the informer privilege ... It is only where innocence is at stake that the privilege yields and information tending to reveal the identity of the informant can be disclosed." (para. 43) This could arise in the context of a challenge to the validity of the reasonable grounds for securing a search warrant or an authorization from a judge to conduct a wiretap.

Because the safety of an informant might be at stake, judges recognize that it is not just the Crown prosecutor and police officer that would have to be involved in a decision whether or not to disclose the informant's identity. Justice Fish explained in the *Basi* case that, "... the informer privilege belongs jointly to the Crown and to the informant. Neither can waive it without the consent of the other". (para. 40) The court procedure for determining if a claim of informer privilege is legitimate is an exceptional one. Obviously, this cannot be done in a public hearing and, unusually, neither an accused person nor his or her lawyer can attend. As Justice Fish explains, the existence of informer privilege, "... must be determined by the court *in camera* at a 'first stage' hearing ... Ordinarily, only the putative informant and the Crown may appear before the judge". (para. 38) The standard used for assessing privilege is a balance of probabilities. If the judge decides to override the claim of privilege in a case where the accused's innocence is at stake, the judge could allow the prosecution the choice of withdrawing the criminal charge so that the identity of the informant can be protected.

R. v. Anderson, [2013] S.J. No. 528, 2013 SKCA 92 was a complex drug trafficking case that involved a lengthy investigation using search warrants, wiretaps and video surveillance. When Mr. Anderson's defence lawyer discovered that one of the confidential police informants had died, he sought disclosure of the identity of this informer, claiming that informer privilege should not survive death. Both the trial judge and the Saskatchewan Court of Appeal disagreed, with Justice Ottenbreit of the Court of Appeal stating: "Courts have recognized that protection does not just include the informer personally, but also the family and friends associated with that person." (para. 142) Informer privilege can survive the death of the informant.

All others who claim *privilege* for confidential information (doctors, counsellors, priests, journalists, *etc.*), are assessed by judges on a case-by-case basis using four criteria, first suggested by Professor Wigmore in an Evidence text he wrote back in 1961, and adopted by Canadian judges in a number of common law precedents (*i.e., Slavutych v. Baker,* [1976] S.C.J. No. 29, [1976] 1 S.C.R. 254 at para. 260).

If all four criteria are not met, it is likely that the court will order the witness to disclose the confidential information. The "Wigmore Rules" are basically that:

(1)   The initial communication was made in confidence;

(2)   Confidentiality is an essential part of the relationship between the parties;

(3)   The relationship is one that society would want to protect; and

(4)   Injury from disclosure is greater than the benefit to society from the correct outcome of the trial.

If you consider these criteria carefully, you will see that the fourth one is the one most likely to cause a judge to order the person claiming privilege to disclose the information despite the claim. Consider the situation of a priest, who has heard the confession of someone who is alleged to have murdered a child. Perhaps the other evidence pointing in the direction of this accused is less than conclusive. There is no doubt that his or her communication was made in confidence and that confidentiality is an essential part of the relationship between priests and people who come to confession. It may also be that society would want to protect the sanctity of this sort of spiritual or religious relationship. Nevertheless, is a judge going to be willing to protect this confidential relationship if it means that a child killer might avoid conviction? In cases involving serious criminal charges and potentially crucial information, judges are more likely to order disclosure than they are to protect claims of privilege.

This may not be true in civil cases, where the issue is usually one of financial compensation, rather than the potential loss of someone's freedom or a dangerous criminal avoiding conviction. In a civil case, a court might be more willing to protect the confidential relationship and uphold a claim of privilege for confidential information. Madame Justice McLachlin of the Supreme Court of Canada made this point in a case called, *M. (A.) v. Ryan,* [1997] S.C.J. No. 13, 143 D.L.R. (4th) 1. Nevertheless, the *Wigmore Rules* have been used to compel disclosure in cases like *Guthrie v. St. Joseph Print Group Inc.,* [2018] O.J. No. 1273, 2018 ONSC 1411. In that case, an employer who was being sued for the wrongful dismissal of a long-term employee tried to claim privilege for communications between upper management and the human relations department. Master Champagne ruled, "I do not find that the first three criteria of Wigmore are met and even if they were...the harm caused by the disclosure of the e-mails in the present case would not outweigh the benefit gained for the correct disposal of the litigation." (paras. 22-23)

WARNING OF THE RISK OF RELYING ON THE UNTRUSTWORTHY "VETROVIC" WITNESS

In *R. v. Connell,* [2017] B.C.J. No. 841 (S.C.), Judge T.S. Woods made the following observation: "It must be acknowledged that criminal acts are not uncommonly committed by and against persons involved in the criminal underworld with only other persons in the criminal underworld present as witnesses. That does not mean that all prosecutions which confront such situations must necessarily fail and that all wrongdoers involved in such situations must necessarily escape liability for their unlawful actions." (para. 51)

Nevertheless, it has become a common practice for judges to provide a "clear and sharp" warning to themselves or jurors about the dangers of relying on the evidence of witnesses who may be considered inherently untrustworthy without some confirmatory evidence backing what they have said. As was stated by Justice Dickson in the foundational case of *R. v. Vetrovec*, [1982] S.C.J. No. 40, [1982] 1 S.C.R. 811 at 831: "...as a matter of common sense something in the nature of confirmatory evidence should be found before the finder of fact relies upon evidence of a witness whose testimony occupies a central position in the purported demonstration of guilt and yet may be suspect by reason of the witness being an accomplice or complainant or of disreputable character."

In *R. v. Carroll*, [2014] O.J. No. 2, 2014 ONCA 2, leave to appeal refused [2014] S.C.C.A. No. 193, Justice Watt observed, "The rationale that underpins a *Vetrovec* caution originates in the concern that for certain types of witnesses, lay members of the jury simply lack the critical experience to adequately gauge the credibility of these types of witnesses and the reliability of their evidence." (para. 78)

While multiple court decisions make it clear that issuing the warning is a matter within the discretion of the trial judge, "...failure to give a *Vetrovec* warning when required amounts to an error of law." (Justice Bastarache at para. 1 in *R. v. Brooks,* [2000] S.C.J. No. 12, [2000] 1 S.C.R. 237) It is somewhat ironic that the *Brooks* case itself adds some confusion to exactly when the discretion to warn should be exercised. Three Supreme Court justices said the trial judge should have provided the warning in relation to two jailhouse informants who testified that the accused had confessed to killing an infant; three ruled a warning was unnecessary in the circumstances. Justice Binnie, the seventh justice, voted to uphold the accused's conviction for murder even though he believed the warning should have been provided. In Justice Binnie's view, there was enough evidence to convict the accused, regardless of the error the trial judge made in not warning jurors.

Justice Major, in his dissenting opinion in *Brooks*, described the jailhouse informants about whom he believed the jurors should have been warned: "Both...were of unsavoury and infamous character. Both had lengthy criminal records of dishonesty.... In addition, B...had a history of substance abuse and an alarming psychiatric history highlighted by ...suicide attempts, paranoia, deep depression and a belief in his clairvoyant ability...both witnesses had histories of offering to testify against other accuseds." (paras. 49-50)

Justice Major also described what a *Vetrovec* warning should entail: "At a minimum, a proper *Vetrovec* warning must focus the jury's attention specifically on the inherently unreliable evidence. It should refer to the characteristics of the witness that bring the credibility of his or her evidence into serious question. It should plainly emphasize the dangers inherent in convicting an accused on the basis of such evidence unless confirmed by independent evidence." (para. 94)

Even a judge sitting alone must be alive to these issues and caution him or herself. The principle was recently applied by Judge Woods in *R. v. Davies*, [2017] B.C.J. No. 2601, 2017 BCPC 392. The accused was facing a charge of aggravated assault, with an allegation that he had stabbed Charles Mackenzie. The victim was the only Crown witness who could testify to the identity of his assailant.

Judge Woods described the victim himself as "manifestly a *Vetrovec* witness". Not only did Mackenzie have a lengthy criminal record involving dishonesty and misleading various courts, he testified that many aspects of statements he had made to police in respect of this incident were lies. Originally, he had told police he was "blackout drunk" and could not identify his assailant, but at trial contended that was a lie, and that he'd been stabbed by his long-time friend, Colton Davies. The only evidence available from an independent witness "further undermined the court's confidence in the testimony given by Mr. Mackenzie." (para. 43). Judge Woods had no difficulty finding that this inherently unreliable evidence fell short of proof beyond a reasonable doubt and acquitted the accused.

SPECIAL TREATMENT FOR COMPLAINANTS IN SEXUAL ASSAULT CASES

Sections 278.1 through 278.91 of the *Criminal Code* set up a process for protecting a complainant (alleged victim) in a long list of sexually assaultive type of offences from having to disclose the contents of psychiatric, counselling, employment or educational records that the person would normally expect to remain private. The aim of these provisions is to minimize additional "victimization" and privacy invasions that could occur during a trial that might make a victim think twice about reporting abuse in the first place, or actually going ahead and testifying in court against his or her abuser.

For the defence lawyer to get access to these types of records pertaining to the complainant, the lawyer would have to convince the judge that the contents would likely be relevant to the case. Before the judge would order any disclosure of this type of information, the judge will examine it privately. The judge will be able to assess the defendant's needs to access this information to mount a defence. Any such need will be balanced with the potential harm to the witness's privacy before the judge will order disclosure. The judge will only allow disclosure of pertinent portions of the private record.

R. v. Quesnelle, [2013] O.J. No. 1365, 2013 ONCA 180, revd [2014] S.C.J. No. 46 is a case where the accused was facing several charges relating to violent sexual assaults of two different victims. Because of a radio documentary about one of the alleged victims, Mr. Quesnelle's lawyer discovered that this complainant had made four or five previous complaints to the police about violent sexual assaults involving other alleged perpetrators. When the lawyer asked for disclosure of the police occurrence reports in relation to these other allegations, the Crown claimed they were private records, protected from disclosure under s. 278.2 of the *Criminal Code*. While the trial judge agreed, the Ontario Court of Appeal did not. Justice MacFarland of the Court of Appeal explained (paras. 33 and 34): "When a victim of a sexual assault speaks to police about the attack, he or she is not doing so in the context of a trust-like, confidential, or therapeutic relationship. ... In my view, there can be no "reasonable expectation of privacy" in information a complainant provides to police and which the police record in one form or another."

The Supreme Court of Canada did not agree; siding with the trial judge. As Justice Karakatsanis said at para. 43 of *R. v. Quesnelle*, [2014] S.C.J. No. 46, [2014] 2 S.C.R. 390: "People provide information to police in order to protect themselves and others. They are entitled to do so with confidence that the police will only disclose it for good reason. The fact that the information is in the hands of the police should not nullify their interest in keeping that information private from other individuals." Whether or not such records will be disclosed involves a trial judge balancing the privacy interests of the witness and the accused's right to make full answer and defence. The judge's decision to protect the privacy of the witness, as occurred in this case, is entitled to deference.

Section 277 prevents an accused's lawyer from using any evidence of the alleged victim's sexual reputation to challenge that witness's credibility. Section 276 strictly limits the use that could be made of any evidence of prior sexual conduct by the alleged victim to show that the witness is less worthy of belief or more likely to have consented to sexual conduct with the accused.

Section 274 of the *Criminal Code* makes it clear that an accused could be convicted on the basis of the testimony of the alleged victim alone (as long as the judge or jury is convinced of guilt beyond a reasonable doubt, of course). There is no necessity for the evidence to be *corroborated* or supported by other evidence and the judge is not to warn jurors of the danger of convicting without such support.

SPECIAL TREATMENT FOR CHILDREN AND WITNESSES WITH DISABILITIES

A public trial in open court is the normal situation in our criminal justice system. We, literally, do not want our criminal matters decided behind closed doors in most circumstances. Nevertheless, s. 486 of the *Criminal Code* allows a judge to exclude members of the public from the courtroom when a witness under 18 is testifying and the accused is charged with a sexual offence or other offence involving violence directed against the young person.

The section also allows the trial judge to make an order banning the publication of the alleged victim's name, or any specific details of the trial that would lead to members of the public being able to identify the victim from media reports of the trial. When the assaultive behaviour is alleged to have been done by a family member, this would include a ban on the publication of the name of the accused, since that might allow the alleged victim to be identified indirectly.

It has also been a principle of our criminal justice system that an accused person is entitled to face his or her accuser. Subsection 486.2(1) allows for an exception to this principle for a witness under 18, or a witness who suffers from a disability if the witness would have a difficult time giving a candid description of an alleged offence with the person who is purported to have victimized him or her in the witness's line of sight. A judge can make arrangements so that the witness could give his or her testimony from behind a screen, or in a location where this sort of eye-to-eye contact is not necessary.

In the British Columbia Court of Appeal case of *R. v. S. (J.Z.)*, [2008] B.C.J. No. 1915, 2008 BCCA 401, affd [2010] S.C.J. No. 1, 2010 SCC 1, the court ruled that allowing two children, aged eight and 11 to testify behind a screen did not violate the accused father's Charter protected rights to a fair trial. In so ruling, Madam Justice Smith mentioned an observation that had been made by Justice Morden of the Ontario Court of Appeal that, "… a screen only blocked the complainant's view of the accused, but did not prevent the accused, the prosecutor or the trial judge from viewing the complainant". (para. 32)

If the witness is under 14, or suffers from a mental disability, a judge can also allow a *support person* to be close to the witness while he or she gives evidence.

Sections 715.1 and 715.2 of the *Criminal Code* allow for the use of a videotape of evidence of an alleged victim or other witness under the age of 18 or a witness who suffers from a disability. There is a requirement that the video be made within a "reasonable" time of the alleged offence and that the witness must be in court at the time of the trial to "adopt" the contents of the video. He or she would also need to be available for cross-examination by the accused's lawyer after the video is shown. Part of the logic behind this statutory assist for children and witnesses who are disabled is that it may be better to record the witness's recollection of the event shortly after it happened, rather than having to wait months or years for a trial, with the possibility of a less accurate memory. In addition, it could reduce the number of times the alleged victim is required to recollect the details of what may have been a very traumatic event.

RELIGIOUS FACIAL COVERINGS

In the Supreme Court of Canada case of *R. v. S. (N.)*, [2012] S.C.J. No. 72, 2012 SCC 72, judges were asked to consider the issue of whether or not a key witness in a criminal trial should be allowed to have her face covered by a veil known as a niqab when testifying. Wearing the niqab, only the witness's eyes would be visible to court participants, the rest of her face would be covered. The defendants, who were charged with sexually assaulting the adult witness when she was a child, had asked a judge holding a preliminary inquiry in the case to order the witness to remove the niqab. Their lawyers argued that allowing the witness to wear the veil was a restriction on their clients's right to make full answer and defence, as protected by s. 7

of the *Canadian Charter of Rights and Freedoms* and the right to a fair and public hearing, as protected by clause 11(*d*) of the *Charter*. The witness, a Muslim woman, responded that requiring her to remove the veil would be a violation of her freedom of religion, a fundamental freedom protected by clause 2(*a*) of the *Charter*.

The 54-page decision in the case at the Ontario Court of Appeal level, followed by a 33-page decision in the Supreme Court of Canada, serves to illustrate what a challenging legal issue this is. One the one hand, Justice Doherty of the Ontario Court of Appeal pointed out that ([2010] O.J. No. 4306 at para. 54, 2010 ONCA 670):

> Covering the face of a witness may impede the cross-examination in two ways. First, it limits the trier of fact's ability to assess the demeanour of the witness. Demeanour is relevant to the assessment of the witness's credibility and the reliability of the evidence given by that witness. Second, witnesses do not respond to questions by words alone. Non-verbal communication can provide the cross-examiner with valuable insights.

On the other hand, Justice Doherty recognized at para. 79:

> N.S. is a Muslim, a minority that many believe is unfairly maligned and stereotyped in contemporary Canada. A failure to give adequate consideration to N.S.'s religious beliefs would reflect and, to some extent, legitimize that negative stereotyping. Allowing her to wear a niqab could be seen as a recognition and acceptance of those minority beliefs and practices and, therefore, a reflection of the multi-cultural heritage of Canada ... Permitting N.S. to wear her niqab would also broaden access to the justice system for those in the position of N.S., by indicating that participation in the justice system would not come at the cost of compromising one's religious beliefs.

In the majority decision at the Supreme Court of Canada, Chief Justice McLachlin cautioned that covering a witness's face may impede both cross-examination and credibility assessment by a judge or jury. At the same time, she recognized that judges also have to consider the societal harms that could occur if there was a blanket policy that a witness must remove a niqab. This could include a reluctance of people with strong religious beliefs to report offences or otherwise participate in the justice system. As a result, Justice McLachlin said that a trial judge must consider the issue on a case-by-case basis, accommodating the religious beliefs if possible, but considering factors such as how central the witness's testimony is to the case, how necessary a full cross-examination might be and whether or not the wearing of the niqab would have a significant impact on the accused person's right to make full answer and defence: "[T]he answer lies in a just and proportionate balance between freedom of religion on the one hand, and trial fairness on the other, based on the particular case before the Court." (para. 31 of the Supreme Court decision) In some cases, this will inevitably result in a trial judge requiring the witness to remove the niqab before testifying.

In a dissenting opinion, Justice Abella of the Supreme Court of Canada made the valid point that the wearing of a niqab is unlikely to affect an assessment of a witness's demeanour any more than if that witness testifies through an interpreter (a *Charter* protected right for a witness who does not speak the language of trial), or if the witness has suffered a stroke which affects facial expressions or has a speech impediment.

TEST YOURSELF

1. Five-year-old Farah told her teacher, "Uncle Zach put his thingie in my private." The teacher called the police. Officers investigated and charged Zach with sexual assault and sexual interference. If there is a trial, will Farah be a *competent* witness to provide evidence at Zach's trial? Should the prosecutor be concerned? Briefly explain.

2. Farah told the police that the incident happened at Uncle Zach's house and that Aunt Eva was home at the time. Aunt Eva lives with Zach as his wife, though they've never been legally married. Could Aunt Eva be *compelled* to testify at Zach's trial? Explain your answer.

3. At Zach's trial, the prosecutor calls one of the investigating officers who charged Zach as her first witness. The first two questions the prosecutor asks the officer are these:

   Q1 — You are Detective Constable Sam Zidane of the Municipal Police Service, is that correct?

   Q2 — How did you first happen to meet the child molester, Zach Beeston?

   Should Zach's defence lawyer *object* to either of these questions? Why or why not?

4. Use a computer to find the Ontario Court of Appeal decision in *R. v. Y. (V.)*, [2010] O.J. No. 3336, 2010 ONCA 544. This case involves two of the Court of Appeal justices ruling that the conviction of the accused for the sexual assault and unlawful confinement of a 13-year-old neighbour should be set aside and a new trial held. Why? One of the Court of Appeal judges disagreed with his fellow judges. What was his reasoning? Which judgment do you find more convincing? Briefly explain.

   BONUS: Check to see if this case was appealed to the Supreme Court of Canada.

Chapter 5

Opinion Evidence and Experts

OPINION EVIDENCE AND THE NON-EXPERT WITNESS

Most witnesses are restricted to testifying about what they have seen, heard, smelled or otherwise experienced. Judges, if prompted by an objection, will generally prevent a witness from adding a personal inference, or *opinion* to his or her testimony covering direct observations. In most circumstances, the courts reject the value of the witness's opinion. The accepted wisdom seems to be that at worst the opinion could mislead the judge or jurors, and at best the opinion is of little value to making a fair assessment of the truth.

For example, we expect a witness to be able to provide a description like this: "The man's hair was hanging in his face. His clothes had dirt on them. He was waving his arms around and loudly shouting swear words." Unless a judge knows a witness has special expertise, the judge will have trouble with the reliability or usefulness of what is being said if the witness tries to add, "In my opinion, this person was insane," or even, "This person was clearly insane." Opposing advocates and the trial judge will usually recognize this type of opinion, whether it comes packaged with warning words or not.

On the other hand, it is not always easy to distinguish between factual accounts and expressions of opinion. If someone testifies that a person appeared to be six feet tall or that a car looked as though it was going over the speed limit, we would probably consider that useful evidence for the judge or jury to consider. However, if you really think about it, most observations that are not based on some type of exact measurement involve an element of speculation and are definitely affected by the unique perspective of the individual making the observation.

Let's face it, the line between observed *fact* and *opinion* is a blurry one. A witness takes the stand and says, "The accused, Paul Atkinson is the person I saw at the scene of the crime." Is this a statement of fact, or an opinion? People who have studied wrongful convictions in the criminal justice system will tell you that faulty eyewitness identifications have played a very significant role in many of these cases. Judges will warn jurors of the risks of relying on this type of evidence. Scientists will tell you there is a subjective, evaluative and inferential element to what we call memory. A memory of an incident or a person is certainly not the same as a photo or videotape. So would a judge exclude an eyewitness identification if an opposing advocate tried to have it categorized as an objectionable opinion? Not likely. As Justice Watt of the Ontario Court of Appeal observed in *R. v. M.C.*, [2014] O.J. No. 3959, 314 C.C.C. (3d) 336 at para. 67 (C.A.): "The law of evidence distinguishes between fact and opinion.

The distinction seems ...ultimately one of convenience rather than objective reality. All sensory data is mediated by our powers of perception, assimilation and expression."

Judges do allow non-expert or *lay* witnesses to provide opinion evidence about many things that we all experience as part of our day-to-day lives. There are simply too many common situations when it is practically impossible to separate inference from observed facts. Courts regularly allow non-expert witnesses to provide opinion evidence about someone's identity, height, weight and apparent age. They might be allowed to express a view on someone's emotional state (*i.e.*, "He looked angry," or "She looked shocked"). A lay witness may also be allowed observations on a person's physical condition (*i.e.*, "She seemed to be sick," or "I'm pretty sure he was drunk").

Non-expert witnesses are regularly allowed to provide estimates of speed and distance. If the witness can demonstrate a basis for familiarity with someone's handwriting, a lay witness may be allowed to identify the handwriting on a document that has significance in a trial.

In a case called *R. v. Graat*, [1982] S.C.J. No. 102, 31 C.R. (3d) 289, the Supreme Court of Canada was asked to assess whether police officer witnesses should have been allowed to express opinions that Mr. Graat's ability to drive a car was impaired by alcohol. Since the accused was facing an impaired driving charge, this amounted to letting the witness express an opinion on the "ultimate issue" for the trial judge dealing with the case. Prior to this case, judges had been reluctant to allow witnesses to go that far in expressing an opinion. Justice Dickson ruled that this type of evidence could be allowed in a situation like this one.

> The judge in the instant case was not in as good a position as the police officers ... to determine the degree of Mr. Graat's impairment or his ability to drive a motor vehicle. The witnesses had an opportunity for personal observation. They were in a position to give the Court real help. They were not settling the dispute. They were not deciding the matter the Court had to decide, the ultimate issue. The judge could accept all or part or none of their evidence ... . It has long been accepted in our law that intoxication is not such an exceptional condition as would require a medical expert to diagnose it.

In his decision, Justice Dickson made it clear that the police officers were not testifying as experts and that this was not the justification for allowing their evidence to be admitted, "Ordinary people with ordinary experience are able to know as a matter of fact that someone is too drunk to perform certain tasks, such as driving a car ... Constable McMullen and Sergeant Spoelstra were not testifying as experts based on their extensive experience as police officers." The fact that they may have seen more drunks than other witnesses did not affect the *admissibility* of their evidence. Of course, a judge or juror would have to decide how much importance, or *weight* such background might add to what they had to say.

In *R. v. Lee*, [2010] S.C.J. No. 52, 2010 SCC 52, the accused was convicted of charges of sexual assault with a weapon and unlawful confinement. It was alleged that he had chased a female victim, whom he had encountered outside a nightclub, and then forced her to perform oral sex at knife point. His defence was that the victim had consented to the sexual act. At trial, a police officer, who was a qualified tracking dog handler, testified that he followed tracks in the snow from the nightclub to the location of the alleged attack. This witness claimed he had expertise in the interpretation of footprints and that it was his opinion that the people who had made the footprints had been running. Neither the witness's expertise, nor his opinion was challenged by the defendant's lawyer during the trial. The trial judge, in rejecting the testimony of the defendant and accepting that of the victim, used the officer's evidence that the footprints made it look, "... as if there was somebody running from the others", as one of 12 points that led her to disbelieve the defendant's version of the event. When the defendant's lawyer tried to challenge the use of this evidence on appeal, seven judges on the Supreme Court rejected the challenge, referring to Crown counsel's comment that, "... any school child would deduce this from the tracks in the snow which the witness observed". The observation required no special expertise.

While judges may allow non-expert witnesses to state opinions on factual issues, Justice Dickson made it clear in the *Graat* case that, "A non-expert witness cannot, of course, give opinion evidence on a legal issue as, for example, whether or not a person was negligent ... An opinion that someone was negligent is partly factual, but also involves the application of legal standards." If there is a jury, it is up to the trial judge as the *trier of fact* to explain legal concepts to jurors. If a judge is hearing the case alone, he or she should not need a witness's opinion on the state of the law (and will have more than enough commentary from the opposing lawyers on relevant legal issues when they make their closing presentations, after all the evidence is in).

EXPERT EVIDENCE

Sometimes, judges or jurors do need *expert* help in understanding the importance or significance of certain pieces of evidence. *Experts* are people who have the special knowledge, training or experience that goes beyond the scope of knowledge of the average juror or judge. For example, an expert in hydrodynamics (the movement of fluids) may be able to provide an *opinion* that a certain type of wound, caused by a particular weapon would result in a projection of blood that would cover an assailant. It is easy to see the relevance and usefulness of this opinion if other evidence placed several potential perpetrators at the scene but only one was found wearing blood-splattered clothing.

Since this expert witness is highly unlikely to have been on the scene when this event occurred, his or her direct observations of the event are non-existent. Nevertheless, this witness can provide useful evidence to the judge or jurors in the form of an *opinion*, formed on the basis of the witness's special expertise. The opinion could relate to an investigation or evidence analysis the expert has conducted on the scene or in a lab after the incident. Or, the expert may simply have used his or her expertise to assess the significance of evidence witnessed or gathered by others. Often, the expert will testify after other witnesses have told the judge or jury about pieces of evidence on which the expert will base the opinion.

We allow experts to provide opinion evidence at trials because their specialized knowledge and training make their opinions relevant and helpful to the judge or jurors who have to decide what happened.

THE PROCESS FOR GETTING EXPERT EVIDENCE ADMITTED

Section 657.3(3) of the *Criminal Code* requires a party who intends to use an expert to provide the other side with 30 days advance notice of the use of the expert. Provincial evidence statutes contain similar provisions that would apply to civil trials.

The *Criminal Code* specifies what should be included in the advance notice. This includes the name of the proposed expert witness, an outline of his or her qualifications and a description of the area of expertise in which he or she will provide testimony. If a prosecutor is calling the expert, disclosure requirements mean that the prosecutor also has to provide the defence with a copy of any report the expert has prepared, or a summary of the opinion the expert will be providing. The report or summary has to be handed over a "reasonable period before the trial". A defence expert's report or summary must be given to the prosecutor no later than the close of the prosecutor's case against the accused. In civil trials, expert reports are usually exchanged well in advance of the trial, with provincial statutes providing specific deadlines.

The lawyer or agent who is using an expert must go through a qualification process in court, before the expert will be allowed to provide the opinion evidence. This occurs in each case, whether the particular witness is testifying as an expert for the first time, or the 40th time. When the witness is called to testify, he or she will first be asked to outline his or her relevant education, training or specialized experience and the trial judge will be asked to *qualify* the witness as an expert in the needed area of expertise. The opposing lawyer or agent will be able to ask questions to challenge the actual expertise of the witness, or to narrow the scope of the area of expertise that the witness will be able to cover when he or she offers an opinion.

As Mr. Justice Watt of the Ontario Court of Appeal stated in *R. v. Abbey*, [2013] O.J. No. 1460, 2013 ONCA 206 at para. 42):

> ... the qualifications of witnesses proposed as experts and, if qualified, the scope of the opinions they may proffer, are determined on a case-by-case basis ... . A party who tenders a witness as an expert on specific issues in one proceeding is not estopped from challenging the same witness' qualifications, or the scope of the witness' testimony, in another proceeding.

The trial judge is actually being called upon to assess two things before the advocate will be able to use the expert to offer opinion evidence. First, the *subject* of the opinion must be so distinctly related to a specialized science or occupation that it is beyond the sphere of knowledge of the average person (a juror). In other words, it has to be something on which only an expert would be qualified to offer a useful opinion. Secondly, the witness must actually have specialized knowledge, skill or experience in that area of expertise so that his or her opinion would be likely to assist the judge or jury in a search for the truth. In other words, the witness must really be an expert.

It is not always academic qualifications that convince a judge to accept a proposed witness's expertise. In *R. v. Reid*, [2017] O.J. No. 3555, 2017 ONSC 4082, the Crown sought to have a Detective Constable qualified as an expert on issues related to the production, valuation and trafficking of cannabis. During his career, the officer had been involved in over 150 marijuana cultivation investigations and had attended "many police training courses" on drug investigation techniques. As Justice Garson observed, "He accepted that his trainers for his courses were police officers and that he relied on them for his opinion that the average adult heavy user consumes 1-3 grams per day...and does not know what qualifications or training the trainers had. He further agrees that he received no accreditation as an expert and there is no regulatory body for police experts." (paras. 13-14)

In allowing the detective to testify as an expert, the judge ruled, "The fact that he is not a doctor, psychologist, pharmacist, statistician, or otherwise more qualified in the areas of scientific research do not detract from his qualifications nor serve as impediments to his ability to testify as an expert." (para. 31)

On the other hand, having academic credentials is no guarantee that a witness will be allowed to testify as an expert. In the Ontario Court of Appeal decision in *R. v. M.C.* (mentioned earlier in this chapter), a trial judge had allowed a clinical psychologist with a PhD to testify about a link between child sexual abuse and utterances made during non-epileptic seizures. The psychologist's opinion was based on the fact that he had read "one survey article that critically reviewed existing literature" on the subject. Justice Watt, writing for the three judges of the Ontario Court of Appeal, ruled , "...a clinical psychologist with neither practical nor academic expertise in NES episodes...A review of a single survey article did not qualify Dr. Wolfe to give an expert opinion outside his field of expertise." (paras. 99-100) A new trial was ordered, which would have to proceed without this testimony.

Even when the expert has been properly qualified, a trial judge must be careful to restrict the expert from getting into irrelevant or anecdotal evidence that is not the proper scope of expert opinion and may be prejudicial to the accused. This is what occurred in *R. v. Sekhon*, [2014] S.C.J. No. 15, 2014 SCC 15, where a police expert who was testifying on the customs and practices of the drug trade was asked a question by the Crown prosecutor about whether any of the drug couriers he had investigated had been unaware of what they were transporting.

His response was to the effect that none of the thousands of couriers he had en-countered had been unaware. Since the main thrust of the defence was that Mr. Sekhon was driving an acquaintance's truck with drugs in a hidden compartment that Sekhon knew nothing about, Justice Moldaver of the Supreme Court of Canada stated at para. 49:

> The impugned testimony ... was not legally relevant because the guilt or innocence of accused persons Sgt. Arsenault had encountered in the past is legally irrelevant to the guilt or innocence of Mr. Sekhon ... . It is trite to say that a fundamental tenet or our criminal justice system is that the guilt of an accused cannot be determined by reference to the guilt of other, unrelated persons ... and it is certainly not a matter that is technical or scientific in nature.

R. v. Belic, [2011] O.J. No. 4775, 2011 ONCA 67, was a murder trial that arose out of a shooting that occurred at a student pub in Oshawa, Ontario. An expert from the Centre for Forensic Sciences was qualified to testify as an expert in the area of firearms identification and the marking created on ammunition fired from a particular weapon. He linked ammunition found in the possession of Mr. Belic to weapon that was used to shoot the victim. When the defence lawyer cross-examined this witness, he pressed him to offer an opinion as to whether or not eyewitnesses would be able to connect a muzzle flash to any one individual who was standing in the midst of a group of people when the gun was fired. The expert responded several times by saying, "That's really beginning to be outside my area of firearms expertise" and "... it's dealing with peoples' perceptions which I'm not comfortable commenting on." (para. 8) However, when pressed further, the expert finally said that he didn't think it was possible to identify the shooter in a group of people from a muzzle flash.

The defence lawyer tried to make a big deal out of this point in his closing argument, but the trial judge told the jurors that this was not something that required an expert opinion and that the jurors could form their own opinion about what the eyewitnesses may have been able to see. The Court of Appeal ruled that the trial judge had acted correctly in limiting the subject matter of the expert's opinion in this way.

NEW AREAS OF EXPERTISE

Experts have to be qualified each time they are called to testify and trial judges have an opportunity in each trial to decide whether or not a certain field of expertise is required by the judge or jury in that trial. As a result, it could be said that the qualification of an expert in one trial does not really set a precedent that the same expert and his or her field of expertise will be accepted in another trial. Nevertheless, some fields of science and expertise have established a level of validity and credibility that trial judges will recognize and that opposing lawyers or agents may not be able to effectively challenge when an expert is called.

The Supreme Court of Canada has made it clear that when lawyers or agents try to introduce witnesses claiming expertise in new fields of study, trial judges must subject these offers of expert opinion evidence, "... to special scrutiny to determine whether it meets a basic threshold of *reliability*" (emphasis added to Justice Sopinka's quote from *R. v. Mohan*, [1994] S.C.J. No. 36, 89 C.C.C. (3d) 402 at para. 28).

In *R. v. Mohan*, a doctor was charged with sexually assaulting four young patients. The defence lawyer wanted to call a psychiatrist who was going to say that the defendant did not fit the "personality profile" of a pedophile, someone who would be sexually attracted to children. The trial judge refused to allow the witness to testify. The judge felt that it was not clear that these types of "personality profiles" were actually part of a reliable body of science. The Supreme Court of Canada supported the trial judge's refusal to admit this evidence, stating that trial judges must act as "gatekeepers" to keep "junk science" out of our trials.

Another example arose in a second Supreme Court of Canada case involving alleged sexual assaults against children, called *R. v. J. (J.-L.)*, [2000] S.C.J. No. 52, [2000] 2 S.C.R. 600. In this case, defence lawyers tried to offer the expert opinion of a sexologist, who had conducted tests on the defendant using a device called a plethysmograph. This device was designed to measure "penile swelling" when a subject was exposed to sexually arousing sights and sounds involving children. Based on the defendant's lack of arousal during the test sessions, the sexologist was prepared to testify that the defendant was unlikely to be a pedophile.

When the proposed expert admitted during the qualification process that the testing device only worked "between 47.5 per cent and 87 per cent" of the time, the trial judge refused to qualify the expert, using this "junk science". The Supreme Court of Canada supported the trial judge's stance, stating that the evidence did not meet the high standard of reliability required for expert evidence to be useful in court.

In *R. v. Abbey*, [2009] O.J. No. 3534, 2009 ONCA 624, leave to appeal refused [2010] S.C.C.A. No. 125, the Crown prosecutor wanted to call an expert on street gangs, named Dr. Totten, who was prepared to testify to the meaning of a teardrop tattoo for gang members, based on interviews he had done with 81 gang members with teardrop tattoos. Seventy-one of these interviewees were in jail for murdering rival gang members. Warren Abbey, who was on trial for the alleged murder of a rival gang member, had a tattoo of this type inscribed on his face a couple of months after the event.

The trial judge would not allow this expert evidence in his role as a gatekeeper, claiming he didn't find Dr. Totten's study sufficiently reliable and categorizing it as a *novel scientific theory*. He cited the fact that theories respecting the meaning of teardrop tattoos among gang members had neither been published nor peer-reviewed. The trial judge also found fault with the small size of the study, Dr. Totten's inability to provide an error rate for his analysis and the fact that none of the interviews had been conducted with members of the gang known as the Malvern Crew. This was the gang to which Warren Abbey belonged.

When the jury acquitted Mr. Abbey, the Crown appealed the trial judge's ruling on the exclusion of this expert evidence. The Ontario Court of Appeal ruled that the trial judge had applied the wrong standard in deciding on admissibility. Citing factors like error rates and peer-review of studies, it was clear that the trial judge was referring to reliability factors that had been considered in the American case of *Daubert v. Merrell Dow Pharmaceuticals Inc.*, 509 U.S. 579. This is a case that had been mentioned with approval by the Supreme Court of Canada in *R. v. J. (J-.L.)*, [2000] S.C.J. No. 52, [2000] 2 S.C.R. 600 discussed above. It has been used to assess expert opinions that are based on the scientific method.

As Justice Doherty noted, "Dr. Totten did not pretend to employ the scientific method ... . Dr. Totten's opinion flowed from his specialized knowledge gained through extensive research, years of clinical work and his familiarity with the relevant academic literature." (para. 108) In remarking that most expert evidence routinely heard by courts cannot be scientifically validated, Justice Doherty said that the proper question to be answered in assessing the reliability of Dr. Totten's opinion was, "... whether his research and experiences had permitted him to develop a specialized knowledge about gang culture ... that was sufficiently reliable to justify placing his opinion as to the potential meanings of the teardrop tattoo in that culture before the jury". (para. 117) The Court of Appeal felt Dr. Totten's evidence should have been admitted and ordered a new trial.

The second trial of Warren Abbey does not mark the end of this analysis of expert evidence. Following the second trial, in which Abbey was convicted, his lawyers discovered fresh evidence, calling into question the impartiality of Dr. Totten and the reliability of his expert opinion on the meaning of teardrop tattoos. The Ontario Court of Appeal had to deal with the issue once again in *R. v. Abbey*, [2017] O.J. No. 4083, 2017 ONCA 640.

Interestingly, the ammunition for challenging Dr. Totten was provided in another trial of a man named Gager, in which the *defence* attempted to call him as an expert on street gangs and to offer the opinion that the accused in the case did not have the characteristics of a gang member. This trial was held after *Abbey's* second trial. The Crown aggressively challenged Dr. Totten's expertise during the *voir dire* to determine if he was qualified to provide this expert evidence at all. The Crown challenged all of the statistical information that had been included in studies Dr. Totten had purportedly conducted into street gang culture.

The new evidence presented to the Ontario Court of Appeal now clearly demonstrated that Dr. Totten had grossly exaggerated the number of gang members he claimed to have interviewed in the "studies" on which he based his expert evidence about the tattoos. He had similarly exaggerated the number of interviewees who had been convicted of homicide, and the fact that his studies had generated any valid statistics about teardrop tattoos on the gang members he had interviewed. As Justice Laskin of the Ontario Court of Appeal concluded, "I agree with Abbey's submission that the fresh evidence is sufficiently cogent that if it had been put before the trial judge he would have ruled Totten's opinion evidence about the meaning of a teardrop tattoo inadmissible." (para. 109)

Justice Laskin went on to rule, "The fresh evidence…shows that Totten's evidence is too unreliable to go to a jury…and the prejudice and harm from admitting it would be great both because it would consume too much valuable court time and because the jury would likely be unable to effectively and critically assess the evidence." (para. 121). The Court was forced to order yet another new trial for Warren Abbey.

DNA analysis as an investigative tool has become so notorious that it is easy to forget that the science is relatively new and experts being allowed into Canadian criminal courts to express opinions based on this analysis really started with the murder trial reviewed by the Ontario Court of Appeal in the late 1990s, *R. v. Terceira*, [1998] O.J. No. 428, 123 C.C.C. (3d) 1, affd [1999] S.C.J. No. 74, 142 C.C.C. (3d) 95. Justice Finlayson of the Court of Appeal stated that the trial judge was correct in admitting DNA evidence at the trial and that the judge had properly assessed the reliability of the scientific methodology as a technique that had gained acceptance in the scientific community and could be validated as reliable.

Of course, the science itself had been used in criminal investigations since Dr. Alec Jeffreys had first become involved in analyzing blood samples related to the sexual assaults and murders of two teenage girls in Narborough, England in 1986. Dr. Jeffreys' DNA analysis helped police eliminate one young suspect who had been wrongfully accused and ultimately led to the confession of the real killer. The science had developed, its acceptance in the scientific community expanded and its use in criminal investigations had spread broadly in the 12 years before it was accepted as a valid basis for expert opinion evidence in the *Terceira* trial in Ontario. If properly done, expert evidence based on DNA analysis meets the criteria for the admission of scientifically sound evidence laid out in the *Daubert* case.

With the legalization of marijuana in Canada, there will inevitably be a heightened focus on the ability of police to assess whether or not a driver of a vehicle is impaired by a drug other than alcohol. Under s. 254 (3.1) of the *Criminal Code,* a police officer with reasonable grounds to believe that person has been driving while impaired by a drug can request the suspect submit to an evaluation by an "evaluating officer". Such officers receive special training and are certified as "drug recognition experts" (DRE) under the Code and Evaluation of Impaired Operation (Drugs and Alcohol) Regulations, SOR/2008-196. They utilize a 12-step process to determine if the driver has indications of drug impairment.

In the recent case of *R. v. Bingley,* [2017] S.C.J. No. 12, [2017] 1 S.C.R. 170, the Supreme Court of Canada was asked to decide whether a DRE could testify about his or her findings without a *voir dire* to assess the DRE's expertise. The majority of the Supreme Court ruled that a *voir dire* would not be necessary; "…s. 254(3.1) and the legislative and regulatory scheme that accompanies it conclusively answer the question of expertise. The DRE is established by Parliament to possess special expertise outside the experience and knowledge of the trier of fact. He is thus an expert for the purpose of applying the 12-step evaluation and determining whether the evaluation indicates impairment…" (para. 27)

THE RULE AGAINST OATH-HELPING

Judges in Canada have been very reluctant to allow experts to testify as to whether or not a particular witness is telling the truth. This has been described as a "rule against oath-helping". In *R. v. Beland*, [1987] S.C.J. No. 60, 60 C.R. (3d) 1 at para. 17, Justice McIntyre of the Supreme Court of Canada stated that the rule exists because, "… judges and juries are capable of assessing credibility". Case reports make it clear that judges want jurors to continue to do this sort of assessment on their own, without giving in to the allure of relying on an expert. The expert whose evidence was rejected in the *Beland* case had administered a polygraph (lie detector) test to the accused. The defence hoped to call the expert to testify that the test indicated that the accused was telling the truth when claiming innocence. In rejecting this type of evidence, the Supreme Court left it to the trial judge or jurors to decide whether or not to believe the accused if he chose to testify.

Expert witnesses have been allowed to offer opinions that would help the judge or jury understand the behaviours of certain types of witnesses, like child sexual abuse victims or battered women, but this testimony cannot cross the line to suggest that a particular witness should be believed because he or she is a member of that group. It has been used to help explain why complaints of abuse might be delayed or how an alleged victim could continue to live with an abuser in a generalized context, but should not be directed at the credibility of a specific witness. Chief Justice McLachlin of the Supreme Court of Canada discussed these issues in a minority opinion in *R. v. D.D.*, [2000] S.C.J. No. 44, [2000] 2 S.C.R. 275 and for the majority in *R. v. Marquard*, [1993] S.C.J. No. 119, [1993] 4 S.C.R. 223 at 249. This may be a tough distinction for jurors to make and critics of the cases that have allowed this type of expert testimony have pointed out that its prejudicial effect may well outweigh any probative value.

LIMITS ON THE USE OF EXPERT WITNESSES

Judges are usually mindful of the impact that the testimony of an expert with an impressive array of credentials might have on jurors. They will warn jurors that they still have a responsibility to assess the *weight*, or importance that should be given to each witness's testimony, regardless of the witness's declared expertise. Jurors are reminded before they start their deliberations that they can accept or reject any portion of any witness's testimony.

In order to prevent our trials from simply becoming a battle of experts, evidence statutes limit the number of experts that any party can call at a trial. Section 7 of the *Canada Evidence Act* stipulates that if the defence or prosecution wants to use more than five experts, they must ask for special permission from the trial judge. Many of the provincial evidence statutes that govern civil trials and criminal trials related to provincial and municipal offences reduce the number of experts to three unless a judge permits more.

Ontario's *Rules of Civil Procedure* make it clear that an expert's primary duty is to assist the court, *not* whichever party plans on calling the witness (even though one of the parties is likely paying for the expert's time in preparing a written report and attending court to testify). In a clear attempt to curtail lawsuits that involve a 'battle of experts', the rules go as far as to give a judge the power to require opposing experts to meet in advance of the trial in order to clarify different interpretations of the evidence and to narrow the contentious issues as much as possible.

Ontario's *Rules* require expert witnesses to sign a "Form 53", on which the witness will commit to an obligation to the court to be "fair, objective and non-partisan". This does not mean that a lawyer for the party who is calling the witness cannot help the expert to understand the justice process in which he or she will be immersed. Nor does it prevent the lawyer reviewing an expert's draft report. As the Ontario Court of Appeal explained in *Moore v. Getahun*, [2015] O.J. No. 398, 2015 ONCA 55, leave to appeal refused [2015] S.C.C.A. No. 119 : "Consultation and collaboration between counsel and expert witnesses is essential to ensure that the expert understands the duties reflected...in Form 53... Reviewing a draft report enables counsel to ensure that the report (i) complies with the *Rules*...(ii) addresses and is restricted to the relevant issues and (iii) is written in a manner and style that is accessible and comprehensible." (para. 63)

The Supreme Court of Canada's decision in *White Burgess Langille Inman v. Abbott and Haliburton Co.*, [2015] S.C.J. No. 23, 2015 SCC 23 provides additional cautions that trial judges must decide, "...whether expert evidence that meets the preconditions of admissibility is sufficiently beneficial to the trial process to warrant its admission ..." The Court went on to emphasize that a judge should consider any lack of impartiality or bias by the expert. Justice Cromwell explained:

> The expert's opinion must be impartial in the sense that it reflects an objective assessment of the question at hand. It must be independent in the sense that it is the product of the expert's independent judgment, uninfluenced by who has retained him or her or the outcome of the litigation. It must be unbiased in the sense that it does not unfairly favour one party's position over another. (para. 32)

Justice Hourigan of Ontario's Court of Appeal made this observation in a recent civil case, *Bruff-Murphy (Litigation guardian of) v. Gunawardena*, [2017] O.J. No. 3161, 2017 ONCA 502, leave to appeal dismissed [2017] S.C.C.A. No. 343: "The law regarding expert witnesses has evolved considerably over the last 20 years. Gone are the days when an expert served as a hired gun or advocate for the party that retained her." (para. 1) The trial judge had allowed a psychiatrist to testify for the defence in a case that had to determine if the plaintiff was entitled to financial compensation for injuries suffered in a car accident. Justice Hourigan noted that the psychiatrist's expert report, "...goes beyond a mere lack of independence and appears to have adopted the role of advocate for the defence. Given the paucity of psychiatric analysis in the report versus the high degree of potential prejudice in wrongly swaying the jury...Dr. Bail should have been excluded from testifying." (para. 47) A new trial was ordered.

The requirement for impartiality of the expert was applied in a recent drug trafficking prosecution, *R. v. McManus*, [2017] O.J. No. 1372, 2017 ONCA 188. Police had seized an iPhone and Blackberry from the accused, from which they extracted a large number of text messages. The Crown called one of the investigating officers to testify as an expert on the meaning of words used in the text messages. At trial, he provided an opinion that phrases such as "are you good" and "what ya want" had drug-related connotations, and that words like, "bling", "work", "cake" and "cook" did also. On appeal, the accused's lawyer challenged the bias and partiality of this expert and the opinion provided.

Justice van Rensburg of the Ontario Court of Appeal pointed out that the officer's prior involvement in the investigation "...would immediately give rise to a concern about the officer's ability...to provide an impartial opinion." (para. 70) The Court went on to note, "The evidence that D.C. Bullick provided could easily have been offered by another witness who had no connection to the case." (para. 73). The evidence should not have been admitted. A new trial was ordered.

In *R. v. Livingston*, [2017] O.J. No. 5009, 2017 ONCJ 645, Justice Lipson refused to qualify a Crown expert on the operation of computer systems because the retired O.P.P. officer had been involved throughout the investigation of the crime in question, even proposing additional charges that could be laid against the accused. In addition, the proposed expert had sent e-mails to other investigators that demonstrated his lack of independence and impartiality. The trial judge, characterized "Mr. Gagnon's comments to be the kind one would expect to hear from a partisan police investigator, not a supposedly independent and unbiased expert." (para. 60)

EXPERTS AND EYEWITNESS TESTIMONY

R. v. Frimpong, [2013] O.J. No. 1765, 2013 ONCA 243 is a recent case in which the accused was convicted of two counts of first degree murder by a jury. A key element of the evidence against the accused was the testimony of an eyewitness named Chammas, who identified Mr. Frimpong as the shooter in an attempted robbery that turned into a scuffle between the robbery target and one of the perpetrators. Chammas, who was in the hotel room where the incident occurred, testified that Frimpong fired a shot at the participants in the scuffle that resulted in the death of both. It was alleged that Frimpong had arrived at the room as an accomplice of the robber who died.

During the trial, Frimpong's defence lawyer attempted to call an expert, Dr. Roderick Lindsay to explain to the jurors general frailties and dangers inherent in eyewitness identification evidence. In addition, Dr. Lindsay hoped to describe concepts called "change blindness" and "unconscious transference" which could explain how Mr. Chammas could have honestly but mistakenly believed that Mr. Frimpong was the shooter, having seen him in the presence of the dead robber earlier in the evening. The trial judge ruled that this expert's evidence did not meet the necessity criteria; in other words, the jury did not need an expert to tell them about the inherent frailties of eyewitness testimony. Frimpong appealed this ruling to the Ontario Court of Appeal.

In upholding the trial judge's refusal to allow the expert to testify, Justice Doherty of the Court of Appeal effectively said that standard warnings which trial judges are required to make about the "notorious unreliability" of eyewitness testimony, together with the defence lawyer's closing arguments on the issue, were all the jury needed. In so ruling, Justice Doherty also mentioned that he saw no reason to depart from the reasoning of his own Court of Appeal some 16 years earlier in *R. v. McIntosh*, [1997] O.J. No. 3172, 35 O.R. (3d) 97.

The *McIntosh* case involved multiple charges, including attempted murder and robbery, and was also dependent on eyewitness testimony. The defence had tried to call a professor of psychology, Dr. Alexander Yarmey who was prepared to discuss problems with cross-racial identification, photographic line-ups, in-court identifications and post-event contamination of memory that were factors in the case. He had been qualified to provide this type of opinion in a number of court cases in the U.S. In rejecting the need for this expert opinion, Justice Finlayson of the Ontario Court of Appeal stated, "I have some serious reservations as to whether the 'Psychology of Witness Testimony' is an appropriate area for opinion evidence at all." (para. 19) He went on to add: "This opinion evidence is directed to instructing the jury that all witnesses have problems in perception and recall with respect to what occurred during any given circumstance that is brief and stressful. Accordingly, Dr. Yarmey is not testifying to matters that are outside the normal experience of the trier of fact: he is reminding the jury of the normal experience." (para. 20) Justice Finlayson also believed that, "... the well established warnings in the standard jury charge on the frailties of identification evidence" were more than adequate. (para. 22)

This seems like a questionable premise indeed. As was pointed out by Justice Rosenberg of the Ontario Court of Appeal in *R. v. Hanemaayer*, [2008] O.J. No. 3087, 2008 ONCA 580: "Mistaken eyewitness identification is the overwhelming factor leading to wrongful convictions. A study in the United States of DNA exonerations shows that mistaken eyewitness identification was a factor in over 80 per cent of the cases." (para. 29) Anthony Hanemaayer had actually entered a guilty plea to a sexual assault he did not commit, owing to the confident testimony of an honest, but mistaken eyewitness and his fear that a conviction following a trial would result in a longer sentence.

Judges know that eyewitness identification evidence is *notoriously unreliable* (*R. v. Jack*, [2013] O.J. No. 519, 2013 ONCA 80). They also know that it is the reliability of the identification, not the credibility of the eyewitness that is often the problem (*R. v. Alphonso*, [2008] O.J. No. 1248, 2008 ONCA 238). Judges are expected to understand that interracial identification and identifications made in stressful situations are problematic (*R. v. McDonald*, [2012] O.J. No. 243, 2012

ONCA 40). They should also be aware of issues that can be created by improper police procedures in conducting photo or live line-up identifications (Justice Peter Cory, *The Inquiry Regarding Thomas Sophonow*). Judges should know that in-court identifications of someone prominently placed in the prisoners' dock is of little value (*R. v. Hibbert*, [2002] S.C.J. No. 40, 2002 SCC 39), and that generic descriptions and a failure to notice distinctive features should set off warning bells (*R. v. Yigzaw*, [2013] O.J. No. 4091, 2013 ONCA 547). But judges still get it wrong (*R. v. Gough*, [2013] O.J. No. 973, 2013 ONCA 137).

Is it ridiculously naïve to believe that members of the public who are called to sit as jurors can be sufficiently informed of this array of eyewitness identification problems through a judge's instructions alone? Many of the cases mentioned in the preceding paragraph necessitated re-trials owing to inadequate instructions. Eyewitness identification experts regularly testify in the U.S. and other jurisdictions. Is it time for Canadian courts to make more extensive use of this area of expertise?

GATHERING EVIDENCE FOR EXPERT ANALYSIS

Several sections of the *Criminal Code* facilitate the gathering of evidence on which experts may conduct studies that could result in generating opinion evidence. Section 487.092 enables a judge to issue a warrant authorizing police officers to obtain handprints, fingerprints, footprints or tooth impressions. Section 487.05 allows a judge to issue a warrant to enable a peace officer to obtain a bodily substance from a suspect for DNA analysis. This can be done by plucking hairs, pricking the skin for blood, or swabbing the inside of the mouth. The impression obtained by s. 487.092 can be used for any criminal offence. The DNA sample section applies to a designated list of offences, but it is a long list. It includes murder, sexual assault, kidnapping and arson, among many other charges. The Supreme Court of Canada upheld the constitutional validity of using the DNA warrant provision in *R. v. B. (S.A.)*, [2003] S.C.J. No. 61, 2003 SCC 60.

The federal *Identification of Criminals Act* authorizes the police to collect fingerprints and photographs from anyone charged with an offence that is classified as *indictable*. This, of course, includes many of the more serious charges under the *Criminal Code* and *Controlled Drugs and Substances Act*. Since it is a *charge* that triggers the possibility of gathering this evidence, *hybrid* offences (those that can be treated as either indictable or summary conviction matters once the prosecutor gets an opportunity to make that choice), are also covered by the statute. Copies of the fingerprints gathered are kept in a central repository that is operated by a branch of the R.C.M.P. This collection can be accessed in order to make comparisons with fingerprint evidence that has been collected at a crime scene.

Section 254 of the *Criminal Code* allows a police officer to demand that a person suspected of impaired driving provide a breath sample for analysis of blood alcohol content. Officers who have received certification as breathalyzer technicians can then use an approved device to analyze the breath sample and issue a report. The Code specifies that this report can be used as evidence of blood alcohol content and the technician's attendance will only be required if the defence provides notice that they want the technician in attendance at the trial for cross-examination purposes.

If the suspect is incapable of producing a breath sample, a police officer can demand a blood sample for analysis purposes. The blood sample must be taken by a qualified medical practitioner or technician. If the suspect is in no condition to agree to a breath or blood sample, s. 256 of the *Criminal Code* allows a judge or justice of the peace to issue a warrant to authorize a police officer to require a medical practitioner to take a blood sample for analysis purposes. This type of warrant could be obtained over the phone.

TEST YOURSELF

1. A trial is being held to determine whether or not a dead man had written a document that appeared to be his will. Some members of the family are claiming that it is a forgery. In this situation:

   (a) only a handwriting expert would be allowed to testify as to whether or not the writing on the document is that of the deceased;

   (b) handwriting is not a science or profession that has experts, so only family members of the deceased would be allowed to testify;

   (c) probably both a handwriting expert and someone like the dead man's wife could give opinion evidence on the handwriting;

   (d) the trial judge or jurors could compare handwriting samples to the document themselves to determine who wrote it.

2. An expert in sexual behaviour is called to testify at a *bestiality* trial for the defence. The accused, Arnold Ziffle is alleged to have engaged in sex with a goat. The evidence the expert is prepared to present is based on studies he has conducted related to the sexual behaviour of Canadians. The expert is willing to say that sex with members of the sheep family is normal behaviour for the majority of Canadians. Is it likely the expert will be able to present this evidence to the jury if the Crown objects? Briefly explain.

3. An evidence professor was found lying on his back, on the floor of his office, dead. Further investigation revealed that someone apparently poisoned the bottle of rum the professor kept in the bottom drawer of his desk to "sweeten" his tea. An autopsy confirms that the professor's blood system was full of a lethal combination of rum and rat poison.

   One of the professor's colleagues reported seeing a student leaving the professor's empty office the day before the professor's body was discovered. The student appeared to be carrying a small bottle. A search of this student's locker reveals a small bottle with a label reading, "POISON". Many of the student's classmates have described the student as "psycho" and "totally deranged".

   (a) If the student is charged with murdering the professor, describe the experts the prosecutors will likely want to call as witnesses at the trial.

   (b) Would the defence also wish to call expert witnesses? Briefly describe the fields of expertise that may be helpful from the defence perspective.

Chapter 6

Character and Similar Fact Evidence

PREJUDICIAL EFFECT VERSUS PROBATIVE VALUE

If prosecutors in our criminal justice system were able to present evidence that demonstrated that an accused person had a well-deserved reputation as a bad person, or had previously done bad things, this would undoubtedly make it easier to convince a trial judge or jury that the defendant was responsible for whatever bad action he or she was accused of this time. In fact, they may become convinced of guilt without any substantial evidence that the accused actually committed this offence. It could become so bad that the judge or jury may overlook legitimate evidence pointing to the accused's innocence. Is this sort of evidence liable to lead to the truth about this offence, or to obscure the truth?

This is not to say that information about an accused person's criminal background or reputation is irrelevant. A judge or jury may find it very relevant to know that a person accused of committing the assault they are being asked to attribute to this individual has been convicted of committing 10 prior assaults or that everyone in the neighbourhood is afraid of this person because of his or her violent reputation. The problem, of course, is that the prejudicial effect that this evidence may have on the judge or jury outweighs the probative value in establishing beyond a reasonable doubt that the person committed this assault. It would be fundamentally unfair to an accused person to allow prosecutors to use this sort of evidence in a criminal trial.

Think of it another way. When police officers "round up the usual suspects", they will undoubtedly find the actual perpetrators of specific offences. Unfortunately, they may also end up leveling false accusations against downtrodden people with few societal allies who will be poorly equipped to mount any kind of an effective challenge. Surely, a criminal "justice" system should be designed to avoid this sort of systemic bias against people who have been in trouble in the past.

CHARACTER EVIDENCE AND PREVIOUS CONVICTIONS

Character or reputation evidence is simply proof that the accused is the type of person who could have committed such an offence. The general rule is that prosecutors cannot introduce evidence of an accused person's bad character or previous convictions because the prejudicial effect of this type of evidence outweighs its probative value.

There are exceptions to the general rule. Section 666 of the *Criminal Code* makes it clear that the gloves come off for the prosecution if the accused is the first to make his or her character an issue. For example, if the accused presented evidence that he or she would never do such a thing, this would open the door to the prosecutor presenting evidence of the accused's prior convictions as a form of rebuttal. Court decisions make it clear that courts may also open the door to evidence of previous behaviours for which there were no criminal charges, as long as the evidence that these incidents actually occurred is convincing.

Judges also allow prosecutors to produce character evidence if the defence lawyer or agent challenges the character of the alleged victim or other prosecution witness during the trial. It is also possible for an accused person to attack the character of a co-accused in an effort to make it appear more likely that this individual committed the offence. Making character an issue opens the door to responding evidence directed toward the accused.

In *R. v. Jackson*, [2013] O.J. No. 4677, 2013 ONCA 632 (C.A.), affd [2014] S.C.J. No. 30, 2014 SCC 30, the accused was convicted of the second degree murder of a drug dealer named Campbell. Mr. Jackson's primary defence was that he had acted in self-defence in shooting Campbell. He alleged that Campbell had threatened him and was reaching for a concealed gun when Jackson responded with the series of shots that resulted in Campbell's death. The police who investigated the murder never found any guns at the scene, not the gun that Campbell was alleged to have in his possession nor the gun that Jackson used.

During the jury trial, the defence lawyer had asked the judge for permission to present evidence of the deceased victim's criminal record, which included some four-year-old charges for possession and transfer of firearms. The defence hoped that this would provide evidence of the fact that the deceased may have been likely to have a gun in his possession at the time of the incident as Jackson alleged and that Campbell was likely the aggressor. The trial judge refused to admit evidence of the deceased's record, questioning both relevance and the fact that its admission, "...would trigger a side issue that would consume an undue amount of time and would distract the jury unduly from the main issue in the case". (para. 29)

Justice Gillese of the Ontario Court of Appeal agreed with the trial judge, adding at paras. 46 and 47:

> ... if the deceased's convictions had been admitted into evidence, the door would have been opened to the Crown to adduce evidence of all of the appellant's offences involving guns and violence, including his convictions as a youth for two robberies, assault with a weapon, and careless use of a firearm ... . Further, the door would have been opened to the Crown to introduce the facts underlying ... including his aggravated assault conviction stemming from an attempted murder incident in which the appellant shot a number of people.

It is hard to imagine how Mr. Jackson would have benefitted from opening that can of worms.

We all know that the defendant has a right to remain silent and, as a result, there is never an obligation for the defendant to take the stand to testify. If the defendant has a criminal record, there is a real risk created by s. 12 of the *Canada Evidence Act*. This section states that, "A witness may be questioned as to whether the witness has been convicted of any offence." The section is used primarily as a challenge to the *credibility* of a witness with a criminal background. Technically speaking, the *credibility*, or believability of a witness is a different issue than the character of the witness and is relevant when anyone is testifying in court. Nevertheless, the Supreme Court of Canada in *R. v. Corbett*, [1988] S.C.J. No. 40, 64 C.R. (3d) 1, made it clear that if the witness is the defendant, a judge has a discretion to exclude evidence of prior convictions as a form of challenging credibility *if* the prejudicial effect of that evidence outweighs its probative value. Let's face it, unless the record is for perjury or a trust-related offence like fraud, how much real relevance does the simple fact the witness has a record have on whether or not the defendant is likely to be telling the truth? On the other hand, the potential prejudicial effect of painting the defendant as a criminal prior to the jury deliberating on guilt or innocence on this charge is pretty clear.

Defence lawyers are allowed to make a *Corbett* application, requesting a trial judge to exclude evidence of the defendant's prior convictions <u>before</u> the defendant runs the risk of taking the stand to testify. In *R. v. Underwood*, [1997] S.C.J. No. 107, [1998] 1 S.C.R. 77, the Supreme Court ruled that the defence lawyer can make the application after the case for the prosecution ends and prior to any defence evidence being called. If the case involves a jury, the trial judge could ask them to leave and hold a *voir dire*, or mini hearing to assess the appropriateness of barring the prosecutor from using the defendant's convictions should he or she choose to testify. Obviously, the trial judge's ruling on this application may well influence whether the accused person chooses to testify or not.

The Ontario Court of Appeal decision in *R. v. Bomberry*, [2010] O.J. No. 3286, 2010 ONCA 542 provides an interesting example of these principles. Kirsten Bomberry was an admitted sex trade worker and crack cocaine addict, charged with the murder of one of her sex trade clients. Bomberry testified at her trial and admitted to being with the deceased earlier on the night in question, but she denied having killed him, or even being present when he was murdered in his vehicle. A police officer who had been locked up with the accused in her cell testified about Bomberry's violent nature, including comments that she was afraid of Ms. Bomberry, who demonstrated a tough persona while in jail. The trial judge did not provide any limiting warning to the jury about the risk of using such bad character evidence, or the fact that Bomberry was a crack addict and prostitute in assessing Ms. Bomberry's guilt with respect to the stabbing death of the victim. The Ontario Court of Appeal ruled that this was a mistake. As Justice O'Connor wrote: "The evidence was prejudicial to the appellant and there was a real risk that it would divert the jury from the task of deciding the case on the basis of the admissible evidence legally relevant to proving the charge…". (para. 34)

In addition, despite a pre-trial *Corbett* application to exclude prejudicial information about her extensive criminal record, the trial judge allowed the Crown to present evidence that Ms. Bomberry had four assault convictions, and several other charges. As the Court of Appeal ruled, this was also a mistake: "Not only were the assault convictions unnecessary for the task of assessing the appellant's credibility, but they were also potentially very prejudicial to her in terms of opening the door to propensity reasoning. … [T]hey portrayed the appellant as a person prone to violence." (para. 48) Because of the trial judge's errors, the Ontario Court of Appeal set aside Ms. Bomberry's conviction for murder and ordered a new trial.

In *R. v. Chamot*, [2012] O.J. No. 6267, 2012 ONCA 903, the accused was charged with eight counts of sexual assault involving three children, two boys and a girl. The offences were alleged to have occurred over several years when the children were living with the accused. The children's mother had come from Poland to live with Chamot and the children accompanied her.

During the trial, the jury not only heard evidence about the specific incidents that formed the basis for the charges, but the testimony of the children and the mother also included a great deal of other evidence that put Chamot in a bad light. The gist of this evidence was that, "… Chamot was a cruel and brutal person who terrorized three young children virtually from the time they arrived in Canada." (para. 59) While Justice Doherty of the Ontario Court of Appeal ruled that much of this evidence was necessary and admissible to provide context for the children's testimony and to assist the jury in assessing their credibility and reliability, the trial judge had failed to adequately warn the jury about the risk of using the evidence improperly (para. 62):

> …the trial judge must make it clear that the jury cannot use the evidence to infer that the accused is a bad person worthy of punishment regardless of his or her culpability on the specific allegations. The trial judge must also tell the jury that it cannot infer from that evidence that because the accused is the kind of person likely to abuse children, he or she is therefore guilty of the specific allegations.

Because of the lack of such limiting instructions to the jury, the Ontario Court of Appeal ruled that the accused was entitled to a new trial.

Section 360 of the *Criminal Code* is directed at people who are accused of possession of property obtained by crime. Subsection (1) specifies that if the accused has been convicted of theft or possession of stolen property in the five years prior to the current charge, these previous convictions can be used as proof that they knew the property found in their possession was "unlawfully obtained". It does seem a little strange that the federal government has chosen to legislate an exception to the common law only in relation to this charge. A couple of trial judges have ruled that treating this charge differently is a violation of the principles of fundamental justice that are protected in s. 7 of the *Canadian Charter of Rights and Freedoms*. I have not found evidence that Crown prosecutors wanted to challenge these rulings at the Court of Appeal level. Perhaps there simply have not been very many cases where prosecutors felt they needed evidence of prior offences to secure a conviction. This makes one wonder if there is really any pressing need for this legislated exception at all.

SIMILAR FACT EVIDENCE

The prejudicial effect of allowing a prosecutor to prove that an accused person has done similar bad things in the past usually outweighs the probative value of the evidence and, as a result it is usually excluded. Nevertheless, judges have long recognized that there may be circumstances where the probative value of this sort of evidence on a relevant issue is actually so great that it will be admitted, despite the potential prejudicial effect. Judges must evaluate the unique circumstances that exist in each case, but by looking at some of the leading cases where similar fact evidence has either been admitted or excluded, you can gain an understanding of the factors they will consider important in making these decisions.

One of the earliest cases where similar fact evidence was admitted originated in Australia and worked its way all the way around the world to the British Privy Council. This was the last court of appeal for many Commonwealth countries at the time, including Canada. The Privy Council supported the trial judge's decision to admit some very disturbing similar fact evidence owing to the probative value of the evidence in establishing a pattern of behaviour that seemed to indicate that an odd couple from down under were turning a profit by accepting small payments to care for unwanted infants which they quickly murdered, then buried. *Makin v. Attorney General for New South Wales*, [1894] A.C. 57 (P.C.) involved the trial of a couple named John and Sara Makin, charged with the murder of one infant named Horace Murray. The Makins had accepted a small sum of money from the child's unwed mother, 16-year-old Amber Murray. Formal adoption processes and adoption agencies were unknown at the time and it was shameful in many communities for unwed young mothers to keep their "illegitimate" children. The Makins appeared to have viewed these circumstances as an opportunity for profit. When asked what he had been arrested for, John Makin apparently told a cellmate, "baby farming".

When the police investigated the Makins, they found they had moved regularly and left the bodies of 13 infants, including Horace Murray buried in backyards and basements. Police were able to locate four other unwed mothers who had given their children up to the Makins in very similar circumstances to those described by Amber Murray. Unfortunately, given the state of forensic science at the time and the decomposition of most of the infant remains, the only child the police were able to positively identify was Horace Murray. Hence, there was only one murder charge.

At the trial, in an effort to prevent a defence claim that tiny Horace had simply died of natural causes, the prosecutor wanted to produce evidence from the other four mothers of the Makins' "adoption" routine. In addition, the prosecutor wanted to be able to show that the other 12 infant bodies had been buried at three homes the Makins had occupied for short periods of time. In ruling that the evidence was properly admitted by the trial judge, Lord Herschell of the Privy

Council laid the groundwork for the principles of similar fact evidence that have developed since:

> It is undoubtedly not competent for the prosecution to adduce evidence tending to show that the accused has been guilty of criminal acts other than those covered by the indictment, for the purpose of leading to the conclusion that the accused is a person likely from his criminal conduct or character to have committed the offence for which he is being tried. On the other hand, the mere fact that the evidence adduced tends to show the commission of other crimes does not render it inadmissible if it be relevant to an issue before the jury, and it may be so relevant if it bears upon the question whether the acts alleged to constitute the crime charged in the indictment were designed or accidental, or to rebut a defence which would otherwise be open to the accused.

Judges have also made it clear that the probative value of similar fact evidence may outweigh its prejudicial effect and make it admissible when a pattern of behaviour, a very distinctive *modus operandi*, demonstrates that it is quite likely that the person who committed the past acts also committed the current one. In the case of *R. v. Straffen*, [1952] 2 Q.B. 911 (C.C.A.), the English Court of Criminal Appeals had to deal with the strange strangulation of a young girl named Linda Bowyer. She had apparently been strangled by hand, without any attempt at sexual interference and with no attempt to conceal the body, which was left in a public place. The accused, Thomas Straffen, had briefly escaped from a facility for the criminally insane, located close to the murder scene. He was in the vicinity at the time of the offence. Mr. Straffen quickly became a person of interest to investigators. This was not surprising, as he had been sent to the psychiatric facility a year earlier after admitting to murdering two other young girls in very similar circumstances. Straffen was not prepared to admit that he had also killed Linda Bowyer. At his trial for that murder, the prosecutor tried to introduce evidence of the previous slayings. Justice Slade ruled that it was appropriate to admit evidence of these other acts, "… not for the purpose of showing … that the appellant was 'a professional strangler', but to show that he strangled Linda Bowyer; in other words, for the purpose of identifying the murderer of Linda Bowyer as being the same individual as the person who had murdered the other two little girls in precisely the same way".

The Supreme Court of Canada decision in *R. v. Arp*, [1998] S.C.J. No. 82, [1998] 3 S.C.R. 339, involved similar fact evidence of two murders that were tried at the same time, though the victims had been killed some three and a half years apart. Both incidents involved drunken women who had been offered a ride. When their corpses were found in remote areas, it was clear that the killer had used a sharp instrument to remove articles of clothing, which were then spread around the murder scene. Mr. Justice Cory said that in a case involving more than one count, "… the link between the accused and any one count will be relevant to the issue of identity on the other counts which disclose a striking similarity in the manner in which those offences were committed." (para. 53)

It is important that if multiple charges are going to be tried together, there should be some relevant similarity. In *R. v. Last*, [2009] S.C.J. No. 45, [2009] 3 S.C.R. 146, Gregory Last was charged with two sexual assaults involving two different victims that occurred about a month apart. The jury trial of both assaults was held together, despite the fact that there was no similarity between the way the two attacks were alleged to have occurred and despite Mr. Last's application to have the trials of each count held separately. After Last was convicted of both assaults by the jury, he appealed, claiming that he was unduly prejudiced by the joint trial. The Supreme Court of Canada agreed, ruling that the risk of prejudice to the accused was significant because of both a risk of credibility cross-pollination and prohibited propensity reasoning on the part of the jury members. The Supreme Court felt that the judge's instruction to the jury seeking to limit the effect of prejudice and prohibited propensity reasoning was not enough in this case and that the charges should have been tried separately. Administration of justice efficiency in holding a joint trial was not a good enough rationale in light of the significant risk of prejudice to Mr. Last.

R. v. Quesnelle, [2013] O.J. No. 1365, 2013 ONCA 180 presents a contrasting situation. Mr. Quesnelle was charged with sexually assaulting two different victims and the trial judge denied his application for a severance of the trials. The Ontario Court of Appeal ruled there was no reason to interfere with the trial judge's ruling on this point . The Court of Appeal noted a long list of similarities between the individual events. Both complainants were drug addicts who testified they had been driven to the same location in a dirty van. Both claimed they were then led to the basement of a Laundromat in a shopping plaza where there was a soiled mattress on the floor. They each alleged they were given drugs, punched and forced to have anal intercourse. Both claimed the accused bragged of membership in the Hell's Angels and his preference for forced sex. Both were dropped off after the respective incidents at a bus stop.

The case of *R. v. Shearing*, [2002] S.C.J. No. 59, [2002] 3 S.C.R. 33, provides an interesting application of these principles. The accused was a cult leader, who was alleged to have indecently assaulted several young cult members and his housekeepers' children over a 25-year period. He faced 20 charges, involving 11 different complainants. The sheer number of charges would have made the case interesting enough, but the role of the spiritual beliefs of the cult provided an intriguing additional element. Cult teachings, promoted by Mr. Shearing as cult leader included a belief that the path to spiritual enlightenment included sexual experience. The accused used his status in the cult to teach young girls that they could reach such enlightenment through sexual contact with him. It took years before many of the now grown complainants triggered the investigation that led to the charges.

A key issue at trial was whether or not the evidence of each allegation of sexual misconduct was admissible as similar fact evidence in relation to the other charges. As with any similar fact evidence, the probative value of this evidence would have to outweigh the obvious prejudicial effect the multiple charges could have on portraying the accused as a sexual predator. It should be noted that the defendant admitted touching all of the complainants except his housekeepers' children. His defence to the charges was that the girls had consented to the touching.

When the case eventually worked its way through the appeal process to the Supreme Court of Canada, Justice Binnie wrote the majority decision on the use of the similar fact evidence. He first addressed the probative value of the evidence, concluding that it was strong enough to justify admission of each allegation in relation to the other charges:

> ... the cogency of the similar fact evidence rests on the validity of the double inference that firstly, the accused had a situation-specific propensity to groom adolescent girls for sexual gratification by exploiting the cult's beliefs and its domestic arrangements, and secondly, that he proceeded in that way with each complainant. Similarity and unity of the incidents ... lay in the accused's *modus operandi*, his abuse of power and the theme of quack spiritualism.

Justice Binnie recognized that in the circumstances, where all the alleged victims knew one another, there was an opportunity for *collusion*. In other words, there was a possibility that they could have gotten together and concocted the allegations against the accused. However, he also thought the evidence of this actually happening was weak and felt it was fair for the trial judge to raise the issue with the jurors and let them decide whether or not this factor should diminish the value of the evidence of each of the complainants.

Evidence of collusion had a different impact on the admissibility of similar fact evidence in the case of *R. v. Handy*, [2002] S.C.J. No. 57, [2002] 2 S.C.R. 908. The accused was facing a charge of sexual assault causing bodily harm. His defence was that the sex had been consensual. The complainant admitted that she had consented to vaginal sex, but not anal sex, or other acts that hurt her. The prosecutor called the defendant's ex-wife to provide similar fact evidence. She was prepared to say that Mr. Handy enjoyed engaging in painful sex, particularly anal sex. Her testimony would also be that, when aroused, her husband would not take "no" for an answer.

Although the trial judge admitted the ex-wife's evidence, the Ontario Court of Appeal and the Supreme Court of Canada ruled that the judge was wrong to do so. First, the "similar facts" alleged by the ex-wife were not all that similar. In fact, several of the acts she was prepared to describe were worse than the allegation that was the subject of the trial. This meant that their prejudicial effect was high. In addition, there were more dissimilarities than similarities in the actual incidents, including the fact that none of the alleged attacks on the ex-wife started with consensual sex, which was a key element in the trial. Overall, the probative value of the similar fact evidence of the ex-wife was low.

In the opinion of Justice Binnie of the Supreme Court of Canada, the probative value of the similar fact evidence was further lowered by the very real possibility of collusion between the current complainant and the ex-wife. The ex-wife admitted she had spoken to the woman several months before the incident that was the subject of the trial. During that meeting, the ex-wife provided details of her former husband's criminal record and boasted that she had received $16,500 from the Criminal Injuries Compensation Board for his attacks on her.

The trial judge had thought it was appropriate to simply leave the possibility of collusion to the jury, the approach that was followed in *R. v. Shearing*. Justice Binnie, who had also written the decision in *R. v. Shearing*, said that would be the correct approach if there was only a possibility of collusion (*R. v. Handy* at para. 111):

> Here there is something more. It is the whiff of profit. The ex-wife acknowledged that she had told the complainant of the $16,500 she received from the Criminal Injuries Compensation Board on the basis, she agreed, that, "[a]ll you had to do was say that you were abused". A few days later the complainant, armed with this information, meets the respondent and goes off with him to have sex in a motel room.

Justice Binnie ruled that here the evidence of collusion affected the probative value of the similar fact evidence and the trial judge should have kept the ex-wife's evidence out. This was enough for the Supreme Court of Canada to rule that there should be a new trial.

In *R. v. Doodnaught,* [2017] O.J. No. 5263, 2017 ONCA 781, the accused doctor was an anesthesiologist who assisted with operations at North York General Hospital. He underwent a 76-day trial involving 21 counts of sexually assaulting patients while they were on the operating table, undergoing lower body surgeries. As unlikely as the circumstances sound, there was evidence that during such surgeries, the anesthesiologist works in the vicinity of the patient's head, while separated from other doctors and nurses in the operating room by non-transparent drapes. These serve as a barrier, protecting the sterile area where the surgery is going on from a non-sterile area where the anesthesiologist monitors the patient's level of consciousness.

In convicting the accused of all 21 counts of sexual assault, the trial judge pointed out that none of the individual complainants knew each other, so the risk of collusion was non-existent. Though there were 25 anesthesiologists who worked at NYGH, no reports of sexual misconduct were ever alleged against anyone other than Dr. Doodnaught. As Justice Watt of the Court of Appeal observed, the probative value of the similar fact evidence of the 21 separate allegations in this case exceeded its prejudicial effect, "...because the force of similar circumstances defies coincidence or other innocent explanation." (para. 149) The Court of Appeal ruled that each of the individual allegations could be used in support of the others; "Even if a reasonable doubt existed in relation to each allegation considered in isolation, the individual allegations remain mutually supportive and capable of establishing proof beyond a reasonable doubt." (para. 157)

EVIDENCE OF GANG INVOLVEMENT

R. v. Perrier, [2004] S.C.J. No. 54, [2004] 3 S.C.R. 228 and *R. v. Chan*, [2004] S.C.J. No. 53, [2004] 3 S.C.R. 245, are two related cases that involved multiple break and enter and robbery charges against two individuals who were alleged to be members of a gang that committed a series of three home invasions. The *modus operandi* for all of the robberies involved some strikingly similar elements. In each, the home of a middle-aged Asian woman was approached by a person pretending to be a postal worker with a package. After knocking on the door to gain entry, this person was joined by several other gang members, some Asian, some Caucasian, who would bind the homeowner with duct tape prior to searching for valuables.

Descriptions of the invaders provided by each of the victims varied. It appeared as though membership in the gang might have altered from robbery to robbery. There did not seem to be any consistency to the descriptions of individuals playing particular roles, like that of the fake postman either. Despite these discrepancies, the trial judge directed the jury that they could use the evidence from each of the robberies as similar fact evidence serving to identify the two accused as participants in each of the other robberies.

The Supreme Court of Canada said that the trial judge had misdirected the jury and ordered new trials. While the evidence was certainly strikingly similar enough to demonstrate that the acts had been committed by one gang, the prejudicial effect of the evidence outweighed its probative value in establishing the identity of the accused as a participant in each of the crimes. As Justice Major ruled (at para. 25 of *R. v. Perrier*):

> ... the fact that an individual may have been a member of the gang on one occasion proves nothing more than a mere possibility that he was a member on another occasion. In this case the evidence of a group activity must be accompanied by evidence linking the individual to each of the group's offences for which he has been charged, either by virtue of the distinctiveness of his role or by other independent evidence. Without this additional link, the required nexus between the similar fact evidence and the acts of a particular accused is absent, and the similar fact evidence will not have sufficient probative value to outweigh the prejudice caused.

Another issue the courts have had to deal with is the prejudicial effect on an accused of being labelled as a member or associate of a known criminal gang during the course of the prosecution's case. The Manitoba Court of Appeal was faced with an interesting set of circumstances in the case of *R. v. Lamirande*, [2002] M.J. No. 133, 164 C.C.C. (3d) 299 (C.A.). Three men and one woman faced charges in relation to the robbery of a grocery store in Winnipeg in which a person who tried to intervene in their escape was shot and killed. The actual shooter was found guilty of second degree murder in a separate trial. The driver of the getaway vehicle cut a deal with the Crown and agreed to testify against Norman Guimond and Sheri Lamirande at their manslaughter trial. This key prosecution witness, in describing what had happened, explained the relationship between each of the players in the robbery and how they had come together to commit the offence. He explained that he, the shooter and Guimond were all members of a notorious local street gang called the Indian Posse and that Ms. Lamirande "hung around with them".

He went on to explain that the three gang members and another member had planned to rob a jewelry store. When the fourth member of the planned robbery failed to show up, they recruited Ms. Lamirande, who was with them at the time. All participants were aware that they would commit the robbery armed with a sawed-off shotgun and a metal bar. When they discovered the jewelry store was closed, they shifted their attention to the grocery store where the shooting took place.

In addition to this testimony, the prosecution also used letters and poems seized from Sheri Lamirande at the time she was admitted to the local jail, following her arrest. These documents also mentioned the Indian Posse, seeming to confirm her association with the gang.

Defence lawyers tried to argue that the evidence of this gang association had little or no probative value in relation to identifying the two accused as participants in the robbery and shooting. At the same time, it was felt that there was great prejudice to each of the accused in allowing the jury to hear about their association with a notorious local gang. It was pointed out that neither Guimond nor Lamirande had done anything to put their character into issue in the trial.

The trial judge accepted the prosecutor's position that the evidence had great probative value in establishing a connection between each of the participants and the robbery, enough to outweigh any prejudicial effect that would be caused.

Justice Scott of the Manitoba Court of Appeal agreed, stating at para. 85:

> In my opinion, the evidence was properly admitted to provide the essential background and context within which Lamirande and the others came together, planned, and executed the robbery. It was relevant and necessary to place into context Desjarlais' evidence which detailed the sophisticated robbery plans, the use of a get-away [*sic*] vehicle, and the agreement to 'smoke' any person who chose to get in the way. Without it, the Crown's case would have made little sense.

Sections 467.1 through 467.13 of the *Criminal Code* establish specific offences related to committing offences for the benefit of a criminal organization. Obviously, evidence indicating a defendant's involvement with such an organization is a necessary element of any such charge. In the Ontario Superior Court case of *R. v. Lindsay*, [2005] O.J. No. 2870, 66 W.C.B. (2d) 454 (S.C.), affd [2009] O.J. No. 2700, 97 O.R. (3d) 567 (C.A.), both accused were convicted of extortion in association with a criminal organization, the Hell's Angels. Considerable evidence going to the issue of the Hell's Angels being a criminal organization was admitted, along with evidence that both accused were members. There was further evidence that the act of extortion was committed while the defendants were wearing gang clothing and that threats were made where five other guys would be sent to the victim's house, who were "the same kind of mother fuck as I am".

In murder trials, such as *R. v. Abbey*, [2009] O.J. No. 3534, 2009 ONCA 624, leave to appeal refused [2010] S.C.C.A. No. 125 (discussed in Chapter 5) and *R. v. Williams*, [2013] O.J. No. 2421, 2013 ONSC 3100 (discussed in Chapter 3), evidence of gang involvement of the accused and the deceased was considered relevant and admissible because the killings were allegedly linked to gang rivalry.

AN ACCUSED'S GOOD CHARACTER EVIDENCE

Although it triggers the possibility of a prosecutor's response, there are cases where the accused will want to present evidence of his or her good character. This could be done through reputation evidence, expert testimony or through the accused's own testimony.

The permitted use of reputation evidence involves calling a witness who is familiar with the accused and knows his or her reputation in the community. If it is relevant to the issues of the case, this could include a general reputation for honesty, for being non-violent or for having the morals that would tend to raise doubt about involvement in the alleged criminal behaviour. The witness is not allowed to testify about specific acts the accused has done. This could open up a confusing side argument about the accused's involvement in these matters that would have limited relevance to the main trial issues.

Experts might be called to express an opinion about a characteristic of the accused that would make it unlikely he or she committed the offence alleged. This could, perhaps, be a psychiatric condition that would create an aversion for that type of activity.

A straight denial of having committed the offence by the accused person is not taken by the courts to be an assertion of good character that triggers a rebuttal by the prosecutor. Embellishing the denial can create difficulties. In the Ontario Court of Appeal case of *R. v. Dussiame*, [1995] O.J. No. 962, 98 C.C.C. (3d) 217 (C.A.), the accused was a teacher who was alleged to have sexually assaulted a student. In testifying, Mr. Dussiame insisted that he was a happily married man, inferring that because of his happy marital situation he would not be the type of person who would have to target a student for sexual gratification. The trial judge allowed the prosecutor to call several rebuttal witnesses to say that the accused had complained to them about problems in his marriage.

ATTACKING THE CHARACTER OF THE VICTIM

In Chapter 4, we discussed the statutory protections provided to alleged victims in sexual assault cases. Sections 276 and 277 of the *Criminal Code* prevent attacks on complainant credibility based on sexual reputation or prior sexual conduct.

Most other alleged victims are open to attacks on their character. If an accused raises self-defence in response to a charge involving assaultive behaviour or even homicide, it is not unusual for a judge to accept evidence portraying the alleged victim as a person with a reputation for violence, or indicating that it is likely that the purported victim was actually the aggressor in the incident.

A useful example is the case of *R. v. Pintar*, [1996] O.J. No. 3451, 110 C.C.C. (3d) 402 (C.A.), an Ontario Court of Appeal decision. Late one night, Joe Pintar, who lived in a remote location, was confronted at his front door by two large drunken men who were threatening to kill him. They made repeated attempts to get in and Mr. Pintar grabbed a rifle to scare them off. In the struggle that ensued, both intruders ended up dead and Joe Pintar found himself charged with wrongfully causing their deaths. In using self-defence as a response, Pintar was able to present a great deal of evidence about the violent reputation of the main aggressor in the situation and about repeated threats this individual had made on his life.

The Supreme Court of Canada extended the concept of self-defence to include the use of the "Battered Woman Syndrome" in the murder case of *R. v. Lavallee*, [1990] S.C.J. No. 36, 55 C.C.C. (3d) 97. The use of this defence involves portraying the deceased victim as a bad person who has repeatedly abused the defendant to the extent that she has acquired a sense of helplessness that prevents her from fleeing from her abusive situation. Eventually, she comes to see the only possible recourse to save herself, and perhaps children and other family members, is to kill the abuser. While the use of this defence and the expert opinions that initially justified its acceptance is controversial, it has been an element in many cases since the *R. v. Lavallee* decision. It is impossible to mount without calling evidence to attack the character and reputation of the victim.

R. v. Leon, [2018] O.J. No. 1251, 2018 ONSC 1482, is a recent case in which the accused, who was charged with second degree murder, wished to present evidence of both a criminal record and uncharged allegations of violence that had been levelled against his victim, Tevin James. This would bolster Mr. Leon's claim of self-defence. At the same time, Mr. Leon sought to prevent the Crown from presenting any evidence of his own prior convictions for robbery, one of which included its own element of violence.

In ruling on these issues, Justice Spies highlighted the risks to an accused in a circumstance like this one; "In my view there is a need to balance the picture …The purpose of the evidence I have ruled is admissible with respect to Mr. James is that he had a disposition to easily become violent and use a weapon if available. If I do not permit the Crown to lead any evidence of Mr. Leon's robbery convictions, then the jury will have no evidence that Mr. Leon has ever acted violently if he chooses not to testify." (para. 95)

CHARACTER EVIDENCE IN CIVIL TRIALS

Character evidence seldom seems to be relevant in civil trials. When it is, courts still apply the rule that its probative value must outweigh its prejudicial effect before it will be admitted.

0984394 B.C. Ltd. v. Sticky's Candy Holdings Ltd., [2017] B.C.J. No. 1962, 2017 BCSC 1760 is a recent civil case in which the plaintiff's president claimed that she was induced to get involved with a candy store franchise because of negligent misrepresentations made by the defendant's primary promoter. In the plaintiff's statement of claim, it was alleged that the promoter had made similar misrepresentations to other "potential, current and former Sticky's Candy franchisees". The defendant sought to prevent the production of such evidence as being unnecessarily prejudicial.

In ruling that the similar fact evidence could be utilized, Justice Iyer stated,

"I find that they would be probative of whether Mr. Burnette had a scheme as alleged and that he made the representations to Ms. Larson." (para. 14), The judge also cited an Ontario decision in a case called *Prism Data Services Ltd. v. Neopost Inc.*, [2003] O.J. No. 2994 (S.C.J.), where it was ruled, "Such allegations are proper as long as the added complexity resulting therefrom does not outweigh the probative value." (para. 8)

A lawsuit that is based on *defamation*, where the plaintiff is claiming that the defendant has damaged his or her reputation is obviously a situation where evidence that deals with the plaintiff's reputation is going to have high probative value.

TEST YOURSELF

1. Two people close to Mr. Kahn died in very mysterious circumstances. His sister's body was found in a large freezer in his home. Four years later, his wife was found dead in the bathtub. Both appeared to have died from a lack of oxygen and Mr. Kahn was the beneficiary on both of their life insurance policies.

   If Mr. Kahn was charged with murdering both women, could the wrongful death of the one be used as similar fact evidence with respect to the wrongful death of the other? Why or why not?

2. A man named Morrissey shot and killed his girlfriend after she told him they were breaking up. When he was charged with murder, Mr. Morrissey claimed that the shooting was an accident that occurred when he was trying to kill himself. He wants to call evidence during his trial to show that he tried to commit suicide when two previous girlfriends had broken up with him. Should this evidence be admissible? Briefly explain.

3. An evidence professor is killed when he is struck in the head with an apple as he enters the cafeteria. No one claims to have actually seen the apple being thrown, but a student has been identified as rushing from the scene shortly after the incident. When police investigate, they discover that this student had been doing poorly in the professor's class and her evidence notebook is covered with remarks like, "I hate this guy" and "This boring S.O.B. should die." In addition, the student has a previous conviction for assault. It seems that she was charged after throwing an orange at a child she was babysitting. She entered a guilty plea to the assault and was given a short period of probation.

   If the student is charged with murdering the professor, will the prosecutor be able to present evidence of the student's prior conviction? Briefly explain.

Chapter 7

Hearsay

THE BASIC HEARSAY RULE

A witness cannot repeat a statement originally made outside the courtroom by someone else, *if* this evidence is being used to prove the *truth* of the contents of that statement.

THE RATIONALE BEHIND THE EXCLUSION OF HEARSAY

R. v. Khelawon, [2006] S.C.J. No. 57, 2006 SCC 57, is an important Supreme Court of Canada decision, in which Justice Charron made a number of very clear statements about hearsay evidence, including this one at para. 2:

> While no single rationale underlies its historical development, the central reason for the presumptive exclusion of hearsay statements is the general inability to test their reliability. Without the maker of the statement in court, it may be impossible to inquire into that person's perception, memory, narration or sincerity. The statement itself may not be accurately recorded. Mistakes, exaggerations or deliberate falsehoods may go undetected and lead to unjust verdicts. Hence, the rule against hearsay is intended to enhance the accuracy of the court's findings of fact, not impede its truth-seeking function.

If we do not have the person who originally made the statement in court, we have no way of judging the validity of what was said or the credibility of the person who initially said it. We cannot test the accuracy of the statement and we lose a key component of our adversarial system of justice, where witnesses and their testimony are regularly challenged through *cross-examination*. Professor Wigmore (source of the "Wigmore Rules" discussed in Chapter 4) once said that, "Cross-examination is the greatest legal engine ever invented for ascertaining the truth." This has been repeated so often in Canadian courts that no one really questions the fundamental importance of being able to cross-examine the person who originally made a statement that will be used as evidence.

In *R. v. Baldree,* [2013] S.C.J. No. 35, [2013] 2 S.C.R. 520, Justice Fish of the Supreme Court of Canada listed some of the nuances that can be missed when hearsay evidence is admitted and cross-examination is circumvented:

> First, the declarant may have *misperceived* the facts to which the hear say statement relates; second, even if correctly perceived, the relevant facts may have been *wrongly remembered;* third, the declarant may have narrated the relevant facts in an *unintentionally misleading manner;* and finally, the declarant may have *knowingly made a false assertion*. The opportunity to fully probe these potential sources of error arises only if the declarant is present in court and subject to cross- examination. (para. 32)

Let's face it, our justice system provides some pretty strong hints that all testimony is potentially unreliable. That is why we require most witnesses to swear an oath or solemn affirmation and why society has made lying in court, or *perjury*, a crime. How could we possibly rely on evidence when the original speaker or writer is not subject to these safeguards because he or she is not even in the courtroom?

EXCEPTIONS TO THE BASIC RULE OF EXCLUSION

Judges have developed a number of *common law* exceptions to the rule requiring the exclusion of hearsay. In other words, sometimes hearsay statements are repeated in court with a judge's permission. There are also statutory exceptions to the general rule. Many of the exceptions depend on the circumstances in which the original statement was made and whether or not the dangers of inaccuracy or misleading fabrication are reduced by those circumstances. A primary exception is based on the use that will be made of the evidence. Practically, the exceptions could be divided into four main categories, with the third including a number of subcategories.

1.   The Purpose Exception

The first significant exception to the exclusion of hearsay comes from the wording of the rule itself. We do not allow witnesses to repeat statements that were originally made outside the courtroom *if* that evidence is being used to establish the *truth* of what was said. How about a situation where a witness is simply trying to demonstrate that an out-of-court statement was made; not trying to show that the contents of that statement were true? If the fact of the statement being made is relevant, this evidence should be admissible.

How did a police officer decide he had reasonable and probable grounds to conduct a search? A statement from a reliable source might constitute such grounds. This was an issue in the important case of *R. v. Collins*, [1987] S.C.J. No. 15, [1987] 1 S.C.R. 265, which we discussed in Chapter 3 and which will come up again in Chapter 10. When an undercover officer tackled Ruby Collins and wrestled her to the ground, seizing a balloon containing heroin, he was not acting on reasonable grounds created from his observations of her, but on information he had received. Though the trial judge initially prevented the officer from speaking about these out-of-court statements, the Supreme Court of Canada ruled his testimony about the source of his grounds for acting was both relevant and admissible.

At what point in time did a victim die? A person who heard the deceased utter any kind of statement at a particular time could help to establish the timeline between life and death. In *R. v. Ferber*, [1987] A.J. No. 343, 36 C.C.C. (3d) 157 (C.A.), the Alberta Court of Appeal ruled that a witness should be allowed to testify to the fact of a phone conversation with an individual who would soon become a murder victim. It was useful to establish that this person was still alive at the time and that the murder had to have occurred later. The contents of the conversation were irrelevant.

R. v. Bentley, [2013] B.C.J. No. 1790, 2013 BCSC 1125 involved a perjury charge against one of the police officers who had confronted Robert Dziekanski in the well-publicized incident that occurred at the Vancouver Airport in 2007, during which Mr. Dziekanski died. It was alleged that Bentley had lied on multiple occasions during his testimony at a public inquiry into Mr. Dziekanski's death. Not only were the officer's notes on the incident and statements made at the inquiry contrary to the video evidence recorded by a bystander, it appeared as though this officer's notes bore strikingly similar inaccuracies to those of the other officers involved in the incident. The Crown was alleging that the officers had colluded in producing an inaccurate account which exaggerated the deceased's aggression and attempted to justify the officers' excessive use of force. The Crown had sought to have these other officers' notes admitted at Bentley's trial, not for the truth of the contents, but rather to demonstrate that the officers had colluded on fabricating a false account of what had occurred. Justice McEwan of British Columbia's Supreme Court admitted the other officers' notes for that purpose.

A person, who is accused of assaultive behaviour, or even murder, may have acted in self defence after hearing a threat. Should he or she be able to tell the court about the threat? What if something the alleged victim said could have provoked the defendant's attack? It would seem to be both reasonable and relevant to allow the witness to discuss statements that were made outside the courtroom in these situations. This type of evidence was admitted in both *R. v. Pintar*, [1996] O.J. No. 3451, 110 C.C.C. (3d) 402 (C.A.) and *R. v. Lavallee*, [1990] S.C.J. No. 36, 55 C.C.C. (3d) 97, cases which were discussed in Chapter 6.

How about a situation where the police raid the residence of someone who they believe has been trafficking drugs? They seize a quantity of drugs, but while they are on the scene they also answer repeated calls to the residence phone. Each of the callers asks for their suspect and indicates that they are looking for drugs. Should the officers be able to testify about the phone calls they had received on the scene? The Ontario Court of Appeal in a case called *R. v. Edwards*, [1994] O.J. No. 1390, 34 C.R. (4th) 113 (C.A.), affd [1996] S.C.J. No. 11, [1996] 1 S.C.R. 128, ruled that the officers could testify to the fact that such phone calls were received while they were in the residence. With the accused facing a charge of possession *for the purpose of trafficking*, the evidence of drug deal phone calls was relevant without getting into the details of each call.

What if there is only one intercepted phone call? This was the situation in *R. v. Baldree*, [2013] S.C.J. No. 35, 2013 SCC 35, where the Supreme Court of Canada ruled that if the Crown was relying on this one call as evidence that drugs were possessed by the accused for the purpose of trafficking, the police officer's second-hand information about the contents of the call must be considered hearsay and subject to an analysis of whether or not this evidence is *necessary and reliable*. These concepts will be discussed in more detail, later in this chapter.

2.   Statements by a Party

Another major exception to the general exclusion of hearsay arises when the out-of-court statement a witness wishes to repeat was originally made by one of the *parties* involved in the court case. The rationale for this exception is, of course, that a *party* to the trial will be in court to refute, or challenge the accuracy of the hearsay statement if he or she wishes to do so. The party can direct his or her lawyer or agent to challenge the witness's accuracy of recall and can take the stand to deny making the statement, or to explain the context or true meaning if he or she chooses. The judge or jury can then assess the relative credibility of the witness and the party.

A witness may be allowed to repeat a relevant out-of-court statement by the accused in a criminal case or by plaintiff or defendant in a civil case. The out-of-court statement may include *admissions* (*i.e.*, "I was in the neighbourhood that night," or "I had been meaning to get the brakes fixed, but just never got around to it"), or *confessions* (*i.e.*, "Damn right I killed that Evidence professor," or "I guess I did let little Waldo play with the explosives").

In criminal cases, there are serious concerns that overly aggressive tactics by agents of the government could result in false admissions and confessions. There are also issues related to fundamental *Charter*-protected rights to silence and to the assistance of a lawyer that arise. We will discuss the special rules that ensure that a defendant's confessions or admissions are *voluntary* and that *Charter* protections are observed in Chapter 8.

It is also important to remember that a victim is <u>not</u> a *party* in a criminal case (the parties are society, represented by Crown prosecutors, and the defendant). As a result, out-of-court statements by the victim cannot be repeated by another witness through reliance on this exception. Victim statements may be admissible under other common law exceptions, but not this one. We will see another exception being used to admit a victim's out-of-court statement in the case of *R. v. Griffin*, [2009] S.C.J. No. 28, 2009 SCC 28, which is discussed below.

3.   Original Declarant Unavailable

Other common law exceptions have developed to allow for the repetition of statements that were originally made outside the courtroom when:

(a)   the original statement maker is unavailable; and

(b)   the original statement was made in circumstances that a judge feels lends reliability to the statement, without the need for the normal challenges to accuracy and trustworthiness provided by cross-examination.

(i)   Dying Declarations

There is a special exception to the exclusion of hearsay that only applies in homicide trials. Statements that were originally made by someone who is now dead can be repeated by another witness *if* it can be demonstrated that the deceased had a "hopeless, settled expectation of imminent death" at the time the statement was made. There is no doubt it would often be helpful to the prosecution to admit a statement like, "Joe shot me," particularly if there was no one else around to see what happened.

This common law exception has been around for hundreds of years and is based on the premise that someone would be unlikely to lie if he or she was on death's doorstep. Clearly, some of this rationale stems from a time when most people shared religious beliefs in the afterlife, with the possibility of eternal damnation for last-second lies. As described in an English case from 1789, dying declarations are, "...made in the extremity, when the party is at the point of death, and when every hope of this world is gone: when every motive to false-hood is silenced, and the mind is induced by the most powerful considerations to speak the truth..." (Justice Eyre in *R. v. Woodcock* (1789), 168 E.R. 352)

Critics have suggested that with religious affiliations being far less common in today's society, the exception no longer makes sense. While that may be true, you could also argue that the exception never really made sense since the truthfulness of the deceased is just one of the concerns that is addressed through cross-examination. If the statement maker is dead, how do you assess what opportunity he or she had to see the assailant? Was it dark? Was the victim attacked from behind? Is the victim simply assuming an attack from someone he or she feared, or did the victim actually see "Joe" pull the trigger? A defence lawyer will never be able to explore those issues with the statement maker.

Judges do strictly apply the limitation that the statement maker has to know that he or she is dying. Examples include a victim who had been doused in gasoline and set on fire (*R. v. Hall*, [2011] O.J. No. 5109, 2011 ONSC 5628) and a victim who had been stabbed 29 times, with intestines spilling from his body and a neck nearly severed (*R. v. Nurse*, [2014] O.J. No. 5003, 2014 ONSC 2340). If the evidence tended to show that the victim was unaware that he or she was fatally wounded, the statement would not be admitted using this exception.

The case of *R. v. Nurse* is an interesting one because the "hearsay" in question was not a statement at all, but a gesture. The victim, who died in an ambulance *en route* to the hospital, had pointed to one of the accused while police were attending to him. The police had asked him who had stabbed him, but the victim was unable to speak because of the severe lacerations to his neck. As Justice Coroza noted in admitting evidence of the gesture, "...an out of court statement may be verbal, written or implied. An 'implied statement' is any assertion not expressed by language, but rather is revealed through action." (at para 37)

In a Nova Scotia case, called *R. v. Muise*, [2013] N.S.J. No. 290, 2013 NSSC 141, it was the defence that sought to have a dying declaration admitted. Evidence showed that the victim had likely been shot from a distance of over 50 metres, by a gunman obscured by large boulders. There were three potential shooters on the scene. It was a dark, windy, rainy night. Police, who had attended the fatally wounded victim, asked him several times who had shot him. Between repeatedly stating, "I can't breathe – I'm going to die", the victim also clearly said, "I don't know." Mr. Muise's lawyer believed this could be useful evidence for his client's defence. The trial judge ruled it could be admitted under the dying declaration hearsay exception.

(ii)   Statements of Mental State

Courts have admitted out-of-court statements of a person's state of mind as an exception to the hearsay rule. Of course, the original declarant has to be unavailable to testify in court and his or her expressed state of mind must be relevant. This exception was used in *R. v. Griffin*, [2009] S.C.J. No. 28, 2009 SCC 28, a murder trial involving allegations that the accused had killed a man named Poirier because Poirier owed him a significant sum of money in relation to a drug deal. Shortly before being shot to death, Poirier had told his girlfriend that he had gone into hiding because he feared for his life and "... if anything happens to me, it's your cousin's family". The girlfriend was prepared to repeat this out-of-court statement during the trial and to testify that she understood Poirier to be referring to Poirier's fear of the accused, John Griffin, who was indirectly related to the girlfriend.

Why was this statement relevant? Justice Charron, writing for a majority of the Supreme Court of Canada said, "... Poirier's fearful state of mind is probative of the nature of the relationship between he and Griffin in the time period immediately preceding the murder." (para. 63) This took on added significance because, during the trial, defence lawyers had tried to suggest that in the dead man's drug-dealing life, several people other than the accused may have had a motive to kill Poirier. Justice Charron noted, "... the trial judge correctly observed that Poirier's particularized fear of Griffin was evidence that tended to rebut the defence proposition that someone other than Griffin might have had a motive to kill Poirier in January 2003. While Poirier's fear of Griffin was not conclusive on this issue, the evidence was highly relevant to the question of identity." (para. 65)

(iii)   Business Records

Statements that have been made outside the courtroom and will potentially be treated as *hearsay* include written documents. In other words, the legal concept of *hearsay* is broader than a dictionary definition of "something that is overheard". Judges have long accepted the admissibility of business records that were prepared by someone who is dead, and many years ago Canadian courts expanded that restriction to include records made by employees who were missing and could not be located at the time of trial. They believe that we can trust the reliability of a written record *if* it was made right around the time of the event, recorded by someone with personal knowledge of what occurred and a work-related duty to gather that information. These circumstances tend to remove any suspicion that the information in the document would have been fabricated.

The *Canada Evidence Act* and provincial and territorial evidence statutes provide for the admission of business records. There are some differences between the statutes. Subsection 30(10) of the federal statute specifically states that business records made "... in the course of an investigation or inquiry", or "... in the course of obtaining or giving legal advice or in contemplation of a legal proceeding" are not admissible. Provincial and territorial statutes do not all add this qualifier. Many of the provincial and territorial statutes require advance notice to the opposing lawyer or agent before business records can be used. The federal statute does not.

(iv) Testimony from a Prior Hearing

Section 715 of the *Criminal Code* and some provincial rules of court allow testimony that has been recorded at a previous court hearing involving the same parties to be admitted if the witness who testified at that hearing is now unavailable. The *Criminal Code* provision contemplates situations where the witness is now refusing to testify, is dead, mentally incompetent or missing.

In *R. v. Abbey*, [2013] O.J. No. 1460, 2013 ONCA 206, the accused was alleged to have murdered a rival gang member. Abbey was acquitted by a jury at his first trial, but the Crown appealed and Abbey was convicted during a second trial on the same charge. During the second trial, the Crown attempted to call another gang member who had testified against Abbey at his first trial. When this gang member refused to testify again at the second trial, the Crown relied on s. 715 to have this witness's testimony from the first trial "read in" at the second trial.

The primary rationale behind admitting this type of hearsay evidence is the likelihood of reliability because the evidence has been given under oath and accurately recorded.

A key requirement of these provisions is that there must have been a full opportunity for the opposing party to cross-examine the witness at the previous hearing. If that party chose not to take advantage of this opportunity, the evidence might still be admissible.

As a result, it is a risky tactic for a lawyer to not cross-examine a prosecution witness at a *preliminary inquiry*. If the witness dies, or becomes unavailable prior to the actual trial, his or her evidence may be admissible.

The application of section 715 of the *Criminal Code* was the key issue in a case called, *R. v. Saleh*, [2013] O.J. No. 5554, 2013 ONCA 742. The accused was charged with the murder of a drug associate. Two other associates of the accused, named Yegin and Esrabian were also charged with the same murder and were tried separately. Esrabian was convicted at his trial, while Yegin was acquitted of the murder. With their own trials concluded, both refused to testify at Saleh's trial and the Crown sought to have evidence which they had given at preliminary inquiries admitted. During his preliminary inquiry testimony, Yegin, an admitted enforcer for drug dealers, provided the only evidence that placed Saleh at the scene of the murder. In addition, though Yegin admitted transporting the victim to the scene of the crime, he claimed that Saleh had shot the deceased and that this action had come as a surprise to Yegin.

Yegin's version of the events had not only changed several times prior to his preliminary inquiry testimony, but after the preliminary inquiry and Saleh's lawyer's opportunity to cross-examine him, Yegin had negotiated for a withdrawal of his own murder charge in exchange for showing the police the location of the body. It was also obvious that Yegin, who had been charged with the same murder, had an incentive to minimize his own role to secure the deal with the prosecution team. As a result, Saleh's lawyer argued that it had been unfairly prejudicial of the trial judge to admit a video and transcript of Yegin's preliminary inquiry testimony when the lawyer could have no chance to cross-examine Yegin in front of the jury at Saleh's trial.

The Ontario Court of Appeal agreed with Saleh's lawyer, ruling that the trial judge had failed to properly consider Yegin's unreliability, and the unfairness created by Saleh's lawyer's inability to confront Yegin in the jury's presence. They made it clear that even when s. 715 might otherwise apply, a judge still needs to weigh the prejudicial effect versus the probative value of the admission of such evidence.

(v) *Res Gestae* Statements

Common law courts determined that it would be safe to admit spontaneous statements that were made while an event was occurring, which is what *res gestae* means. The rationale behind this exception is that the statement is likely to be reliable because the person making the statement has not had any time to think up a fabrication.

As expressed by the Ontario Court of Appeal in *R. v. Khan,* [1988] O.J. No. 578 27 O.A.C. 142, affd [1990] S.C.J. No. 81, [1990] 2 S.C.R. 531, "A spontaneous statement made under the stress or pressure of a dramatic or startling event and relating to such an occasion may be admissible as an exception to the hearsay rule. The stress or pressure of the act must be such that the possibility of concoction or deception can be safely discounted." (p. 148)

In the recent case of *R. v. Carty,* [2017] O.J. No. 5169, 2017 ONCA 770, the Ontario Court of Appeal ruled a trial judge should have assessed a murder victim's statement that he had been shot by "Sniper" (Carty's nickname) as a *res gestae* hearsay exception.

(vi) Statements against Interest

If a person makes an out-of-court statement that could be harmful to the person making the statement, either from a financial perspective, or because he or she could go to jail, if believed, is it likely that person would lie? Several courts have said that it is unlikely, and on this basis have admitted such statements when the original speaker was unavailable to testify at trial.

In *R. v. Underwood*, [2002] A.J. No. 1558, 2002 ABCA 310, Garry Underwood was convicted of murdering Patrick Campbell. As part of Underwood's defence, his lawyers had sought to have statements that had been made by Kenneth Phillips to his wife and another witness that Phillips owned the murder weapon and that when he heard of Underwood's arrest had said, "They got the wrong guy on that charge." Phillips had then purportedly pointed to himself as the killer.

By the time of Underwood's trial, Kenneth Phillips was dead, having succumbed to a lifetime of drug and alcohol abuse. The trial judge refused to admit these hearsay statements by Phillips under the "against penal interest" exception, but the Court of Appeal ruled they fit that exception and ordered a new trial. As Justice Conrad wrote:

> ...a party hoping to rely on the penal interest exception to justify the admission of out-of-court statements by a dead person must show three things: (a) ...the declaration was against his or her penal interest; (b) that the statement was made in circumstances where the declarant should have known it is against penal interest; and (c) that the potential for penal consequences was not too remote. (para. 36)

(vii) The Principled Approach

The Supreme Court of Canada made a decision in 1990 that expanded the possibility of hearsay being admitted in any circumstance where it can be established by the party who wants to use it that the evidence is *necessary* and *reliable*. The case is called *R. v. Khan*, [1990] S.C.J. No. 81, 59 C.C.C. (3d) 92, and involved a charge of sexual assault laid against a doctor who was alleged to have victimized a three-year-old patient. The child was alone with the doctor for several minutes. Afterwards, the child told her mother that the doctor, "... put his birdie in my mouth, shook it and peed in my mouth". (*R. v. Khan* at para. 4) The child had a wet spot on her clothing and when this was later analyzed, it was found to be made up of saliva and semen. From your careful reading of Chapter 4, you will be aware that the prosecutor probably realized there may be a problem getting the child's evidence of the assault admitted. Even though the child would age between the time of the incident and the trial, she was still very young. Before she could testify, the trial judge would have to decide whether or not she was *competent*. She was not.

Should the mother be allowed to testify as to what the child had told her? This would obviously be hearsay. Did it fit any of the common law exceptions that we have discussed so far? The trial judge found that it did not and refused to allow the mother to testify. The Crown prosecutors were not happy with this result and appealed the decision all the way to the Supreme Court of Canada. There, Madam Justice McLachlin ruled that there should be a new, principled approach to hearsay. If there was a *necessity* for the evidence and if it was likely to be *reliable*, a trial judge should admit it.

In the *Khan* case, necessity was created by the child's inability to testify and the central importance of this evidence in relation to a charge of sexual assault. A number of factors contributed to the belief that the evidence was likely reliable. The discovery of semen on the child's clothing certainly supported the hearsay story of what happened. Would a three-year-old invent a twisted sexual situation like this? It was more likely her innocent way of explaining a remarkable event that had just occurred. Justice McLachlin ruled that the mother's account of what the child had told her should have been admitted. It would be admissible at a new trial.

In the recent case of *R. v. Bridgman,* 2017 ONCA 940, police seized a cellphone when they executed a search warrant on the residence of a man they believed was trafficking prescription drugs, including oxycodone. They extracted incoming text messages that they believed were orders for drugs. The trial judge was prepared to admit these incoming text messages under the principled exception to the hearsay rule.

On the necessity issue, the judge accepted evidence of an investigating officer that he hadn't bothered to locate the sources of the incoming texts because people purchasing drugs often have fake names associated with their phones, and would be unlikely willing to testify for fear of being labelled as snitches, even if they could be located. On the reliability issue, the judge noted the sheer volume of the requests for drugs, the similarities between the message requests, and the fact that one of the messages was addressed to "Art". The accused's first name was Arthur.

When defence counsel challenged the necessity finding at the Court of Appeal level, due to the investigating officer making no effort to locate the original sources of the texts, Justice Fairburn rejected the argument. Not only was it reasonable for the trial judge to accept the officer's justification for this lack of effort, "…threshold reliability and necessity work in tandem. The more reliable a statement, the less important the necessity analysis may become." (para. 63). It was felt the quantity of similar text messages made them highly reliable and admissible under the principled approach.

In *R. v. Starr*, [2000] S.C.J. No. 40, 147 C.C.C. (3d) 449, Justice Iacobucci wrote the majority decision for the Supreme Court of Canada in another look at the principled approach to hearsay. He ruled that previously existing common law exceptions should not be eliminated by this approach. However, if the admissibility of the evidence is challenged by an opposing advocate, the trial judge should assess that evidence using the concepts of necessity and reliability.

In *R. v. Khelawon*, [2006] S.C.J. No. 57, 2006 SCC 57, Justice Charron dealt with the principled approach once more and added a reminder that even evidence that appears to be necessary and reliable could be excluded if the prejudicial effect of the evidence is out of proportion to its probative value or if it would be unfair to the accused to admit the hearsay evidence when there would be no chance to cross-examine the original statement-maker. The defendant was the manager of a retirement home and faced charges of assault with a weapon, aggravated assault, assault causing bodily harm and uttering death threats in relation to five elderly residents. Charges were based on statements that the alleged victims had made to several people, including a cook in the facility and four statements made to the police that had been videotaped. One of the elderly residents had testified at a *preliminary inquiry* held in relation to the charges.

By the time of the trial, over two years after the charges were laid, four of the alleged victims were dead and the fifth was no longer mentally competent to testify. Because they were not available to testify and the information they had provided to others was central to the charges, the prosecutors asked the trial judge to admit a total of 10 out-of-court statements of the five, including the videotapes of the statements made to the police.

The trial judge ruled that this hearsay evidence was both necessary and reliable. The finding that the evidence was reliable was based on the "striking similarities" between the various accounts of assaultive and threatening behaviour by the accused. The judge convicted the accused of charges related to attacks on two of the victims and acquitted him on the other counts. Sentences imposed totalled four and a half years in jail.

The defendant's appeal to the Ontario Court of Appeal focused on the admissibility of the hearsay evidence. The majority of the appeal court ruled that none of the hearsay should have been admitted and acquitted Mr. Khelawon on all the charges. One of the appeal court judges dissented and would have maintained a conviction in relation to charges involving a victim named Skupien, whose allegations had been videotaped by the police prior to his death. The split decision gave the prosecutors the right to appeal the acquittals and the hearsay decision to the Supreme Court of Canada.

The Supreme Court of Canada ruled that the majority of the appeal court was correct in excluding the hearsay evidence. While it was easy enough to recognize the necessity of using the hearsay statements, there were serious questions related to the reliability of the evidence. For example, at the time Mr. Skupien had given his videotaped statement to the police, there were already serious questions in relation to his mental competence. He had been encouraged to visit the police by the retirement home's cook, who was a disgruntled employee with reasons to dislike the defendant, Khelawon, the facility manager. Had this influenced the old man's statement? The defence would never get an opportunity to explore this issue through the cross-examination of Mr. Skupien, who was dead. While a doctor had examined Mr. Skupien shortly after the alleged assaults and discovered injuries, these injuries would also have been consistent with a fall, so offered little in the way of support for the reliability of the out-of-court allegations. Justice Charron added, "The statements made by other complainants posed even greater difficulties and could not be substantively admitted to assist in assessing the reliability of Mr. Skupien's allegations." (para. 7)

At the Ontario Court of Appeal level of this case, Justice Rosenberg noted that the *Criminal Code* provides a potential solution for preserving evidence if investigators or prosecutors fear that a key witness may die or become otherwise unavailable prior to the trial. Sections 709 through 714 set up a procedure for recording the evidence in front of a *commissioner*. This might be a judge or justice of the peace who is located in the geographic vicinity of the witness. The beauty of the process is that the defendant and his or her lawyer would be present during the recording of the evidence and the lawyer can cross-examine the witness at that time, thereby protecting the defendant's right to challenge the witness's evidence. At the Supreme Court of Canada, Justice Charron supported the use of this alternative as a method of avoiding the exclusion of out-of-court statements that occurred in the *Khelawon* case.

R. v. Bradshaw, [2017] S.C.J. No. 35, 2017 SCC 35, is a recent Supreme Court decision that sets a new standard for assessing whether corroborative evidence is useful in resolving the threshold reliability element in the principled approach to the admission of hearsay evidence. Robert Bradshaw was charged with two murders he allegedly committed with a career criminal named Roy Thielen. In statements to the police, Thielen had first claimed to have shot the victims himself. In a second statement to undercover officers involved in a Mr. Big sting, Thielen claimed he shot one of the victims and Bradshaw the other. In a subsequent re-enactment of the murders, videotaped by police, Thielen implicated Bradshaw in both murders.

After entering guilty pleas to second degree murder of the victims at his own trial, Thielen then refused to testify at Bradshaw's trial. The Crown sought to use the video of the murder re-enactment Thielen had done in place of Thielen's testimony in open court.

Because Thielen wouldn't testify, the "necessity'"requirement for using the video was met, but Justice Karakatsanis at the Supreme Court level ruled the trial judge had failed to give the question of threshold reliability of this hearsay evidence sufficient scrutiny. In particular, the majority of the Supreme Court agreed that evidence capable of corroborating the key details of Thielen's video re-enactment of the murders was lacking. Justice Karakatsanis recommended a four-step process for determining whether such corroborative evidence could assist in assessing threshold reliability. A trial judge should:

1. Identify the material aspects of the hearsay statement that are tendered for their truth.
2. Identify the specific hearsay dangers...in the...circumstances of the case.
3. Based on the circumstances and these dangers, consider alternative, even speculative, explanations for the statement.
4. Determine whether...the corroborative evidence led at the *voir dire* rules out these alternative explanations such that the only remaining likely explanation ... is the declarant's truthfulness about...the material aspects of the statement. (at para. 57)

In this case, Justice Karakatsanis found there were "serious reasons to be concerned that Thielen lied about Bradshaw's participation in the murders". Thielen "had a strong incentive to minimize his role in the crime and to shift responsibility...a motive to implicate Bradshaw to reduce his own culpability..."

(paras. 65-67) None of the corroborative evidence eliminated this alternative explanation for Thielen's out-of-court efforts to implicate Robert Bradshaw. The Supreme Court ruled that the trial judge had erred in admitting the re-enactment video. A new trial was ordered for Bradshaw.

Many cases have already applied the *Bradshaw* criteria, including Judge Anne Derrick's decision in *R. v. W. (N.)*, [2017] N.S.J. No. 292, 2017 NSPC 33. W. (N.) was accused of murder. Another youth, identified as M.C.O., told police investigators during a lengthy interrogation involving another crime that W. (N.) admitted to M.C.O. that he killed the victim. M.C.O.'s four-hour interrogation was videotaped.

When called as a Crown witness at the trial of W. (N.), M.C.O. claimed to have no memory of the interrogation (despite being shown the video). He also claimed to have been "drunk and high" and that this distorted everything he may have said during this interrogation. In court, M.C.O. refused to repeat that the accused had confessed a murder to him.

In light of M.C.O.'s intransigence at trial, the Crown applied to have the videotape of M.C.O.'s interrogation admitted to prove the truth of the fact that W. (N.) had confessed to the murder. Applying *Bradshaw*, Judge Derrick refused this request, stating,"The concern I have with M.C.O.'s statement about W. (N.)'s confession is not that he may have been mistaken or have wrongly remembered, but that he was lying." (para. 90).

M.C.O. originally told police that he knew nothing about the murder W. (N,) was accused of committing. As M.C.O.'s own interrogation continued over several hours, M.C.O. repeatedly told the officers that he would "do anything" to facilitate going home and being released from his own charges. Police continued to pressure him for anything W. (N.) had said to him about the murder. This clearly provided an alternative explanation for M.C.O.'s statement about W. (N.)'s "confession". It was quite possible he provided this nugget hoping he would be allowed to go home. None of the potential corroborative evidence proposed by the Crown negated this possibility.

As Judge Derrick observed, "There is no question that a witness like M.C.O. throws a spanner into the works of the criminal justice process. It is a challenge the criminal justice process has to confront without lowering its admissibility standards...A criminal trial can be hobbled by the lying, obstructionist, feigning witness. The jurisprudential answer to that problem has not been to loosen the fetters around hearsay." (paras. 113-114)

There may be circumstances where hearsay evidence may be admissible because there is no real need to provide the defendant with an opportunity for cross-examination. *R. v. Nicholas*, [2004] O.J. No. 725, 182 C.C.C. (3d) 393 (C.A.), involved charges of break and enter and sexual assault. The alleged victim had made a 911 call shortly after the event in which she stated that she had been sexually assaulted. All such calls are recorded. She also provided a videotaped statement to the police within hours. At trial, her psychologist testified that this complainant was too traumatized to give evidence in court about the incident and if she was forced to testify, might commit suicide. The prosecutor tried to have the hearsay evidence of her 911 call and videotaped statement admitted without her being made available to the defence for cross-examination purposes.

The trial judge refused to admit the hearsay evidence, but the Ontario Court of Appeal ruled that this was a mistake in the circumstances. The taped evidence did nothing more than establish that the alleged victim had been assaulted. She did not try to identify her attacker during these statements and would not have been able to do so in court. Apparently, her head had been covered by a pillow during the assault. The prosecutor was going to establish the identity of her attacker using comparisons of DNA evidence, not the testimony of this woman. The Ontario Court of Appeal ruled that there would be no prejudice to the defendant if the hearsay evidence was admitted and his lawyer was not able to cross-examine, since there would be little value to the cross-examination of this complainant anyway.

4.   Prior Inconsistent Statements

Common law courts have always allowed opposing lawyers and agents to use evidence of previous inconsistent statements made by a witness outside the courtroom to challenge the witness's *credibility*. Evidence statutes also authorize the use of such hearsay evidence for this and other purposes.

Section 9 of the *Canada Evidence Act* allows an advocate to confront his or her own witness with prior inconsistent statements. This is the process for having a witness declared *adverse*. This basically means that a witness the lawyer was depending on to say one thing has now come to court and changed his or her story. Once the use of the out-of-court statement demonstrates to the judge what is going on, the judge may allow the advocate to cross-examine his or her own witness. This is an exception to the basic rule of questioning your own witnesses, discussed in Chapter 4. Cross-examination is used to challenge the new position the witness is taking. It is a technique that was used by the prosecutor in the Nova Scotia case of *R. v. W. (N.)*, [2017] N.S.J. No. 292, 2017 NSPC 33, discussed above. However, even when cross-examined by the Crown and confronted with a video of his out-of-court interrogation, the witness remained uncooperative, "You can show me the video a thousand times – I don't remember."(para. 4)

Section 10 of the *Canada Evidence Act* allows an advocate to cross-examine an opposing witness using prior inconsistent statements made outside the courtroom. These might be statements made in writing or recorded in some other way. If the witness denies making the prior statement, s. 11 allows the advocate to confront the witness with proof that the statement was made.

Since the Supreme Court of Canada decision in *R. v. B. (K.G.)*, [1993] S.C.J. No. 22, 79 C.C.C. (3d) 257, this type of evidence may also be admitted for the truth of the prior statement and not just to challenge the accuracy of current testimony.

The case involved a teen who was charged with murder for stabbing another young man. Three friends of the accused, who were with him at the time of the incident, gave videotaped statements to the police in the presence of adults of their choice and a lawyer. All three stated that the defendant had done the stabbing. When they were called to testify at trial, all three said the out-of-court statements were lies and refused to identify the accused as the murderer. Without having the prior videotaped statements admitted for their truth, the prosecutor would be unable to secure a conviction. While the trial judge refused to admit the out-of-court statements for their truth, the Supreme Court of Canada said they could be admitted, again based on principles of necessity and reliability.

Obviously, in this case, necessity was not created by the witness being unavailable. Instead, Justice Lamer said the prior inconsistent statements were necessary to assist the court in figuring out what really happened. In a sense, the necessity is created by the reversal on what the witness has told investigators. The reliability of the out-of-court statements was dependent on the fact that they were made under a commitment to tell the truth and accuracy was assured by the fact that the statements had been videotaped in their entirety. The witnesses were in court and could be cross-examined on both statements, the one made out-of-court and the contrary version given during the trial. Justice Lamer said that in these circumstances, a judge or jury could assess the *comparative reliability* of the two statements.

The principle was used again by the Supreme Court of Canada in the case of *R. v. U. (F.J.)*, [1995] S.C.J. No. 82, 42 C.R. (4th) 133. In this case, the defendant had been accused of sexually assaulting his daughter. During the investigation, both the daughter and the defendant had given statements to the police that were "strikingly similar" in terms of describing the details of what had occurred and when the assaults had taken place. Unfortunately, neither of their out-of-court statements was recorded using either a video or audio tape. At trial, both the father and daughter denied that any sexual activity had happened, though the daughter did admit making the original statement to the police. She was now suggesting that her original statement was a lie.

Of course, as we discussed earlier in this chapter, the statement the father made during the investigation could be admitted at trial as an "admission of a party". In order to admit the daughter's earlier statement for its truth, the Supreme Court applied the principles discussed in *R. v. B. (K.G.)*. In this case, reliability could be found in the striking similarity between the original statements provided by the father and daughter.

R. v. Youvarajah, [2013] S.C.J. No. 41, 2013 SCC 41 is a case that comes to a different conclusion about the use of a prior statement. Mr. Youvarajah and a youth, who can only be identified by the initials D.S., met a person named Andrew Freake in a park for the purported purpose of consummating a drug deal. Freake was shot dead during this transaction. There was no dispute that the fatal shots were fired by the youth, D.S. Both Youvarajah and the youth were charged with murder. It was the Crown's contention that while D.S. was the shooter, he had been supplied with the gun by Youvarajah, who also instructed D.S. to shoot Freake in retribution for some previous shady drug transactions.

Since D.S. was a youth he had to be tried separately in Youth Court. During this trial, D.S. entered a guilty plea to second degree murder and "adopted" an Agreed Statement of Facts (ASF), which the Crown prosecutor had drafted, but

D.S. had signed. The signing of the ASF was not preceded by an oath, nor was the process videotaped. The ASF submitted at the youth trial served to minimize D.S.'s role by stating that Youvarajah had supplied him with the gun, ordered him to kill Freake and then demanded the gun's return.

When the Crown called D.S. to testify at Youvarajah's trial, his story was significantly different. D.S. claimed the gun was his own, having acquired it during a previous crime. D.S. also testified that he did not shoot Freake because Youvarajah had told him to do so; he did it because Freake had disrespected him. Nor did D.S. turn the gun over to Youvarajah after the shooting; he threw it into the river.

Faced with this new version of the events, the Crown tried to have the Agreed Statement of Facts from D.S.'s trial admitted for the truth of its contents at Youvarajah's trial. Justice Flynn, the trial judge, refused to admit the ASF, ruling that it did not meet the threshold requirement of reliability. Having been drafted by the Crown, it was not in D.S.'s own words nor had it been signed under oath. Additionally, D.S. was now claiming that he did not understand the words "acknowledge" or "accurate", used when he was purported to have adopted the ASF at his own trial. D.S. would not waive his solicitor-client privilege concerning discussions he had with his own lawyer prior to signing the ASF, so he could not be cross-examined on that issue.

With little other evidence pointing to Youvarajah being the directing actor in Feake's shooting, Youvarajah was acquitted. When the Crown appealed, the Ontario Court of Appeal ruled that the ASF could have been admitted and ordered a new trial. When the defence appealed this decision, the Supreme Court of Canada supported the trial judge's ruling and reinstated Youvarajah's acquittal.

Justice Karakatsanis of the Supreme Court reasoned that it was hard to fault Justice Flynn's finding of unreliability in relation to the ASF, noting: "Criminal law is generally and rightfully suspicious of allegations made by a person against an accomplice. It has long been recognized that evidence of one accomplice against another may be motivated by self-interest and that it is dangerous to rely on such evidence absent other evidence which tends to confirm it." (para. 62) In this case, "[t]he trial judge identified D.S.'s incentive to minimize his own involvement in order to obtain a youth sentence for second degree murder. Indeed, D.S. testified that he agreed to facts ... which he knew to be wrong in order to secure his plea bargain." (para. 66)

5. Prior Consistent Statements

In the Supreme Court of Canada decision in *R. v. Stirling*, [2008] S.C.J. No. 10, [2008] 1 S.C.R. 272, Justice Bastarache stated: "It is well established that prior consistent statements are generally inadmissible ... This is because such statements are usually viewed as lacking probative value and being self-serving". (para. 5) For example, if an accused person testifies at his or her criminal trial, he or she will certainly be allowed to proclaim his or her innocence. In most circumstances, however, the accused would not be able to present evidence that he or she had also made this proclamation on previous occasions outside the courtroom. The reason, of course, is that this would add little value to the court's decision-making process and, as was cynically expressed in the Ontario Court of Appeal case of *R. v. Divitaris*, [2004] O.J. No. 1945, 188 C.C.C. (3d) 390 (C.A.) (and quoted by Justice Bastarache), "… a concocted statement, repeated on more than one occasion, remains concocted".

Justice Bastarache went on to point out that there are some exceptions to this general rule and the *Stirling* case provides an example. Beau Stirling had been charged with criminal negligence causing death and bodily harm, based on allegations that he was the driver of a car that was involved in a single-vehicle crash that killed two passengers and injured a third. The key issue raised at trial was whether it was Stirling who was driving at the time of the crash or the other survivor, a young man named Harding.

Harding testified at trial that he was in the back seat at the time of the accident while Stirling was driving. Stirling's lawyer challenged Harding's testimony by suggesting he had a motive to lie, to avoid the consequences of the potential criminal charges arising out of the accident (and other unrelated drug charges that had been dropped shortly before the trial) and because he was suing Stirling for injuries suffered in the crash. In response to this allegation of fabrication, the Crown prosecutor asked the judge to admit evidence that Harding had made out-of-court statements shortly after the accident that were consistent with his trial testimony, including a statement made in the hospital, while still heavily medicated.

The defence lawyers agreed that it was valid for a trial judge to admit the prior consistent statements to refute the suggestion of recent fabrication, but argued that the trial judge had gone further and had used prior consistent statements for the truth of their contents. As Justice Bastarache states: "… a prior consistent statement that is admitted to rebut the suggestion of recent fabrication continues to lack any probative value beyond showing that the witness's story did not change as a result of a new motive to fabricate. Importantly, it is impermissible to assume that because a witness has made the same statement in the past, he or she is more likely to be telling the truth …". (para. 7) The Supreme Court did not agree with the defence lawyer that the trial judge had used the evidence for this improper purpose: "It is clear from the reasons of the trial judge that he was aware of the limited value of Mr. Harding's prior statements." (para. 8)

In *R. v. S. (D.G.)*, [2013] M.J. No. 261, 2013 MBCA 69, the accused was charged with the sexual assault of his stepdaughter when she was under the age of 14. The stepdaughter had not reported the assaults to the police until 10 years after the alleged incidents. Prior to the trial, the Crown had sought the judge's permission to present evidence that the stepdaughter had mentioned these incidents to two of her friends much earlier (two and three years after the alleged assaults). The Crown claimed these hearsay statements were necessary, not for the truth of their contents, but rather to rebut an anticipated defence of recent fabrication *or* as part of a "narrative" exception that had been used in a line of cases running from the Ontario Court of Appeal decision in *R. v. Curto*, [2008] O.J. No. 889, 2008 ONCA 161. The cases had allowed such evidence in circumstances of delayed reporting of child sexual assault to help juries understand the reasons for delay, the timing of disclosure and to assess truthfulness of the alleged victim in explaining a delay in reporting.

In *R. v. S. (D.G.)*, the trial judge granted the Crown permission but limited the evidence to the fact the disclosures had been made to the two friends and when, without any details of the alleged incidents of sexual assault being included. This protected the hearsay from being used for the truth of its contents. The Manitoba Court of Appeal approved of the trial judge's approach, especially in light of the defence's stated intention to challenge the complainant's credibility on the basis that she had not previously mentioned the alleged assaults to close family members.

TEST YOURSELF

1. The communications dispatcher at police headquarters received this call:

   "This is Maria Marseille. I'm at 87 Norwood Drive. My ex is trying to break down the door. Please come quickly! HURRY!"

   By the time officers arrive at the scene, Maria is dead. She had been beaten with a blunt object. Her ex-husband is on trial for murder, even though there was no one on the scene, except the corpse, when police arrived. The dispatcher is being called to testify about the contents of the phone call. Is it admissible? Why or why not? Would it make any difference if the conversation was taped?

2. Lester is on trial for murder, for allegedly beating a man to death with his bare hands. He does not deny hitting the victim, but intends to use the defence of provocation. He wants to testify that the alleged victim told him:

   "Go ahead, hit me, you fag. Your old lady already told me you're no man. That's why she needs me to satisfy her."

   Should the prosecutor object? Will an objection be successful? Briefly explain.

3. Bob is a bouncer at the Last Dance Saloon. He "escorted" a rowdy patron named Marvin to the exit one night. Marvin is now suing Bob and Bob's employer, claiming Bob assaulted him. Marvin suffered a concussion, broken jaw, broken ribs and has lost the sight in one eye.

   Marvin claims he has no memory of what happened on the night in question, but intends to call a witness who can testify that he heard:

   (a) Marvin tell Bob to, "Ease up. I'll go willingly. Please stop punching me";
   (b) Bob tell Marvin, "I'm going to beat the living crap out of you, you mouthy little weasel!"

   Would each of these pieces of evidence be admissible? Kindly explain your answer. Would your answer change if this were a criminal trial? Why?

4. Rather than paying the expense of a doctor to come and testify about the extent of his injuries, Marvin from question 3 is planning to submit a letter to the judge from his doctor that outlines the nature of his injuries, their likely cause and the prognosis? Would the letter be admissible? Why or why not?

5. Go online and find the Ontario Court of Appeal decision called *R. v. Mohammed*, [2007] O.J. No. 2642, 2007 ONCA 513. Read the case and consider these questions. Which of the common law justifications was used to admit the hearsay evidence used in this trial? Would the hearsay evidence have been admissible using the "testimony from a prior hearing" exception? Briefly explain why or why not.

Chapter 8

Admissions, Confessions and Charter Protections Against Self-Incrimination

ADMISSIONS AND CONFESSIONS

An admission could be an oral or a written statement, or it might even be conduct by a party to a lawsuit or the defendant in a criminal trial that links the person to a material fact that tends to show legal responsibility or guilt. Indeed, that is certainly a mouthful. A few examples should help.

Say a person hears a gunshot and rushes to the scene. She notices a young man, standing close to a body on the floor. She also notices a weapon nearby. "Is this your gun?" she asks the young man. The young man nods his head in a positive response. This could be a useful piece of evidence if the gun turns out to be the murder weapon and the young man is charged with homicide. It would be considered an admission.

A *confession* is simply a more specific type of admission, going right to the heart of the matter. In the incident above, if the young man had said, "I shot this useless S.O.B. and I'm proud of it," this would be considered a confession, with or without the expression of pride in accepting responsibility for the death.

Admissions can be either *inculpatory* or *exculpatory*. The first indicates that a person was involved in some way with the incident, while the other is a form of denial. Either could be relevant.

The statement, "I was at the scene of the crime that night," is an example of an *inculpatory* admission. A statement like, "I don't know how those stolen goods got into my garage," might indicate knowledge of the fact that the goods are stolen, even though the statement maker is trying to deny involvement in a crime. This would be considered an admission, even with the effort to deny criminal behaviour, which is normally considered *exculpatory*.

As discussed in Chapter 7, admissions or confessions made outside of court by a party to a lawsuit or a defendant in a criminal trial are generally an admissible type of hearsay evidence. After all, the original speaker will be in court and can take the stand to refute the contents of a statement or the implication attached to his or her actions, or could explain the context if he or she chooses. Admissions that are made to someone who is considered to be a *person in authority* are given closer scrutiny by a judge before they can be used in a criminal court.

PERSONS IN AUTHORITY

Years ago, judges started to express a concern that *persons in authority*, like police officers, customs officers or correctional personnel might be able to intimidate, or coerce admissions or confessions from people and that these sorts of admissions might not, as a result, be a reliable form of evidence. Such admissions started to be treated differently than admissions made to others. Before they could be used at all, a judge would assess the *voluntariness* of these admissions in a *voir dire*.

Justice Cory of the Supreme Court of Canada dealt with the threshold issue of who is a person in authority in a case called *R. v. Hodgson*, [1998] S.C.J. No. 66, [1998] 2 S.C.R. 449 at para. 16. It potentially includes the majority of people employed in our criminal justice system; as a general rule, a person in authority is someone engaged in "the arrest, detention, examination or prosecution of the accused".

In the *Hodgson* case, the Supreme Court of Canada ruled that even if the parents of a young girl confronted the accused about sexually assaulting their daughter, this did not turn them into *persons in authority*. There was a similar view expressed in *R. v. T. (S.G.)*, [2010] S.C.J. No. 20, [2010] 1 S.C.R. 688, where a stepfather accused of sexually assaulting a teenaged girl had written an email of apology to the girl's mother. The trial judge had admitted the email as evidence without examining the issue of whether or not the mother could be considered a person in authority. The Supreme Court of Canada confirmed that there was no reason to do so in the circumstances.

In *R. v. Glessman*, [2013] A.J. No. 204, 2013 ABCA 86, the accused was alleged to have sexually assaulted his roommate's girlfriend. When the roommate confronted him and told him the only way the young woman was not going to press charges was if he apologized, and then added, "You better plead for your fucking life", the accused apologized. The defence lawyer questioned the voluntariness and admissibility of this apology and a subsequent statement to the police, in which the accused acknowledged that he had made the apology.

The trial judge ruled that there was no evidence that the accused believed that either the roommate or the complainant were persons in authority, so the question of the voluntariness of the apology was not an issue. Citing *Hodgson*, the Alberta Court of Appeal upheld the trial judge's ruling, stating at paragraph 8 of the decision, "... voluntariness does not become an issue if the receiver of the statement is not a person in authority".

On the other hand, in *R. v. Wells*, [1998] S.C.J. No. 67, [1998] 2 S.C.R. 517, the father of young boy held a knife to the throat of Sidney Walwyn Wells, whom he believed had sexually assaulted his son. The father extracted an inculpatory statement and an apology. Since the father had already discussed the incident with the police and had devised this knife-wielding plan to trick Wells into a confession, the Supreme Court ruled that a trial judge should at least consider the issue of whether or not the father should be considered a *person in authority* before ruling on the admissibility of the admissions.

In *R. v. MacDonald-Pelrine*, [2014] N.S.J. No. 16, 2014 NSCA 6, the trial judge operated on the assumption that Ms. MacDonald-Pelrine's employment supervisor and auditors who had reviewed suspicious financial transactions in which she was involved should be considered persons in authority when they asked her to provide an explanation for missing funds. Before admitting evidence of the statements that she gave in response to their inquiries at Ms. MacDonald-Pelrine's fraud trial, the judge checked to ensure that neither the supervisor nor the auditors had threatened the accused or offered any inducements. The Nova Scotia Court of Appeal endorsed the trial judge's approach, stating: "... the decision by the trial judge on voluntariness is sound". (para. 39)

It is an important aspect of the *person in authority* concept that the person would have to be perceived as such by the defendant when the statement was made or action witnessed. What if the statement was made to an undercover police officer, when the accused had no idea that the person to whom he or she was speaking was a police officer? In the case of *R. v. Rothman*, [1981] S.C.J. No. 55, [1981] 1 S.C.R. 640, a police officer named McKnight was disguised as a trucker when he was placed in a cell with the suspected drug trafficker, Mr. Rothman. Rothman admitted his involvement in trafficking activities to his cellmate. Justice Martland ruled that "... McKnight was not a person in authority because he was not regarded as such by the appellant". As a result, the court did not have to examine the voluntariness of the statement that Rothman made to McKnight. (As we will soon discuss, there are other, *Charter* issues that would have to be addressed if a situation like this arose today.)

R. v. Welsh, [2013] O.J. No. 1462, 2013 ONCA 190, leave to appeal refused [2013] S.C.C.A. No. 383, considered a situation where an undercover police officer involved in a murder investigation posed as a spiritual advisor named Leon who practiced Obeah, a form of mysticism common among people of Caribbean descent. One aspect of the belief system is that the spirit of a person who died in uncertain circumstances can bring harm, bad luck and distress to the living. The undercover officer portrayed himself to the family of several young men who were thought to be involved in the murder as someone who could protect them from such harm and from the justice system. Although there was no evidence that the young men had been adherents of this belief system before their family was approached, two of them admitted to the undercover officer that they were at the scene of the killing, seeking whatever protection from the police this spiritual advisor might be able to provide.

The Ontario Court of Appeal ruled that the issue of voluntariness of the admissions did not arise because the suspects saw "Leon" as a spiritual advisor, not a person in authority. The court also rejected defence arguments that the police tactic was a "dirty trick" that would bring the administration of justice into disrepute, or that it violated the religious beliefs of the suspects. Both the trial judge and the appeal court judges pointed out that the young men were speaking to this Obeah man in an effort to get assistance in thwarting the police investigation, not to fulfil a religious purpose: "... the appellants' corrupt purpose significantly undermines any religious element there may have been in their relationship with Leon". (para. 104)

All three Court of Appeal judges added this proviso (para. 73):

> We wish to state clearly that this decision does not stand for the proposition that the police are entitled to pose as religious advisers and expect that statements obtained from religiously-motivated suspects will be admitted. In cases where suspects have sincere religious beliefs and seek counseling from a supposed religious adviser for non-corrupt religious reasons, the result could well be different.

This was an acknowledgement of comments made by Mr. Justice Lamer in the *Rothman* case, where he had recognized that it was sometimes necessary for police investigators to resort to "tricks or other forms of deceit". However, Justice Lamer had added: "What should be repressed vigorously is conduct on their part that shocks the community. That a police officer pretends to be a lock-up chaplain and hear a suspect's confession is conduct that shocks the community; so is pretending to be the duty legal-aid lawyer eliciting in that way incriminating statements." (*R. v. Rothman*, [1981] S.C.J. No. 55, [1981] 1 S.C.R. 640 at 697)

"Tricks or other forms of deceit" are employed by undercover officers on a long-term, rather epic scale when they employ a "Mr. Big" operation in an attempt to elicit a confession from a suspect. The technique has been utilized by the R.C.M.P. and other police organizations in hundreds of cases, particularly cold case murders, where alternative evidence of the suspect's guilt had proven elusive.

In the lead Supreme Court of Canada decision on the admissibility of Mr. Big confessions, *R. v. Hart*, [2014] S.C.J. No. 52, [2014] 2 S.C.R. 544, Justice Moldaver described a typical operation:

> A Mr. Big operation begins with undercover officers luring their suspect into a fictitious criminal organization of their own making. Over the next several weeks or months, the suspect is befriended by undercover officers. He is shown that working for the organization provides a pathway to financial rewards...There is only one catch. The crime boss...must approve the suspect's membership...
>
> The operation culminates with an interview-like meeting between the suspect and Mr. Big. During the interview, Mr. Big brings up the crime the police are investigating and questions the suspect about it. Denials of guilt are dismissed...it becomes clear to the suspect that by confessing to the crime, the big prize – acceptance into the organization – awaits. (paras. 1-2)

As Justice Abella of the Supreme Court previously pointed out in *R. v. Grandinetti*, [2005] S.C.J. No. 3, [2005] 1 S.C.R. 27, the suspect, "...believed that the undercover officers were criminals, not police officers...The statements, therefore, were not made to a person in authority...a *voir dire* on voluntariness became unnecessary." (paras. 44-45)

Nevertheless, by the time the *Hart* case was decided, the Supreme Court recognized concerns expressed by legal experts that these misleading tactics could generate false confessions, particularly if they were directed at particularly vulnerable suspects. In addition, the fact that the scenarios utilized demonstrate that the suspect was willing to participate in the faux criminal activities of the Mr. Big organization could prejudice the trier of fact (jurors or judge) toward the suspect/accused at trial. As a result, Justice Moldaver formulated a new common law rule to address the issue. Mr. Big confessions are now presumed to be inadmissible, but the Crown is permitted to justify their admission by establishing that the probative value of the confession outweighs the prejudicial effect. Many are admitted on this basis (*i.e., R. v. Randle,* [2016] B.C.J. No. 526, 2016 BCCA 125, leave to appeal refused [2016] S.C.C.A. No. 176; *R. v. Yakimchuk,* [2017] A.J. No. 312, 2017 ABCA 101).

People do not necessarily fit the legal concept of a *person in authority* just because they would be viewed as authority figures by the accused. For example, a teacher, school principal, parent or an employer could be an authority figure, but not closely involved in investigating an incident with the objective of generating evidence to lay a criminal charge. In this context, these people would not be considered persons in authority. On the other hand, any of these individuals could fit the definition in a specific situation, if he or she was acting on behalf of the police, or intentionally gathering information so that a criminal prosecution could be pursued. Some school boards have initiated zero tolerance policies that compel teachers and principals to report any incidents that may have a criminal component to the police. This may draw school authorities over the line and create closer scrutiny of any statements they take from students.

VOLUNTARINESS

The foundation of the Canadian courts' approach to voluntariness was set way back in 1914 in an English case, called *Ibrahim v. R.,* [1914] A.C. 599 (P.C.). Lord Sumner of the British House of Lords put the onus on prosecutors who wanted to use such a statement to show it was, "... a voluntary statement, in the sense that it has not been obtained from him either by fear of prejudice or hope of advantage exercised or held out by a person in authority".

Canadian cases quickly identified the need to look at the characteristics of a particular accused when assessing the probable effect of a threat or an inducement made by someone in authority. As Justice Rand said in *R. v. Fitton,* [1956] S.C.J. No. 70, [1956] S.C.R. 958:

> The cases of torture, actual or threatened, or of unabashed promises are clear; perplexity arises when much more subtle elements must be evaluated. The strength of mind and will of the accused, the influence of custody or its surroundings, the effect of questions or of conversation, all call for delicacy in appreciation of the part they have played behind the admission ...

Judges have made it clear that admissions that are not the product of a properly operating mind are involuntary and inadmissible. In a case called *R. v. Ward*, [1979] S.C.J. No. 29, [1979] 2 S.C.R. 30, the Supreme Court of Canada examined a situation where Ward made a confession relating to a car accident in the back of a police cruiser, shortly after regaining consciousness. Even though the police officers did not know it at the time, Ward was in a state of shock when he made the statement. The trial judge refused to admit this as a voluntary confession and the Supreme Court agreed with the trial judge's assessment.

If a person is really drunk, police investigators should probably wait until the person has sobered up before trying to take a statement. In *R. v. Clarkson*, [1986] S.C.J. No. 20, [1986] 1 S.C.R. 383, Ms. Clarkson admitted shooting her husband during a police interrogation. She had also agreed to have a blood sample taken that indicated that her blood alcohol level was three times more than the legal driving limit. Could anyone really say she had an operating mind at the time she was interrogated? The Supreme Court of Canada decided that her confession was inadmissible because her *Charter*-protected right to counsel was violated (primarily because she was too drunk to understand it), but Justice Wilson also discussed the unfairness of conducting an interview when the accused was in this state.

In *R. v. Horvath*, [1979] S.C.J. No. 54, [1979] 2 S.C.R. 376, a confession was generated through an extremely intense form of interrogation that incorporated hypnosis techniques. The Supreme Court of Canada found this statement to be involuntary and inadmissible.

Many cases suggest that the diminished mental capacity of the person being questioned could have an influence on whether any statement he or she makes is voluntary. From reading cases like the Supreme Court of Canada decision in *R. v. Whittle*, [1994] S.C.J. No. 69, 32 C.R. (4th) 1, it would seem that a mental illness would have to be pretty severe to affect the voluntariness of a statement. Whittle was a schizophrenic who confessed to murder. At the time of his confession he was mentally unstable to the point that he was hallucinating. In fact, he mentioned the fact that voices in his head were compelling him to speak. Nevertheless, the Supreme Court ruled that his confession was voluntary because he was capable of understanding that the statement could be used against him during a trial.

The Supreme Court spent a great deal of time discussing the key concepts related to voluntariness in a case called, *R. v. Oickle*, [2000] S.C.J. No. 38, 147 C.C.C. (3d) 321. The case involved a Nova Scotia man who police interrogated until he confessed to committing a series of arsons. As part of the court's decision that the confession was admissible, Justice Iacobucci discussed a number of factors that a court should consider in deciding whether or not a statement to a person in authority should be admitted. These would include whether an accused's choice to speak had been overwhelmed by inducement, oppressive circumstances, police trickery or the lack of an operating mind.

The Supreme Court provided examples of inducements that could cause questions about the voluntary nature of a statement. Police offers of lenient treatment, holding out the possibility of a reduced charge or sentence in return for a statement, are situations that were mentioned. Oppressive circumstances would obviously include confessions extracted using violence, but could also include an accumulation of factors.

The Ontario Court of Appeal case of *R. v. Hoilett*, [1999] O.J. No. 2358, 136 C.C.C. (3d) 449 (C.A.), involved Mr. Hoilett's confession to a sexual assault. Hoilett was drunk when he was arrested and was left naked in a cold cell for several hours. Police woke him up after a brief sleep and subjected him to an intense interrogation. He was not given adequate clothing and was refused food or even Kleenex for his runny nose. When he repeatedly fell asleep during the interrogation process, he was awakened and pressured until he eventually confessed. The Ontario Court of Appeal ruled that these oppressive circumstances rendered his confession involuntary and inadmissible.

VOIR DIRE

Before the prosecution can use an out-of-court admission that has been made to someone like a police officer, customs officer or correctional personnel, the judge will hold a *voir dire*, or mini hearing to examine the circumstances and assess whether or not the admission was made voluntarily. As stated by Justice Charron of the Supreme Court of Canada in *R. v. Singh*, [2007] S.C.J. No. 48, [2007] 3 S.C.R. 405 at para. 25, "... the Crown bears the burden of establishing voluntariness beyond a reasonable doubt and the exclusion is automatic if the test is not met ...".

If it is not so obvious that the person who will be repeating the statement or discussing his or her observations of conduct is a person in authority, it is up to the defendant's lawyer or agent to raise the issue with the judge. Justice Charron addressed this matter in *R. v. T. (S.G.)*, [2010] S.C.J. No. 20 at para. 22, [2010] 1 S.C.R. 688:

> To be considered a person in authority, the accused must believe that the recipient of the statement can control or influence the proceedings against him or her, and that be-lief must be reasonable. Because the evidence necessary to establish whether or not an individual is a person in authority lies primarily with the accused, the person in au-thority requirement places an evidential burden on the accused. While the Crown bears the burden of proving the voluntariness of a confession beyond a reasonable doubt, the accused must provide an evidential basis for claiming that the receiver of a statement is a person in authority.

The judge would then start the *voir dire* by listening to evidence on whether or not a person in authority is involved.

The jury, if there is one, would be removed from the court while the *voir dire* is held. This allows the accused to testify with respect to his or her perception of the disputed person in authority, or the voluntariness of his or her statement or actions, without giving up the right to remain silent in the main part of the trial.

If, following the *voir dire*, the judge decides that the admission is admissible, the witness who will be allowed to testify may have to repeat a great deal of the information about the circumstances surrounding the taking of the statement when the jury returns to court. The jury can still assess the value, or weight, they will give to this evidence, based in part on the circumstances under which the admission occurred.

A case from Nova Scotia called *R. v. Mantley*, [2013] N.S.J. No. 66, 2013 NSCA 16, leave to appeal refused [2013] S.C.C.A. No. 208, provided an interesting scenario. Elwood Mantley had been arrested as a result of highly suspicious behaviour when he had tried to force his way into his wife's hospital room at the Dartmouth Hospital. He had an array of weapons with him at the time. Security guards claimed he was making threats to harm his wife. Mr. Mantley was ultimately charged with attempted murder.

After his arrest, Mantley had been placed in an interview room at the police detachment that was equipped with audio and video recording devices. At several intervals, the arresting officer who was conducting an interrogation interview with Mr. Mantley left the room. During these periods alone in the interview room, Mantley was speaking to himself in a loud voice: "All of the utterances, in a profanity-laced rant to himself, make reference to Mr. Mantley's intention to kill Ms. Mantley." (para. 29)

The trial judge admitted video of these utterances Mantley made to himself as admissions of a party, without holding a *voir dire* to determine whether they were made voluntarily. Since Mr. Mantley was in police custody and locked in an interview room at the time, Justice Farrar of the Nova Scotia Court of Appeal stated: "There is a danger introducing monologues or soliloquies, such as those made by Mr. Mantley without first looking at the circumstances under which the utterances are made ... to determine whether they are voluntary. In my view, the trial judge erred in failing to hold a *voir dire* ...". (paras. 35 and 36)

THE EFFECT OF *CHARTER* SECTIONS 7 AND 10

Section 7 of the *Canadian Charter of Rights and Freedoms* protects an accused person's right to remain silent as one of the principles of fundamental justice and probably also provides a constitutional element to the confession rule itself, requiring statements to persons in authority to be voluntary in order to be admissible. Clauses (*a*) and (*b*) of s. 10 of the *Charter* add rights for people who are arrested or detained. Clause (*a*) is a requirement that the person be promptly informed of the reason for the arrest. Clause (*b*) guarantees the right to retain the services of a lawyer and to be informed of this. Court decisions have made it clear that violations of any of these *Charter*-protected rights may have an impact on whether or not admissions can be used as evidence in court.

The Supreme Court of Canada decision in *R. v. Hebert*, [1990] S.C.J. No. 64, 77 C.R. (3d) 145, made it clear that the right to remain silent provides a broader protection for an accused person than the rule requiring that confessions made to persons in authority be voluntary. Mr. Hebert was a robbery suspect who told police he did not wish to speak to them, effectively exercising his right to remain silent. As in the pre-*Charter* case of *Rothman*, discussed above, an undercover police officer was placed in the cell with Hebert. Unlike in *Rothman*, when the undercover police officer's questioning of Hebert elicited information about the robbery, the prosecutor discovered that this admission could not be used at trial. Justice McLachlin of the Supreme Court said (at para. 75) that the police cannot act to, "… subvert the suspect's constitutional right to choose not to make a statement".

The undercover officer was perceived only as a cellmate by Mr. Hebert, not as a person in authority. That, however, is not the key issue when looking at a potential *Charter* violation of the right to remain silent. The *Charter* protects everyone from overly intrusive actions by the government and their agents. When assessing whether or not constitutional rights have been violated, judges will be focusing on the actions of *agents of the state*. Obviously, a police officer is an *agent of the state* whether someone in custody perceives the officer to be one or not. Court decisions have made it clear that the police can also recruit agents for specific tasks and that their actions may also be controlled by the *Canadian Charter of Rights and Freedoms.*

In *R. v. Broyles*, [1991] S.C.J. No. 95, [1991] 3 S.C.R. 595, Mr. Broyles was facing a charge of murdering his grandmother and informed police that he was going to exercise his right to remain silent. Police recruited a friend of the accused to visit him in the lock-up. The friend was equipped with a hidden recording device and told by the police to get the accused talking about the murder. The tape recording showed that the friend came very close to interrogating Broyles during their conversation and did get him to make admissions. In assessing whether or not the tape-recorded conversation should be admissible, Justice Iacobucci of the Supreme Court of Canada found that in the circumstances Broyles' friend was acting as an agent of the state (clearly the friend would not have been seen as a person in authority by Broyles, so the general confession rule did not apply). In actively drawing the statements from Broyles, this agent of the state had violated Mr. Broyles' right to remain silent and the tape could <u>not</u> be used in court. Justice Iacobucci stated that it was necessary to, "… limit the use of the coercive power of the state to force an individual to incriminate himself".

The actual actions of the agent of the state are crucial in assessing whether or not a person's right to remain silent has been violated. The case of *R. v. Liew*, [1999] S.C.J. No. 51, [1999] 3 S.C.R. 227, provides a useful example. Mr. Liew was arrested with an undercover police officer to whom he had been trying to sell cocaine. They were placed in the same interview room. Liew had no inkling that he was with a police officer. Liew started a conversation about the circumstances of his arrest and the officer continued it with comments that the Supreme Court of Canada later found were simply in keeping with the role he was playing as a drug purchaser, like, "What happened?" and, "They got my fingerprints on the dope." In response to the second comment, the defendant admitted his prints were also on the drugs. The majority of the Supreme Court of Canada ruled that this admission could be used at Liew's trial because the officer had not actively elicited the statement. In accepting the role of an undercover police officer as a valid investigative tool, Justice Major, writing a decision for an 8-1 majority, stated at para. 45:

> It is of no consequence that the police officer was engaged in subterfuge, permitted himself to be misidentified, or lied, so long as the responses by the appellant were not actively elicited or the result of interrogation. In a more perfect world, police officers may not have to resort to subterfuge, but equally, in that more perfect world, there would be no crime.

An effort by a suspect to exercise his right to remain silent combined with his right to speak to a lawyer before saying anything to the police were the twin issues in the Supreme Court of Canada case of *R. v. Manninen*, [1987] S.C.J. No. 41, [1987] 1 S.C.R. 1233. When police started to question Ronald Manninen about his role in an armed robbery at a convenience store, Mr. Manninen replied, "… I ain't saying anything until I see my lawyer. I want to see my lawyer."

In spite of this attempt to exercise his rights, police continued their questioning; asking him what he had done with the knife he used in the robbery. Manninen's response to that suggestion was, "He's lying. When I was in the store I only had the gun …". The prosecutor was anxious to make use of this admission at Mr. Manninen's trial, but the Supreme Court of Canada ruled that it was inadmissible. Once a person attempts to exercise a right to retain and instruct counsel, protected by clause 10(*b*) of the *Charter*, the police must stop their questioning until the person has had a reasonable opportunity to do so. Any statement acquired in violation of this right will be excluded.

R. v. D. (G.T.), [2018] S.C.J. No. 7, 2018 SCC 7 is a recent Alberta case that involved an accused who was charged with sexually assaulting a former intimate partner, with whom he had fathered two children. After arresting D. (G.T.) at an Edmonton homeless shelter, the arresting officer from the Edmonton Police Service read the accused a "standard Charter warning" from his police notebook. When asked, as part of this process, if he wanted to speak with a lawyer, the accused invoked his right to counsel by saying, "Yes".

Following this request, rather than facilitating access to a lawyer, the officer continued to read from the same warning card, adding specifics related to the charge: "You may be charged with sexual assault and breach. You are not obliged to say anything unless you wish to do so, but whatever you say may be given in evidence. *Do you wish to say anything?*" (Italics added).

The accused responded with what the prosecutor at trial would argue was an admission, "I didn't think it would be raping because we have our two boys together." The issue that worked its way through to the Supreme Court of Canada was should this response have been admissible during D. (G.T.)'s trial?

Citing the Supreme Court of Canada's decisions in *R. v. Prosper*, [1994] S.C.J. No. 72, [1994] 3 S.C.R. 236 and *R. v. Ross,* [1989] S.C.J. No. 2, [1989] 1 S.C.R. 3, Justice Veldhuis, in a dissenting opinion at the Alberta Court of Appeal, pointed out that once a detainee exercises his or her right to counsel, state agents must refrain from eliciting incriminating evidence from the person until he or she has had a reasonable opportunity to consult with a lawyer. In this case, by asking the direct question, "Do you wish to say anything?", the officer's question "…was not merely the functional equivalent of an interrogation – in effect, it was an interrogation, albeit a very brief and non-confrontational one". ([2017] A.J. No. 879, 2017 ABCA 274 at para. 73)

Justice Veldhuis added that, "Until the detainee has a reasonable opportunity to speak with counsel, the police must not ask one eliciting question, ten eliciting questions, or ten hours of questions." (para. 74). Justice Veldhuis believed the accused's purported admission should never have been admitted during his trial, and felt a new trial was in order, without this piece of evidence available to the prosecution.

A majority of the Supreme Court of Canada agreed with Justice Veldhuis that once D. (G.T.) invoked his right to counsel, the arresting officer violated his "duty to hold off" by asking additional questions before the right could be exercised. The fact that the question had been printed on a "standard Charter warning card" issued to officers by the Edmonton Police Service did nothing to make it Charter- compliant. A new trial was ordered.

The power of s. 10 of the *Charter* was further illustrated in the case of *R. v. Black*, [1989] S.C.J. No. 81, [1989] 2 S.C.R. 138. Ms. Black was arrested for stabbing a young woman and initially charged with assault with a weapon. When she was given an opportunity to contact a lawyer, she mistakenly phoned a lawyer who did not practise criminal law. This was of no value in getting help with respect to her dilemma. Things became worse when her victim died and police told her that she was now facing a murder charge. Ms. Black asked for another chance to contact a lawyer. Officers would only allow her one phone call and the lawyer was not available to speak to her until the next day. The police continued their questions in relation to the stabbing anyway, assuming that they had done enough to allow Ms. Black to exercise her right to counsel. No doubt they were pleased when she directed them to the murder weapon and admitted stabbing the victim.

This pleasure would have surely turned to disappointment when the Supreme Court of Canada ruled that Ms. Black's admissions could not be used during her trial. Continuing to question her before she had a chance for any meaningful discussion with a lawyer was ruled to be a violation of her s. 10 right to counsel. There was no urgency and the police should have waited until Ms. Black had a real opportunity to exercise this right.

Her first opportunity to speak to a lawyer, when the charge she was facing was assault with a weapon would not have covered her admissions in relation to the more serious charge of murder, even if she had spoken to a lawyer with knowledge of criminal law. Once her victim died, the new punishment ramifications required fresh notifications of the reason for her detention under clause 10(*a*) of the *Charter* and her right to retain and instruct counsel under clause 10(*b*). Her initial conversation when the risk involved assault with a weapon charge would not have satisfied these *Charter* protections.

In *R. v. T. (D.)*, [2013] O.J. No. 1766, 2013 ONCA 166, a 16-year-old was arrested in a stolen vehicle and charged with possession of stolen property under $5000. Back at the police detachment, one of the arresting officers told him of his right to remain silent, his right to counsel and of his right to have a parent present during questioning (because of the additional protections afforded youth under the *Youth Criminal Justice Act*). The young man confirmed that he understood his rights and that he wished to make a statement without speaking to a lawyer or his mother, who had arrived at the police station. This waiver of his rights and his subsequent interview were videotaped.

The interview initially dealt with the theft of the car, but eventually the police officer started to ask the young man about the contents of the car, mentioning several iPods. First, the young man said one of the iPods was stolen from a house, then went on to add that he had also stolen a bag of marijuana from that house and intended to sell the dope to make some money. As a result of these details, several additional charges were laid, including break and enter and possession of marijuana for the purpose of trafficking. At trial, the video of his entire interview was admitted as evidence and the youth was convicted of all of the charges.

On appeal, a lawyer for the youth argued that once the interview shifted from the stolen car, the youth's jeopardy increased and the police officer should have halted the interview until the youth was re-advised of his rights. Justice MacPherson of the Ontario Court of Appeal agreed, stating: "… police must reiterate the right to counsel if they want to ask questions that go beyond an exploratory stage in connection with a related but significantly more serious offence, or a different and unrelated offence. This obligation to re-advise applies even where, as here, the detainee brings up the other offences". (para. 28) Any parts of the youth's statement that went beyond the initial car theft should have been excluded from use at trial. The Court of Appeal ordered that a new trial must be held on these charges, without the use of the youth's confession.

Terry Burlingham was under investigation for two murders of young women in Cranbrook, British Columbia when he phoned a lawyer for advice. The lawyer told him to exercise his right to remain silent and Burlingham told the police of his intention to do so and that he did not want to talk to them until his lawyer could come to the lock-up and speak to him. Nevertheless, the police continued to question Burlingham for hours and to make derogatory comments about the lawyer. Eventually, they offered him a "deal" and said that this opportunity would be off the table if he waited to speak to his lawyer before giving the officers the information they were seeking. Burlingham was convinced to confess and show the police where a murder weapon had been dumped in the Kootenay River.

Justice Iacobucci of the Supreme Court of Canada ruled that the evidence the police extracted could not be used at trial. Their violations of Burlingham's right to counsel were flagrant. It is imperative to keep, "… improperly obtained evidence from being admitted to the trial process when it impinges upon the fairness of the trial". (*R. v. Burlingham*, [1995] S.C.J. No. 39, [1995] 2 S.C.R. 206 at para. 25)

It is clear from these cases and others that the *Charter*-protected right to retain and instruct counsel is not a hollow right that simply requires being informed. The Supreme Court decision in *R. v. Bartle*, [1994] S.C.J. No. 74, [1994] 3 S.C.R. 173, emphasized that officers must make an effort to ensure a person understands the right and that he or she be informed about free legal informational services or legal aid, including information about any toll-free numbers that could be accessed.

The courts will ensure that a defendant has a real opportunity to exercise the right, practical assistance in making contact with a lawyer and that investigating officers back off until a person asking to exercise the right is given every opportunity to do so. The Supreme Court has stated in the *Clarkson* case, mentioned above and in *R. v. Prosper*, [1994] S.C.J. No. 72, [1994] 3 S.C.R. 236, that a person can only validly waive his or her right to counsel if the person is capable of understanding what is being given up.

One case is particularly useful in demonstrating the effect of a series of *Charter* violations involving the right to counsel and the right to be informed of this right. In *R. v. Wittwer*, [2008] S.C.J. No. 33, [2008] 2 S.C.R. 235, a 71-year-old was charged with three counts of sexual interference involving children. Dieter Wittwer had first made a statement about the behaviour while being questioned by an RCMP officer when he was locked up in the Kamloops Correctional Centre on an unrelated charge. The officer had failed to inform Wittwer of his right to counsel at the time, so police understood that it would be unlikely that this statement could be used at trial. When a second officer returned to question Wittwer about the sexual interference incidents, this officer informed Wittwer of his right to counsel, but then made no effort to accommodate such consultation. A tape recording of this statement was also of very poor quality. The RCMP decided it would be wise to discuss the circumstances of the sexual interference with Wittwer a third time, in case this second statement was also ruled to be inadmissible at any trial.

An experienced police interrogator named Sergeant Skrine was sent in for the third round of questioning of Mr. Wittwer in relation to the sexual interference allegations. This time, Wittwer refused to discuss the incidents with the RCMP sergeant for over four hours. Frustrated with the impasse, Sergeant Skrine decided to confront Mr. Wittwer with his knowledge of the first, likely inadmissible statement that Wittwer had made to the first RCMP officer. In this way, Skrine extracted a third statement from Wittwer related to the sexual interference charges.

A trial judge admitted this third statement and Wittwer was initially convicted of all three charges, but his lawyers appealed, arguing that this third statement was tainted by the earlier *Charter* violations. A 7-0 panel of the Supreme Court of Canada agreed. As Justice Fish wrote at para. 26 of the decision:

> With a view to obtaining these incriminating admissions from the accused, the police knowingly and deliberately made use of an earlier statement that they themselves had obtained from the appellant in a manner that infringed his constitutional rights under the *Charter*. This alone is sufficient to taint the subsequent statement and to cry out for its exclusion ... To hold otherwise is to invite the perception that the police are legally entitled to reap the benefit of their own infringements of a suspect's constitutional rights. And this, in my view, would bring the administration of justice into disrepute.

NARROWING THE PROTECTIONS OF *CHARTER* SECTIONS 7 AND 10

A trilogy of cases considered by the Supreme Court of Canada in 2010, and *R. v. Singh*, [2007] S.C.J. No. 48, [2007] 3 S.C.R. 405 seem to place significant limits on the right to silence and the right to counsel in order to, "... strike the proper balance between the public interest in the investigation of crimes and the suspect's interest in being left alone" (quoting Chief Justice McLachlin and Justice Charron in *R. v. Sinclair*, [2010] S.C.J. No. 35, 2010 SCC 35 at para. 63). These recent rulings have attracted expressions of concern and criticism, even from within the Supreme Court itself. As Justice Binnie stated in a dissenting opinion in the *Sinclair* case at para. 98:

> What now appears to be licenced ... is that an individual (presumed innocent) may be detained and isolated for questioning by the police for at least five or six hours without reasonable recourse to a lawyer, during which time the officers can brush aside assertions of the right to silence or demands to be returned to his or her cell, in an endurance contest in which the police interrogators, taking turns with one another, hold all the important legal cards.

Jagrup Singh was arrested in relation to the shooting death of an innocent bystander, outside a pub in British Columbia. The incident occurred in 2002, but it would be five years before the Supreme Court of Canada resolved the key evidence issue that arose in relation to the case. When interrogated by a police sergeant, Mr. Singh refused to talk about the incident, beyond denying his involvement, asserted his right to remain silent *18* times and asked to be returned to his cell when the officer continued with the interrogation. This request was denied and Singh eventually identified himself on a security video that had been taken inside the pub on the night in question. He never confessed to the crime, but this admission, coupled with the evidence of eyewitnesses to the shooting, led to Singh being convicted of second degree murder by a jury.

The one appeal issue that took the case to the Supreme Court of Canada was whether or not Jagrup Singh's right to silence, as protected by s. 7 of the *Charter* was violated when the interrogation continued despite his repeated insistence on not discussing the incident. Singh's lawyers argued that if this right was violated, Singh's self-identification in the security video should have been excluded from use at trial. As Justice Charron, writing for a 5-4 majority of the Supreme Court of Canada put it, "... Mr. Singh asks that the Court impose on the police a correlative obligation ... to stop questioning a suspect whenever he or she clearly asserts the right to silence." (para. 42) Justice Charron rejected this suggestion, stating that "... Mr. Singh's proposition ignores the state's interest in the effective investigation of crime." (para. 45) At para. 46 of the majority's ruling, Justice Charron cites with favour a quote from the Supreme Court of Canada's decision in *R. v. Hebert*, [1990] S.C.J. No. 64, [1990] 2 S.C.R. 151: "Police persuasion, short of denying the suspect the right to choose or depriving him of an operating mind, does not breach the right to silence." (at para. 73) Justice Charron refused to find that the officer's actions in continuing the interrogation to the point of the admission went beyond these limits and supported the trial judge's finding that Jagrup Singh's admission was both voluntary and admissible.

Justice Fish and three other Supreme Court of Canada judges who joined in a dissent were disturbed by the majority's decision. In discussing the continued interrogation after repeated requests by Singh to remain silent, Justice Fish wrote, "A right that need not be respected after it has been firmly and unequivocally asserted *any* number of times is a constitutional promise that has not been kept." (para. 70) More powerfully, the dissenters added, "What is at stake ... is the Court's duty to ensure that a detainee's right to silence will be respected by interrogators once it has been unequivocally asserted, and not disregarded or insidiously undermined by an investigative 'stratagem'". (para. 57) In this case, the interrogator had admitted during the *voir dire* on the admissibility of Singh's self-identification that he had decided to continue discussing the case with Singh, "... in an effort to get him to confess, no matter what".

In the case of *R. v. Willier*, [2010] S.C.J. No. 37, 2010 SCC 37, an Alberta man was arrested and charged with murdering a woman with whom he had a prior relationship. Informed by police of his right to counsel, and that he could get free legal advice using a toll free number operated by the Legal Aid program, Mr. Willier had a brief conversation with a Legal Aid lawyer. The next day, a Sunday, Willier asked if he could speak to a specific criminal defence lawyer, but when he made the phone call could only connect with an answering machine in the lawyer's office. The trial judge suggested that a police officer then actively discouraged Willier from waiting until Monday to speak to his lawyer of choice and encouraged him to use the free Legal Aid line instead. Willier did so and after just one minute on the phone with duty counsel, the police engaged him in "an investigative interview". Others would call it an interrogation. During the interview/interrogation, Willier admitted to involvement in the death of the victim. The trial judge ruled that Willier had been denied a reasonable opportunity to consult with counsel of his choice, contrary to subs. 10(*b*) of the *Charter*, and excluded the interview admissions from use at trial.

The Crown appealed the trial judge's ruling and the Alberta Court of Appeal stated that there had been no *Charter* violation, ordering a new trial. When Willier appealed this decision to the Supreme Court of Canada, the highest court in the land supported the Alberta Court of Appeal's view of the matter. Justices McLachlin and Charron stated that the *Charter*, "... does not guarantee detainees an absolute right to retain and instruct a particular counsel at the initial investigative stage ...". (para. 24) The judges added that while police have to give a detainee a reasonable opportunity to contact counsel and to facilitate their doing so, the police should not be expected, "... to monitor the quality of the advice once contact is made." (para. 41) After the person has spoken to a lawyer (Legal Aid supplied duty counsel or not), police could commence an interview, "... unless a detainee indicates, diligently and reasonably, that the advice he or she received is inadequate ...". (para. 42)

In *R. v. McCrimmon*, [2010] S.C.J. No. 36, 2010 SCC 36, Donald Russell McCrimmon was arrested in relation to the abduction, drugging and sexual assault of five women in Chilliwack, British Columbia. He expressed a desire to speak to a particular lawyer, but again, when unable to reach the lawyer, agreed to speak to duty counsel on the 24-hour advice line provided by Legal Aid. After this brief contact with duty counsel, an experienced police interrogator questioned McCrimmon for over three hours. During this interrogation, the accused was told about the evidence the police had compiled against him and McCrimmon repeatedly said he did not want to discuss the topic until he had spoken to his lawyer, would like to have his lawyer present and asked to be taken back to his cell. The interrogator responded by telling him that he had already spoken to a lawyer, that he could not have the lawyer with him in the interview room, and though McCrimmon could exercise his right to silence, the officer felt it was his job to tell him about the evidence investigators had compiled and would not return him to his cell. After two hours into this interrogation, McCrimmon began to admit his involvement in the assaults.

When McCrimmon's lawyer attempted to use *Charter* challenges to keep these admissions out of the trial, the trial judge rejected the challenges and admitted the evidence. The appeals of this ruling went all the way to the Supreme Court of Canada.

The majority of the Supreme Court justices ruled, like in *Willier* that there had been no s. 10(*b*) violation of McCrimmon's right to speak to a particular lawyer, because the accused had accepted the consultation with Legal Aid duty counsel when his preferred choice was not immediately available. In relation to McCrimmon's request for further consultation with a lawyer once the interrogation started, the Supreme Court ruled, unlike in the *Black* case discussed above, "… there was no change in circumstances triggering a right to renewed consultation with counsel." (para. 4)

Perhaps, most importantly, the Supreme Court ruled, "… we reject Mr. McCrimmon's submission that s. 10(*b*) requires the presence, upon request, of defence counsel during a custodial interrogation …". (para. 16) This is a fundamental difference from the approach taken by courts in the United States, which have allowed suspects to have their lawyers present during police interrogations since at least the time of the decision in *Miranda v. Arizona*, 384 U.S. 436 (1966). The Canadian Supreme Court's denial that this is part and parcel of the right to counsel guaranteed in s. 10 of the *Charter* is discussed in more detail in *R. v. Sinclair*.

Trent Terrence Sinclair's case caused a 5-4 split decision in the Supreme Court of Canada, with strong dissenting opinions being written by Justices Binnie, LeBel and Fish. Mr. Sinclair was initially charged with second degree murder and eventually convicted of manslaughter. The incident involved a booze and cocaine fuelled fight over drugs and money. A frying pan and knife were used in the fray. The key issue in the case revolved around statements Sinclair made after undergoing a five-hour interrogation by an experienced police sergeant, named Skrine.

Yes, it would seem this is the same Sergeant Skrine, the RCMP endurance questioner who had interrogated Dieter Wittwer for over four hours in the case discussed in the previous section.

Sinclair spoke to a lawyer of his choice on the phone for about three minutes prior to Sergeant Skrine starting his interrogation. Once the interrogation began, Sinclair repeatedly expressed discomfort in discussing the case without his lawyer present and his intention to remain silent on subjects related to the homicide. While Sergeant Skrine told Sinclair he could choose to talk or not, the Sergeant also said Sinclair did not have the right to have his lawyer present and that his three-minute phone call had satisfied his right to counsel. Eventually, Sergeant Skrine extracted the admissions he was seeking. After the interrogation, Sinclair made a further admission to an undercover officer posing as his cellmate and participated in a re-enactment of the killing at the scene. The trial judge ruled that all Sinclair's statements were voluntary and that his s. 10 right to counsel had been satisfied by the three-minute phone call. All statements were ruled to be admissible at trial and are likely to have contributed to Sinclair's conviction.

The British Columbia Court of Appeal agreed with the trial judge, as did five of nine judges at the Supreme Court of Canada level. In rejecting Sinclair's lawyers' assertions that s. 10 should include a *Miranda*-like right to have a lawyer present during an interrogation, the Supreme Court majority mentions that "*Miranda* came about in response to abusive police tactics then prevalent in the U.S. ...". (para. 39) It is hard to understand what makes a majority of the Supreme Court think that Canadian police are immune to these same abusive tactics. Only time and future cases will demonstrate if the Supreme Court has opened this door. As Justice Binnie wrote in dissent, "Many confessions obtained in extended police interrogations are true, but too many are not". (para. 78)

Barring a change in circumstances (*e.g.*, new charges emerging), or non-routine procedures, "... like participation in a line-up or submitting to a polygraph ..." (para. 50), the Supreme Court of Canada has ruled that the purpose of s. 10(*b*), "... is achieved by a single consultation at the time of detention or shortly thereafter." (para. 47) They somewhat disingenuously add, "The police, of course, are at liberty to facilitate any number of further consultations with counsel." (para. 49) Do these judges actually believe that the police will be more respectful of a suspect's right to consult a lawyer than the Supreme Court requires them to be? As Justices LeBel and Fish wrote in a strong dissent at para. 172:

> In our view, the right to counsel, and by extension its meaningful exercise, cannot be made to depend on an interrogator's opinion in this way. Detainees are constitutionally entitled to consult counsel without having to persuade their interrogators that their wish to do so is *valid* or *reasonable*. And no detainee is bound, simply because an interrogator sees no valid need for further consultation, to submit to the unrelenting questioning of an interrogator, bent on extracting a confession to be relied on in prosecuting the detainee.

Have some of the Supreme Court of Canada judges lost sight of the cornerstone underlying *Charter*-protected rights for suspects, the presumption of innocence? Justice Binnie in dissent, has aptly expressed the risk when police, who often operate from a different presumption, are allowed too much leeway; "Convinced (wrongly) of the detainee's guilt, the police will take whatever time and ingenuity it may require to wear down the resistance of the individual they just *know* is culpable. As this Court recognized in *R. v. Oickle* ... innocent people are induced to make false confessions more frequently than those acquainted with the phenomenon might expect". (para. 90)

CLAUSE 11(*c*) OF THE *CHARTER*

So far in this chapter, we have discussed common law and constitutional protections against the use of statements made by a defendant outside court. Clause 11(*c*) of the *Canadian Charter of Rights and Freedoms* protects a defendant from being forced to testify in court. It provides that, "Any person charged with an offence has the right not to be compelled to be a witness in proceedings against that person in respect of the offence." This, of course, means that the prosecution cannot force an accused person to testify at his or her own trial or at a preliminary inquiry held in relation to charges against that person.

This section does not prevent a defendant from choosing to testify on his or her own behalf. We learned in Chapter 4 that the *Canada Evidence Act* and provincial evidence statutes specifically make the defendant a competent witness for such a purpose. The risk of taking the stand to testify is that the defendant could then be required to answer incriminatory questions from the prosecutor on cross-examination. The Supreme Court of Canada, in a case called *R. v. Arradi*, [2003] S.C.J. No. 22, [2003] 1 S.C.R. 280, ruled that a defendant who refused to answer the prosecution's questions could be held in contempt of court and face the appropriate punishment for the refusal.

Legally, corporations are considered to be legal "persons", separate from the people who own the shares in the corporation and the officers that run the business. The Supreme Court of Canada has ruled in *R. v. Amway Corp.*, [1989] S.C.J. No. 3, 68 C.R. (3d) 97, that when a corporation is charged with an offence, corporate officers cannot use clause 11(*c*) as a basis for a refusal to testify. In other words, since the officers of the corporation are considered to be separate legal persons from the corporation itself, a corporate officer could be ordered to attend court through the use of a *subpoena* and compelled to testify against the corporation. Refusal could result in contempt charges.

SECTION 13 OF THE *CHARTER*

Section 13 of the *Canadian Charter of Rights and Freedoms* provides that: "A witness who testifies in any proceedings has the right not to have any incriminating evidence ... used to incriminate that witness in any other proceedings ...".

This means you could testify that, "Paul Atkinson and I robbed the bank together", at my trial, without a risk that this statement could then be used at your trial if you were later put on trial for the same robbery.

It also protected a man by the name of Dubois from having a statement he made at his first murder trial used against him when an appeal resulted in a new trial. In *R. v. Dubois*, [1985] S.C.J. No. 69, 48 C.R. (3d) 193, the accused admitted he had killed the victim at his first trial, but claimed it was done in self-defence. When a new trial was ordered, the prosecutor tried to use this evidence from the first trial to identify Dubois as the killer. Justice Lamer of the Supreme Court of Canada ruled that this would be a violation of s. 13 of the *Charter*. In addition, if this were allowed, it would also violate clause 11(*c*) since it would have the same effect as allowing the prosecutor to compel the defendant to testify against himself.

R. v. Henry, [2005] S.C.J. No. 76, [2005] 3 S.C.R. 609, also involved a murder charge. The accused testified at his first trial and was convicted. When a new trial was ordered on appeal, the defendant chose to testify again at his second trial. The Crown prosecutor used a transcript of Henry's evidence from his first trial to challenge his credibility. Much of the evidence used from the first trial was incriminating. Henry's defence lawyers tried to argue that using his testimony from the first trial for cross-examination purposes was a violation of the protection provided by s. 13 of the *Charter*.

Justice Binnie, writing for a unanimous panel of the Supreme Court of Canada disagreed. Justice Binnie pointed out that the purpose of s. 13 is to protect individuals from being indirectly compelled to incriminate themselves, as the prosecutor had tried to do in the *Dubois* case. If the defendant chooses not to testify at the retrial, the prosecutor cannot use the defendant's testimony from the first trial to incriminate him or her. Section 13 is not available to a defendant who chooses to testify at his retrial on the same indictment. Being confronted with the prior testimony is part of the risk of choosing to testify.

Could s. 13 of the *Charter* be used for nefarious purposes? Suppose I am charged with a crime that the evidence shows was committed by one perpetrator. I convince you, my close personal friend, to testify at my trial that I could not have committed the offence because you did. Does s. 13 protect you from having any such confession used at your own trial if the police decide to charge you with the offence after I am acquitted?

The prosecutor was thinking of this issue in a case called *R. v. Jabarianha*, [2001] S.C.J. No. 72, [2001] 3 S.C.R. 430. A defence witness took the stand and claimed that he was the sole perpetrator of a theft for which Jabarianha was on trial. The prosecutor wanted to cross-examine the witness on his knowledge of the protection offered by s. 13 as a method of questioning the truth of his testimony. The trial judge allowed this line of questioning, but when they had a chance to review this, the Supreme Court of Canada said the trial judge was mistaken. The Supreme Court decided that the probative value of this type of questioning was low, while the prejudicial effect on the witness's testimony is high. They pointed out that s. 13 offers a pretty limited form of protection since it is directed solely at the testimony that is given at the previous trial. The witness could still be charged and convicted on other evidence that pointed to his or her guilt. In addition, if the witness chose to testify at his or her own trial, he or she could be confronted with any conflicting testimony provided in the original trial as a means of challenging the witness's credibility. The court was also not comfortable with the prosecutor trying to use knowledge of a constitutionally-protected right as a method of suggesting dishonesty.

Section 13 specifically allows testimony given at an earlier trial to be used if the witness is charged with perjury in relation to that testimony. This, of course, is logical since the testimony is the key component of the *actus reus* of the perjury charge.

TEST YOURSELF

1. A police officer is investigating a series of break-ins. She goes to Eric Erratic's home to question him as a suspect, due to a tip from a local informant. Eric is in the driveway, removing items from the trunk of a car as the officer approaches. Consider each of the following scenarios and decide whether or not you think the evidence would be admissible if Eric goes on trial in relation to the break-ins.

    (a) Eric sees the officer approach. He throws a blanket over some tools in the trunk of the car (crowbar, hammer, screwdrivers, *etc.*). Eric refuses to say anything to the officer.

    (b) Before the officer can speak, Eric blurts out, "I didn't have nothin' to do with them B. & E.'s, if that's what you're here for!"

    (c) The police officer provides the standard warnings and advises Eric of his rights, then says, "You better tell me the truth, you useless little piece of dog crap!" Eric makes a statement similar to his erudite comment described in (b).

    (d) Same as (c), but the officers words are, "We'll go easy on you, if you admit you did the break-ins."

    (e) Same as (c), but the officer, who is accompanied by three large partners, says, "Now be a good little boy and tell us what you've been up to with those tools."

2. Joe's mother suspects that her little Joey has been molesting little girls in the area. It's all over the newspapers and the police are stymied in their search for the perpetrator. Mom corners 15-year-old Joe in his bedroom and says, "Joey, I think you have a problem. Tell me if you did the diddling. We can get you some help." When Joe confesses, Mom immediately calls the police. Joe refuses to say anything to the officers when they arrive and asks to speak to a lawyer.

3. Marta has become a very popular young woman at her high school, selling a variety of illegal drugs. The vice principal is trying to clean up the school and notices a lot of suspicious activity around Marta's locker. She calls Marta into her office and tells Marta she is going to be expelled from school unless she explains the source of her classmates' blank stares. Marta replies, "I can't lie to you. It was Mr. Jones (a popular physical education teacher). He put me up to it. He gets the stuff and takes a big cut of all the money."

Chapter 9

Search and Seizure and
Section 8 of the Charter

BALANCING PRIVACY EXPECTATIONS AND CRIMINAL CONTROL

The Canadian justice system and other common law jurisdictions have long recognized the importance of balancing society's interest in investigating and solving crime with individual rights to be free from state intrusions on privacy. Few of us want to give police officers or government inspectors the right to drop in uninvited, whether we are sitting around watching the hockey game or *C.S.I. Miami*, or rolling a joint. Some of you may not mind an intrusion on the joint rollers, but you'd fight like the dickens to protect your right to watch the Calgary Flames, or the Ottawa Senators in your birthday suit, since they won a game the last time you did it and you do not want to risk messing up the good luck. You are not at all sure that anyone, including the police, should see you when you are helping out the team in this way. As the Supreme Court of Canada declared in *R. v. Dyment*, [1988] S.C.J. No. 82, [1988] 2 S.C.R. 417 at 427: "The restraints imposed on government to pry into the lives of the citizen go to the essence of a democratic state." Justice Binnie of the Supreme Court liked this quote so much that he repeated it in the 2008 case known as *R. v. M. (A.)*, [2008] S.C.J. No. 19 at para. 35, 2008 SCC 19.

Mr. Justice Dickson of the Supreme Court of Canada quoted an author by the intriguing name of Polyvios Polyviou on this issue in the case of *R. v. Genest*, [1989] S.C.J. No. 5 at para. 1, 45 C.C.C. (3d) 385:

> The privacy of a man's home and the security and integrity of his person and property have long been recognized as basic human rights, enjoying both an impressive history and a firm footing in most constitutional documents and international instruments. But much as these rights are valued they cannot be absolute. All legal systems must and do allow official power in various circumstances and on the satisfaction of certain conditions to encroach upon rights of privacy and security in the interests of law enforcement, either to investigate an alleged offence or to apprehend a lawbreaker or to search for and seize evidence of crime.

The balancing of these two competing interests has become a key part of the Canadian Constitution through s. 8 of the *Canadian Charter of Rights and Freedoms*, which guarantees that: "Everyone has the right to be secure against unreasonable search and seizure." This provision is obviously aimed at limiting the powers of government agents like police officers, customs officers, fish and game officers, taxation and food inspectors in relation to the privacy interests of members of the public, but only when the agents are acting unreasonably. The section has an enormous potential impact on evidence-gathering processes and the use of evidence, particularly in criminal trials. Examining court decisions that review real life applications of this constitutionally-protected balancing act is necessary to fully grasp the implications of s. 8 on the law of evidence.

REASONABLE EXPECTATION OF PRIVACY

Shortly after the *Canadian Charter of Rights and Freedoms* was enacted, the Supreme Court of Canada got involved in clarifying the objective of s. 8. In *Hunter v. Southam*, [1984] S.C.J. No. 36, 14 C.C.C. (3d) 97, Justice Dickson said the section is intended, "… to protect individuals from unjustified state intrusion upon their privacy". It is a powerful protection in that most searches by agents of the state that invade a person's privacy interests will require prior authorization by a judge. Justice Dickson stated that warrantless searches would be considered unreasonable unless the prosecution could justify the failure to secure a warrant in advance.

Justice Dickson went on to note that the protection is not as narrow as the common law protections that had developed around property interests and the rights to control the intrusions of trespassers. As he pointed out, s. 8 of the *Charter* "… protects people and not places".

Justice La Forest, mentioned in the Supreme Court of Canada's decision in *R. v. Dyment*, [1988] S.C.J. No. 82, [1988] 2 S.C.R. 417, that individual privacy interests could fit into three categories: territorial or spatial, which could be tied to places; personal, which would involve bodily integrity; and private information. In *R. v. Patrick*, [2009] S.C.J. No. 17, [2009] 1 S.C.R. 579, police in Calgary reached into the airspace over Russell Patrick's property to snatch garbage bags placed on a platform adjacent to his back alley for the municipal garbage collectors. They riffled through the garbage bags, discovering drug-making paraphernalia. The police reach, snatch and exploration of garbage bag contents was done without a warrant. The police used the evidence discovered in the garbage bags to secure a warrant to search his house. Patrick was charged with producing, possessing and trafficking ecstasy, contrary to the *Controlled Drugs and Substances Act*. In analyzing the incident, Justice Binnie of the Supreme Court of Canada spoke of the reach and snatch as a territorial or spatial issue. The exploration of the contents of the garbage bags fit the private information category.

In *R. v. Edwards*, [1996] S.C.J. No. 11, 104 C.C.C. (3d) 136, Justice Cory of the Supreme Court of Canada specified that the starting point for dealing with any alleged violation of s. 8 by state agents is to determine whether or not the person alleging a violation has occurred had a "... reasonable expectation of privacy". According to Justice Cory (at para. 45):

> The factors to be considered in assessing the totality of the circumstances may include, but are not restricted to, the following:
>
> (i)   presence at the time of the search;
>
> (ii)   possession or control of the property or place searched;
>
> (iii)   ownership of the property or place;
>
> (iv)   historical use of the property or item;
>
> (v)   the ability to regulate access, including the right to admit or exclude others from the place;
>
> (vi)   the existence of a subjective expectation of privacy; and
>
> (vii) the objective reasonableness of the expectation.

Mr. Edwards had been charged in relation to the possession of illegal drugs. The drugs had been seized during a warrantless search of his girlfriend's apartment and defence lawyers asked the court to exclude this evidence due to a violation of s. 8 of the *Charter.* The Supreme Court ruled that Edwards did not have a reasonable expectation of privacy in the girlfriend's apartment. He had a key and kept a few of his things in the apartment, but he did not contribute to the rent or other expenses and had no authority to control anyone else's access to the apartment. The Supreme Court judges decided that when you took all of the factors into account, Edwards was nothing more than a "privileged guest" in the apartment and could not legitimately claim a reasonable expectation of privacy with respect to the space.

In the *Edwards* case, the Supreme Court of Canada pointed out that if an accused person asks a judge to exclude evidence because of a s. 8 violation, he or she has the onus of establishing the privacy interest. When you look at the last two factors listed above from Justice Cory's decision, this will include not only asserting his or her subjective expectation of privacy, but also that this is a reasonable expectation when viewed by an objective bystander. These two factors have been re-emphasized by the Supreme Court of Canada in many cases, including *R. v. Tessling*, [2004] S.C.J. No. 63, 2004 SCC 67 (involving the use of FLIR technology to measure heat emanating from a home using an airplane); *R. v. Kang-Brown*, [2008] S.C.J. No. 18, 2008 SCC 18 (sniffer dogs checking luggage for drugs in a bus depot); *R. v. Patrick*, [2009] S.C.J. No. 17, [2009] 1 S.C.R. 579 (garbage bags set out near an alleyway, behind a home); *R. v. Gomboc*, [2010] S.C.J. No. 55, 2010 SCC 55 (electricity usage, measured with a digital recording ammeter, attached to a cable, just beyond the property line); *R. v. Marakah,* [2017] S.C.J. No. 59, [2017] 2 S.C.R. 608 (text messages retrieved from the recipient's cell phone) and *R. v. Jones,* [2017] S.C.J. No. 60, [2017] 2 S.C.R. 696 (text messages stored by a service provider).

Obviously, the context of a claim for an expectation of privacy is important. A person's expectation of privacy in his or her own home, apartment or hotel room would be relatively high. The Supreme Court of Canada has emphasized that most searches in these settings would require prior authorization by a judge, often in the form of a warrant, to be considered reasonable under s. 8. Nor is it just the physical space of one's home that carries a high expectation of privacy. As Justice Binnie of the Supreme Court of Canada stated in the *R. v. Patrick* case, "... in the case of information about activities taking place in the home, such an expectation is presumed ...". (para. 37)

Personal electronic devices can carry a significant expectation of privacy. In *R. v. Morelli*, [2010] S.C.J. No. 8, 2010 SCC 8, Justice Fish of the Supreme Court of Canada wrote: "It is difficult to imagine a search more intrusive, extensive, or invasive of one's privacy than the search and seizure of a personal computer." (para. 2) In *R. v. Cole*, [2012] S.C.J. No. 53, 2012 SCC 53, Justice Fish of the Supreme Court of Canada ruled that even a school teacher using a board-issued computer, "... had a reasonable expectation of privacy in his Internet browsing history and the informational content of his work-issued laptop, any non-consensual examination by the state was a 'search' and any taking, a 'seizure'." (para. 59)

Cases like *R. v. TELUS Communications Co.*, [2013] S.C.J. No. 16, 2013 SCC 16, *R. v. Marakah and R. v. Jones* (noted above) and *R. v. Hiscoe*, [2013] N.S.J. No. 188, 2013 NSCA 48 (C.A.) touch upon the issue of privacy expectations in relation to text messages and the contents of cellphones, with judges consistently operating on the presumption of the reasonableness of such an expectation.

In *R. v. Nolet*, [2010] S.C.J. No. 24, 2010 SCC 24, the Supreme Court of Canada had to consider if a transport truck driver would have a reasonable expectation of privacy with respect to the sleeping compartment in the cab of a tractor-trailer. Mr. Justice Binnie, writing for all nine judges of the Supreme Court said, "... the court may presume that individuals would expect a measure of privacy in what, for a long-distance trucker, suffices as a temporary home". But, Justice Binnie went on to add that "... the level of expectation is necessarily low because the cab of a tractor-trailer rig is not only a place of rest but a place of work, and the whole of the cab is therefore vulnerable to frequent random checks in relation to highway transport matters." (para. 31) The Supreme Court of Canada made it clear that in a mode of transportation used in a highly regulated industry, there could not be a very high expectation of privacy.

In *R. v. Loewen*, [2011] S.C.J. No. 100, 2011 SCC 21, the Supreme Court of Canada reviewed a trial judge's decision where the judge had pointed out that a privacy interest in a vehicle would be lower than that in a home. The judge noted the additional factor that Loewen was not the owner of the car he was driving when drugs were found in the vehicle. The S.C.C. supported this reasoning.

In *R. v. Johnson*, [2013] O.J. No. 1308, 2013 ONCA 177, Patrick Johnson was the lone backseat passenger in a car that was stopped for highway traffic violations. While processing the driver's tickets, police engaged Johnson in a conversation and noticed a handgun protruding from a knapsack on the seat beside Mr. Johnson. He was charged with a number of weapons offences. The judges who assessed whether the handgun should be admissible noted that it was discovered "in plain view" during a routine investigation and "[t]here was a low expectation of privacy given Johnson was a passenger in a car he did not own, and the gun was found in a knapsack he did not own." (para. 27) Sadly for Mr. Johnson there was evidence that he did own the gun.

The expectation of privacy may also be lower in a high school hallway. The Supreme Court ruled that marijuana found on a student frisked by a vice principal could be used as evidence during a criminal trial as long as the school official was acting within the scope of his or her authority to maintain a safe school environment and had reasonable grounds to believe the student was violating a school rule (see *R. v. M. (M.R.)*, [1998] S.C.J. No. 83, [1998] 3 S.C.R. 393). On the other hand, when police and their sniffer dogs conducted a random search of student backpacks, without any reasonable grounds to believe an offence was being committed, the Supreme Court ruled that the students' reasonable expectation of privacy and s. 8 of the *Charter* had been violated and excluded drug evidence from use at trial (*R. v. M. (A.)*, [2008] S.C.J. No. 19, 2008 SCC 19).

Similarly, someone's reasonable expectation of privacy may be relatively low at an international border crossing or airport. In *R. v. Chehil*, [2009] N.S.J. No. 515, 2009 NSCA 111, the Nova Scotia Court of Appeal ruled that it was permissible for police officers to view an airline's flight manifest without a warrant. They were looking for passengers flying alone from British Columbia, who had paid for their tickets in cash and were only carrying one piece of luggage. Such passengers fit a police profile of individuals who may be transporting narcotics. Using information secured in this way, they then had a sniffer dog check a particular passenger's luggage and the dog indicated the presence of drugs and charges were laid. The Court of Appeal ruled that a passenger buying an airplane ticket had no reasonable expectation that the airline's flight manifest, containing this type of information, was private. A unanimous panel of the Supreme Court of Canada supported the Nova Scotia Court of Appeal's analysis of these issues (*R. v. Chehil*, [2013] S.C.J. No. 49, 2013 SCC 49).

On the other hand, when police officers, acting only on an anonymous tip, violated several of an airline passenger's *Charter* rights, including conducting a highly intrusive rectal search, heroin discovered in a condom located in his rectum was excluded from use at trial (*R. v. Greffe*, [1990] S.C.J. No. 32, [1990] 1 S.C.R. 755).

In *R. v. Monney*, [1999] S.C.J. No. 18, [1999] 1 S.C.R. 652, an airline passenger who a customs officer had reason to believe was importing narcotics was detained in a "drug loo facility" until he voided 84 pellets containing 5 grams each of heroin into a bedpan. The Supreme Court of Canada ruled that this was a reasonable type of customs search, being far less intrusive than what had been done in *Greffe*.

The main message from the cases seems to be that while there will be diminished expectations of privacy in public settings, allowing some types of searches to be conducted without any prior authorization by a judge, it would be a mistake to think that searches in these settings do not still have to be conducted reasonably.

WHAT IS A SEARCH?

In *R. v. Wise*, [1992] S.C.J. No. 16, 70 C.C.C. (3d) 193, a case that dealt with the issue of whether or not the installation of a monitoring beeper to track a suspect's movements constituted a *search*, the Supreme Court of Canada made it clear that the concept of a *search* could include a broad spectrum of investigative processes, "[i]f the police activity invades a reasonable expectation of privacy, then the activity is a search." (at para. 3)

In *R. v. Evans*, [1996] S.C.J. No. 1, [1996] 1 S.C.R. 8, a case that involved a police officer sniffing for the odour of marijuana when Evans answered the door of his residence, the Supreme Court of Canada focused on the intention of the officer in undertaking the activity: "... the intention of the police in approaching the individual's dwelling is relevant in determining whether or not the activity in question is a 'search' within the meaning of s. 8". (at para. 20) Since the officer in this case was following up on a suspicion that there was drug activity on the premises, he approached the home with the intention of gathering more evidence. As a result, his sniffing amounted to a search.

In *R. v. MacDonald*, [2014] S.C.J. No. 3, 2014 SCC 3, police went to the door of Mr. MacDonald's condominium to ask him to turn his music down as a result of a noise complaint. After the resident slammed the door on the officer and swore at her, the officer called her supervisor. The supervisor and officer returned to the unit, knocking and kicking at the door to get Mr. MacDonald to answer. When he finally did, the door was only opened a bit and the officer noticed something bright and shiny, partially hidden behind MacDonald's leg. After asking the resident what it was and receiving no response, the officer pushed the door open further and observed a gun. The officers then forced their way into the condominium and disarmed MacDonald, who was charged with handling a firearm in a careless manner. The case was analyzed in the context of the police efforts in forcing the door open a few inches amounting to a search.

In *R. v. Kang-Brown*, [2008] S.C.J. No. 18, 2008 SCC 18, all of the judges on the Supreme Court of Canada ruled that a sniffer dog's sniffing of luggage in a bus depot amounted to a search within s. 8 of the *Charter*, even though they were split on whether or not drug evidence obtained in this way should be excluded. The majority decided to exclude the evidence. In *R. v. M. (A.)*, [2008] S.C.J. No. 19, 2008 SCC 19, seven of nine Supreme Court judges ruled that a sniffer dog's sniffing of a student's backpack amounted to a search and six of them ruled that drug evidence discovered in this way should be excluded from use at trial.

A search could begin with questioning and could even include the assistance of the suspect being investigated. The case of *R. v. Mellenthin*, [1992] S.C.J. No. 100, 76 C.C.C. (3d) 481, dealt with an individual whose car was stopped as part of a random stop-check by police. The officer asked Mr. Mellenthin what was in an open gym bag that was on the front seat. Mellenthin said that the bag contained food, but also opened the bag further for the officer, who noticed glass vials. Now suspicious that the bag contained drugs, the officer continued to search the bag and the car, discovering cannabis resin. The Supreme Court of Canada concluded that this entire process amounted to a search, including the questioning and the opening of the bag by the defendant, since this was done at the request of the police officer. Supreme Court judges also ruled that the evidence discovered should be excluded from use at trial because the search was an unreasonable invasion of Mellenthin's privacy in these circumstances.

There was a similar result in the Ontario Court of Appeal case of *R. v. Young*, [1997] O.J. No. 2431, 116 C.C.C. (3d) 350 (C.A.). Police were investigating a break-in that had taken place at a neighbourhood store, when they noticed Mr. Young in the vicinity. Young appeared to be drunk. Officers asked him where he was going and asked him to empty his pockets. He removed a wad of cash and underestimated how much he had on him when questioned. Officers later found that cash had been stolen from the store in an amount that approximated Young's pocket contents. He was charged with the break and entry of the store. The Ontario Court of Appeal ruled, "... the officer put into motion what became an illegal search by simply inviting the appellant to permit an intrusion on his person in the form of emptying his pockets. It was the same as if the officer had reached out and physically emptied the pockets." (at para. 16)

WHAT IS A SEIZURE?

Justice La Forest of the Supreme Court of Canada provided a definition for a *seizure* in relation to s. 8 of the *Charter* in the *R. v. Dyment* case mentioned earlier in this chapter. The definition of a seizure is pretty straightforward, "... the taking of a thing from a person by a public authority without that person's consent".

In *Quebec (Attorney General) v. Laroche*, [2002] S.C.J. No. 74, 2002 SCC 72, the Supreme Court had to consider whether or not a court-ordered freeze on selling off real estate believed to have been purchased with proceeds from crime could be considered a seizure. Justice LeBel ruled that this should be considered a seizure, even though there was no physical change in the possession of the property. The order would prevent the owner from dealing with it freely.

In *R. v. Gettins*, [2003] O.J. No. 4758, 181 C.C.C. (3d) 304 (C.A.), blood samples were taken from the accused for medical purposes after he was involved in a fatal car accident. When the hospital no longer needed the blood samples for treatment purposes, police put "Centre for Forensic Sciences" sealing labels on the glass vials. This was done to preserve the integrity of the evidence while they secured a search warrant authorizing the seizure of the samples from the hospital so they could be tested for blood alcohol content. Based on the evidence from the investigation, the accused was charged with impaired driving causing death.

On appeal to the Ontario Court of Appeal, Gettins' lawyer tried to argue that the evidence from the blood samples should have been excluded from the trial because placing the seals on the vials prior to securing the warrant constituted an illegal seizure under s. 8. The Ontario Court of Appeal rejected that argument and said that placing the seals on the vials did not intrude on any protected privacy interest. The court noted that, "There was no interference with the appellant's physical integrity because the blood had already been taken." (para. 17) In addition, "The sealing of the vials of blood did not amount to an unreasonable search or seizure of the appellant because it did not interfere with the appellant's spatial interests, dignity, physical integrity or his interest in controlling the release of information about himself." (para. 20)

AGENTS OF THE STATE

There is no question that police officers, customs officers, correctional personnel, fisheries officers and income tax investigators would all be considered agents of the state controlled by s. 8 of the *Charter*.

In the last chapter, we discussed *R. v. Broyles*, [1991] S.C.J. No. 95, [1991] 3 S.C.R. 595, where the Supreme Court of Canada ruled that a friend of the accused could be considered an agent of the state when recruited by police to assist in gathering evidence. The Supreme Court established a simple test for deciding whether or not the friend was acting as an agent of the state: "... would the exchange between the accused and the informer have taken place, in the form and manner in which it did take place, but for the intervention of the state or its agents?" The Supreme Court decided that the friend's conversation with Broyles would have been significantly different if the police had not hooked the friend up to a recording device and directed the friend to steer the conversation to Broyles' role in the death of his grandmother.

What about school authorities? Teachers and principals are paid with tax dollars, but they are certainly not normally involved in the criminal justice process as a regular part of their duties. Should they be mindful of s. 8 of the *Canadian Charter of Rights and Freedoms* when they search students for illegal drugs or weapons? In the case of *R. v. M. (M.R.)*, [1998] S.C.J. No. 83, 129 C.C.C. (3d) 361, a principal searched a student for drugs in the presence of a police officer. In deciding that s. 8 did <u>not</u> apply to this search, the Supreme Court of Canada focused on the fact that school personnel had a provincial *Education Act* duty to enforce school discipline and ensure a safe, drug-free environment for the whole student body. This was the primary motive for the principal's actions, and in applying the test established in the *Broyles* case, Justice Cory of the Supreme Court of Canada decided there was nothing about the way the search was conducted that changed just because the police officer was present. Since the prime motive for the search was disciplinary and not to gather evidence for a criminal prosecution, s. 8 did not apply to the search conducted by the principal. The drug evidence was admissible at the youth's trial on a possession charge.

Several cases have focused on the role of private security officers in gathering evidence. In *R. v. Buhay*, [2003] S.C.J. No. 30, 174 C.C.C. (3d) 97, bus station security guards thought they smelled marijuana in a rented locker. Without calling police initially, they decided to investigate further and got bus company employees to open the locker for them. Inside, they discovered a duffel bag, containing the dope. At this stage, they put the duffel bag back in the locker and called police.

The Supreme Court of Canada ruled that the actions of these private security guards were not limited by s. 8 of the *Canadian Charter of Rights and Freedoms*: "In the case at bar, there is nothing in the evidence which supports the view that the police instructed the security guards to search locker 135 and therefore the security guards cannot be considered state agents." (para. 30)

Interestingly, the actions of the police, when they arrived on the scene did violate s. 8 of the *Charter*. Rather than using the information supplied by the security guards to get a warrant before reopening the locker, they simply got the bus company employees to open the locker again and seized the duffel bag of drugs. The police were obviously directing this illegal search. There was a reasonable expectation of privacy over a closed duffel bag, locked in a bus terminal locker. Police actions were ruled to be an unreasonable seizure in the circumstances, rendering the seized evidence inadmissible at Mr. Buhay's trial.

The Alberta Court of Appeal dealt with the actions of a mall security guard in seizing 44 ecstasy pills from the occupant of a car parked in the mall parking lot in *R. v. Chang*, [2003] A.J. No. 1281, 180 C.C.C. (3d) 330 (C.A.). The guard testified that she had approached the suspicious vehicle as part of her role in promoting the safety and protection of customers' property while on the mall's premises. When it appeared as though the driver was trying to conceal something in his hand, the guard said she was concerned about safety issues and asked to see what the driver was holding. He passed over a plastic pill container. When the security guard noticed that the gel caplets did not match the description on the pill's container, she phoned the police, who arrived within minutes.

Justice Russell of the Alberta Court of Appeal ruled that in these circumstances, the security guard was not acting as an agent of the state. Her actions were not being directed by the police, since they were not involved until after her initial seizure of the drugs. Her investigation involved a safety motivation linked to her role as a security guard, rather than an intention to gather evidence for a criminal prosecution. The guard's actions were not affected by s. 8 of the *Charter*. Since the trial judge had initially excluded the evidence on this basis, the Alberta Court of Appeal ordered that the prosecution should be entitled to a new trial and that the seized drugs could be used as evidence.

There is an intriguing aside to this case. As part of the analysis of the way events transpired, Justice Russell did indicate that once the security guard handed the drugs over to the police, this became a seizure that was subject to s. 8 scrutiny. Nevertheless, the judge also ruled that there was nothing unreasonable about the police taking control of the drugs passed along by the security guard. If you were to apply this reasoning to the facts of the *Buhay* case, it becomes apparent that the police in that scenario may have been in a better position if the security guards had never placed the duffel bag back in the locker, but had simply turned it over to the police when they arrived.

In *R. v. Terry*, [1996] S.C.J. No. 62, [1996] 2 S.C.R. 207, agents of the Canadian government asked U.S. police in California to assist them by arresting a murder suspect they believed was responsible for a homicide in British Columbia. California police arrested Mr. Terry and also questioned him about the incident. At his Canadian trial on the murder charge, Mr. Terry's lawyer tried to have the statements he made to the American police excluded due to violations of the *Canadian Charter of Rights and Freedoms*. Justice McLachlin of the Supreme Court refused to decide that foreign police officers could ever be considered agents of the Canadian government, but did rule that Canadian law would <u>not</u> apply to any actions taken by these foreign officers within their own country anyway. "The gathering of evidence by these foreign officers or agency is subject to the rules of that country and none other. Consequently, any cooperative investigation involving law enforcement agencies of Canada and the United States will be governed by the laws of the jurisdiction in which the activity is undertaken …". (para. 19)

WARRANTLESS SEARCHES

Section 8 of the *Canadian Charter of Rights and Freedoms* protects individuals from unreasonable searches and seizures. When would a search or seizure be considered reasonable? In *Hunter v. Southam Inc.*, [1984] S.C.J. No. 36, 14 C.C.C. (3d) 97, Justice Dickson established that the key to initiating such an investigation is a matter of having reasonable and probable grounds to believe an offence has been committed and that evidence related to that offence can be secured. "The state's interest in detecting and preventing crime begins to prevail over the individual's interest in being left alone at the point where credibly-based probability replaces suspicion." (at paras. 114-115)

This is the criteria for getting a judge or justice of the peace to issue a warrant authorizing a search and it is also the requirement in circumstances where common law or a statute allows a search or seizure to occur without a warrant. Since Justice Dickson also stated that under s. 8 warrantless searches are presumed to be unreasonable, under what circumstances could a prosecutor convince a judge that a warrantless search or seizure was the reasonable thing to do?

Justice Sopinka of the Supreme Court of Canada dealt with an important exception to the need for a warrant in the case of *R. v. Grant*, [1993] S.C.J. No. 98, 84 C.C.C. (3d) 173 at para. 30. He ruled that a warrantless search could be conducted where *exigent* circumstances render obtaining a warrant impracticable. What is an exigency? Where there is, "… imminent danger of loss, removal, destruction or disappearance of the evidence sought …". In such a circumstance, if the officers took the time to get a warrant, the evidence would be gone. Other exigencies could arise when police officers have to act quickly to protect life, or for the safety of the officers themselves or members of the public. There are many court cases providing useful examples of exigencies that have been found to justify warrantless searches and others where a lack of an exigency made a warrantless search a violation of s. 8 of the *Charter*.

The courts have always found a person's home to be a place where there is a high expectation of privacy, even if the home is a ramshackle trailer. *R. v. Feeney*, [1997] S.C.J. No. 49, 115 C.C.C. (3d) 129, is a Supreme Court of Canada decision that became notorious in police circles because a great deal of evidence was excluded from a murder trial when an investigating officer violated a suspect's privacy rights in relation to his home.

Police were investigating the grisly murder of an elderly gentleman in a rural community in British Columbia. Money and cigarettes had been stolen from the victim's home and his vehicle was found abandoned on the roadside. Officers had no more than a suspicion that a man named Feeney might be involved, because a witness had seen him in the vicinity of the abandoned vehicle. When the investigating officer followed up on this tip, he learned that Feeney was living in a trailer on a relative's property. The officer went to the house and knocked on the door and announced it was the police. Receiving no answer, the officer entered the trailer and noticed Feeney asleep. Soon, he also noticed that Feeney was wearing a blood-spattered shirt and that other pieces of potential evidence were scattered on the floor. Feeney was arrested.

The Supreme Court of Canada ruled that entering the trailer had been a violation of s. 8 of the *Charter*. There was no exigency in the circumstances and a warrant should have been obtained before any attempt was made to invade Feeney's reasonable expectation of privacy with respect to his dwelling. Even though other evidence was gathered from the house after securing a warrant, the warrant was issued by a judge based on evidence that had been acquired illegally during the initial violation of Mr. Feeney's rights. None of the evidence connected to this initial illegal action could be used at trial.

In *R. v. Paterson,* [2017] S.C.J. No. 15, 347 C.C.C. (3d) 280, police responded to a 911 call from a woman who was crying and apparently injured. Before they reached Brendan Paterson's apartment, the officers were told by the building manager that the woman had already been taken to the hospital. After knocking on Mr. Paterson's door, Paterson came to the door and satisfied the officers that there was no one in the residence in need of assistance. The officers did note an odour of marijuana in the residence and asked Mr. Paterson its source. He told them he had some unconsumed portions of marijuana roaches in the apartment.

Officers explained that they would have to seize the roaches, but that this would be a 'no case' seizure. This meant that they were not going to charge him with anything in relation to the marijuana roaches. When Paterson said he would retrieve the roaches and attempted to close the door, the officer prevented the door closure and followed Paterson into the apartment. At trial, the officer claimed to have done so out of concern that Paterson would destroy the roaches and for "officer safety".

In the apartment, the police officer observed a bullet-proof vest on a couch, a handgun on an end table and a bag of pills on a speaker stand. He arrested Paterson and called to obtain a telewarrant to continue a search. In executing the search, various illegal drugs, four loaded weapons and a large amount of cash were seized.

Writing for a majority of the Supreme Court of Canada, Justice Brown found that, where the police had determined that the situation of the marijuana roaches was not serious enough to justify an arrest, "...it cannot have been serious enough to intrude into a private residence without a warrant." (para. 39) He concluded that it was important for the Court to not condone such conduct and that, "...the evidence obtained as a result of the entry and search of the appellant's residence should be excluded as its admission would bring the administration of justice into disrepute." (para. 57)

R. v. Golub, [1997] O.J. No. 3097, 117 C.C.C. (3d) 193 (C.A.), was a situation where the Ontario Court of Appeal found there was an exigency, justifying the police actions in entering a residence without a warrant. Police had received a tip that Mr. Golub was upset because of a domestic break-up. They were also told that he had an Uzi submachine gun and that he had threatened others. Police rushed to Mr. Golub's apartment complex, planning to arrest him. They evacuated the rest of the building and located Golub just outside his apartment, placing him under arrest. Officers continued to enter the apartment in an attempt to locate the weapon and any other associates of Golub who may have been on the scene. They found no one else on the scene, but located a loaded gun in the bedroom. Had they violated s. 8 of the *Charter* by entering the apartment without a warrant?

Justice Doherty of the Ontario Court of Appeal said no, even though, "... searches of a home as an incident of an arrest ... are now generally prohibited subject to exceptional circumstances ..." (para. 41) In this case, the decision to enter the home was made in the heat of the moment based on concerns for public and officer safety because the weapon had not been located and police suspected someone else might be in the apartment. This was a sufficiently exceptional situation, rendering the search of the home reasonable.

The Ontario Court of Appeal decision in *R. v. Lee*, [2017] O.J. No. 4302, 2017 ONCA 654 involved a review of police actions when they responded to a 911 call that an Asian male in a brown hat was parked in a car in a liquor store parking lot, holding what appeared to be a gun. The caller also reported that the person may have been selling drugs and had visited the car's trunk, in which a large bag was observed. The informant provided a description of the car, including the licence plate number. Police dispatch, having checked the licence number, notified responding officers that the car was a rental.

When police arrived at the scene, the car had moved, but was parked on a nearby road. Officers asked the lone occupant to exit the vehicle and conducted a pat-down search. When no gun was found, the officers continued a search of the interior of the car. Still no gun. They used a remote, inside latch to pop the trunk, locating a heavy duffle bag. Thinking there may be guns inside, they unzipped the bag. Though no gun was found, the bag held 23 kilos of cocaine. Mr. Lee, the car's occupant, was charged with possession of a narcotic for the purpose of trafficking. He challenged whether or not the search of the trunk of the vehicle was reasonable in the circumstances.

Both the trial judge and the reviewing judges in the Court of Appeal ruled that in responding to the report of a gun in possession of the car's driver, "Once the police had searched the appellant's person and the car's cabin, it was not an unreasonable inference that the gun might be in the trunk." (para. 58) There was a justifiably reasonable belief that public safety might be at risk, "...because had the police not searched the trunk ...and had the appellant been allowed to leave, he would still have had access to any firearm in the trunk simply by pressing a lever and re-opening the trunk...The only way the police could complete their duty to protect the public from the risk of harm was to search the trunk." (para. 59)

It should be noted that Justice Weiler of the Court of Appeal cautioned that, "...this decision must not be read as condoning an unlimited search of a car for police or public safety purposes whenever there is an investigative detention... it is the totality of the circumstances that must be considered in very case." (para. 64)

In *R. v. Godoy*, [1998] S.C.J. No. 85, 131 C.C.C. (3d) 129, there was a 911 emergency call to the police dispatcher. The call was disconnected before the caller had a chance to speak. When the dispatcher was able to trace the call, officers were sent to the scene immediately. Mr. Godoy answered the door, but told police that nothing was wrong. As this conversation was going on, officers heard a woman crying. They forced their way past Godoy and entered the home. They found a bruised woman curled up on the floor and arrested Mr. Godoy for assault. The Supreme Court of Canada was asked to decide whether or not this entry violated a reasonable expectation of privacy in the Godoy home, contrary to s. 8 of the *Charter*. The Court had no difficulty finding that it did not: "This interference is authorized at common law as it falls within the scope of the police duty to protect life and safety and does not involve an unjustifiable use of the powers associated with this duty." (para. 28)

The British Columbia Court of Appeal examined a case where two police officers entered a residence without a warrant to preserve evidence. In the case of *R. v. Duong*, [2002] B.C.J. No. 90, 162 C.C.C. (3d) 242 (C.A.), police initially went to the Duong home during a routine investigation of a home invasion that had occurred in the neighbourhood. While they were at the door, the officers noticed the strong smells of growing marijuana and some that was burning. Putting two and two together, the officers believed that they had happened upon a grow-op. They feared that if they left to get a warrant, the residents of the home may have disappeared or destroyed any evidence on the scene. Rather than risking this, the officers arrested Mr. Duong at the door and continued into the home where they located a woman, who was also arrested. Other evidence of the grow-op was apparent, so one officer was left in the home while the other officer left to get a warrant to authorize a continuation of the search. Was the initial entry of the residence unreasonable?

The British Columbia Court of Appeal said no, "... the conclusion that there were exigent circumstances justifying the entry of the house to effect the arrests and justifying the warrantless initial search is supported by the evidence and I see no basis upon which we could interfere." (para. 31) The Court of Appeal ruled that the trial judge had been correct in allowing evidence gathered to be admitted in these circumstances.

There is common law authority for the premise that police officers can also make a warrantless entry into a home if they are in "hot pursuit" of someone they would be authorized to arrest under the arrest powers in s. 495 of the *Criminal Code*. The issue was addressed by the Supreme Court of Canada in *R. v. Macooh*, [1993] S.C.J. No. 28, 82 C.C.C. (3d) 481 at para. 19:

> [I]t would be unacceptable for police officers who were about to make a completely lawful arrest to be prevented from doing so merely because the offender had taken refuge in his home or that of a third party. ...The offender is then not being bothered by the police unexpectedly while in domestic tranquility. He has gone to his home while fleeing solely to escape arrest. ... The flight of the offender, an act contrary to public order, also should not be thus rewarded.

The common law and s. 489 of the *Criminal Code* allow for the seizure of evidence of an offence if it is in "plain view" when an officer is lawfully on the premises in the first place.

Justice Jackson of the Saskatchewan Court of Appeal dealt with the issue in a case called *R. v. Spindloe*, [2001] S.J. No. 266, 154 C.C.C. (3d) 8 (C.A.). In that case, police had entered a record store looking for drug paraphernalia. They had a search warrant that was later ruled to be defective. Nevertheless, while they were on the scene, officers seized several items of evidence that were on display in the public part of the store. Justice Jackson ruled that this evidence was admissible at trial. There could be no reasonable expectation of privacy in the public parts of the store during hours when the store was open. These items were in plain view, and the police like anyone else could legally enter this part of the store during business hours. Other items that police had seized from locked cupboards were not admissible because the warrant was defective.

A SEARCH "INCIDENT TO AN ARREST"

In *Cloutier v. Langlois*, [1990] S.C.J. No. 10, 53 C.C.C. (3d) 257 at para. 53, the Supreme Court of Canada made it clear that a warrantless search of a person who has been arrested is reasonable and will generally not violate s. 8 of the *Canadian Charter of Rights and Freedoms*.

> ... a search of the accused for weapons or other dangerous articles is necessary as an elementary precaution to preclude the possibility of their use against the police ... Further, the process of the arrest must ensure that evidence found on the accused and in his immediate surroundings is preserved.

In *R. v. Fearon*, [2013] O.J. No. 704, 2013 ONCA 106, police conducted a cursory search of the contents of a cellphone they had seized incidental to the arrest of Kevin Fearon in relation to the robbery of a jewelry stall at a flea market. Two men had held up the stall operator with a gun. Eyewitnesses provided descriptions of the robbers and the licence plate of their getaway vehicle. Police soon connected the vehicle to the accused and his alleged accomplice. They were arrested together. When police conducted a pat down search of Fearon, they discovered a cellphone. The phone was on and was not password protected or otherwise "locked". Officers did a cursory search of the contents, hoping to discover some evidence indicating the location of the gun and/or jewelry. They found a picture of a gun and a draft text message that referred to the jewelry robbery.

Mr. Fearon's defence lawyer challenged the admissibility of this evidence on the basis that the search of the contents of the cell phone went beyond what could be justified as a search "incident to an arrest". In analyzing the situation, Justice Armstrong of the Ontario Court of Appeal cited the Supreme Court of Canada's decision in *R. v. Caslake*, [1998] S.C.J. No. 3, [1998] 1 S.C.R. 51 as describing the parameters of this common law doctrine. At paragraph 44 of that decision, Chief Justice Lamer had stated that police, "... must have some reason related to the arrest for conducting the search at the time the search was carried out, and that reason must be objectively reasonable".

Applying this rationale to the *Fearon* situation, the trial judge had concluded that the police did reasonably believe that examining the contents of the cell phone would yield evidence relevant to the robbery. Justice Armstrong of the Court of Appeal agreed, while providing a cautionary proviso (paras. 57 and 58):

> The initial search at the time of the arrest involved a cursory look through the contents of the cell phone to ascertain if it contained such evidence. The subsequent examinations of the contents of the cell phone at the police station are more difficult ... . [T]he proper course for the police was to stop the examination of the contents of the cell phone when they took the appellant to the police station and then proceed to obtain a search warrant.

The Nova Scotia Court of Appeal largely agreed with the *Fearon* analysis in a case called *R. v. Hiscoe*, [2013] N.S.J. No. 188, 2013 NSCA 48. In that situation, the police had Jamie Hiscoe under surveillance when he was arrested at a drive-in theatre where police observed what appeared to be a drug transaction occurring between two adjacently parked cars. They seized Hiscoe's cellphone and did a cursory examination for evidence of drug trafficking communications at the time of the arrest. This was followed by a more thorough examination of the contents of the phone back at the police station, and a full 'content dump' performed by a forensics investigator a month later. No warrant for these searches had been obtained.

The trial judge refused to admit any evidence beyond that acquired in the cursory search conducted incidental to the arrest. Both the trial judge and the Nova Scotia Court of Appeal believed that there was no reason to conduct any further search beyond that without first obtaining a warrant. Failure to do so violated Hiscoe's privacy interest in the contents of his cellphone and section 8 of the *Charter.* Justice Oland of the Nova Scotia Court of Appeal only really deviated from Justice Armstrong's reasoning in *Fearon* in noting in an addendum (para. 81):

> I am not persuaded that the password protection is as significant a factor as Justice Armstrong states. ... Whether such a security feature exists or is turned on is not substantively helpful in determining the privacy interests of the accused in the contents of his cell phone, nor the propriety of a police search. Just because a password is not on

at the very moment the police seize a cell phone cannot mean that the state is welcome and free to roam through its contents.

In *R. v. Mann*, [2004] S.C.J. No. 49, 2004 SCC 52, the Supreme Court of Canada extended the concept marginally beyond "a search incident to an arrest" by recognizing that a security-related pat-down could also be appropriate in a situation where police were conducting an initial investigative detention of a person who matched the description of a suspect in a recent break and entry. However, the Court ruled that drug evidence had to be excluded from the trial of Mr. Mann when an officer went beyond a search for weapons by reaching into the pouch pocket of Mr. Mann's hoody after detecting something soft during the pat-down.

The *Mann* decision was applied by the Ontario Court of Appeal in a case called, *R. v. McGuffie*, [2016] O.J. No. 2504, 131 O.R. (3d) 643 (C.A.). In the Court's decision, Justice Doherty cautioned: "A brief detention on the street to question an individual implicated in a criminal investigation involving ongoing events may be justifiable under the *Mann* criteria, but under those same criteria imprisonment in a police cruiser while handcuffed for some indefinite period while an officer carries out other aspects of a criminal investigation could not be justified." (para. 38) A subsequent "safety search" of the individual that resulted in drugs being located on his person was ruled to be unreasonable and the evidence excluded from use at trial; "If there was any danger to Constable Greenwood when he conducted the second search, it flowed directly from his unlawful detention of the appellant and not from anything Constable Greenwood was doing in the lawful exercise of his duty." (para. 54)

In *R. v. Golden*, [2001] S.C.J. No. 81, [2001] 3 S.C.R. 679, the Supreme Court of Canada considered whether strip searches should be part of the arrest process. The Court decided that they should only be used if the police have reasonable and probable grounds to believe that the strip search is necessary, not simply because of a blanket policy. In addition, the Court added that any such search should be done reasonably and with respect for the dignity of the person being searched, generally in the relative privacy of the police station; "Strip searches conducted in the field could only be justified where there is a demonstrated necessity and urgency to search for weapons or objects." (para. 102)

In *R. v. Stillman*, [1997] S.C.J. No. 34, 113 C.C.C. (3d) 321, the Supreme Court of Canada ruled that taking bodily samples (like hair or saliva for DNA testing) without permission or a warrant would be unreasonable. They cannot simply be taken as part of the arrest process. As the Supreme Court pointed out, there is no exigency since there is no danger that the evidence is going to disappear if the person is in custody. As we discussed in Chapter 5, s. 487.05 of the *Criminal Code* authorizes judges to issue warrants to compel the collection of this type of evidence in the appropriate circumstances.

R. v. Saeed, [2016] S.C.J. No. 24, [2016] 1 S.C.R. 518 might seem to be a somewhat shocking departure from the approach taken by the Supreme Court in the *Golden* and *Stillman* decisions, but is supported by an interesting rationale. Early in the morning of a day in May of 2011, police received a report that a

15-year-old group home resident had been violently sexually assaulted by an older man, outside a party she had attended. Mr. Saeed was quickly arrested and taken to the police station. A detective asked the accused to provide a penile swab in the hope that any DNA of the victim that may show up from the swab would help to pinpoint her assailant as the suspect in custody. Mr. Saeed's lawyer challenged this "search incident to the arrest" (and conducted without a warrant) as being unreasonable under s. 8 of the Charter.

Justice Moldaver, writing for a majority of the Supreme Court of Canada, pointed out that the *Stillman* decision dealt with seizing samples from the accused's own body and the need for a warrant in that circumstance. In the *Saeed* situation, "The evidence sought is not personal information relating to the accused...accused persons do not have a significant privacy interest in the complainant's DNA..." (para. 47) Justice Moldaver went on to point out that a penile swab is neither invasive nor penetrative; "...while there is no disputing that a penile swab intrudes on an accused's privacy, the intrusion is limited. In my view, it is not so substantial as to require the police to obtain consent or a warrant." (para. 61)

OTHER JUSTIFICATIONS FOR WARRANTLESS SEARCHES

Warrantless searches can be undertaken if the person in control of the evidence consents. In an Ontario Court of Appeal decision called *R. v. Wills*, [1992] O.J. No. 294, 70 C.C.C. (3d) 529 (C.A.), Justice Doherty emphasized the importance of the prosecutor being able to establish that the person has waived their privacy rights with full knowledge of the consequences. The waiver must be proven to be voluntary, "... not the product of police oppression, coercion or other external conduct which negated the freedom to choose ...". (para. 69).

Warrantless searches may also be valid because of a very low expectation of privacy in some circumstances. In *R. v. Simmons*, [1988] S.C.J. No. 86, 45 C.C.C. (3d) 296, the Supreme Court of Canada considered sections of the federal *Customs Act* which allowed for warrantless searches based on "suspicion" of a person having items hidden on his or her body, as opposed to the normal requirement of reasonable probability. The Supreme Court ruled that because "... personal privacy reasonably expected at customs is lower than in most other situations", the reduced standard in the statute was reasonable. In addition, the Supreme Court judges concluded that, "... questioning by customs officers, searches of luggage, frisk or pat searches, and the requirement to remove in private such articles of clothing as will permit investigation of suspicious bodily bulges ... are not unreasonable within the meaning of s. 8". (para. 50)

The case of *R. v. Beaulieu*, [2010] S.C.J. No. 7, 2010 SCC 7, presents an interesting scenario. RCMP officers in Montreal were involved in an extensive drug trafficking investigation when they obtained a judge's authorization to intercept Georges Beaulieu's private conversations. This included an authorization to install listening devices in his car. While engaged in the installation of listening devices, the police officers became intrigued by hidden electrical switches under the dashboard of the car, with wires leading to the console. The officers decided to dismantle the console, though of course this was clearly not part of the court-authorized installation of listening devices. The officers discovered a hidden compartment in the console. In the hidden compartment was a leather case. With curiosity spurring them on, the officers opened this case and found a loaded gun. Not wanting to interrupt the ongoing drug investigation, the officers rendered the gun unusable and simply put it back in its hiding place. A year later, Georges Beaulieu was charged with possession of a loaded firearm, contrary to s. 95 of the *Criminal Code*.

Had the police found this gun through an unreasonable search in violation of s. 8 of the *Charter*? Both the trial judge and the Supreme Court of Canada said yes. As Justice Charron of the Supreme Court of Canada expressed it at paragraph 3 of their decision, "It is not disputed that the judicial authorization did not give the police carte blanche to search the vehicle in a manner or for a purpose that exceeded the terms of the judicial order." Nevertheless, the trial judge went on to say that the *Charter* violation was "… at the less serious end of the spectrum". The trial judge also focused on the location, noting that Mr. Beaulieu had a somewhat reduced privacy interest in his car. Overall, the trial judge concluded that admitting the evidence of the gun in these circumstances would *not* bring the administration of justice into disrepute under subs. 24(2) of the *Charter* and Mr. Beaulieu was convicted. The Supreme Court of Canada supported the trial judge's approach.

When the police in *R. v. Patrick*, [2009] S.C.J. No. 17, [2009] 1 S.C.R. 579, took away Russell Patrick's garbage bags to conduct a search, the fact that the householder had placed the garbage at the edge of his property line for garbage collectors was considered significant. Justice Binnie, in speaking for the Supreme Court of Canada, said "I believe the householder has sufficiently abandoned his interest and control to eliminate any objectively reasonable privacy interest." (para. 63) Justice Binnie went on to add: "Given that the act of abandonment occurred prior to the police gathering the garbage bags, there was no privacy interest in existence at the time of the police intervention …". (para. 69) Further, "[L]ifestyle and biographical information was exposed, but the effective cause of the exposure was the act of abandonment by the appellant, not an intrusion by the police …". (para. 71) As a result, a warrant was not needed to secure this evidence.

USE OF TECHNOLOGY TO SEARCH

The use of most types of electronic devices to intercept private communications is specifically rendered illegal in s. 184 of the *Criminal Code*. Any such interception by investigators can only be done with the prior authorization by a superior court judge. Wiretaps of phone calls or the use of recording devices and boom mikes all fall under the *Criminal Code* limitations.

In *R. v. Duarte*, [1990] S.C.J. No. 2, 53 C.C.C. (3d) 1, the Supreme Court of Canada ruled that it was a violation of s. 8 of the *Charter* for agents of the state to intercept or record private communications without the prior authorization of a judge, even if one of the parties to the discussion had consented.

In *R. v. Wong*, [1990] S.C.J. No. 118, [1990] 3 S.C.R. 36, the Supreme Court ruled that video surveillance of a hotel room without a judge's prior authorization was an unreasonable form of search and hence a violation of s. 8: "... the very reason we rent such rooms is to obtain a private enclave where we may conduct our activities free of uninvited scrutiny". (at para. 21)

There is no reasonable expectation of privacy where the public has access, such as outside commercial buildings, or inside convenience stores. Evidence generated from video cameras in these locations would be admissible. This was pointed out in the Quebec Court of Appeal decision in *R. v. Elzein*, [1993] J.Q. no 802, 82 C.C.C. (3d) 455, and the Supreme Court of Canada decision in *R. v. Nikolovski*, [1996] S.C.J. No. 122, 3 C.R. (5th) 362, where the potential value of such evidence became clear when an eyewitness was unable to identify a thief, but it was ruled that the trial judge could rely on the video for identification.

The New Brunswick Court of Appeal ruled that low level surveillance of the yard of a home from a helicopter without prior authorization by a judge was an infringement on the residents' reasonable expectation of privacy in a case called *R. v. Kelly*, [1999] N.B.J. No. 98, 169 D.L.R. (4th) 720 (C.A.). In some ways, this decision would seem to be consistent with the Supreme Court of Canada decisions in *R. v. Grant*, [1993] S.C.J. No. 98, 84 C.C.C. (3d) 173 and *R. v. Plant*, [1993] S.C.J. No. 97, [1993] 3 S.C.R. 281, which found s. 8 *Charter* violations when "perimeter" searches were conducted from the yards of residences without warrants (though neither of the Supreme Court cases involved the use of any technology).

On the other hand, the Supreme Court of Canada decision in *R. v. Tessling*, [2004] S.C.J. No. 63, 2004 SCC 67, supports the use without prior authorization of a type of technology that detects heat emanating from a building. Police used an airplane and Forward-Looking Infrared technology to detect whether or not unusually large levels of heat were emanating from the home of Mr. Tessling, whom they suspected of running a marijuana grow-operation. The Supreme Court decided the key question was; "... does FLIR technology in fact intrude on the reasonable sphere of privacy of an individual?" (para. 34) They ruled that it did not: "These devices are passive instruments which are sensitive to only thermal radiant temperature. The devices do not see into, or through structures." (para. 34)

This type of reasoning was extended to approve drug investigators soliciting the assistance of an electrical utility company in installing a digital recording ammeter (or DRA) to measure the electricity flow to a home they suspected of housing a marijuana grow-op in the 2010 Supreme Court of Canada case, *R. v. Gomboc*, [2010] S.C.J. No. 55, 2010 SCC 55.

USE OF SNIFFER DOGS AND REASONABLE SUSPICION

Are drug detection dogs capable of invading the privacy interests of individuals? Context seems important. The Alberta Court of Appeal case of *R. v. Lam*, [2003] A.J. No. 811, 178 C.C.C. (3d) 59 (C.A.) involved a situation where police officers with a drug-detecting sniffer dog were in the Calgary bus terminal when they decided to follow a couple who went into the locker area. When the dog indicated the scent of drugs at the woman's locker, police proceeded to search the couple's luggage and bags that were in the locker. They seized a large amount of cash and drugs. The trial judge and the Alberta Court of Appeal found the use of the sniffer dog in this situation to be a violation of a reasonable expectation of privacy in the locker, contrary to s. 8 of the *Charter*. As the Alberta Court of Appeal ruled, "The police had nothing more than suspicion when Constable Bouey approached the locker with the police dog, and the purpose of the dog-sniff was to determine what was in the bag inside the locker. In these circumstances, the police were obliged to leave her alone." (para. 49) In using the sniffer dog, the court decided police, "... were using a technique that enabled them to see what would have remained private were they to rely on their ordinary senses." (para. 34)

There was a similar outcome in the Supreme Court of Canada decision in *R. v. Kang-Brown*, [2008] S.C.J. No. 18, 2008 SCC 18. Evidence discovered by a sniffer dog in luggage at a bus depot was excluded because police had initiated the search, "... based on speculation rather than objectively verifiable evidence supporting reasonable suspicion." (LeBel J. at para. 60) The officer's testimony made it clear that engaging the accused and the resulting search was triggered by little more than an "elongated stare".

The new "reasonable suspicion" standard referred to by Justice LeBel in *Kang-Brown* was applied in a case involving a sniffer dog search of airport luggage. In *R. v. Chehil*, [2013] S.C.J. No. 49, 2013 SCC 49, RCMP officers at the Halifax airport had examined a flight manifest for a flight from Vancouver to Halifax. They discovered that Mr. Chehil had purchased a ticket shortly before the plane's departure, had paid cash and had only checked one bag. The officers testified at trial that they believed these to be indicators of illegal transporting and trafficking in narcotics.

When the flight arrived at the airport, the police had a drug detection dog scan an array of bags from the flight. The dog "indicated" for the presence of drugs in front of Chehil's bag. When the accused claimed his bag, the police arrested him for possession of a narcotic and the locked bag was forced open. No warrant had been obtained. The bag was found to contain 3 kilograms of cocaine. The charge justifying Chehil's arrest was revised to possession for the purpose of trafficking.

The trial judge in the case found that there was not sufficient evidence of the dog's reliability in detecting drugs and, as a result, ruled the search unreasonable, excluding the drug evidence. The Nova Scotia Court of Appeal rejected this reasoning, found the search to be reasonable and ordered a new trial. The accused appealed this finding to the Supreme Court of Canada.

In assessing whether the process followed was appropriate, Justice Karakatsanis, writing for a unanimous Supreme Court of Canada, ruled that because a dog sniff of luggage involves a relatively minimal intrusion, it could be conducted based on a *reasonable suspicion* of criminal activity. A positive indication by a dog that has been proven reliable, combined with other factors could then contribute to reasonable and probable grounds to make an arrest. Since an actual physical search of the contents of luggage is more intrusive than the external dog sniff, this could only be done once the reasonable and probable grounds for making an arrest had been satisfied. The Supreme Court had decided in *R. v. Caslake*, [1998] S.C.J. No. 3, [1998] 1 S.C.R. 51 that a warrantless search of this type could be made incidental to a proper arrest.

Justice Karakatsanis clarified that compared to reasonable and probable grounds, "... reasonable suspicion is a lower standard, as it engages the reasonable possibility, rather than probability, of crime". (para. 27) Nevertheless, she cautioned that, "... profile characteristics are not a substitute for objective facts that raise a reasonable suspicion of criminal activity". (para. 40) She also added that it would be a mistake, "... to say that hunches or intuition grounded in an officer's training will suffice ...". (para. 47)

After re-reading the police officers' justifications for using the sniffer dog in the *Chehil* case, it is tempting to quote Shakespeare in commenting on Justice Karakatsanis provisos that the judge "doth protest too much". There isn't much beyond drug dealer profiling and a police hunch in the "reasonable suspicion" that Justice Karakatsanis endorsed in ordering a new trial for Mr. Chehil.

The Supreme Court of Canada was far from unanimous in recognizing reasonable suspicion in the companion case of *R. v. MacKenzie*, [2013] S.C.J. No. 50, 2013 SCC 50. The warrantless sniffer dog search of a motor vehicle, conducted by two R.C.M.P. officers in Saskatchewan, generated a 5-4 split decision in the highest court in the land.

The officers had pursued a car travelling on the Trans Canada Highway between Calgary and Regina, despite the fact that when the car came over the crest of a hill toward them, their radar only recorded the vehicle's speed as being 2 kilometres per hour over the speed limit. The officers justified their pursuit by claiming they thought the driver had braked aggressively when he saw their marked cruiser. They planned to simply warn the driver about speeding, not issue a ticket. In an act of courtesy he undoubtedly came to regret, Mr. MacKenzie actually came to a stop for the pursuing cruiser before the officers had signalled him to do so. In retrospect, one of the police officers would view this cooperation as suspicious. As the next paragraph will show, police can use this issue either way; they'll view you with suspicion if you cooperate, or if you don't.

One officer approached the vehicle and asked for MacKenzie's licence and registration. At trial, this officer testified that the driver seemed extremely nervous when he handed over his documents. He further testified to observing that MacKenzie appeared to be sweating and had a pinkish colour to his eyes; leading the officer to suspect the driver might be involved in a drug offence. This prompted the officer to ask MacKenzie to get out of the vehicle and for permission to search the car. Mr. MacKenzie did not consent to a search – a suspicious lack of cooperation?

Unfortunately for Mr. MacKenzie, his refusal to consent to a search was rendered moot. The officers just happened to have a drug detection dog with them on traffic duty! Brought from the cruiser, the dog was soon 'indicating' the scent of drugs at the hatch area of the vehicle. Now, hot on the trail, the officers conducted a warrantless search of the car's interior. Finding several gift-wrapped boxes in the hatch area, their curiosity demanded an unwrapping. While someone's birthday may have just been rendered less exciting, the police were not disappointed. The boxes contained over 30 pounds of marijuana.

Prior to his trial for possession for the purpose of trafficking, Mr. MacKenzie asked the trial judge to exclude the marijuana evidence because the police had violated section 8 of the *Charter* in using the sniffer dog without sufficient justification. The trial judge applied the "reasonable suspicion" standard and found that the factors the police had taken into account prior to using the dog fell short. As a result, the trial judge found that the use of the dog amounted to an unreasonable search and excluded the drug evidence.

When the Crown appealed the trial judge's decision to the Saskatchewan Court of Appeal, those judges ruled that the case was "very close to the line", but were satisfied that the "constellation of objective factors" met the reasonable suspicion standard. As a result, they set aside MacKenzie's acquittal and ordered a new trial.

In agreeing with the Saskatchewan Court of Appeal's assessment, Justice Moldaver, writing for a five judge majority of the Supreme Court of Canada, stated, "… while it is critical that the line between a hunch and reasonable suspicion be maintained to prevent the police from engaging in indiscriminate or discriminatory practices, it is equally vital that the police be allowed to carry out their duties without … their every move be[ing] placed under a scanning electron microscope." (para. 65)

In writing a dissenting opinion for a four judge minority of the Supreme Court of Canada, Justice LeBel responded: "The relatively low standard of reasonable suspicion, which allows police officers considerable latitude, increases the need for careful review of police action … ." (para. 95) Justice LeBel added: "The police cannot simply draw on their experience in the field to create broad categories of 'suspicious' behaviour into which almost anyone could fall. … In order to uphold and reinforce privacy rights, courts must not fail to hold police accountable when they stray from the proper exercise of their power and draw broad inferences of criminality without specific, individualized suspicion that can be objectively assessed." (para. 97)

To bring the sniffer dog cases full circle, the Alberta Court of Appeal dealt with another search conducted at the Calgary bus terminal in *R. v. Navales*,

[2014] A.J. No. 156, 2014 ABCA 70. Eric Navales had arrived in Calgary on an overnight bus from Vancouver. Sadly for him, RCMP officers were conducting a training exercise in the bus terminal with their drug detection dogs. A plain-clothes officer noticed that Navales, who had been heading toward a restroom, changed direction and made for the exit when he noticed the dogs. The officer followed Navales outside and engaged him in conversation, seeking to get him to agree to have his luggage searched. While this was never accomplished, the officer did manage to extract quite a lot during this "conversation".

The officer learned that Navales had purchased his ticket just 45 minutes before departure and that he had paid cash. The officer also noticed that the name on the ticket was Salazar, not Navales and that there appeared to be a large quantity of $100 bills in Navales' wallet. With Navales showing signs of becoming increasingly nervous, the officer called one of the dog handlers over and the dog "indicated" for drugs in front of Navales' bag. The officer searched the bag, finding 10 kilo-bricks of cocaine.

During his trial of possession for the purpose of trafficking, Mr. Navales asked the trial judge to rule that the use of the sniffer dog and subsequent search of his bag violated his section 8 *Charter* right to protection from an unreasonable search. The trial judge rejected this claim and Navales appealed. The Alberta Court of Appeal waited until the Supreme Court of Canada had released their decisions in *Chehil* and *MacKenzie*, and then applied the "reasonable suspicion" reasoning from those cases to dismiss Mr. Navales' appeal.

The most interesting aspect of the *Navales* decision is the critical comments by Justice Berger of the Alberta Court of Appeal. Justice Berger accepts that the outcome of the *Navales* case was inevitable because of the binding nature of the majority decisions of the Supreme Court of Canada in *Chehil* and *MacKenzie*. However, he laments the watered down standard of reasonable suspicion being based on the mere "possibility" of criminality. Quoting Chief Justice Warren of the U.S. Supreme Court, Justice Berger warns that this, "… invites 'intrusions upon constitutionally guaranteed rights based on nothing more substantial than inarticulate hunches'." (para. 38)

USE OF WARRANTS TO CONDUCT SEARCHES

Many pieces of legislation, including the *Criminal Code* and the *Controlled Drugs and Substances Act* provide for a wide variety of warrants and judicial authorizations to search for and seize particular types of evidence. Because of the way the courts have interpreted s. 8 of the *Canadian Charter of Rights and Freedoms*, any investigator who could be considered an agent of the state is wise to follow the requirements of the appropriate statute and get prior authorization from a judge whenever possible. As the Supreme Court of Canada made clear in *R. v. Patrick*, [2009] S.C.J. No. 17, [2009] 1 S.C.R. 579: "A warrantless search of a private place cannot be justified by the after-the-fact discovery of evidence of a crime." (para. 32)

As we will discuss in the next chapter, if you come to a trial and try to argue that you conducted a search or seized evidence without a warrant because you did not think you had the reasonable and probable grounds to justify getting a judge or justice of the peace to issue one, the evidence is likely to be excluded from trial anyway. The real answer to not yet having reasonable and probable grounds is simply to work harder and dig deeper. Reasonable and probable grounds are the threshold criteria for securing a warrant and for warrantless searches. Anything less will be considered an unreasonable violation of *Charter*-protected privacy interests.

The Supreme Court of Canada decision in *R. v. Morelli*, [2010] S.C.J. No. 8, 2010 SCC 8, makes it clear that the necessary documentation to secure a warrant or judge's authorization to search needs to be prepared carefully. Justice Fish of the Supreme Court of Canada described an "information to obtain" (ITO) a search warrant prepared by the investigators in that case as "… carelessly drafted, materially misleading, and factually incomplete." (para. 4) Justice Fish found the resulting warrant to be defective and ruled that child pornography evidence obtained from a computer using this warrant had to be excluded from use at trial under subs. 24(2) of the *Charter*. As a result, the accused, who was originally convicted at trial, was acquitted on appeal.

In *R. v. Strauss,* [2017] O.J. No. 4084, 2017 ONCA 628, the Ontario Court of Appeal were dealing with significant police misconduct, including disclosure in an ITO that "was not full and frank". In the ITO, the officer who drafted it suggested that the key evidence justifying the issue of a warrant had been collected when police had previously entered a rural property and barn, without obtaining a warrant, "as there was no house apparently attached to the property and no persons around". As Justice Benotto of the Ontario Court of Appeal observed: "This was not true. First, there was a house on the property. Second, the police officers' evidence made it clear that the decision to enter the property was made when they set out from the station…; it had nothing to do with the fact that there were 'no persons around'." (para. 49)

The Ontario Court of Appeal was not impressed; "A senior investigating officer and his team made a conscious decision to 'gamble' with the law and the courts. To admit the evidence under these circumstances would reward and ultimately permit this conduct." (para. 54) Appeal judges ordered that the seizure of a significant stash of guns, ammunition, cash and drugs would have to be excluded from use at trial as a result. The Court of Appeal quashed multiple convictions and entered acquittals on all counts.

Judges of the Supreme Court of Canada have added a caution about the need for careful drafting of an ITO when the police wish to search more than one unit of a multi-unit residence. In *R. v. Campbell*, [2011] S.C.J. No. 32, 2011 SCC 32, police had conducted a search of all four units in a townhouse that operated as a rooming house. A female tenants' body had been found close the townhouse and the police secured a search warrant during their murder investigation. Although another tenant was eventually convicted of the murder, the police had found a sawed-off shotgun in Mr. Campbell's unit during their search. Campbell was charged with a number of weapons offences. There was no suggestion the gun was connected in any way to the murder.

When Mr. Campbell challenged the validity of the warrant and his appeal reached the Supreme Court of Canada, Justice Charron wrote: "It is important to stress ... that Mr. Campbell's expectation of privacy in his room within the townhouse is just as high as that of a resident of a single dwelling unit. In drafting ITOs proposing to search more than one unit within a multi-unit dwelling, this principle should be reflected by clearly setting out reasonable and probable grounds for each unit to be searched." (para. 15)

R. v. Le, [2013] B.C.J. No. 2247, 2013 BCCA 442, is a British Columbia Court of Appeal case that dealt with the scope of a search warrant. In this case, Ms. Le was in her sister's home when the police arrived to execute a search warrant that was secured because of the sister's suspected drug activity. Because Ms. Le was not the suspect, the police allowed her to leave the house while they continued their search. However, when Ms. Le picked up her purse from the kitchen table on the way out, officers decided to search the purse before she left. The officers discovered crack cocaine in the purse and Ms. Le was arrested.

The question for the trial and appeal court judges became, did a search warrant for a home in which a purse was found authorize a search of the purse which belonged to someone who was not the target of the investigation? The trial judge pointed out that the warrant authorized the police to search and seize "things" found in the home. As a result, if the purse had not been picked up by Ms. Le, they would have no way of knowing who owned it and could have searched it pursuant to the warrant. Did the simple act of picking up the purse cause Ms. Le's reasonable expectation of privacy in relation to the contents of the purse to override the authority of the warrant to search "things" found in the home? Justice Chiasson of the BCCA ruled that it did not, "... the search was authorized by law and was reasonable". (para. 28)

In *R. v. Vu*, [2013] S.C.J. No. 60, 2013 SCC 60, police had acquired a search warrant to search a home in relation to theft of electricity and marijuana production. Even though their ITO had mentioned an intention to search for "computer generated notes", the warrant that was issued did not specifically authorize the search of computers. The Supreme Court of Canada ruled that because of the heightened privacy interest in the contents of a personal computer, police must have specific authorization to search the data. If police come across a computer in the course of a general search warrant, they can seize it to ensure the integrity of the data, but they must obtain a separate warrant to scan the contents.

USE OF FORCE

When a warrant to search is properly obtained, significant force can be used in executing the search if that is deemed reasonable in the circumstances. Justice Weiler's decision in the case of *R. v. Burke*, [2013] O.J. No. 2920, 2013 ONCA 424 contains a discussion of some of the general principles. The starting point is a conservative one, aimed at reducing the possibility that a startled householder will react violently when his or her personal space is invaded. As Justice Weiler points out, this approach was first articulated by the Supreme Court of Canada in *Eccles v. Bourque*, [1974] S.C.J. No. 123, [1975] 2 S.C.R. 739: "The general rule for the execution of a search warrant on a person's home is that the police must knock, announce their authority, and announce the reason for entry." (para 41 of *Burke*)

Justice Weiler goes on to explain: "The police are permitted to depart from the 'knock and announce' principle only in exigent circumstance, including if there is a need to prevent the destruction of evidence, or to ensure the safety of the police or the occupants ... . The onus is on the police to justify a departure from the knock and announce principle". (para. 41)

In the *Burke* case, the police had secured a warrant to enter Burke's home to seize his computer to search for evidence of child pornography. Around supper time, Mr. Burke was at home, watching T.V. with his door unlocked when, "[w]ithout warning, uniformed officers kicked in the door and stormed into his apartment. ... [T]hey pointed guns at him and some of them were masked. ... They shouted at the appellant to get to the ground. He was terrified and believed if he made a wrong move he could be killed." (para. 34)

The officer in charge of the investigation testified that she had determined that a no-knock entry was necessary because of the ease with which digital files could be destroyed or encrypted. Police feared this could be done before the accused answered the door if they had simply knocked. She didn't have as much of an explanation for why eight officers with body armour, semi-automatic weapons and balaclavas were needed.

Justice Weiler commented that: "In the absence of a concern for police safety, the element of intimidation accompanying the use of masks and drawn weapons may be unnecessary and is a cause for judicial concern." (para. 58) Nevertheless, she was not prepared to overturn the trial judge's decision that there was no section 8 *Charter* violation, citing Justice Cromwell of the Supreme Court of Canada, who said in the *Cornell* case (discussed below): "... [h]aving determined that a hard entry is justified, I do not think that the court should attempt to micromanage the police's choice of equipment." (para. 31 of *Cornell*)

This reasoning was also followed by the Ontario Court of Appeal in *R. v. Rutledge*, [2017] O.J. No. 4032, 2017 ONCA 635. A justice of the peace had granted telewarrants for a farmhouse, occupied by Mr. Rutledge. The ITO to secure the warrants was based on information from a confidential informant who had provided detailed information about drug dealing from the premises, numerous people with access and weapons, including a semi-automatic rifle on site.

The officer in charge of the search determined that it would be safest to approach undetected and to flush occupants from the residence to avoid an armed standoff. As Justice Watt observed, "To execute the warrants, the police came loaded for bear. Equipment of a dynamic entry. Tactical units. Night vision eyewear. Loud hailers...And tear gas." (para. 6). Officers approached the house with caution, broke a window and tossed in a tear gas canister. Rutledge, the sole occupant at the time, fled the residence and the search continued without incident.

At his trial on a variety of firearms charges, Mr. Rutledge raised the issue of whether the use of tear gas rendered the search unreasonable, particularly since the gas was not mentioned in the ITO to secure the warrant. As the Court of Appeal ruled in rejecting this claim, "...police decisions about the manner in which a search will be carried out fall to be adjudged by what was or should reasonably have been known to them at the time the search was conducted, not through the lens of how things turned out...Hindsight is not our measuring stick. ... police are entitled to some latitude...This is no place for the Monday morning quarterback." (paras. 25-26).

The case of *R. v. Cornell*, [2010] S.C.J. No. 31, 2010 SCC 31, provides an interesting discussion of this issue by two different factions of the Supreme Court. The split decision had four Supreme Court judges ruling that the search of the Cornell residence, believed to be a stash house for a cocaine distribution operation, was reasonable, while three Supreme Court justices found the techniques used by the police unreasonable. The scenario they were analyzing was described succinctly by Justice Fish, in dissent, at para. 46:

> Loaded weapons in hand, nine masked members of a police tactical unit smashed their way into the appellant's home in a residential Calgary neighbourhood. They forced the appellant's brother, who has a mental disability, face-down to the floor and cuffed his hands behind his back. They dented the front door with their battering ram and broke the door frame, destroyed some of the interior doors, pried locks off a garage door and rendered the garage door itself inoperable.

Writing for the majority of the Supreme Court of Canada, Justice Cromwell ruled: "The police had well-grounded concerns that the use of less intrusive methods would pose safety risks to the officers and occupants of the house and risk the destruction of evidence." (para. 2) Justice Cromwell went on to add, "...the police must be allowed a certain amount of latitude in the manner in which they decide to enter premises. They cannot be expected to measure in advance with nuanced precision the amount of force the situation will require". (para. 24)

In many ways, the dissenting opinion of Justice Fish is more convincingly expressed. It almost makes you wonder if the judges were ruling on the same situation. At para. 121:

> The absence of any prior investigation regarding the Cornell home and its occupants; the violence and destructiveness of the entry; the force used to subdue the sole, mentally disabled occupant of the house; the total failure to justify departure from the "knock and announce" rule in respect of the Cornell residence; the use of masks without justification; the use of drawn weapons without any reason to suspect that their physical security was at risk; ... and all the other facts and circumstances I have mentioned leave me with no doubt that the police in this case violated the right of the appellant, enshrined in s. 8 of the *Charter*, "to be secure against unreasonable search or seizure".

TEST YOURSELF

1. You're working as a drug officer. One night, when you're off duty, you attend a major junior hockey game at the community arena. While you're there, you notice a notorious local drug trafficker sitting with someone whom you have long suspected is the regional boss of an international motorcycle gang. Believing they may be conducting "business", you flash your I.D. and ask the T.V. crew for the cable network that will be televising the game if you can borrow their parabolic microphone and recording equipment for a few minutes. After a brief lesson on how it is used, you direct the mike toward your targets. You intercept and record this conversation:

   > Gang Boss: "Two thousand hits, 15 large."
   > Local Drug Dealer: "When and where?"
   > Gang Boss: "Midnight, tonight, Canadian Tire dumpster."

   Using this information, you arrest the local drug dealer, picking two discarded food containers (which you later learn are stuffed with fentanyl tablets) from the dumpster, as he deposits a kitchen waste bag containing a significant sum of cash. You also intend to charge the motorcycle gang boss with trafficking and conspiracy. If you do so, will you be able to use the tape of the conversation you recorded at the hockey game as evidence at the trial?

2. You're still working as a drug officer when you receive an anonymous phone call, providing information that a well known local musician is producing large quantities of MDMA (ecstasy) and crystal meth in the barn and basement of a farmhouse he rents, just outside town.

   (a) Is this likely to be a sufficient basis for obtaining a search warrant to further investigate this tip?

   (b) Could you go on to the farm property to gather more evidence before attempting to get a warrant?

   (c) Can you go up, knock on the door and simply sniff and look around to obtain further evidence to justify a search warrant?

   (d) Is it a good strategy to snatch the musician's garbage bags from the side of the road before the trash collector arrives on garbage pick-up day?

3. You're a police officer, walking a downtown beat. As you pass a small apartment building, you hear female screams. You zero in on a particular apartment when this is followed by a male voice, swearing loudly. You can distinctly hear a thumping sound, as well. What, if anything, should you do in this situation? Briefly explain.

4. Go online and locate the Supreme Court of Canada's decision in *R. v. Cole*, [2012] S.C.J. No. 53, 2012 SCC 53. What was the nature of the charge the accused was facing? Should this affect the analysis of the *Charter* issues raised in the case? Do you find the reasoning of Justice Fish (for the majority) or Justice Abella (in dissent) more compelling? Why?

Chapter 10

Other Charter Rights and Remedies

RIGHT TO DISCLOSURE

As discussed in Chapter 1, criminal trials are skewed contests where the full resources of society can be used in an attempt to prove that an individual has committed a criminal offence. Partially in response to the potential imbalance of the criminal justice process, s. 7 of the *Canadian Charter of Rights and Freedoms* protects everyone's "... life, liberty and security of the person ..." and a person cannot be, "... deprived thereof except in accordance with the principles of fundamental justice". Court decisions have made it clear that one of these constitutionally-protected principles of fundamental justice is the right of an accused person to disclosure of any evidence that police or other government agents and prosecutors have gathered during the investigation.

This protection has also been described as the right of an accused person *to make full answer and defence*. If public money has been expended to gather evidence against an individual, that person should be entitled to know what he or she is up against, but also should have access to any evidence generated through public expenditure that may be used to raise a reasonable doubt about the person's guilt. In other words, the accused is entitled to disclosure of all potentially relevant evidence, whether the prosecutor plans to use the evidence or not. Justice Sopinka of the Supreme Court of Canada, in the important case of *R. v. Stinchcombe*, [1991] S.C.J. No. 83, [1991] 3 S.C.R. 326 at 336, described this right as "... one of the pillars of criminal justice on which we heavily depend to ensure that the innocent are not convicted".

In *R. v. O'Connor*, [1995] S.C.J. No. 98, [1995] 4 S.C.R. 411, Justice L'Heureux-Dubé of the Supreme Court of Canada tied the duty of disclosure to the prosecutor's special role in the justice system: "... full and fair disclosure is a fundamental aspect of the Crown's duty to serve the Court as a faithful public agent, entrusted not with winning or losing trials but rather with seeing that justice is served". (at para. 101)

There is no doubt that the duty extends to evidence in the possession of the police and other government investigative agencies. *R. v. Taillefer*; *R. v. Duguay*, [2003] S.C.J. No. 75, [2003] 3 S.C.R. 307, is a case that came to the Supreme Court of Canada because of a failure to disclose significant quantities of evidence in the control of the Quebec provincial police service, the Surete de Quebec. Both of the accused were charged with the first degree murder of a 14-year-old girl. Taillefer was convicted at a trial in 1991, as was Duguay. Duguay's murder conviction was overturned on appeal, but he entered a guilty plea to manslaughter in 1995, rather than facing another trial for second degree murder. Eight years later, the Poitras Commission, which was investigating the provincial police service, discovered a great deal of evidence in the possession of the police that had never been disclosed to the defence, either prior to their initial trials in 1991, or before Duguay's guilty plea in 1995.

In reviewing the circumstances of this case, Justice LeBel of the Supreme Court of Canada said: "To determine whether there is an infringement of the right to make full answer and defence, the accused will have to show that there was a reasonable possibility that the failure to disclose affected the outcome at trial or the overall fairness of the trial process." (para. 71) The failure to disclose evidence in this case meant that Taillefer's conviction was quashed and a new trial was ordered. In the case of Duguay, who had already served eight years of a 12-year sentence for manslaughter, he was allowed to withdraw his guilty plea, his conviction was quashed and a *stay* of proceedings was ordered. This meant that he could not be re-tried for the homicide.

SECTION 9 OF THE *CHARTER*

Section 9 of the *Canadian Charter of Rights and Freedoms* states that: "Everyone has the right not to be arbitrarily detained or imprisoned." Violations of this right could affect the admissibility of evidence gathered at the time of the arbitrary arrest or detention.

In the breathalyzer case of *R. v. Ladouceur*, [1990] S.C.J. No. 53, [1990] 1 S.C.R. 1257, the accused's vehicle had been stopped as part of a random roadside spot-check program to check for impaired drivers. Ladouceur's lawyer claimed that this was an arbitrary detention and tried to have the evidence produced as a result excluded from use at his trial. The prosecutor argued in response that even if the spot-check program did involve an arbitrary detention; this was a reasonable limit on the rights of motorists, which would be permissible under the provisions of s. 1 of the *Charter.* That section specifies that *Charter* rights are guaranteed, but are subject to, "… such reasonable limits prescribed by law as can be demonstrably justified in a free and democratic society".

The Supreme Court of Canada sided with the prosecution. A roadside stop-check could be considered an arbitrary detention, contrary to s. 9 of the *Charter*, but it was justified under s. 1 because of the legitimate societal concern with protecting society from impaired drivers. Evidence generated during this type of very temporary detention would be admissible.

Of course, not all arbitrary forms of detention will be justifiable. The Supreme Court of Canada decision in *R. v. Harrison*, [2009] S.C.J. No. 34, 2009 SCC 34, involved an Ontario police officer's unjustified stop of a rental car, registered in Alberta. The officer originally stopped the vehicle because it did not have a front licence plate, required for vehicles registered in Ontario, but not for Alberta vehicles. The officer realized that the car had a rear Alberta plate prior to any contact with the driver, but continued his detention and investigation anyway. When the officer learned that the driver of the vehicle was operating it even though his driver's licence was suspended, the officer arrested the driver and proceeded with a warrantless search of the vehicle and its contents, including two sealed cardboard cartons, located in the cargo area. In a 6-1 decision, the Supreme Court of Canada ruled that in acting as he did, the police officer had violated the s. 9 protection against arbitrary detention and the s. 8 protection against an unreasonable search. The judges also ruled that 35 kilograms of cocaine discovered in the cardboard cartons should have been excluded from use at trial due to the *Charter* violations and, as a result, Mr. Harrison was acquitted of a nasty trafficking charge.

In *R. v. Mellenthin*, [1992] S.C.J. No. 100, [1992] 3 S.C.R. 615, the Supreme Court of Canada pointed out that roadside stops are authorized by legislation to check for sobriety, valid licences, ownership, insurance and the fitness of the vehicle. Nevertheless, driver and passenger searches beyond these purposes would not be permissible without some additional justification, based on the reasonable probability that evidence of an offence would be discovered.

In the case of *R. v. Belnavis*, [1997] S.C.J. No. 81, [1997] 3 S.C.R. 341, the Supreme Court justices pointed out that even if a vehicle were stopped for a legitimate reason and the driver was arrested pursuant to an outstanding traffic warrant, this would not justify a search of the trunk of the vehicle without a warrant.

The Supreme Court of Canada decision in *R. v. Nolet*, [2010] S.C.J. No. 24, 2010 SCC 24, seems to suggest that due to the heavily regulated nature of the trucking industry, things may be different if a person is driving a commercial vehicle, like a tractor-trailer. An R.C.M.P. officer in Saskatchewan, acting under the provincial *Highways and Transportation Act*, randomly stopped a truck registered in Quebec. The officer noted an expired fuel sticker on the exterior of the truck and discovered the vehicle was not registered for commercial trucking in Saskatchewan, after requesting the vehicle's registration from the driver. Both of these constitute regulatory offences for truck operators in Saskatchewan and the provincial statute authorizes police to search a commercial vehicle for evidence of an offence and to seize evidence discovered. In this case, the warrantless search of the cab and trailer turned up something entirely different than trucking regulation violations — $115,000 in cash and 392 pounds of marijuana. Two truck operators, Nolet and Vatsis were charged with trafficking and possession of proceeds of crime. The Supreme Court ruled that in this situation there was no violation of either ss. 9 or 8 of the *Charter*.

The Supreme Court spent a considerable period of time analyzing the legal definition of "detention" in *R. v. Grant*, [2009] S.C.J. No. 32, 2009 SCC 32, mentioning the importance of the concept, not only in relation to s. 9 of the *Charter*, but also because the rights protected by s. 10 for an individual to be informed of a reason for an arrest or detention and of the right to retain counsel are triggered by a detention occurring. Justices McLachlin and Charron, writing the majority decision, stated (at para. 44) that:

> Detention under ss. 9 and 10 of the *Charter* refers to a suspension of the individual's liberty interest by a significant physical or psychological restraint. Psychological detention is established either where the individual has a legal obligation to comply

with the restrictive request or demand, or a reasonable person would conclude by reason of the state conduct that he or she has no choice but to comply.

In *R. v. Suberu*, [2009] S.C.J. No. 33, 2009 SCC 33, the Supreme Court of Canada recognized that there may be circumstances where the police are engaged in preliminary investigative questioning that comes short of detention. In the *Suberu* case itself, a police officer arrived at a liquor store where employees had phoned in a report of two individuals trying to use a stolen credit card. The officer asked a few preliminary questions of Musibau Suberu, who was exiting the store and requested that Suberu not leave. Mr. Suberu provided answers to the officer's questions that indicated some knowledge of the crime. At this stage, the trial judge ruled that the officer was "... engaged in a general inquiry and had not yet zeroed in on the individual as someone whose movements must be controlled". (para. 31) As a result, the Supreme Court agreed with the trial judge that there was no detention and hence no obligation to outline Mr. Suberu's right to counsel just yet. When the officer subsequently received additional information indicating that Suberu matched the description of one of the suspects and arrested Suberu, the officer provided the appropriate explanation of s. 10 rights. The Supreme Court found this course of action correct in the circumstances. Evidence acquired prior to the detention was admissible.

CHARTER SUBSECTION 24(1) REMEDIES

Section 24 is the key remedy section of the *Charter* that is likely to have an impact on the admissibility of evidence. While we will soon discuss subs. 24(2), which was drafted specifically to provide the remedy of the exclusion of evidence for some *Charter* right violations, subs. 24(1) provides for a broad spectrum of remedies which may be triggered by an abuse of rules of evidence, or may also restrict the use of evidence.

The spectrum of remedies available in subs. 24(1) is restricted only by the creativity of the judges who are called upon to apply it. The subsection provides that, "Anyone whose rights or freedoms ... have been infringed or denied may apply to a court of competent jurisdiction to obtain *such remedy as the court considers appropriate and just in the circumstances.*" (Emphasis added)

It was this subsection that allowed the Supreme Court of Canada to tailor remedies specific to each of the accused in the cases of *Taillefer* and *Duguay* discussed above. Both had been impacted by a violation of their rights to disclosure under s. 7 of the *Charter*, but the distinctions in the way they had been dealt with in the criminal justice process resulted in different remedies being granted by the Court. Taillefer's first conviction was quashed and a new trial was ordered. For Duguay, who had already served the major portion of the sentence imposed for his conviction, he was allowed to withdraw his guilty plea; his conviction was also quashed, but the prosecution could not subject him to the possibility of another trial after the Court ordered a *stay* of the charges against him. Those were the remedies that the Supreme Court of Canada determined were "appropriate and just in the circumstances".

A *stay* was also considered to be the appropriate remedy in the Ontario Court of Appeal decision in *R. v. Salmon*, [2013] O.J. No. 1461, 2013 ONCA 203. The accused was facing 17 charges, including living off the avails of prostitution and human trafficking. "The trial judge found that police had fabricated evidence to make it appear that two pieces of false identification in the name of the complainant had been found in [Salmon's] wallet at the time of his arrest, and that at least one police officer lied about it in testimony." (para. 1 of Justice MacPherson's decision).

The trial judge ruled that this was an abuse of process and also a violation of Salmon's rights under s. 7 of the *Charter*. The police actions were such a fundamental violation of notions of justice that they undermined the integrity of the justice system and stopping the prosecution was the appropriate remedy. The Court of Appeal agreed with the trial judge's ruling that "... the police conduct ... was so egregious that only a stay could serve society's interest in preserving the integrity of the justice system". (para. 9).

In *R. v. Bellusci*, [2012] S.C.J. No. 44, 2012 SCC 44, the Supreme Court of Canada reviewed a situation where a trial judge had granted a stay of proceedings because of the action of a prison guard. Riccardo Bellusci was chained, shackled, handcuffed and defenceless when a prison guard provoked him and possibly endangered his life by telling other prisoners that Bellusci was a sex offender. Bellusci responded by threatening the guard's family. In response to Bellusci's threats, the guard beat the crap out of the bound and defenceless prisoner, but it was Bellusci facing a charge of "intimidating a justice official" because of his threats.

The trial judge stayed the proceeding, ruling that the guard's actions were an egregious violation of Mr. Bellusci's right to security of the person under section 7 of the *Charter*. The judge also felt the integrity of the justice system was further tarnished by the "sclerotic solidarity" of the other prison guards who testified about the incident. A 9-0 panel of the Supreme Court of Canada ruled that the trial judge had considered the appropriate factors in granting the stay.

R. v. Babos, [2014] S.C.J. No. 16, 2014 SCC 16 is a contrasting case where a majority of the Supreme Court of Canada ruled that a trial judge's stay of proceedings was not a necessary remedy. Justice Moldaver pointed out that only in "the clearest of cases" would a stay for an abuse of process be warranted: "... the question is whether the state has engaged in conduct that is offensive to societal notions of fair play and decency and whether proceeding with a trial in the face of that conduct would be harmful to the integrity of the justice system." (para. 35)

In this case, a Crown prosecutor, who was no longer involved in the case by the time it went to trial, had threatened the accused with more charges if he did not enter a guilty plea to the ones he was already facing. In addition, the trial judge had decided that two police officers had colluded in misleading the court as to whether or not the accused had consented to a search of the trunk of his car in which a firearm was found.

In considering the original prosecutor's threats, Justice Moldaver made it clear that, "[w]ithout question, the bullying tactic to which Ms. Tremblay resorted was reprehensible and unworthy of the dignity of her office. It should not be repeated by her or any other Crown." (para. 61) However, Justice Moldaver also said it was appropriate to consider the fact that this prosecutor was no longer involved in the case and her actions 18 months earlier really didn't affect the fairness of the trial. With respect to the police officers' apparent collusion, that could have been addressed by excluding the one piece of evidence acquired as a result. There was a great deal more evidence involved in the large number of charges the accused was facing.

Deciding whether to grant a stay, "… requires weighing the seriousness of the misconduct against the societal interest in having a trial." In this case, the accused was facing 22 charges, involving drugs, guns and organized crime: "When the impugned misconduct … is weighed against society's interest in a trial, I am satisfied that this is not one of the 'clearest of cases' where the exceptional remedy of a stay of proceedings is warranted." (para. 69)

In *R. v. Bjelland*, [2009] S.C.J. No. 38, 2009 SCC 38, Jason Bjelland was charged with importing 22 kilograms of cocaine when custom officers discovered the drugs under the bumper of a trailer he was towing behind his car when he crossed into Alberta from the U.S. Long after the preliminary inquiry, and shortly before his trial was to start, the Crown disclosed significant "new" evidence from two alleged accomplices. The Crown argued that the evidence, although available, could not have been disclosed earlier since that would have compromised an ongoing investigation and might endanger a witness. Bjelland's lawyer claimed this late disclosure violated the s. 7 *Charter* right to make full answer and defence and asked the trial judge for a stay of the proceedings or, failing that, the exclusion of the evidence disclosed under subs. 24(1). The trial judge refused the stay, but did order that the evidence involved in the tardy disclosure be excluded from use at trial. Bjelland was acquitted and the Crown appealed the trial judge's decision to exclude the evidence.

When Justice Rothstein dealt with the issue for the majority of the Supreme Court of Canada, he stated that: "While the exclusion of evidence will normally be a remedy under s. 24(2), it cannot be ruled out as a remedy under s. 24(1). However, such a remedy will only be available in those cases where a less intrusive remedy cannot be fashioned to safeguard the fairness of the trial process and the integrity of the justice system." (para. 19) Justice Rothstein pointed out that society also has an interest in preserving the truth-seeking function of trials. In this case, "… an adjournment would have preserved society's interest in a fair trial while still curing the prejudice to the accused". (para. 38) A new trial was ordered for Mr. Bjelland.

In the case of *R. v. White*, [1999] S.C.J. No. 28, [1999] 2 S.C.R. 417, Ms. White was involved in a car accident and filed a report of the accident with the police, as she was required to do under a provincial statute. When the prosecutor tried to use this statement as evidence at a trial of a criminal charge related to the accident, Ms. White's lawyer argued that this would be a violation of her right not to incriminate herself. This right is one of the principles of fundamental justice, covered by s. 7 of the *Charter*. The trial judge decided to exercise his prerogative to provide an appropriate remedy, using subs. 24(1) of the *Charter*. The judge ruled that the statement provided under the requirement of the provincial statute could not be used by the prosecution in the criminal trial.

In approving the trial judge's approach, the Supreme Court of Canada mentioned that subs. 24(2) provides the normal remedy for the exclusion of evidence, but requires that the evidence, "… was obtained in a manner …" that violated *Charter* rights. In this case, where the statement was provided under a provincial statute that required it for purposes other than a criminal charge, there was no violation of a *Charter* right in the way the evidence was obtained. It would be the use of the evidence in the criminal trial that would affect trial fairness. Both ss. 11(*d*) and 7 of the *Charter* ensure trial fairness. Subsection 24(1) is broad enough to allow for the exclusion of evidence in a circumstance like this, where trial fairness would be affected by the admission of evidence.

In *R. v. Nasogaluak*, [2010] S.C.J. No. 6, 2010 SCC 6, police violated Lyle Nasogaluak's s. 7 right to security of his person when they beat him badly while arresting him after a high speed chase. The police broke Lyle's ribs and punctured a lung. Though the accused entered a guilty plea to impaired driving and flight from police charges, the trial judge used subs. 24(1) of the *Charter* to justify a sentence reduction on the charges below a statutory minimum laid out in the *Criminal Code*. The Supreme Court of Canada found that a sentence reduction could be used in response to evidence of police misconduct, but also stated that this could be accomplished in the Nasogaluak case through general sentencing discretion principles which did not lower the accused's sentence below the statutory minimum. Nevertheless, Justice LeBel of the Supreme Court of Canada did leave the door open to this sort of remedy in future cases at para. 6:

> A sentence reduction outside statutory limits does not generally constitute an "appropriate" remedy within the meaning of s. 24(1), unless the constitutionality of the statutory limit itself is challenged. However, the remedial power of the court under s. 24(1) is broad. I therefore do not foreclose the possibility that, in some exceptional cases, a sentence reduction outside statutory limits may be the sole effective remedy for some particularly egregious form of misconduct by state agents in relation to the offence and the offender.

In *Vancouver v. Ward*, [2010] S.C.J. No. 27, 2010 SCC 27, a lawyer in Vancouver was mistakenly arrested and subject to a strip search after police received a tip that someone was planning on assaulting the Prime Minister with a pie at a public function. After several hours in custody, the police realized they had no evidence to support a charge of attempted assault against Mr. Ward and he was released without any criminal charges being laid. Ward sued the Vancouver police, alleging that the strip search was an unreasonable search under s. 8 of the *Charter* and claiming a financial compensation remedy under subs. 24(1). The trial judge ruled that such a remedy was appropriate, ordering that Mr. Ward be paid $5,000 for the violation of his *Charter* rights. The Supreme Court of Canada agreed that such a financial remedy was appropriate in this situation.

CHARTER SUBSECTION 24(2) REMEDY

Subsection 24(2) of the *Canadian Charter of Rights and Freedoms* is the key remedy section, providing for the exclusion of evidence that is, "... obtained in a manner that infringed or denied any rights or freedoms guaranteed by this *Charter*...". Exclusion of the evidence is not automatic. The subsection goes on to direct a judge to consider all the circumstances and to exclude the evidence if, "... the admission of it ... would bring the administration of justice into disrepute".

The case of Ruby Collins (*R. v. Collins*, [1987] S.C.J. No. 15, [1987] 1 S.C.R. 265), which we have already discussed a number of times in this book, and *R. v. Stillman*, [1997] S.C.J. No. 34, 113 C.C.C. (3d) 321, became the Supreme Court of Canada's foundation cases in setting out factors a judge should consider in assessing whether or not admitting the evidence would bring the administration of justice into disrepute. The factors discussed in these and other Supreme Court cases included:

- What kind of evidence was obtained?
- Which *Charter* right was violated?
- Was the *Charter* violation deliberate, wilful, flagrant or done inadvertently in good faith?
- Did the violation occur in urgent circumstances?
- Were other investigatory techniques available?
- Would the evidence have been obtained anyway?
- Is the charge a serious one?

Chief Justice McLachlin and Madame Justice Charron of the Supreme Court of Canada streamlined the number of factors for consideration in *R. v. Grant*, [2009] S.C.J. No. 32 at para. 71, 2009 SCC 32. The Justices said that when faced with an application for exclusion of evidence:

> ... a court must assess and balance the effect of admitting the evidence on society's confidence in the justice system having regard to: (1) the seriousness of the *Charter*-infringing state conduct, (2) the impact of the breach on the *Charter*-protected interests of the accused, and (3) society's interest in the adjudication of the case on its merits.

While it is the *Collins* factors that the courts applied in deciding to admit or exclude evidence in many of the *Charter* cases decided prior to 2009, the *Grant* decision provides the parameters utilized in the more recent cases.

R. V. GRANT REJECTS A CONSCRIPTIVE OR NON-CONSCRIPTIVE EVIDENCE FOCUS

Since an accused is not obligated to assist investigators or prosecutors in any way in securing his or her own conviction, judges prior to the decision in *R. v. Grant*, [2009] S.C.J. No. 32, 2009 SCC 32, consistently mentioned that a *Charter* violation that involves *conscripting* an accused to supply evidence against himself or herself was more likely to render a trial unfair if that evidence was used. It is a principle of fundamental justice, secured by s. 7 of the *Charter*, that an accused is protected from any form of self-incrimination that would be part of the violation of the accused's rights. As a result, *conscriptive* evidence was most likely to be excluded from use at a trial because letting it in would bring the administration of justice into disrepute.

In Chapter 8, we discussed a number of cases where statements taken from an accused person in violation of *Charter* rights were considered *conscriptive* and excluded. *R. v. Manninen*, [1987] S.C.J. No. 41, [1987] 1 S.C.R. 1233, involved a suspect who made a statement during continued questioning after he had asked to exercise his right to speak to a lawyer. In *R. v. Hebert*, [1990] S.C.J. No. 64, [1990] 2 S.C.R. 151 and *R. v. Broyles*, [1991] S.C.J. No. 95, [1991] 3 S.C.R. 595, statements were unfairly elicited from incarcerated people who had tried to exercise their right to remain silent.

The *Stillman* case discussed above involved bodily samples (hair and saliva) taken from a suspect without consent or a court order after a defence lawyer had expressly told the police investigators that Stillman would not be co-operating by providing statements or any other evidence. The Supreme Court of Canada considered this a flagrant violation of the rights of the accused and ruled that the *conscriptive* evidence should be excluded.

In *R. v. Grant*, [2009] S.C.J. No. 32, 2009 SCC 32, Chief Justice McLachlin and Justice Charron of the Supreme Court of Canada stated that, "… the approach to admissibility of bodily evidence under s. 24(2) that asks simply whether the evidence was conscripted should be replaced by a flexible test based on all the circumstances, as the wording of s. 24(2) requires." (para. 107) Nevertheless, they go on to say that, "… it may be ventured in general that where an intrusion on bodily integrity is deliberately inflicted and the impact on the accused's privacy, bodily integrity and dignity is high, bodily evidence will be excluded, notwithstanding its relevance and reliability." (para. 111)

Because *real* evidence, like the victim's cigarettes and money found in the suspect's trailer in *R. v. Feeney*, [1997] S.C.J. No. 49, [1997] 2 S.C.R. 13, discussed in Chapter 9, exist regardless of any co-operation by the accused; such evidence was normally considered to be *non-conscriptive*. The courts prior to *Grant* consistently said that this type of evidence was more likely to be admitted than *conscriptive* evidence, though the *Feeney* case provided an illustration that even *non-conscriptive* evidence was excluded from use at trial if its discovery occurs in the context of very serious *Charter* violations by investigators.

Real evidence may be admissible even if there is a *Charter* violation if a court concludes that it would have been discovered anyway if the investigators had followed proper procedures. In *R. v. Black*, [1989] S.C.J. No. 81, [1989] 2 S.C.R. 138, discussed in Chapter 8, police violated the female murder suspect's right to counsel by continuing to question her before she had a realistic chance to speak to a lawyer. During the questioning, she not only made admissions with respect to the stabbing, but directed officers to the location of the knife used in the incident. The knife was located in her home and the Supreme Court concluded that it would likely have been located without the *Charter* violation. They had no doubt that in these circumstances a warrant-authorized search of Black's residence would have occurred at some point.

R. v. Burlingham, [1995] S.C.J. No. 39, [1995] 2 S.C.R. 206, also discussed in Chapter 8, provides a contrasting situation. Officers also violated Mr. Burlingham's s. 10(*b*) right to counsel, extracting admissions in relation to a murder and having Mr. Burlingham show them where he had thrown the murder weapon into the Kootenay River. Because the murder weapon would never have been located without Burlingham's co-operation, the Supreme Court of Canada ruled that the firearm discovered under the ice of the frozen river was *derivative conscriptive* evidence and should be excluded from use at trial. The test for *derivative conscriptive* evidence is that the evidence would not have been discovered but for the evidence conscripted from the accused by the state.

Writing for the majority of the Supreme Court of Canada in *R. v. Grant*, Justices McLachlin and Charron stated at para. 120:

> The conscription-discoverability doctrine has been justifiably criticized as overly speculative and capable of producing anomalous results ... In practice, it has proved difficult to apply because of its hypothetical nature and because of the fine-grained distinctions between the tests for determining whether evidence is "derivative" and whether it is "discoverable".

They reject the old approach. They recommend replacing any focus on conscription and derivative evidence with "... a flexible test based on all the circumstances, as the wording of s. 24(2) requires". (para. 107) The Supreme Court now insists that judges "... must pursue the usual three lines of inquiry". (para. 123) This, of course, refers to the Court's own preference for reference to the seriousness of the *Charter*-infringing conduct, the impact of the breach on the *Charter*-protected rights of the accused and society's interest in the adjudication of the case on its merits.

Interestingly, the *Grant* case itself involved violations of Donnahue Grant's right to freedom from arbitrary detention under s. 9 and his right to counsel under s. 10, though the Supreme Court judges admitted that the police were operating in an area of legal uncertainty around the concept of when detention actually occurs. (A concept which they claimed to clear up and warned police in future not to act as the officers in this case did.) As a result of these violations, the police learned that young Mr. Grant was in possession of a loaded gun. Under the old analysis, the gun would most certainly be considered derivative evidence. Using its new tripartite standard of assessment, the Supreme Court found that, "... the police conduct was not egregious. The impact of the *Charter* breach on the accused's protected interests was significant, although not at the most serious end of the scale. Finally, the value of the evidence is considerable." (para. 140) Overall, they found that the decision to allow the evidence of the gun to be used at trial was a close call, but admitting this evidence would *not* bring the administration of justice into disrepute.

The Supreme Court of Canada came to the opposite conclusion in the *R. v. Paterson* case ([2017] S.C.J. No. 15), discussed in chapter 9, where police had followed Mr. Paterson into his private residence to seize marijuana roaches, though they had no intention of laying a criminal charge in relation to their possession. In that case, Justice Brown of the Supreme Court emphasized that it is, "...important not to allow the third *Grant 2009* factor of society's interest in adjudicating a case on its merits to trump all other considerations, particularly where...the impugned conduct was serious and worked a substantial impact on the appellant's *Charter* right." (para. 56)

ACTIONS OF THE INVESTIGATORS

In *R. v. Kokesch*, [1990] S.C.J. No. 117, 61 C.C.C. (3d) 207, police conducted a perimeter search of a residence, knowing that they did not have reasonable grounds to secure a warrant. Justice Sopinka of the Supreme Court of Canada emphasized the importance of police officers complying with statutes and the common law: "The police must be taken to be aware of this Court's judgments in *Eccles v. Bourque*, [1975] 2 S.C.R. 739 and *Colet v. R.*, [1981] 1 S.C.R. 2 ... Either the police knew they were trespassing, or they ought to have known. Whichever is the case, they cannot be said to have proceeded in 'good faith'...". (paras. 51-52)

Justice Sopinka added that the purpose of considering the seriousness of the *Charter* violation is to assess whether or not the administration of justice would be brought into disrepute by allowing the evidence to be admitted. "The court must refuse to condone, and must dissociate itself from, egregious police conduct". (para. 43) The more egregious the conduct, the more likely that evidence will be excluded.

Justice Sopinka re-emphasized that evidence gathering, either with or without a warrant must be based on reasonable and probable grounds for believing that an offence has been committed and that relevant evidence will be discovered as a result of the investigators' actions. "Where the police have nothing but suspicion and no legal way to obtain other evidence, it follows that they must leave the suspect alone, not charge ahead and obtain the evidence illegally and unconstitutionally." (para. 46)

Evidence may well be admissible despite a *Charter* violation if the police have acted in good faith. In *R. v. Evans*, [1996] S.C.J. No. 1, 104 C.C.C. (3d) 23, the Supreme Court of Canada had a chance to review the actions of police officers who had received an anonymous tip of a marijuana grow operation at the Evans residence. When investigative efforts failed to generate more evidence, they decided to take advantage of an "implied licence" that courts have recognized homeowners extend to people who would otherwise be considered trespassers to come to their door for the purpose of communicating with the residents.

Of course, the police officers were not going to the door to simply communicate. They were hoping to generate more evidence in relation to a grow operation, which was accomplished as the officers were met by the strong odour of growing marijuana when Evans opened the door. The officers arrested Evans just inside the door, where they were also able to see marijuana plants. Using the tip, the odour and what they had seen of the plants, the officers then obtained a search warrant for the residence. Using the warrant, they seized plants and grow equipment.

The Supreme Court of Canada ruled that the implied licence to approach someone's door did not extend to police investigators who were there for the purpose of gathering evidence. As a result, the doorway sniff search was ruled to be unreasonable under s. 8 of the *Canadian Charter of Rights and Freedoms.* In spite of this, the Court added that the *Charter* breach was not particularly serious. In the circumstances, which included a lack of common law direction on this use of an implied licence in this context and society's need to control illegal drug production, the officers had acted in good faith. The Supreme Court decided that evidence generated should still be admissible at Evans' trial: "... the exclusion of the evidence in this case would tarnish the image of the administration of justice to a much greater extent than would its admission." (para. 31)

It is important to realize that once the Supreme Court has said that this sort of sniff search is an unreasonable search under s. 8, police investigators would <u>not</u> be acting in good faith if they tried to use this investigative technique in the future. Evidence would be excluded from a new case based on the same facts. Arguably, the Supreme Court provided the same warning with respect to unlawful detentions in *R. v. Grant.* In the case of *R. v. Paterson* ([2017] S.C.J. No. 15), discussed in chapter 9, Justice Brown of the Supreme Court of Canada cautioned, "...that negligence in meeting *Charter* standards cannot be equated to good faith." (para. 44).

The Supreme Court of Canada decision in *R. v. Côté*, [2011] S.C.J. No. 46, 2011 SCC 46 is a murder case that involves an excellent analysis of the way case law can be applied to the actions of investigators in determining whether or not evidence should be excluded from use at trial. As Justice Cromwell stated in that decision, "... it must not be forgotten that the purpose of the *Charter's* protection against unreasonable searches is to prevent them before they occur, not to sort them out from reasonable intrusions on an *ex post facto* analysis ...". (para. 84) The case provides a great deal of useful direction for investigators and, as a result, has been included in its entirety as Appendix 3.

TEST YOURSELF

1. You work as an investigator for a defence lawyer who is representing B.M. (Buttermilk) Sampson, a basketball star accused of murdering his wife. Prior to trial, you were feeling good about the case for the defence. Your investigation of the information disclosed by the prosecutor showed that there were no eyewitnesses and that the key piece of evidence was a bloody pitchfork found at the scene. Forensic investigation disclosed no fingerprints, footprints, fibres or other evidence linking your client to the scene. When you asked your client about the pitchfork, he laughingly told you, "I don't know which end of those things is up. It sure ain't my fork." Your client is prepared to testify that he was on a flight to Detroit when the murder occurred.

   The trial has started. The prosecutor has called a surprise witness who is prepared to testify that your client won the pitchfork in question at a celebrity hay-baling contest, set up to raise money for 4-H clubs. The witness will claim that he was the person who presented the distinctive prize pitchfork to your client. Is there anything that can be done to prevent the admission of this evidence? Might the judge consider a different remedy than exclusion of the evidence? Briefly explain.

2. You're working as a police officer in a remote community in the far north. Late on the evening of December 24, you receive an anonymous phone call from someone who is either disguising his voice or sounds like a child. The caller tells you that he's working on a large farm and toy-making operation in the area. "Everybody thinks my boss is a saint, but you should see the marijuana grow-op he has in the basement. This is not medical marijuana and the old man has no legal right to grow this much stuff. He'll be gone all night. If you get here right away, you'll have him by those long, white whiskers!" After providing directions, he hangs up. Based on this call, what should you do? Why?

3. Regardless of your answer to question 2, your first move is to go look around the farm. From the road, you can see a strange, blue light coming from the basement windows. You also notice a large barn, with lights shining inside. You enter the farmyard and look in the barn windows. You notice two dwarves, pitch-forking feed into a manger. There are several old reindeer munching on the stuff. If you're not mistaken, the feed looks an awful lot like baled marijuana.

   Would you be able to use the fruits of your investigation to get a valid search warrant to return and seize evidence? Discuss the ramifications of your actions on the trial if you charge the homeowner with cultivating excessive quantities of marijuana.

4. Read the decision of the Supreme Court of Canada in *R. v. Côté*, [2011] S.C.J. No. 46, 2011 SCC 46, included as Appendix 3. According to the original trial judge and the majority of the Supreme Court of Canada,

which of Armande Cote's *Charter* rights were violated by the manner in which the investigation was conducted? Outline the evidence that was excluded pursuant to s. 24(2) of the *Charter* as a result. How would the Quebec Court of Appeal and Justice Deschamps of the Supreme Court of Canada have dealt with these issues?

Chapter 11

Gathering and Organizing Evidence

JUDICIAL NOTICE

We expect judges and juries to come equipped with a general body of knowledge about facts that are so commonly accepted in the local community that it would be unreasonable to question their reliance on this knowledge or to require one of the parties to present evidence on the matter. In a sense these are "evidence freebies".

In an adversarial system, the concept of allowing the judge or jury to take *judicial notice* of such accepted facts is an anomaly. If a judge or jury is using their own knowledge of such a fact, there is no opportunity for the party least likely to receive a benefit from this knowledge to cross-examine or otherwise challenge the legitimacy of the information. As a result, courts have been very strict about limiting the use of this concept to matters that really are non-controversial, or incapable of being legitimately called into question. They also occasionally allow judges or juries to rely on facts that could be easily confirmed by checking a dictionary or a calendar.

The Supreme Court of Canada dealt with the issue of judicial notice in a case called, *R. v. Krymowski*, [2005] S.C.J. No. 8, [2005] 1 S.C.R. 101. Several accused were charged with the wilful promotion of hatred against an identifiable group, the Roma. They were involved in public demonstrations where they carried signs with slogans like, "Honk if you hate Gypsies". Defence lawyers called no evidence, but argued at the conclusion of the prosecution's case that there had been no evidence presented that Roma and Gypsies are the same group. The Crown prosecutor argued that the judge could take judicial notice of the shared meaning of the terms and pointed to the fact that five different dictionaries linked the words. The trial judge refused to take judicial notice of the fact and acquitted the defendants. The prosecutor pursued an appeal all the way to the Supreme Court of Canada.

Justice Charron, for all nine judges of the Supreme Court ruled that: "The dictionary definitions presented to the trial judge hence showed that 'gypsy' can refer to an ethnic group properly known as 'Roma' ... I see no reason why the trial judge should not have taken judicial notice of that fact ...". (para. 24) New trials were ordered for the defendants.

In arriving at this conclusion, Justice Charron relied on Chief Justice McLachlin's definition of judicial notice from the Supreme Court of Canada decision in *R. v. Find*, [2001] S.C.J. No. 34 at para. 48, [2001] 1 S.C.R. 863:

> Judicial notice dispenses with the need for proof of facts that are clearly uncontroversial or beyond reasonable dispute. Facts judicially noticed are not proved by evidence under oath. Nor are they tested by cross-examination. Therefore, the threshold for judicial notice is strict: a court may properly take judicial notice of facts that are either: (1) so notorious or generally accepted as not to be the subject of debate among reasonable persons; or (2) capable of immediate and accurate demonstration by resort to readily accessible sources of indisputable accuracy.

Of course, we also expect our judges to know all relevant statutes and common law. Since, as we discussed back in Chapter 1, they are always the *triers of law* at a trial, lawyers and agents acting as advocates are not required to present evidence to a judge about the law that applies to a particular case. This point is also addressed in the federal and provincial Evidence Acts.

Lawyers and agents as a practical measure will often draw a judge's attention to statutes or court decisions that are most helpful to their client's position during closing arguments if there is no jury present. Providing photocopies of the relevant law is simply considered effective advocacy. You will remember from Chapter 4 that nothing the advocate says during the trial is considered evidence anyway.

If there is a jury, the judge is responsible for explaining the applicable law to the jurors. As a result, any specific reminders from lawyers to the judge about which law applies will be made in written submissions, or without the jury being present.

CERTIFICATES AND AFFIDAVITS – ALTERNATIVES TO LIVE WITNESSES

As discussed in Chapter 2, the *Criminal Code* (R.S.C. 1985, c. C-46) and the *Controlled Drugs and Substances Act* (S.C. 1996, c. 19) allow prosecutors to use certificates of analysis produced by qualified technicians as evidence to establish blood/alcohol levels detected from breath or blood samples or the scientific identity of controlled drugs seized in a criminal investigation. In one sense, this is an attempt to ease the time demands on busy technicians, who could be sitting around innumerable courtrooms, waiting to provide evidence that may or may not ever be challenged by the defence. The statutes require advance notification to the defendant who will be affected by the use of certificate evidence. If a defendant wants the analyst to be present for cross-examination purposes, that request must be made in advance of the trial in a method described on the notification. Otherwise, the certificate can be used without the analyst being there, foreclosing the opportunity for cross-examination.

Provincial and territorial statutes and Rules of Civil Procedure allow for evidence to be presented at some types of hearings through the use of *affidavits*. An *affidavit* is a document, outlining relevant evidence in written form. It is intended to be used in place of oral testimony that would normally be given during a court procedure. The document is set up to make it clear that the information is being given under oath. It must be signed by the person who has provided the information in the presence of a *commissioner of oaths* or a *notary public*. Commissioners and notaries are licensed by the province or territory to supervise the signing of sworn documents and to ensure the person signing the document understands the seriousness of their undertaking that the information is true.

Affidavits are used most commonly for procedural hearings that are held to deal with things that the court must resolve to move a matter along toward trial, rather than during the trial itself, when courts will be making final rulings on disputes between the parties. Copies of the affidavits will be provided to opposing parties in advance of the hearing. If the opponent wants the person who has provided the information for the affidavit to be present for cross-examination purposes during the hearing, they can make this request prior to the hearing date.

Any affidavit or written report could be submitted to the court for consideration as evidence if both sides to the dispute agree that it can be used without the person who prepared it being present for cross-examination purposes. If there is non-contentious information that both sides agree the judge or jury should take into account, this would be an efficient method to submit it and speed up the trial process. Of course, a document that is not supported by the testimony of a witness might not have the impact of live testimony.

DOCUMENTS AND OTHER REAL EVIDENCE

Real evidence, as mentioned briefly in Chapter 1, would include items like a gun, knife, broken glass or documents that have relevance in a trial.

The relevance of a particular item or document is usually explained through a witness who can identify the real evidence and explain the relevance to the judge or jury. Once it has been identified and before it is discussed further, the advocate who is using the document will ask the judge's permission to have it marked as an *exhibit*. The other party could raise any objection he or she may have to the use of the item or document as a piece of evidence at this stage. If the judge allows its use and grants permission to have it marked as an exhibit, it will be given an identification number for easier reference and retrieval when it is needed throughout the trial. The court clerk will maintain control over these items or documents once they are admitted for use as evidence.

As we have already discussed in Chapter 7, documents may have to fit a hearsay exception before they can be used. Of course, documents such as letters or contracts are often relevant information for a judge or jury to consider in arriving at a decision.

Courts have always taken a "best evidence" approach to documents. What this means is that they will expect a party to use the original document if this is available. If a document is a copy, either both sides should agree on its admission in advance of the trial, or the party who wants to use it will have to have a witness who can testify that the document is a true copy that has not been altered in any way. If the witness could also provide an explanation as to why the original is not available, that would be helpful.

The federal, provincial and territorial Evidence Acts provide for the use of certified copies of government documents and some types of business records. A certified copy will be affixed with a stamp and signed by the appropriate government or business record-keeper attesting to the authenticity and accuracy of the copy.

PHOTOS AND VIDEOTAPE

In 1967, the Nova Scotia Court of Appeal, in *R. v. Creemer*, [1967] N.S.J. No. 3, [1968] 1 C.C.C. 14 (S.C. [C.A.]), set standards for the use of photographs as evidence, that have also been consistently used by the courts for videotape as its use has become more and more common. Photos or video must be an accurate representation of the facts, without any distortion or attempt to mislead. As a result, it is necessary for these types of evidence to be introduced through a witness who can attest to the accuracy of what is being depicted.

Recently, the admissibility standard for photographs was applied in *R. v. Tello,* [2018] O.J. No. 195, 2018 ONSC 356. The accused faced multiple charges, including conspiracy to import a thousand kilos of cocaine. A large segment of the Crown case rested on 1000 pages of digital photos that had been taken of text messages from Blackberry phones. Undercover officers had photographed the messages because the encrypted nature of the system used to transmit them prevented police from downloading the electronic content.

The officer who had taken the photos testified to the method and equipment she had used. As Justice Campbell "...oral testimony confirmed the accuracy, reliability and overall fairness of the collection of text messages that were placed before the jury...*viva voce* testimony established the pre-conditions of the admissibility of the photographs of the text messages." (para. 12)

In the Newfoundland Court of Appeal case of *R. v. Penney*, [2002] N.J. No. 70, 210 Nfld. & P.E.I.R. 209 (C.A.), the federal Department of Fisheries and Oceans charged a seal hunter with failing to kill a seal quickly, a violation of a marine mammal regulation. The charge was laid after the ministry received a videotape of a seal killing from the International Fund for Animal Welfare. This video had been in the possession of a professional film editing studio for 10 months before it was delivered to the government officials. In addition, the film involved short sequences of filming, with gaps and no time code to assess how much editing may have been done. This was particularly troubling to the Court of Appeal when the specific charge the accused was facing, and what the video was alleged to depict, was failing to kill a seal quickly. In addition, the trial judge had ruled that the witness who had done the filming was not credible when he said the video had not been altered.

In these circumstances, Justice Welsh of the Newfoundland Court of Appeal ruled that, "The Crown has failed to establish that the video provides an accurate representation of the facts. It follows that the video lacks the necessary probative value to be admitted as evidence ...". (para. 30)

The Supreme Court of Canada decision in *R. v. Nikolovski*, [1996] S.C.J. No. 122, [1996] 3 S.C.R. 1197, provides an interesting contrast. The trial judge was able to view a video taken from a convenience store security camera that depicted a convenience store robbery. The camera operated automatically and continuously during the event and the clerk from the store was able to testify that it was an accurate depiction of what occurred during the robbery. As Justice Cory ruled (para. 28):

> Once it is established that a videotape has not been altered or changed, and that it depicts the scene of a crime, then it becomes admissible and relevant evidence ... It can and should be used by a trier of fact in determining whether a crime has been committed and whether the accused before the court committed the crime. It may indeed be a silent, trustworthy, unemotional, unbiased and accurate witness who has complete and instant recall of events.

DEMONSTRATIVE EVIDENCE

Charts and diagrams and even computer models can assist a witness in providing clear evidence to the trier of fact. As with photos and video an attempt to use any of these could be met with objections by an opposing party if they are not an accurate depiction of a scene or event, or are misleading.

In Chapter 3, we briefly discussed some trial level court decisions that have approved and rejected the use of this type of evidence. *R. v. Suzack*, [1995] O.J. No. 4237, 5 O.T.C. 12 (Gen. Div.), was an Ontario trial where the judge allowed a pathologist to illustrate bullet wounds suffered by a victim on a computer-generated video. The pathologist was able to attest to the accuracy of the video and the trial judge pointed out that it was less prejudicial to the accused in the case than if the pathologist had provided the evidence using bloody photographs of the victim.

Green v. Winnipeg (City) Police Department, [1996] M.J. No. 219, 109 Man. R. (2d) 168 (Q.B.), was a Manitoba trial involving a lawsuit against police officers. The trial judge ruled that a computer-generated "re-enactment" prepared on behalf of the police unfairly depicted only their version of the event and that it would be misleading and prejudicial to admit it.

ENSURING THAT WITNESSES ATTEND

It is crucial that each witness be served with a *subpoena*, well in advance of the trial. The subpoena is actually prepared by the advocate who wishes to secure the attendance of a particular witness according to a format that is provided in the forms at the end of the *Criminal Code* or the *Rules of Civil Procedure* for each province or territory and is then signed by a judge, justice of the peace or the clerk of the relevant court, prior to being served on the witness. The format can require that the witness bring relevant documents or items of real evidence that he or she may have in his or her possession or control.

The subpoena is a court order, requiring the witness's attendance, and if the witness fails to appear at the time and place designated for the trial or other hearing, a warrant could be issued to arrest the witness and have the witness brought to court forcibly. Of course, an advocate would want to avoid the need for this step since such a witness may not be in a particularly good mood to co-operate with the advocate when forced to attend. The advocate who is calling the witness to testify should be meeting with the witness in advance of trial to assist in preparing the witness to testify (as we will discuss in the next chapter). This is a good opportunity to clarify when the witness will be needed and to make sure that the witness can attend and has transportation to the court.

The real advantage of ensuring that each witness has been properly served with a subpoena is that the advocate may be able to justify asking the judge for an adjournment if, for whatever reason the witness does not make it. If this procedural step has not been taken, the judge is unlikely to be sympathetic and may order the advocate to proceed without the evidence that this witness could provide.

TEST YOURSELF

1. Should a judge take *judicial notice* of these things, or will it be necessary to present evidence on the issue?

   (a) Prosecution witnesses have mentioned that the accused was driving a Ford Focus, but no one has actually testified that this is a motor vehicle. The charge is impaired operation of a motor vehicle.

   (b) The accused has been charged under s. 351(1) of the *Criminal Code* with possession of tools for the purpose of breaking into homes. Testimony has made it clear that he had a crowbar and four screwdrivers at the time of his arrest, but no one has specified how they would be used to break into a house.

   (c) A police officer has testified that his radar detection device clocked the accused driving 84 km/h in a 50 km/h zone. Will the officer have to explain how a radar detection device operates?

2. An accused has been charged with sexual assault. The victim did not see the face of her assailant, who was wearing a balaclava at the time of the attack in her apartment. A doctor did a vaginal swab of the victim and a semen sample was taken. The accused was pinpointed when an anonymous tipster provided police with his name and description and specific details of witnessing this person entering the victim's apartment at the time of the offence. This witness has not been located. The accused refused to speak to the police, but did consent to providing a hair sample that was subjected to DNA analysis at the Centre for Forensic Sciences. The DNA in the hair sample "matches" the semen left on the victim.

   If you are the prosecutor preparing this case, outline a list of witnesses you will need to call at the criminal trial and describe other evidence that will be presented during their testimony.

3. Locate and read Justice Campbell's decision in *R. v. Granados-Arana*, [2017] O.J. No. 2578, 2017 ONSC 2123. It provides a useful analysis of the admissibility of crime scene and autopsy photos.

Chapter 12

Some Parting Tips for Investigators, Advocates and Witnesses

INVESTIGATORS

It is important to understand your role in the evidence gathering and presentation process. You are not an advocate and you are not a judge. Your function is to do the very best job you can in gathering any and all potentially relevant evidence. It is crucial that you turn over all potentially relevant evidence to the advocate you are working for, whether this is a prosecutor or a lawyer in private practice. If you try to anticipate the evidence that might be excluded from use at trial, you may leave out evidence that could get in through an exception you are not aware of, or one that has not yet been developed but which may be formulated by the judge dealing with the case you are working on.

It is crucial that you learn and respect the rules of evidence that could affect the admissibility of the evidence you gather, whether you agree with the impact of the rules or not. As a professional investigator, this will require you to keep up with changes to statutes and common law that might impact on your role.

You will learn investigative techniques to locate and preserve real evidence and to ensure a continuity of possession that will allow you to ensure a judge or cross-examiner that no one has tampered with the evidence inappropriately since it came into your possession.

Lots of these techniques require a great deal of time and patience, and as we have discussed many searches and seizures will require the prior authorization of a judge. If you plan to work in the justice system, everything you do will be subject to minute scrutiny and criticism. If you are impatient, feel constrained by the law or need to take short cuts, or if you hate to have others criticizing the way you do your work, this is not the line of work you should be entering.

In order to gather evidence from potential witnesses, you must learn appropriate techniques to ensure that you capture the evidence that they have to provide completely and accurately, without tainting the evidence through your own suggestions or questioning techniques. This is much more difficult than most people realize and requires a great deal of training and discipline. Special attention must be paid to the use of photo-arrays or line-ups as an investigative tool.

Photographs and videotape can be invaluable tools in the gathering and preserving of evidence, but cameras are sophisticated pieces of equipment and you must learn how to operate them properly if they are to enhance your investigative techniques.

When called upon to testify, your professionalism, courtesy and credibility will affect the impact of what you have to say. You must remember that it is not your role to judge the outcome of the case, or to act as an advocate. You are not a *party* to the action and you will not win or lose. If you intend to be in this business for a long time, your professional credibility is far more important than the outcome of any individual case.

ADVOCATES

Advocates have a duty to do their very best for their clients, but they are also considered *officers of the court* and must operate within the parameters of the law.

Advocates organize the presentation of evidence but they do not create it. As an advocate, you and your investigators must locate all the witnesses and real and demonstrative evidence you will need to present your client's case most effectively.

Again, there are no short cuts. You must meet with all potential witnesses, find out what they have to say and help them to say it in the most effective way possible. You will be the expert on the way the court processes work, you will have to tell the witnesses what to expect, how to respond to challenges from your opponent, how to dress and how to speak to the judge or jurors.

You must insist on complete advance disclosure from your client and your opponent, and give considerable thought to the witnesses the opponent will be calling and what you can do to most successfully challenge their testimony.

Once a trial starts, you must be alert and vigilant. In order to prevent an opponent from abusing evidence, you must be prepared to make timely objections before the triers of fact are exposed to evidence they should not be. Advocates should get into the habit of voicing an objection even before you are ready to articulate exactly what is objectionable. The judge will usually give you a few moments to gather your thoughts on the specifics of the objection.

If a court process can be compared to a chess game, you must understand the rules and be able to use them to your benefit and be able to anticipate the moves of your opponent. In fairness, advocacy is far more like work than a game. As a long line of wise advocates have admitted, there is a lot more perspiration than inspiration that goes into effective advocacy.

WITNESSES

As a witness, you are in court or before a tribunal to provide relevant information to the judge or jury. You must tell the truth as you know it.

Your testimony is always provided in response to questions. The advocate who has called upon you to provide evidence should take time before the trial to let you know the questions that he or she will be asking. The lawyer is permitted to assist you in expressing your testimony in as clear a manner as possible.

Hopefully, the advocate will also give you a prediction of the questions that are likely to be asked on cross-examination by the opposing advocate. This, of course, is not always going to be accurate since it requires a significant level of guesswork on the part of the lawyer who is assisting you to prepare.

When you are testifying during the trial or before a tribunal, make sure that you understand each question that is being asked before you attempt to answer. If you are not sure, ask for clarification. If the questioner has asked a multi-part question, request that he or she split it up before attempting to answer.

Witnesses need to answer questions calmly. It is important to avoid arguing with the questioner. If you feel that the questioner is cutting you off from providing necessary clarification, you can ask the judge for permission to clarify. You should never challenge the questioner's right to ask the question based on your own view of the rules of evidence. If a question is improper, it is the role of the opposing lawyer to object. If the objection is valid, it is up to the judge to make that ruling.

If you do not know something, say so. Although it is human nature to try to be helpful; never speculate and try to fill in the gaps. This is going beyond your knowledge base and may well provide a misleading picture to the trier of fact. It may also reduce your credibility if an advocate can successfully draw attention to the fact that you have attempted to exceed the information you can legitimately provide.

During cross-examination, an opposing lawyer may ask if you have discussed your testimony with the lawyer who has called upon you to testify and/or if that lawyer has helped you to prepare for testifying. These are trick questions. The lawyer is trying to get you to deny this through phrasing the accusation as though you have done something wrong. If you say "no", the lawyers and the judge, and eventually the jury, will know that this is not true. It will look as though you are being evasive and that you are prepared to lie. It is a normal, completely legitimate procedure for the lawyer who is calling you to help you prepare. You should freely admit that you have discussed the case with the lawyer. If you deny it because of the accusatory nature of the questioning, you will have reduced your credibility.

If you need to refer to notes to provide accurate answers, you must ask the judge for permission to do so.

RELIANCE ON NOTES WHILE TESTIFYING

Most witnesses must testify without the assistance of any notes or other written material that has been prepared outside the courtroom. Of course, there is absolutely nothing wrong with you reviewing notes you may have made, statements you have provided to the police or other investigators, or the transcript of testimony you gave at a previous hearing before you go into court to testify. This should be done to properly prepare for trial. If a cross-examiner asks you if you have done this, you should freely admit it. The opposing lawyer may ask the judge's permission to see any written material you reviewed before your testimony and the judge will often grant this request.

There are exceptions to the general prohibition to using notes as a memory aid in court, primarily for witnesses like police officers and medical personnel who may have worked on a number of similar cases and may be called upon to testify in court on a regular basis. It is recognized that these witnesses may need a written record of specific events to properly distinguish one case in which they have been involved from another. They may be able to bring their notes into court and refresh their memory if it is first established that:

(1) they need the notes to refresh their memory;
(2) the notes or written record was made by the witness or someone else on the scene as part of their professional duties at the time of the event recorded or shortly thereafter;
(3) if someone else prepared the record it was reviewed for accuracy by this witness at a time very close to the event;
(4) the witness is able to testify to the accuracy of what was originally recorded.

The advocate who has called the witness to testify must establish the need to rely on the notes and the other prerequisites in a series of questions and then ask the judge's permission for the witness to use the notes. If the judge grants the permission, the witness will usually be given a few minutes to go over the notes for a memory refresher and then will be asked questions about the event recorded. The witness is generally not allowed to simply read the notes in response to the questions asked.

If a witness has relied on notes to refresh his or her memory, a cross-examiner would normally be granted permission by the judge to look at the notes and could ask questions about the contents of the notes during cross-examination. The notes do not usually become an exhibit.

There are both professional and judicial expectations with respect to the manner in which police officers make notes. In *R. v. Thompson*, [2013] O.J. No. 1236, 2013 ONSC 1527, Justice Hill stated that as a general rule, "... where multiple officers participate in investigation of an incident, their notes should be made independently and not as a collective and not after a (de)briefing where the incident is discussed as a group." (para. 212)

In *R. v. Narayanapillai*, [2013] O.J. No. 2745, 2013 ONCJ 324, Justice Melvyn Green listened to the evidence of four police officers who testified about an alleged assault that occurred outside a bar. The main issue was the identity of the assailants. In reviewing the evidence of the officers (at para. 38), Justice Green was not at all impressed that,

> ... PC Snow testified that he and his three colleagues "discussed what happened" before or in the course of drafting their notes. This type of collaboration is the antithesis of independent note-making and inevitably compromises the reliability not only of the officers' recorded recollections but, of course, their testimonial accounts which, more than a year later, are largely dependent on those notes.

In *Wood v. Schaeffer*, [2013] S.C.J. No. 71, 2013 SCC 71, the Supreme Court of Canada reviewed two situations in Ontario where police officers had shot and killed members of the public. In Ontario, such incidents are investigated by an independent Special Investigations Unit. Police involved in situations where members of the public have been harmed are required, by regulation, to submit their notes to the SIU. In both cases reviewed, the police officers had consulted with lawyers before submitting their notes. Lawyers reviewed draft notes before the final notes that were ultimately submitted were prepared with the lawyers' assistance. The SIU Director felt this had affected the reliability of the notes as evidence of what happened: "This note writing process flies in the face of the two main indicators of reliability of notes: independence and contemporaneity. The notes do not represent an independent recitation of material events." (para. 17)

Justice Moldaver, writing for a 6-3 majority of the Supreme Court of Canada, stated that allowing police to consult with a lawyer before their notes are prepared, "... creates a real risk that *the focus* of an officer's notes will shift away from his or her *public duty* ... *i.e.* making accurate, detailed and comprehensive notes, and move toward his or her *private* interest, *i.e.* justifying what has taken place ...". (para. 72 – Emphasis in original) In describing one of the officer's notes, Justice Moldaver said, "... Acting Sgt. Pullbrook's notes read like a prepared statement designed, at least in part, to justify his and his partner's conduct ... . [A]n officer's notes are not meant to provide a 'lawyer-enhanced' justification for what has occurred. They are simply meant to record an event, so that others ... can rely on them to determine *what* happened." (para. 80 – emphasis in original)

Justice Cromwell of the Supreme Court of Canada expressed concern with an intentional lack of note-making by a police officer in the case of *R. v. Vu*, [2013] S.C.J. No. 60, 2013 SCC 60. The case involved the execution of a search warrant. Justice Cromwell observed that one of the officers involved in the search, "... admitted in his testimony that he intentionally did not take notes during the search so he would not have to testify about the details. This is clearly improper and cannot be condoned. ... [N]otes of how a search is conducted should ... be kept, absent unusual or exigent circumstances." (para. 70)

The recent decision in *R. v. Clark*, [2017] A.J. No. 1119, 2017 ABQB 643 demonstrates that a failure to make sufficiently-detailed notes contemporaneously to an event can seriously undermine a police witness's credibility when testifying to events that may have occurred years before the eventual trial. Justice Renke observed, "Memory itself is an unreliable record. The mixing of facts from different cases, the recasting of initial recollections into a recalled narrative, and the sheer passage of time reduce the reliability of memory alone. The reliability of Sgt. Forbes' testimony was diminished by the absence of reasonably detailed notes." (para. 19) On a crucial issue of whether or not the accused's Charter rights had been violated, this became critical; "I did not find that Sgt. Forbes was not sincere or that he was not accurately trying to recount what was recalled. I found that his memory was not reliable. This was a consequence, in no small part, of inadequate notes...keeping adequate notes is a police officer's duty." (para. 143)

GO TO COURT

As discussed way back in Chapter 1, our criminal and civil courts and many tribunals operate as public forums. In Canada, we do not believe that the centre stage of our justice system should operate behind closed doors. This provides a wonderful opportunity for investigators, advocates and potential witnesses to attend other peoples' trials. Take advantage of this opportunity.

At the very least, you will become more comfortable with the setting and will not be as intimidated when you make your own first appearance. You can observe first-hand how each judge exercises his or her discretion in controlling what goes on in the courtroom. How do you properly address the judge or jurors? What is the appropriate form of dress for the participants? What is the order of presentation of evidence and how does this process of cross-examination really work? How are objections handled?

You will quickly pick up on the traits of the effective advocates and the witnesses that have the biggest impact. You can also learn from the witnesses and advocates who leave a bad impression and analyze why this occurs. You will see how real and demonstrative evidence is used and may develop your own ideas for increasing the impact of the presentation.

You will be able to see the complex rules of evidence discussed in this book put into practice. The more you see how the rules work, the easier they will be to understand. When there are breaks in the trial or tribunal sessions, ask questions of the participants. If they do not have to violate any confidences to do so, they will often be quite helpful. If you plan to make a career in the justice system, you owe it to yourself and those who will be impacted by your role to gain a thorough understanding of the rules of evidence.

CHALLENGE YOURSELF

1. Develop a practical plan for keeping up with changes to the rules of evidence. How can news reports help you keep abreast of changes? Which professional periodicals or websites might aid in tracking trends in the law? Do you have access to library resources that may help? Who do you know that has better access than you to trends in the justice system? Could you ask to be added to informational mailings or email lists?

2. Attend court and make notes of the good and the bad in terms of evidence presentation. What would you do differently? Why? Be sure to record follow-up questions for someone in the know if you observe steps in the process, or the application of evidentiary rules that you don't understand.

3. Locate and read the Alberta Court of Queen's Bench decision in *R. v. Clark*, [2017] A.J. No. 1119, 2017 ABQB 643.

Appendix 1

Key Portions of the Canada Evidence Act

R.S.C. 1985, c. C-5 (sections 1-24)

An Act respecting
witnesses and
evidence

SHORT TITLE

Short title

1. This Act may be cited as the *Canada Evidence Act.*

R.S., c. E-10, s. 1.

PART I

APPLICATION

Application

2. This Part applies to all criminal proceedings and to all civil proceedings and other matters whatever respecting which Parliament has jurisdiction.

R.S., c. E-10, s. 2.

WITNESSES

Interest or crime

3. A person is not incompetent to give evidence by reason of interest or crime.

R.S., c. E-10, s. 3.

Accused and spouse

4. (1) Every person charged with an offence, and, except as otherwise provided in this section, the wife or husband, as the case may be, of the person so charged, is a competent witness for the defence, whether the person so charged is charged solely or jointly with any other person.

Accused and spouse

(2) No person is incompetent, or uncompellable, to testify for the prosecution by reason only that they are married to the accused.

Communications
during marriage

(3) No husband is compellable to disclose any communication made to him by his wife during their marriage, and no wife

is compellable to disclose any communication made to her by her husband during their marriage.

Offences against young persons

(4) and (5) repealed, 2015

Saving

Failure to testify

(6) The failure of the person charged, or of the wife or husband of that person, to testify shall not be made the subject of comment by the judge or by counsel for the prosecution.

R.S., 1985, c. C-5, s. 4; R.S., 1985, c. 19 (3rd Supp.), s. 17; 2002, c. 1, s. 166; 2014, c. 25, s. 34; c. 31, s. 27; 2015, c. 13, s. 52.

Incriminating questions

5. (1) No witness shall be excused from answering any question on the ground that the answer to the question may tend to criminate him, or may tend to establish his liability to a civil proceeding at the instance of the Crown or of any person.

Answer not admissible against witness

(2) Where with respect to any question a witness objects to answer on the ground that his answer may tend to criminate him, or may tend to establish his liability to a civil proceeding at the instance of the Crown or of any person, and if but for this Act, or the Act of any provincial legislature, the witness would therefore have been excused from answering the question, then although the witness is by reason of this Act or the provincial Act compelled to answer, the answer so given shall not be used or admissible in evidence against him in any criminal trial or other criminal proceeding against him thereafter taking place, other than a prosecution for perjury in the giving of that evidence or for the giving of contradictory evidence.

R.S., 1985, c. C-5, s. 5; 1997, c. 18, s. 116.

Evidence of person with physical disability

6. (1) If a witness has difficulty communicating by reason of a physical disability, the court may order that the witness be permitted to give evidence by any means that enables the evidence to be intelligible.

Evidence of person with mental disability

(2) If a witness with a mental disability is determined under section 16 to have the capacity to give evidence and has difficulty communicating by reason of a disability, the court may order that the witness be permitted to give evidence by any means that enables the evidence to be intelligible.

Inquiry

(3) The court may conduct an inquiry to determine if the means by which a witness may be permitted to give evidence under subsection (1) or (2) is necessary and reliable.

R.S., 1985, c. C-5, s. 6; 1998, c. 9, s. 1.

Identification of accused

6.1 For greater certainty, a witness may give evidence as to the identity of an accused whom the witness is able to identify visually or in any other sensory manner.

1998, c. 9, s. 1.

Expert witnesses

7. Where, in any trial or other proceeding, criminal or civil, it is intended by the prosecution or the defence, or by any party, to examine as witnesses professional or other experts entitled according to the law or practice to give opinion evidence, not more than five of such witnesses may be called on either side without the leave of the court or judge or person presiding.

R.S., c. E-10, s. 7.

Handwriting comparison

8. Comparison of a disputed writing with any writing proved to the satisfaction of the court to be genuine shall be permitted to be made by witnesses, and such writings, and the evidence of witnesses respecting those writings, may be submitted to the court and jury as proof of the genuineness or otherwise of the writing in dispute.

R.S., c. E-10, s. 8.

Adverse witnesses

9. (1) A party producing a witness shall not be allowed to impeach his credit by general evidence of bad character, but if the witness, in the opinion of the court, proves adverse, the party may contradict him by other evidence, or, by leave of the court, may prove that the witness made at other times a statement inconsistent with his present testimony, but before the last mentioned proof can be given the circumstances of the supposed statement, sufficient to designate the particular occasion, shall be mentioned to the witness, and he shall be asked whether or not he did make the statement.

Previous statements by witness not proved adverse

(2) Where the party producing a witness alleges that the witness made at other times a statement in writing, reduced to writing, or recorded on audio tape or video tape or otherwise, inconsistent with the witness' present testimony, the court may, without proof that the witness is adverse, grant leave to that party to cross-examine the witness as to the statement and

the court may consider the cross-examination in determining whether in the opinion of the court the witness is adverse.

R.S., 1985, c. C-5, s. 9; 1994, c. 44, s. 85.

Cross-examination as to previous statements

10. (1) On any trial a witness may be cross-examined as to previous statements that the witness made in writing, or that have been reduced to writing, or recorded on audio tape or video tape or otherwise, relative to the subject-matter of the case, without the writing being shown to the witness or the witness being given the opportunity to listen to the audio tape or view the video tape or otherwise take cognizance of the statements, but, if it is intended to contradict the witness, the witness' attention must, before the contradictory proof can be given, be called to those parts of the statement that are to be used for the purpose of so contradicting the witness, and the judge, at any time during the trial, may require the production of the writing or tape or other medium for inspection, and thereupon make such use of it for the purposes of the trial as the judge thinks fit.

Deposition of witness in criminal investigation

(2) A deposition of a witness, purporting to have been taken before a justice on the investigation of a criminal charge and to be signed by the witness and the justice, returned to and produced from the custody of the proper officer shall be presumed, in the absence of evidence to the contrary, to have been signed by the witness.

R.S., 1985, c. C-5, s. 10; 1994, c. 44, s. 86.

Cross-examination as to previous oral statements

11. Where a witness, on cross-examination as to a former statement made by him relative to the subject-matter of the case and inconsistent with his present testimony, does not distinctly admit that he did make the statement, proof may be given that he did in fact make it, but before that proof can be given the circumstances of the supposed statement, sufficient to designate the particular occasion, shall be mentioned to the witness, and he shall be asked whether or not he did make the statement.

R.S., c. E-10, s. 11.

Examination as to previous convictions

12. (1) A witness may be questioned as to whether the witness has been convicted of any offence, excluding any offence designated as a contravention under the *Contraventions Act*, but including such an offence where the conviction was entered after a trial on an indictment.

Proof of previous convictions

(1.1) If the witness either denies the fact or refuses to answer, the opposite party may prove the conviction.

How conviction proved

(2) A conviction may be proved by producing

(*a*) a certificate containing the substance and effect only, omitting the formal part, of the indictment and conviction, if it is for an indictable offence, or a copy of the summary conviction, if it is for an offence punishable on summary conviction, purporting to be signed by the clerk of the court or other officer having the custody of the records of the court in which the conviction, if on indictment, was had, or to which the conviction, if summary, was returned; and

(*b*) proof of identity.

R.S., 1985, c. C-5, s. 12; 1992, c. 47, s. 66.

OATHS AND SOLEMN AFFIRMATIONS

Who may administer oaths

13. Every court and judge, and every person having, by law or consent of parties, authority to hear and receive evidence, has power to administer an oath to every witness who is legally called to give evidence before that court, judge or person.

R.S., c. E-10, s. 13.

Solemn affirmation by witness instead of oath

14. (1) A person may, instead of taking an oath, make the following solemn affirmation:

I solemnly affirm that the evidence to be given by me shall be the truth, the whole truth and nothing but the truth.

Effect

(2) Where a person makes a solemn affirmation in accordance with subsection (1), his evidence shall be taken and have the same effect as if taken under oath.

R.S., 1985, c. C-5, s. 14; 1994, c. 44, s. 87.

Solemn affirmation by deponent

15. (1) Where a person who is required or who desires to make an affidavit or deposition in a proceeding or on an occasion on which or concerning a matter respecting which an oath is required or is lawful, whether on the taking of office or otherwise, does not wish to take an oath, the court or judge, or other officer or person qualified to take affidavits or depositions, shall permit the person to make a solemn affirmation in the words following, namely, "I, ..., do solemnly affirm, etc.", and that solemn affirmation has the same force and effect as if that person had taken an oath.

Effect

(2) Any witness whose evidence is admitted or who makes a solemn affirmation under this section or section 14 is liable to indictment and punishment for perjury in all respects as if he had been sworn.

R.S., 1985, c. C-5, s. 15; 1994, c. 44, s. 88.

Witness whose capacity is in question

16. (1) If a proposed witness is a person of fourteen years of age or older whose mental capacity is challenged, the court shall, before permitting the person to give evidence, conduct an inquiry to determine

(*a*) whether the person understands the nature of an oath or a solemn affirmation; and

(*b*) whether the person is able to communicate the evidence.

Testimony under oath or solemn affirmation

(2) A person referred to in subsection (1) who understands the nature of an oath or a solemn affirmation and is able to communicate the evidence shall testify under oath or solemn affirmation.

Testimony on promise to tell truth

(3) A person referred to in subsection (1) who does not understand the nature of an oath or a solemn affirmation but is able to communicate the evidence may, notwithstanding any provision of any Act requiring an oath or a solemn affirmation, testify on promising to tell the truth.

No questions regarding understanding of promise

(3.1) A person referred to in subsection (3) shall not be asked questions regarding their understanding of the nature of the promise to tell the truth for the purpose of determining whether their evidence shall be received by the court.

Inability to testify

(4) A person referred to in subsection (1) who neither understands the nature of an oath or a solemn affirmation nor is able to communicate the evidence shall not testify.

Burden as to capacity of witness

(5) A party who challenges the mental capacity of a proposed witness of fourteen years of age or more has the burden of satisfying the court that there is an issue as to the capacity of the proposed witness to testify under an oath or a solemn affirmation.

R.S., 1985, c. C-5, s. 16; R.S., 1985, c. 19 (3rd Supp.), s. 18; 1994, c. 44, s. 89; 2005, c. 32, s. 26; 2015, c. 13, s. 53.

Person under fourteen years of age

16.1 (1) A person under fourteen years of age is presumed to have the capacity to testify.

No oath or solemn affirmation

(2) A proposed witness under fourteen years of age shall not take an oath or make a solemn affirmation despite a provision of any Act that requires an oath or a solemn affirmation.

Evidence shall be received

(3) The evidence of a proposed witness under fourteen years of age shall be received if they are able to understand and respond to questions.

Burden as to capacity of witness

(4) A party who challenges the capacity of a proposed witness under fourteen years of age has the burden of satisfying the court that there is an issue as to the capacity of the proposed witness to understand and respond to questions.

Court inquiry

(5) If the court is satisfied that there is an issue as to the capacity of a proposed witness under fourteen years of age to understand and respond to questions, it shall, before permitting them to give evidence, conduct an inquiry to determine whether they are able to understand and respond to questions.

Promise to tell truth

(6) The court shall, before permitting a proposed witness under fourteen years of age to give evidence, require them to promise to tell the truth.

Understanding of promise

(7) No proposed witness under fourteen years of age shall be asked any questions regarding their understanding of the nature of the promise to tell the truth for the purpose of determining whether their evidence shall be received by the court.

Effect

(8) For greater certainty, if the evidence of a witness under fourteen years of age is received by the court, it shall have the same effect as if it were taken under oath.

2005, c. 32, s. 27.

JUDICIAL NOTICE

Imperial Acts, etc.

17. Judicial notice shall be taken of all Acts of the Imperial Parliament, of all ordinances made by the Governor in Council, or the lieutenant governor in council of any province or colony that, or some portion of which, now forms or hereafter may form part of Canada, and of all the Acts of the legislature of any such province or colony, whether enacted before or after the passing of the *Constitution Act, 1867.*

R.S., c. E-10, s. 17.

Acts of Canada

18. Judicial notice shall be taken of all Acts of Parliament, public or private, without being specially pleaded.

R.S., c. E-10, s. 18.

DOCUMENTARY EVIDENCE

Copies by Queen's
Printer

19. Every copy of any Act of Parliament, public or private, published by the Queen's Printer, is evidence of that Act and of its contents, and every copy purporting to be published by the Queen's Printer shall be deemed to be so published, unless the contrary is shown.

R.S., 1985, c. C-5, s. 19; 2000, c. 5, s. 52.

Imperial proclama-
tions, etc.

20. Imperial proclamations, orders in council, treaties, orders, warrants, licences, certificates, rules, regulations or other Imperial official records, Acts or documents may be proved

(*a*) in the same manner as they may from time to time be provable in any court in England;

(*b*) by the production of a copy of the *Canada Gazette*, or a volume of the Acts of Parliament purporting to contain a copy of the same or a notice thereof; or

(*c*) by the production of a copy of them purporting to be published by the Queen's Printer.

R.S., 1985, c. C-5, s. 20; 2000, c. 5, s. 53.

Proclamations, etc.,
of Governor General

21. Evidence of any proclamation, order, regulation or appointment, made or issued by the Governor General or by the Governor in Council, or by or under the authority of any minister or head of any department of the Government of Canada and evidence of a treaty to which Canada is a party, may be given in all or any of the following ways:

(*a*) by the production of a copy of the *Canada Gazette*, or a volume of the Acts of Parliament purporting to contain a copy of the treaty, proclamation, order, regulation or appointment, or a notice thereof;

(*b*) by the production of a copy of the proclamation, order, regulation or appointment, purporting to be published by the Queen's Printer;

(*c*) by the production of a copy of the treaty purporting to be published by the Queen's Printer;

(*d*) by the production, in the case of any proclamation, order, regulation or appointment made or issued by the Governor General or by the Governor in Council, of a copy or extract purporting to be certified to be true by the clerk or assistant or acting clerk of the Queen's Privy Council for Canada; and

(*e*) by the production, in the case of any order, regulation or appointment made or issued by or under the authority of any minister or head of a department of the Government of Canada, of a copy or extract purporting to be certified to be true by the minister, by his deputy or acting deputy, or by the secretary or acting secretary of the department over which he presides.

R.S., 1985, c. C-5, s. 21; 2000, c. 5, s. 54.

Proclamations, etc., of lieutenant governor

22. (1) Evidence of any proclamation, order, regulation or appointment made or issued by a lieutenant governor or lieutenant governor in council of any province, or by or under the authority of any member of the executive council, being the head of any department of the government of the province, may be given in all or any of the following ways:

(*a*) by the production of a copy of the official gazette for the province purporting to contain a copy of the proclamation, order, regulation or appointment, or a notice thereof;

(*b*) by the production of a copy of the proclamation, order, regulation or appointment purporting to be published by the government or Queen's Printer for the province; and

(*c*) by the production of a copy or extract of the proclamation, order, regulation or appointment purporting to be certified to be true by the clerk or assistant or acting clerk of the executive council, by the head of any department of the government of a province, or by his deputy or acting deputy, as the case may be.

In the case of the territories

(2) Evidence of any proclamation, order, regulation or appointment made by the Lieutenant Governor or Lieutenant Governor in Council of the Northwest Territories, as constituted prior to September 1, 1905, or by the Legislature of Yukon, of the Northwest Territories or for Nunavut, may be given by the production of a copy of the *Canada Gazette* purporting to contain a copy of the proclamation, order, regulation or appointment, or a notice of it.

R.S., 1985, c. C-5, s. 22; 1993, c. 28, s. 78; 2000, c. 5, s. 55; 2002, c. 7, s. 96; 2014, c. 2, s. 5.

Evidence of judicial proceedings, etc.

23. (1) Evidence of any proceeding or record whatever of, in or before any court in Great Britain, the Supreme Court, the

Federal Court of Appeal, the Federal Court or the Tax Court of Canada, any court in a province, any court in a British colony or possession or any court of record of the United States, of a state of the United States or of any other foreign country, or before any justice of the peace or coroner in a province, may be given in any action or proceeding by an exemplification or certified copy of the proceeding or record, purporting to be under the seal of the court or under the hand or seal of the justice, coroner or court stenographer, as the case may be, without any proof of the authenticity of the seal or of the signature of the justice, coroner or court stenographer or other proof whatever.

Certificate where
court has no seal

(2) Where any court, justice or coroner or court stenographer referred to in subsection (1) has no seal, or so certifies, the evidence may be given by a copy purporting to be certified under the signature of a judge or presiding provincial court judge or of the justice or coroner or court stenographer, without any proof of the authenticity of the signature or other proof whatever.

R.S., 1985, c. C-5, s. 23; R.S., 1985, c. 27 (1st Supp.), s. 203; 1993, c. 34, s. 15; 1997, c. 18, s. 117; 2002, c. 8, s. 118.

Certified copies

24. In every case in which the original record could be admitted in evidence,

(*a*) a copy of any official or public document of Canada or of any province, purporting to be certified under the hand of the proper officer or person in whose custody the official or public document is placed, or

(*b*) a copy of a document, by-law, rule, regulation or proceeding, or a copy of any entry in any register or other book of any municipal or other corporation, created by charter or Act of Parliament or the legislature of any province, purporting to be certified under the seal of the corporation, and the hand of the presiding officer, clerk or secretary thereof,

is admissible in evidence without proof of the seal of the corporation, or of the signature or official character of the person or persons appearing to have signed it, and without further proof thereof.

R.S., c. E-10, s. 24.

NOTE; Please go on-line to find any of the remaining sections of the Act.

Appendix 2

Excerpts from the Canadian Charter of Rights and Freedoms

Part I of the Constitution Act, 1982 being Schedule B to the Canada Act 1982 (U.K.), 1982, c. 11

Guarantee of Rights and Freedoms

Rights and Free-
doms in Canada

1. The *Canadian Charter of Rights and Freedoms* guarantees the rights and freedoms set out in it subject only to such reasonable limits prescribed by law as can be demonstrably justified in a free and democratic society.

.....

Legal Rights

Life, liberty and
security of person

7. Everyone has the right to life, liberty and security of the person and the right not to be deprived thereof except in accordance with the principles of fundamental justice.

Search or seizure

8. Everyone has the right to be secure against unreasonable search or seizure.

Detention or
imprisonment

9. Everyone has the right not to be arbitrarily detained or imprisoned.

Arrest or detention

10. Everyone has the right on arrest or detention
(*a*) to be informed promptly of the reasons therefor;
(*b*) to retain and instruct counsel without delay and to be informed of that right; and
(*c*) to have the validity of the detention determined by way of *habeas corpus* and to be released if the detention is not lawful.

Proceedings in
criminal and penal
matters

11. Any person charged with an offence has the right
(*a*) to be informed without unreasonable delay of the specific offence;
(*b*) to be tried within a reasonable time;
(*c*) not to be compelled to be a witness in proceedings against that person in respect of the offence;

(*d*) to be presumed innocent until proven guilty according to law in a fair and public hearing by an independent and impartial tribunal;

(*e*) not to be denied reasonable bail without just cause;

(*f*) except in the case of an offence under military law tried before a military tribunal, to the benefit of trial by jury where the maximum punishment for the offence is imprisonment for five years or a more severe punishment;

(*g*) not to be found guilty on account of any act or omission unless, at the time of the act or omission, it constituted an offence under Canadian or international law or was criminal according to the general principles of law recognized by the community of nations;

(*h*) if finally acquitted of the offence, not to be tried for it again and, if finally found guilty and punished for the offence, not to be tried or punished for it again; and

(*i*) if found guilty of the offence and if the punishment for the offence has been varied between the time of commission and the time of sentencing, to the benefit of the lesser punishment.

Treatment or punishment

12. Everyone has the right not to be subjected to any cruel and unusual treatment or punishment.

Self-crimination

13. A witness who testifies in any proceedings has the right not to have any incriminating evidence so given used to incriminate that witness in any other proceedings, except in a prosecution for perjury or for the giving of contradictory evidence.

Interpreter

14. A party or witness in any proceedings who does not understand or speak the language in which the proceedings are conducted or who is deaf has the right to the assistance of an interpreter.

. . . . .

Enforcement

Enforcement of guaranteed rights and freedoms

24. (1) Anyone whose rights or freedoms, as guaranteed by this Charter, have been infringed or denied may apply to a court of competent jurisdiction to obtain such remedy as the court considers appropriate and just in the circumstances.

Exclusion of
evidence bringing
administration
of justice into
disrepute

(2) Where, in proceedings under subsection (1), a court concludes that evidence was obtained in a manner that infringed or denied any rights or freedoms guaranteed by this Charter, the evidence shall be excluded if it is established that, having regard to all of the circumstances, the admission of it in the proceedings would bring the administration of justice into disrepute.

.....

Application of Charter

Application of
Charter

32.(1) This Charter applies
(*a*) to the Parliament and government of Canada in respect of all matters within the authority of Parliament including all matters relating to the Yukon Territory, Northwest Territories and Nunavut; and
(*b*) to the legislature and government of each province in respect of all matters within the authority of the legislature of each province.

.....

Case Report Sample

CITATION: *R. v. Côté*, 2011 SCC 46,
[2011] 3 S.C.R. 215

DATE: 20111014

DOCKET: 33645

BETWEEN:

Armande Côté

Appellant

and

Her Majesty The Queen

Respondent

- and -

Criminal Lawyers' Association (Ontario)

Intervener

OFFICIAL ENGLISH TRANSLATION: Reasons of Deschamps J.

CORAM: McLachlin C.J. and Binnie, LeBel, Deschamps, Fish, Abella, Charron, Rothstein and Cromwell JJ.

REASONS FOR JUDGMENT:	Cromwell J. (McLachlin C.J. and Binnie, LeBel, Fish, Abella, Charron and Rothstein JJ. concurring)
(paras. 1 to 90)	

DISSENTING REASONS:	Deschamps J.
(paras. 91 to 119)	

R. v. Côté, 2011 SCC 46, [2011] 3 S.C.R. 215

Armande Côté   *Appellant*

v.

Her Majesty The Queen   *Respondent*

and

Criminal Lawyers' Association (Ontario)   *Intervener*

Indexed as: *R. v. Côté*

2011 SCC 46

File No.: 33645.

2011: March 15; 2011: October 14.

Present: McLachlin C.J. and Binnie, LeBel, Deschamps, Fish, Abella, Charron, Rothstein and Cromwell JJ.

ON APPEAL FROM THE COURT OF APPEAL FOR QUEBEC

Constitutional law — Charter of Rights — Enforcement — Exclusion of evidence — Accused charged with second degree murder — Search of accused's home conducted by police without valid warrants — Trial judge finding that police had not acted in good faith and demonstrated blatant disregard for accused's Charter rights throughout investigation — Trial judge concluding that admission of evidence in face of extraordinarily troubling police misconduct, even when decision would lead to acquittal of serious crime, would bring administration of justice into disrepute — Whether Court of Appeal erred in intervening on bases that police had not deliberately acted in abusive manner and that offence was serious — Whether Court of Appeal erred in intervening on basis that evidence could have been obtained legally by warrant without accused's participation — Canadian Charter of Rights and Freedoms, s. 24(2).

Around 9 p.m. on July 22, 2006, C called 9-1-1 to report that her spouse, H, had been injured. The attending physician at the hospital established that H was suffering from head injuries and confirmed the presence of a metal object in H's skull, and communicated this information to the police. The police attended at C's home around midnight. The lights of the house were off and the house was calm. C answered the door in her pyjamas. The police explained that they were there to find out what happened and to make sure the premises were safe, but they did not tell C that they believed that H was suffering from a gunshot wound. The police, accompanied by C, inspected the interior and the exterior of the residence, as well as a gazebo. The police questioned C about the presence of firearms in the house. She confirmed the presence of two firearms but could only locate one, to which she led the police. The police later obtained warrants which were executed at C's residence. A .22 calibre rifle, of the same calibre as the bullet recovered from H's skull, was located by the police.

C was brought to the police station around 3 a.m. but not until 5:23 a.m. was she given a warning as an important witness in the attempted murder of H and advised of her right to counsel. After being warned, C spoke with a lawyer and invoked her right to silence. She then described the events to the police and was placed under arrest for attempted murder. She was cautioned again, advised of her right to counsel, and spoke with a lawyer again. After being placed under arrest, C was interrogated by the police throughout the day. C exhibited extreme anxiety about having the interrogation room closed, seemed to be exhausted and on several occasions told the interrogator that she had had enough, did not want to talk anymore or wanted to go lie down. C's interrogation ended at 8 p.m. on July 23, when she was advised of H's death and charged with second degree murder.

C applied to the trial judge to exclude the evidence against her. The trial judge concluded that the police embarked on a systematic violation of C's rights from the time they first entered onto her property until the end of her interrogation. The trial judge held that the police's entry on C's property, and the search of her house, property and gazebo constituted unreasonable searches and seizures contrary to s. 8 of the *Charter*. He held that the police detained C without telling her why in violation of s. 10(*a*) of the *Charter*, and that the police violated C's right to obtain the assistance of a lawyer and to be advised of that right, in violation of s. 10(*b*) of the *Charter*. He also held that the police violated C's right to silence as protected by s. 7 of the *Charter* and obtained a statement that was not voluntary. The trial judge also found that the investigators had misled a judicial officer to obtain warrants. The trial judge excluded all of the evidence pursuant to s. 24(2) of the *Charter*, finding that its admission would bring the administration of justice into disrepute, and C was acquitted of the charge. The Court of Appeal found that the trial judge was right to exclude C's statements to police. However, it concluded that the trial judge had erred by excluding the observations the police made of the exterior of C's home before the warrants were issued as well as the physical evidence obtained at C's home in execution of the warrants. It ordered a new trial.

Held (Deschamps J. dissenting): The appeal should be allowed and the acquittal restored.

Per McLachlin C.J. and Binnie, LeBel, Fish, Abella, Charron, Rothstein and Cromwell JJ.: The standard of review of a trial judge's s. 24(2) determination of what would bring the administration of justice into disrepute having regard to all of the circumstances is as follows: where a trial judge has considered the proper factors and has not made any unreasonable finding, his or her determination is owed considerable deference on appellate review.

This Court established a revised approach to the exclusion of evidence under s. 24(2) in *R. v. Grant*, 2009 SCC 32 (CanLII), 2009 SCC 32, [2009] 2 S.C.R. 353. This Court held that three avenues of inquiry were relevant to an assessment of whether the admission of evidence obtained in breach of the *Charter* would bring the administration of justice into disrepute: (1) an evaluation of the seriousness of the state conduct; (2) the seriousness of the impact of the *Charter* violation on the *Charter*-protected interests of the accused; and (3) society's interest in an adjudication on the merits. After considering these factors, a court must then balance the assessments under each of these avenues of inquiry in making its s. 24(2) determination to determine whether admission of the evidence would bring the administration of justice into disrepute.

The Court of Appeal erred in intervening on the basis that the police had not deliberately acted in an abusive manner. By its re-characterization of the evidence which departed from express findings by the trial judge which were not tainted by any clear and determinative error, the Court of Appeal exceeded its role. The Court of Appeal also erred in reweighing the impact of the seriousness of the offence. This consideration was fully addressed by the trial judge who was aware of the seriousness of the offence and of the consequences of excluding the evidence.

Furthermore, the Court of Appeal erred by placing undue weight on the "discoverability" of the evidence in its s. 24(2) analysis. Its principal basis for appellate intervention was that the physical evidence could have been obtained legally by warrant, without C's participation. Discoverability is a relevant factor under the current s. 24(2) analysis, however, it is not determinative. A finding of discoverability does not necessarily lead to admission of evidence. In appropriate cases, discoverability may be relevant to the first two branches of the *Grant* analysis.

In the case at bar, with respect to the first branch of the analysis, it is clear that the trial judge considered the officers' misconduct to be very serious. The collection of the evidence pursuant to the warrants was an extension of the earlier, unlawful warrantless searches. The fact that the police could have demonstrated to a judicial officer that they had reasonable and probable grounds to believe that an offence had been committed and that there was evidence to be found, but did not do so, significantly aggravated the seriousness of their misconduct. The police misconduct in obtaining the warrants further aggravated the seriousness of the *Charter*-infringing state conduct. With respect to the second branch of the analysis, the absence of prior judicial authorization constitutes a significant infringement of privacy. Having regard to all of the circumstances, the impact of the police misconduct on C's right to privacy was serious: the unauthorized search occurred in her home in the middle of the night while she was detained and the search was not brief. The breach implicated her liberty, her dignity as well as her privacy interests. Thus, the absence of prior authorization for the search was a serious affront to her reasonable expectation of privacy.

In this case, the trial judge drew the line where the police had continually shown systemic disregard for the law and the Constitution. The trial judge did not err in concluding that the courts must not tolerate this sort of behaviour by those sworn to uphold the law. He took the only course open to him in order to prevent the administration of justice from falling into further disrepute by condoning this disturbing and aberrant police behaviour.

Per Deschamps J. (dissenting): The application of the three-stage test proposed in *R. v. Grant* leads to the conclusion that the physical evidence should not have been excluded. At the first stage of the analysis — that of the seriousness of the *Charter*-infringing state conduct — the police officers' conduct revealed a serious disregard for C's constitutional rights. Not only did the officers not concern themselves with obtaining either a warrant or C's informed consent before conducting their initial search, they also attempted to conceal the constitutional violations of C's rights.

At the second stage — that of the impact of the *Charter* breach on the *Charter*-protected interests of the accused — it is clear that the trial judge did not evaluate the actual impact of the breach. The main interest affected by the unlawful police search was C's expectation of privacy. In this regard, it is not enough to find that the search resulted in an invasion of privacy, as it is also necessary to determine the impact of the failure to obtain prior authorization on C's expectation. To do this, the situation here must be compared with the one that would have prevailed had the search been authorized in advance. It is more specifically the difference in seriousness between the two situations that reveals the extent to which the breach actually undermined the protected interests. In this case, a warrant could have been issued at the start of the investigation and the resulting invasion of C's privacy would, in practice, have been identical to the one that resulted from the warrantless search. Moreover, C did not have the highest expectation of privacy. She was the first and only person to whom the police officers could speak to find out what had happened in the moments before her spouse was taken away by ambulance. Therefore, the visit from the police could hardly be said to have been unexpected.

As for the third stage of the analysis — that of determining whether the search for truth would be better served by admitting the evidence or by excluding it — the evidence in question was reliable physical evidence, and its admission was likely to be of crucial importance to the truth-seeking function and to the conduct of the trial, since the exclusion of the statements made to the police by C meant that it was the only remaining evidence.

After completing all three stages of the analysis, it is necessary to balance the factors that weigh in favour of and against excluding the evidence. Here, the police misconduct, considered as a whole, is serious and the courts must dissociate themselves from it. However, it is possible to do so in respect of the constitutional violations in this case without excluding all the evidence. There are cases of impacts on expectations of privacy that are much more serious. Moreover, where reliable and important evidence exists, society's interest in the search for truth stands out. On the whole, it is the exclusion of the physical evidence that would bring the administration of justice into disrepute.

Cases Cited
By Cromwell J.

Applied: *R. v. Grant*, 2009 SCC 32 (CanLII), 2009 SCC 32, [2009] 2 S.C.R. 353; **referred to:** *R. v. Godoy*, 1999 CanLII 709 (SCC), [1999] 1 S.C.R. 311; *R. v. Evans*, 1996 CanLII 248 (SCC), [1996] 1 S.C.R. 8; *R. v. Tricker* 1995 CanLII 1268 (ON CA), (1995), 21 O.R. (3d) 575; *R. v. Araujo*, 2000 SCC 65 (CanLII), 2000 SCC 65, [2000] 2 S.C.R. 992; *R. v. Grant*, 1993 CanLII 68 (SCC), [1993] 3 S.C.R. 223; *R. v. Harrison*, 2009 SCC 34 (CanLII), 2009 SCC 34, [2009] 2 S.C.R. 494, rev'g 2008 ONCA 85 (CanLII), 2008 ONCA 85, 89 O.R. (3d) 161; *R. v. Beaulieu*, 2010 SCC 7 (CanLII), 2010 SCC 7, [2010] 1 S.C.R. 248; *R. v. Collins*, 1987 CanLII 84 (SCC), [1987] 1 S.C.R. 265; *R. v. Stillman*, 1997 CanLII 384 (SCC), [1997] 1 S.C.R. 607; *R. v. Colarusso*, 1994 CanLII 134 (SCC), [1994] 1 S.C.R. 20; *R. v. Buhay*, 2003 SCC 30 (CanLII), 2003 SCC 30, [2003] 1 S.C.R. 631; *R. v. Nolet*, 2010 SCC 24 (CanLII), 2010 SCC 24, [2010] 1 S.C.R. 851; *R. v. Feeney*, 1997 CanLII 342 (SCC), [1997] 2 S.C.R. 13; *R. v. Greffe*, 1990 CanLII 143 (SCC), [1990] 1 S.C.R. 755.

By Deschamps J. (dissenting)

R. v. Grant, 2009 SCC 32 (CanLII), 2009 SCC 32, [2009] 2 S.C.R. 353; *R. v. Collins*, 1987 CanLII 84 (SCC), [1987] 1 S.C.R. 265; *R. v. Stillman*, 1997 Can-LII 384 (SCC), [1997] 1 S.C.R. 607; *Vancouver (City) v. Ward*, 2010 SCC 27 (CanLII), 2010 SCC 27, [2010] 2 S.C.R. 28; *R. v. Harrison*, 2009 SCC 34 (Can-LII), 2009 SCC 34, [2009] 2 S.C.R. 494.

Statutes and Regulations Cited
Canadian Charter of Rights and Freedoms, ss. 7, 8, 10, 24.
Criminal Code, R.S.C. 1985, c. C-46, s. 488.

APPEAL from a judgment of the Quebec Court of Appeal (Dalphond, Duval Hesler and Gagnon JJ.A.), 2010 QCCA 303 (CanLII), 2010 QCCA 303, 74 C.R. (6th) 130, SOQUIJ AZ-50609169, [2010] Q.J. No. 1162 (QL), 2010 Car-swellQue 15137, setting aside the acquittal entered by Cournoyer J., 2008 QCCS 3749 (CanLII), 2008 QCCS 3749, SOQUIJ AZ-50509743, [2008] J.Q. nº 7951 (QL), 2008 CarswellQue 7931, and ordering a new trial. Appeal allowed, Deschamps J. dissenting.

Carole Gladu, Josée Veilleux and Karine Guay, for the appellant.

Magalie Cimon and Pierre Goulet, for the respondent.

Frank Addario and Kelly Doctor, for the intervener.

The judgment of McLachlin C.J. and Binnie, LeBel, Fish, Abella, Charron, Rothstein and Cromwell JJ. was delivered by

CROMWELL J. —

I.   Introduction

[1]   Evidence obtained in a manner that violates rights guaranteed by the *Canadian Charter of Rights and Freedoms* must be excluded if, having regard to all of the circumstances, its admission would bring the administration of justice into disrepute: s. 24(2). This case raises in stark terms how this requirement applies when the court is faced with serious and systematic disregard for *Charter* rights by the police during the investigation of a serious crime.

[2]   On the appellant's trial for second degree murder, the trial judge, after a five-day hearing, concluded that the police investigators over several hours had violated virtually every *Charter* right accorded to a suspect in a criminal investigation. These violations, he held, were not the result of isolated errors of judgment on the part of the police investigators, but rather were part of a larger pattern of disregard of the appellant's *Charter* rights. The seriousness of this

misconduct was aggravated by the facts that the investigators had misled a judicial officer in order to obtain search warrants and that, as witnesses at trial, they had refused to admit obvious facts, offered improbable hypotheses and tried to justify their actions on untenable grounds. The trial judge found that to admit the evidence in the face of this extraordinarily troubling police misconduct, even when his decision would lead to an acquittal of a serious crime, would bring the administration of justice into disrepute. He therefore ordered its exclusion. In response to this ruling, the Crown stated that it had no other evidence and the appellant was acquitted of the charge.

[3]   The Crown appealed to the Court of Appeal which held that some of the evidence which the trial judge had excluded should have been admitted. The court therefore set aside the trial judge's decision in part and ordered a new trial. On Ms. Côté's further appeal to this Court, the issue is whether the Court of Appeal erred in law in doing so.

[4]   In my respectful view, the appeal must succeed and the decision of the trial judge to exclude the evidence restored. The trial judge drew the line where the police had continually shown systematic disregard for the law and the Constitution. The trial judge did not err in concluding that the courts must not tolerate this sort of behaviour by those sworn to uphold the law. He took the only course open to him in order to prevent the administration of justice from falling into further disrepute by condoning this disturbing and aberrant police behaviour.

II.   Facts, Proceedings and Issues

A.   *Evidence and Decision at Trial, 2008 QCCS 3749 (CanLII), 2008 QCCS 3749 (CanLII)*

(1)   Overview

[5]   The appellant applied to the trial judge to exclude evidence which she claimed had been obtained in a manner that infringed her rights under the *Charter.* The appellant also sought exclusion of her statements to the police on the basis that they had not been made voluntarily. The trial judge essentially agreed with the appellant, finding that the police violated the appellant's rights and misconducted themselves in several respects.

[6]   The trial judge concluded that the police embarked on a systematic violation of Ms. Côté's rights when they entered onto her property at approximately 12:15 a.m. on July 23, 2006, and these violations extended until 8:00 p.m. that evening when her interrogation ended. First, the police officers' entry on the appellant's property, their authorization to enter her home, the search of her house, the peripheral search of the property and the search of her gazebo constituted unreasonable searches and seizures contrary to s. 8 of the *Charter.* Second, within a few moments of their arrival, the police detained the appellant without

telling her why, in violation of s. 10(*a*) of the *Charter*. Third, at that point, and later on in their dealings with the appellant, the police violated her right to obtain the assistance of a lawyer and to be advised of that right, both in violation of s. 10(*b*) of the *Charter*. Fourth, the police violated the appellant's right to silence as protected by s. 7 of the *Charter* and fifth, through their improper questioning, obtained a statement that was not voluntary. In addition, the trial judge found that the investigators had misled a judicial officer to obtain search warrants and had been evasive and unbelievable witnesses at trial. After balancing society's interest in discovering the truth against its interest in maintaining the integrity of the administration of justice, the trial judge excluded all of the evidence, finding that its admission would bring the administration of justice into disrepute.

(2) Evidence and Reasons

[7]   On July 22, 2006, a little before 9:00 p.m., Ms. Côté called 9-1-1 to report that her spouse, André Hogue, had been injured. Mr. Hogue was transported to the Hôtel-Dieu hospital in Sorel and attended to by Dr. Nicolas Elazhary. Dr. Elazhary established that Mr. Hogue had a wound in the back of his head and concluded that he was suffering from head and possibly throat injuries. An X-ray revealed an intracerebral hematoma and a metal image compatible with a projectile. Dr. Elazhary communicated this information to Sergeant François Monetta of the Sûreté du Québec (Tracy Detachment) at 11:08 p.m. Shortly thereafter, Sergeant Monetta sent Constable Alain Hogue to the hospital to speak with Dr. Elazhary. At 11:28 p.m. Dr. Elazhary confirmed the presence of a metal object in the victim's skull and Constable Hogue relayed this information to Sergeant Monetta. At 11:38 p.m. Sergeant Monetta contacted Constable Jean-François Fortier in the Nicolet Detachment of the Sûreté du Québec and communicated the information he had about the victim and the incident, including the observations made by Dr. Elazhary. Thus, from at least 11:38 p.m., before officers arrived at Ms. Côté's residence, the police knew that they were in all likelihood dealing with a bullet wound to the back of the head. They were also aware that the victim had been transported to the hospital from the appellant's address earlier that evening.

[8]   The appellant contacted Dr. Elazhary around 11:30 p.m. She told him that she had left Mr. Hogue beside the gazebo and that when she returned he was lying on the ground. Dr. Elazhary informed the appellant that Mr. Hogue was suffering from head trauma but did not mention the discovery of the bullet wound.

(a) *Investigation of 9-1-1 Call*

[9]   Around 12:15 a.m. patrolling officers Tremblay and Mathieu attended at the appellant's home. All of the lights were off and the house appeared to be calm. Believing the main entrance to be at the rear of the house, the officers went around the back, entered the solarium and rang the doorbell. The appellant answered the door in her pyjamas. The officers explained that they were there to find out what had happened earlier that evening and to make sure the premises

were safe. However, the trial judge was of the view that their explanations did not reflect their true intentions. The trial judge held that

[TRANSLATION] [a]s unpleasant as this might be for a judge, the court did not believe Constables Tremblay, Mathieu and Fortier. They unfortunately failed to display the candour and honesty that are to be expected of police officers responsible for law enforcement. [para. 126]

The officers asked to enter the house and, without responding, the appellant stepped aside. She accompanied the officers as they inspected the interior and exterior of the residence. They did not tell the appellant that they believed that her spouse was suffering from a gunshot wound.

[10] The trial judge found that the violation of the appellant's rights began shortly after the police arrived at her home, when they entered onto her property. The police relied on their power to investigate the 9-1-1 call, and, in particular, to locate the caller, determine his or her reasons for making the call, and provide the required assistance, but the trial judge found that the legitimate ambit of that power to investigate had expired earlier that evening and could not justify their investigation as it unfolded at the appellant's residence: see *R. v. Godoy*, 1999 CanLII 709 (SCC), [1999] 1 S.C.R. 311, at para. 22. In the trial judge's view, the police went to the appellant's house with the intention of conducting a criminal investigation, so they could not claim that, at 12:15 a.m., they were responding to a 9-1-1 call placed at 8:51 p.m. He found it telling that, while seeking the appellant's consent to look around her home, the police had deliberately chosen not to inform her about the gunshot wound to her spouse's head. The trial judge concluded that the police thought the appellant was a suspect in an attempted murder and were not responding to a call for assistance. The trial judge also found it incredible that the police tried to justify their intervention on the basis of ensuring Ms. Côté's safety. If the police had been genuinely concerned for the appellant's safety, he determined that they would not have had her accompany them as they searched the house.

[11] The trial judge explained that even if the parameters set out in *Godoy* were respected during the initial police intervention, this power does not authorize police to search the premises or otherwise intrude on a resident's privacy or property. He concluded that the power recognized in *Godoy* did not authorize the searches of the appellant's house and property and these searches were thus unlawful.

(b)   *Invitation to Knock and Approach*

[12] The Crown also sought to justify the police intervention on the basis of the implied invitation to knock and approach the door for a lawful purpose as set out in *R. v. Evans*, 1996 CanLII 248 (SCC), [1996] 1 S.C.R. 8. This refers to the idea that "the occupier of a dwelling gives implied licence to any member of the

public, including a police officer, on legitimate business to come on to the property" (*Evans*, at para. 13, *per* Sopinka J., citing *R. v. Tricker* 1995 CanLII 1268 (ON CA), (1995), 21 O.R. (3d) 575 (C.A.), at p. 579). The trial judge held that in shutting off the lights in her residence, the appellant had retracted the public and police's implicit invitation to knock and approach. Even if shutting off the lights did not retract this implied invitation, the trial judge found that the police had exceeded the permission accorded by the implied invitation to knock and approach for a lawful purpose. This permission was exceeded because the police had expressly contemplated the possibility of recovering evidence against the appellant when they went to her home, illustrated by the fact that the police deliberately withheld from the appellant the fact that Mr. Hogue had been wounded by a bullet. Given this intention, the police exceeded the implied permission to approach and knock. Therefore, the search was not legally justified on this basis.

(c)   *Appellant's Consent to Enter Her Residence*

[13]   The trial judge also found that the police's failure to provide the appellant with the information they possessed about the nature of her spouse's injuries vitiated her consent to enter her home. It also did not conform to the requirements set out in the jurisprudence for obtaining consent for a warrantless search. The warrantless searches could therefore not be justified on the basis of the appellant's consent.

(d)   *Urgency*

[14]   Finally, the trial judge found that the evidence did not establish urgency. There was no concern for the police or the public's safety, nor was there a concern that some of the evidence would be destroyed. Accordingly, the police officers' entry onto the appellant's property and the warrantless search of her home could not be justified on the basis of urgency.

(e)   *First Search of House and Property*

[15]   After Constables Tremblay and Mathieu entered the appellant's home, she accompanied them as they inspected the interior of the residence. Constable Tremblay then checked the exterior of the house and found that the door to the gazebo was broken and that there appeared to be blood inside the gazebo. Constable Mathieu, accompanied by the appellant, joined Constable Tremblay outside to make sure everything was in order. Constable Mathieu noticed holes in the gazebo's mosquito screen and in the solarium window. The trial judge found that both of these searches were illegal.

[16]   At 12:27 a.m. Constable Tremblay went back to the police cruiser and relayed his observations to Constable Fortier. Constable Mathieu went back inside the house with the appellant. At 12:55 a.m. Constable Tremblay joined the appellant and Constable Mathieu inside the residence and questioned the

appellant about the presence of firearms in the house. Ms. Côté gave some information about the night's events during this encounter. She confirmed the presence of two firearms but could only locate one. She led the officers to her bedroom closet where she showed them a firearm case that she said contained a firearm. Constable Tremblay did not handle the case but assumed that it contained a firearm.

(f)   *Detention*

[17]   The trial judge held that the appellant's detention commenced shortly after Constables Tremblay and Mathieu arrived at her residence. He found that she was detained at 12:27 a.m. when the officers observed holes in the solarium's window and in the gazebo's mosquito screen, failed to tell Ms. Côté about the projectile in Mr. Hogue's head and Constable Mathieu began making surveillance notes with respect to the appellant's behaviour and movements.

[18]   The trial judge found that the police officers had quickly established that Ms. Côté was the only suspect in the attempted murder of Mr. Hogue, which is why they hid from her the fact that they knew about the gunshot wound. The trial judge held that keeping this information from her was a strategic choice to prevent Ms. Côté from being on her guard. The trial judge found that the questions posed and verifications undertaken clearly demonstrated that the goal of the investigation was not to acquire information, but rather to clarify the appellant's participation in the crime. He had the impression that the police officers did not want to admit certain facts because they were afraid that their admissions would lead the court to conclude that Ms. Côté was detained within the meaning of s. 10 of the *Charter* and that she should have been appropriately cautioned. Specifically, he found Constable Mathieu's claim — that if Ms. Côté had wanted to leave, he would have had no choice but to let her go — to be unbelievable. Accordingly, the trial judge found that Ms. Côté's right under s. 10(*a*) of the *Charter* to be informed promptly of the reasons for her detention was violated until she was warned as an [TRANSLATION] "important witness" at 5:23 a.m. (para. 229). He also found that her rights under s. 10(*b*) to retain and instruct counsel upon detention and to be advised of that right were violated.

[19]   At 2:20 a.m. Constable Tremblay spoke to Detective Christian Houle who told him that it would be preferable to bring Ms. Côté to the police station so that she could make a statement given that she was an important person with respect to the incident. At 2:34 a.m. Constables Tremblay and Mathieu took the appellant to the Nicolet police station, giving her the explanation provided by Detective Houle. She remained in the company of Constable Mathieu from her arrival at the police station at 2:54 a.m. until around 4:00 a.m. On a number of occasions, the appellant asked why she was there, why these steps were being taken and why she was not left at home. She was told that she was an important witness, she was more familiar with her spouse than the police were and it was

important for the police to figure out what had happened to Mr. Hogue. At 4:10 a.m. the appellant was asked to write down her version of the evening's events. At 5:23 a.m. Detective Sylvain Bellemare gave the appellant her first warning as an important witness in the attempted murder of André Hogue.

[20] To briefly recap, the appellant's detention began at 12:27 a.m. but the police failed to caution her until 5:23 a.m. and at that point, they only cautioned her as an important witness rather than as a suspect. This violated her s. 10(*a*) and (*b*) rights. The trial judge was very troubled by the fact that throughout their interactions with the appellant, the police constantly minimized her actual legal situation to her and kept her ignorant of the information essential to the exercise of her constitutional rights. He found that they had deliberately failed to caution her correctly and he found this behaviour to be illustrative of a constant and systematic attitude evident throughout their interactions with Ms. Côté.

(g) *Establishment of Security Perimeter and Warrantless Search of Property*

[21] After the appellant was questioned, Constable Mathieu stayed inside the house with her while Constable Tremblay established a security perimeter around the property at 1:15 a.m. At 2:05 a.m. Constables Fortier and Kelly Bellerive arrived on the scene and walked around the property with Constable Tremblay. The trial judge found this to be a warrantless search that violated the appellant's s. 8 rights.

(h) *Enlargement of Security Perimeter*

[22] At 3:10 a.m. Detective Sergeant Luc Briand asked Constable Fortier to enlarge the security perimeter established earlier by Constable Tremblay. Between 3:30 and 3:45 a.m. Constable Fortier expanded the perimeter and took advantage of this opportunity to further search the property. During this search, Constable Fortier observed at least one hole in the gazebo's mosquito screen with the fibres pointing inwards towards the gazebo; a small hole in the interior window of the solarium; a large hole in the exterior window of the solarium; powder residue on the interior of the solarium window; two small holes in the solarium's mosquito screen; and shards of glass on the ground underneath the solarium window. The trial judge found that this constituted an unauthorized perimeter search.

(i) *Issuance of Telewarrants*

[23] At 5:15 a.m. Detective Sergeant Briand drafted requests for telewarrants (a telewarrant for the recording of the 9-1-1 call, a general telewarrant and a search and seizure telewarrant) indicating that he had reasonable and probable grounds to believe that a criminal act, specifically attempted murder with a firearm, had occurred on the night of July 22 at the appellant's home. He indicated

that he had reasonable and probable grounds to believe that the shot had been fired from inside the residence.

[24]   The trial judge noted that Detective Sergeant Briand had failed to fully and frankly disclose all material facts in the Information to Obtain a Search Warrant ("ITO"). For instance, para. 5 of the ITO was misleading because it suggested that some of the observations regarding the solarium and gazebo had been made inadvertently, thereby concealing the fact that Constable Fortier had already made a number of those observations during an earlier unconstitutional search with Constable Tremblay. The trial judge was also troubled by the fact that Detective Sergeant Briand failed to mention the illegal search conducted by Constables Tremblay and Mathieu earlier that evening and the fact that they had refrained from disclosing the bullet wound to Ms. Côté.

[25]   The general telewarrant and the search and seizure telewarrant were executed on July 23, 2006 at 10:35 a.m. at the appellant's house by Detective Sergeant Briand and Constable Alain Gaucher. While searching the house they located a .10 calibre gun in a case in the bedroom closet and a .22 calibre rifle, not in a case in a basement closet. The trial judge noted that the gun found in the basement closet was the same calibre as the bullet recovered from the victim's skull.

[26]   The trial judge held that the general telewarrant and the search and seizure telewarrant were invalid. He found that the police must have identified a problem in Constables Tremblay, Mathieu and Fortier's interventions and sought the warrants to remedy the unconstitutional conduct. He concluded that the warrants were invalid because if the unconstitutionally obtained information was excised from the ITO, the remaining information (paras. 1-3 and 8) did not constitute "some evidence that might reasonably be believed on the basis of which the authorization could have issued" (para. 266, citing *R. v. Araujo*, 2000 SCC 65 (CanLII), 2000 SCC 65, [2000] 2 S.C.R. 992, at para. 51). He also held that the warrants were invalid on the basis of non-disclosure of relevant information as well as the inclusion of deliberately misleading information, such as the wording in para. 5 of the ITO that suggested that Constable Fortier had inadvertently made certain observations while extending the security perimeter when in fact he had made most of those observations earlier while unconstitutionally searching the property with Constable Tremblay. Relying on *R. v. Grant*, 1993 CanLII 68 (SCC), [1993] 3 S.C.R. 223, at pp. 254-55 ("*Grant 1993*"), the trial judge concluded that the entire search process was tainted by the warrantless perimeter searches which violated s. 8.

(j)   *First Police Warning*

[27]   As mentioned above, the appellant was cautioned and advised of her right to counsel at 5:23 a.m. by Detective Bellemare. This was the first time she was so advised even though she had been detained since 12:27 a.m. At that, she was

only cautioned as an "important witness" in the attempted murder of André Hogue. Detective Bellemare used a standard police warning form but struck out the words [TRANSLATION] "arrested or detained" and replaced them with "witness" (evidence of Detective Bellemare, A.R., vol. V, at p. 192). It is notable that the police cautioned the appellant as an important witness at 5:23 a.m. when they had sworn an ITO at 5:15 a.m. stating that they had reasonable and probable grounds to believe that attempted murder had been committed. Given the information that the police possessed at 5:23 a.m., the trial judge found it inexplicable that they only warned Ms. Côté as an important witness. After being warned, she spoke with a lawyer and invoked her right to silence. She then described the day's events to Detective Bellemare and at 5:56 a.m. was placed under arrest for attempted murder. She was cautioned again, advised of her right to counsel and spoke with a lawyer for a second time.

(k) *Interrogation*

[28] After the appellant was placed under arrest for attempted murder at 5:56 a.m., she was transferred to a different police station. After sleeping an hour and eating, she was interrogated first by Detective Bellemare and later by Detective Pierre Samson. At the outset of her interrogation, the appellant exhibited extreme anxiety about having the interrogation room door closed and appeared claustrophobic. She also seemed to be exhausted and on several occasions told the interrogator that she had had enough, she did not want to talk anymore or she wanted to go lie down. She reaffirmed her right to silence over 20 times after consulting various lawyers. At 8:00 p.m. she was advised of Mr. Hogue's death and placed under arrest for murder. This ended her interrogation.

[29] The trial judge concluded that the appellant's right to silence had been systematically violated. He noted that she had been wakened in the middle of the night in the absence of any sort of urgency, the police had deliberately put off warning her appropriately and she was exhausted, claustrophobic and had exercised her right to silence on numerous occasions.

[30] He also faulted the police for having denigrated the work of defence counsel, telling the appellant that she had more life experience than her lawyer and that she was the only person who could help herself. The investigator also counselled her on exercising her right to silence. He told her that if she had planned the murder, like a member of an organized gang would have, he would advise her to remain silent because she would be in serious trouble in that kind of situation. However, given that her situation was very different, the investigator suggested that she need not remain silent. The investigator also suggested that if she had committed an armed robbery he would advise her to remain silent, but again, her circumstances were quite different. In light of this specific behaviour, the whole of the police investigation and the general context of a systematic violation of Ms. Côté's constitutional rights, the trial judge was not convinced

beyond a reasonable doubt that the videotaped statement was made freely and voluntarily.

(l)   *Police Testimony at Trial*

[31] The trial judge made strong, unfavourable findings about the credibility of the police officers' testimony at trial. He did not believe Constables Tremblay, Mathieu and Fortier, characterizing their evidence as lacking in frankness and sincerity. He found that these officers tried to present their intervention at the appellant's house as routine, a simple follow-up to the 9-1-1 call and a verification of the premises, which downplayed their knowledge that Mr. Hogue had likely suffered a bullet wound to the back of the head and that they were conducting a criminal investigation. He also noted that police witnesses refused to admit obvious facts and offered improbable hypotheses to the court. The trial judge had the impression that the officers did this because they did not want him to conclude that Ms. Côté was detained and should have been properly cautioned. As mentioned above, the trial judge found Constable Mathieu's assertion that Ms. Côté was not detained and could have left the police station at any point to be implausible. He found the officers' evidence that the appellant had not been told about the possible gunshot wound because it had not yet been confirmed to be equally unbelievable. Generally, he found that the officers' attitude during their testimony, primarily Constable Tremblay but also Constables Mathieu and Fortier, established that they did not want to admit that one investigative avenue implicated Ms. Côté in the attempted murder of Mr. Hogue.

[32] The trial judge also found that police witnesses tried to downplay the importance of certain evidence. Specifically, they tried to minimize the importance of the information transmitted to them from Dr. Elazhary, illustrated by the fact that Constable Mathieu maintained that the appellant was not detained and was free to leave at any time. The police officers also downplayed the issue of whether the holes in the window of the solarium were bullet holes and claimed that it was important to investigate whether a shot could have come from the river behind the gazebo when this hypothesis was inconsistent with the evidence they had already found. He concluded that the frankness and sincerity that is expected of police officers charged with applying the law was unfortunately lacking in this case.

(m) *Serious and Systematic Violation of Charter Rights*

[33] The trial judge was troubled by the police conduct throughout the investigation; he found that it demonstrated a blatant disregard for the appellant's *Charter* rights. He found that the breaches of the appellant's rights with respect to search and seizure were extremely serious, [TRANSLATION] "flagrant and systematic" (para. 337). They were not, in his view, the product of isolated errors in judgment on the part of the police, but rather were part of a larger pattern

of disregard of the rights guaranteed by the *Charter*. He found that the police had not acted in good faith.

(n) *Exclusion of the Evidence*

[34] Balancing the interests of the state in discovering the truth and the integrity of the administration of justice, the trial judge found that no other result than exclusion of the evidence would prevent further discrediting of the administration of justice. He therefore concluded that the admission of the evidence would bring the administration of justice into disrepute and excluded the oral and written statements given by the appellant, the evidence obtained as a result of the warranted searches at the appellant's home and the observations made by police officers with respect to the exterior of the house before the warrants were issued. In making his decision, he emphasized that the crime in question was serious, that there was a strong societal interest in adjudicating the charge on its merits and recognized that his decision was particularly difficult because it led to the appellant's acquittal.

B. *Court of Appeal, 2010 QCCA 303 (CanLII), 2010 QCCA 303 (CanLII)*

[35] The Court of Appeal found that the trial judge was right to exclude the appellant's statements to police as the police seriously undermined the advice given by Ms. Côté's lawyers in obtaining those statements and this behaviour could not be sanctioned by a court. The Crown conceded, by and large, that the police had committed a number of violations, and that they were serious. It also conceded that the videotaped statements ought to be excluded. However, the court concluded that the trial judge had erred by excluding the observations police made of the exterior of the appellant's home before the warrants were issued as well as the physical evidence obtained at the appellant's home in execution of the two telewarrants.

[36] The Court of Appeal explained that the only issue before it was the admissibility of reliable derivative evidence. In *R. v. Grant*, 2009 SCC 32 (CanLII), 2009 SCC 32, [2009] 2 S.C.R. 353, this Court referred to derivative evidence as "physical evidence discovered as a result of an unlawfully obtained statement" (para. 116). The Court of Appeal seemed to characterize *all* of the physical evidence obtained at the scene as derivative evidence in this sense. The Court of Appeal noted that the trial judge had not had the benefit of this Court's decisions in *Grant* and *R. v. Harrison*, 2009 SCC 34 (CanLII), 2009 SCC 34, [2009] 2 S.C.R. 494, and that these decisions had changed the law in this area. In *Grant*, the Court stated that in determining whether to exclude evidence under s. 24(2) of the *Charter*, a court must assess and weigh the following three factors: (1) the seriousness of the *Charter*-infringing state conduct; (2) the impact of the breach on the *Charter*-protected interests of the accused; and (3) society's interest in the adjudication of the case on the merits (para. 71). The Court of Appeal explained that while derivative evidence was often excluded where an accused's constitutional rights were seriously violated, *Grant* now required the judge "to consider whether admission of derivative evidence obtained through a *Charter* breach

would bring the administration of justice into disrepute" (para. 33, citing *Grant*, at para. 118). The Court of Appeal examined the three factors relevant to the s. 24(2) determination, as set out in *Grant*.

[37] With respect to the first factor (the seriousness of the *Charter*-infringing state conduct), the Court of Appeal acknowledged the trial judge's finding that the *Charter* violations were serious and that the police had systematically violated Ms. Côté's *Charter* rights. However, it concluded that the police officers had not deliberately acted in an abusive manner.

[38] Regarding the second factor (the effect of the violation on the accused's rights), it found that the accused had been seriously affected by a series of police errors. However, the Court of Appeal highlighted the fact that the evidence could have been discovered lawfully without the appellant's participation because the police could have obtained a search warrant. It held that a warrant would have been issued on the basis of the 9-1-1 call and the finding of a bullet in the deceased's head which had entered from the rear, thus eliminating any possibility of suicide. Relying on *Grant*, at para. 122, the Court of Appeal noted that discoverability "retains a useful role ... in assessing the actual impact of the breach on the protected interests of the accused" because the possibility of independent discovery of derivative evidence would mitigate the impact of a *Charter* violation on an accused person (para. 43). The discoverability of the evidence was therefore relevant to the analysis of the second factor. The Court of Appeal held that the admission of the physical evidence would not affect the fairness of the trial or bring the administration of justice into disrepute because the evidence and observations could have otherwise been discovered had the police obtained a warrant when they had grounds to do so.

[39] With respect to the third factor (society's interest in the resolution of the charge on its merits), the court explained that the physical evidence which the trial judge had excluded (e.g. the hole in the gazebo's mosquito screen, the holes in the solarium window, the traces of blood and the firearm registered in the victim's name) was essential to the Crown's case as it included all of the evidence from the scene. The Court of Appeal also underlined that the evidence was reliable. The court found that society's interest in having an adjudication on the merits was extremely important given the seriousness of the alleged crime.

[40] The Court of Appeal took the view that the *exclusion* of the physical evidence, rather than its inclusion, would bring the administration of justice into disrepute. In the Court of Appeal's opinion, all of the physical evidence from the scene would have been discovered without the appellant's assistance, the crime was very serious and the police officers had not deliberately acted in an abusive manner. The court explained that while the police officers' respect for the appellant's constitutional rights had been somewhat fragmented and that the trial judge had not found them to be credible witnesses, they did not intend to act

prejudicially (*pas eu d'"attitude attentatoire"*) (para. 47). Accordingly, the court held that the physical evidence and observations made at the appellant's home should not have been excluded and it allowed the appeal and ordered a new trial.

C. *Issues*

[41] The appellant challenges the Court of Appeal's decision to admit the physical evidence and the evidence concerning the police observations at her home. The Crown concedes, as it must, that the police committed serious breaches of the appellant's constitutional and legal rights. The Crown also does not contest the trial judge's decision to exclude the appellant's statements made to police. However, the Crown supports the Court of Appeal's decision to admit the police observations and the physical evidence obtained at the appellant's home.

[42] The Court of Appeal intervened principally on the basis that the evidence observed or collected at the scene could have been discovered lawfully without the appellant's participation. The Court of Appeal also justified its intervention by suggesting that the police had not deliberately acted in an abusive manner and by emphasizing the seriousness of the offence. It relied on these considerations in re-balancing the relevant lines of inquiry under s. 24(2) and in concluding that the repute of the administration of justice required the admission of some of the evidence. The appeal thus raises two main issues:

1. Did the Court of Appeal err in intervening on the bases that the police had not deliberately acted in an abusive manner and that the offence was serious?

2. Did the Court of Appeal err in intervening on the basis that the evidence was "discoverable"?

III. Analysis

[43] Before discussing the main issues in this case, I will briefly set out the standard of review and the factors relevant to a s. 24(2) determination, as described in *Grant* and its companion cases.

A. *Standard of Review*

[44] The standard of review of a trial judge's s. 24(2) determination of what would bring the administration of justice into disrepute having regard to all of the circumstances is not controversial. It was set out by this Court in *Grant* and recently affirmed in *R. v. Beaulieu*, 2010 SCC 7 (CanLII), 2010 SCC 7, [2010] 1 S.C.R. 248. Where a trial judge has considered the proper factors and has not made any unreasonable finding, his or her determination is owed considerable deference on appellate review (*Grant*, at para. 86, and *Beaulieu*, at para. 5).

B.   The *Grant Analysis*

[45]   This Court established a revised approach to the exclusion of evidence
under s. 24(2) in *Grant*. It explained that s. 24(2) was generally concerned with
"whether the overall repute of the justice system, viewed in the long term, will
be adversely affected by admission of the evidence" (para. 68). As noted earlier,
this Court held that three avenues of inquiry were relevant to an assessment of
whether the admission of evidence obtained in breach of the *Charter* would
bring the administration of justice into disrepute. A court's role when addressing
an application to exclude evidence under s. 24(2) is to balance the assessments
under each of these lines of inquiry and determine, based on all of the circumstances, whether the admission of the evidence would bring the administration
of justice into disrepute.

[46]   In setting out this new framework, this Court made it clear that while these
lines of inquiry did not precisely track the categories of considerations set out in
the earlier jurisprudence, they did capture the factors relevant to the s. 24(2)
determination that had been set out in the earlier cases. In *Beaulieu*, Charron J.,
writing for the Court, emphasized this point, noting that *Grant* did not change
the relevant factors in the s. 24(2) analysis.

[47]   The first line of inquiry involves an evaluation of the seriousness of the state
conduct. The more serious the state conduct constituting the *Charter* breach, the
greater the need for courts to distance themselves from that conduct by excluding
evidence linked to the conduct. The second line of inquiry deals with the
seriousness of the impact of the *Charter* violation on the *Charter*-protected
interests of the accused. The impact may range from that resulting from a minor
technical breach to that following a profoundly intrusive violation. The more
serious the impact on the accused's constitutional rights, the more the admission of
the evidence is likely to bring the administration of justice into disrepute. The third
line of inquiry is concerned with society's interest in an adjudication on the merits.
It asks whether the truth-seeking function of the criminal process would be better
served by the admission or exclusion of the evidence. The reliability of the
evidence and its importance to the prosecution's case are key factors. Admitting
unreliable evidence will not serve the accused's fair trial interests nor the public's
desire to uncover the truth. On the other hand, excluding reliable evidence may
undermine the truth-seeking function of the justice system and render the trial
unfair from the public's perspective. The importance of the evidence to the
Crown's case is corollary to the inquiry into reliability. Admitting evidence of
questionable reliability is more likely to bring the administration of justice into
disrepute where it forms the whole of the prosecution's case, but excluding highly
reliable evidence may more negatively affect the truth-seeking function of the
criminal law process where the effect is to "gut" the prosecution's case.

[48] After considering these factors, a court must then balance the assessments under each of these avenues of inquiry in making its s. 24(2) determination. There is no "overarching rule" that governs how a court must strike this balance (*Grant*, at para. 86). Rather, "[t]he evidence on each line of inquiry must be weighed in the balance, to determine whether, having regard to all the circumstances, admission of the evidence would bring the administration of justice into disrepute" (*Harrison*, at para. 36). No one consideration should be permitted to consistently trump other considerations. For instance, as this Court explained in *Harrison*, the seriousness of the offence and the reliability of the evidence should not be permitted to "overwhelm" the s. 24(2) analysis because this "would deprive those charged with serious crimes of the protection of the individual freedoms afforded to all Canadians under the *Charter* and, in effect, declare that in the administration of the criminal law 'the ends justify the means'" (para. 40, citing 2008 ONCA 85 (CanLII), 2008 ONCA 85, 89 O.R. (3d) 161, at para. 150, *per* Cronk J.A., dissenting). In all cases, courts must assess the long-term repute of the administration of justice.

C. *First Issue*

[49] I turn to the first of the two issues raised on appeal: Did the Court of Appeal err in intervening on the bases that the police had not deliberately acted in an abusive manner and that the offence was serious?

[50] As explained above, the Court of Appeal found that the trial judge had erred in excluding the physical evidence located at the scene. It based its conclusion, in part, on the fact that the police did not intend to act prejudicially nor had they deliberately acted in an abusive manner. It also based this conclusion on the fact that the offence in question was serious. In my respectful view, appellate intervention was not warranted on either of these grounds.

(1) Re-characterization of Police Conduct

[51] The Court of Appeal found that the police did not intend to act prejudicially nor had they deliberately acted in an abusive manner. This constituted a re-characterization of the evidence that was not open to the Court of Appeal. The trial judge made numerous findings to the contrary, specifically that the *Charter* violations were extremely serious, the police had not acted in good faith, the police had demonstrated a continuous and systematic disregard for the appellant's *Charter*-protected rights and had persisted in their misconduct by misleading a judicial officer in obtaining search warrants, by failing to be frank and sincere in their testimony and by trying to justify their actions on untenable grounds. The Court of Appeal, respectfully, exceeded its role by its re-characterization of the evidence which departed from express findings by the trial judge which are not tainted by any clear and determinative error. The Court of Appeal should not have substituted its own view of the police conduct for that of the trial judge.

[52] The respondent spent a considerable portion of its written argument trying to persuade this Court that the trial judge's findings about the nature of the police conduct were unreasonable. The respondent submits that the trial judge went too far in his criticism of the police. More specifically, the respondent submits that it was unreasonable for the trial judge to conclude that the *Charter* violations committed by the police were flagrant without considering the dynamic and evolving nature of the situation. It also submits that the trial judge erred in failing to conclude that the police were faced with a situation of urgency that required immediate action from the patrolling officers. I would not accede to these attempts to reverse the trial judge's findings of fact. A trial judge's findings of fact on a *voir dire* concerning the admissibility of evidence must be respected unless they are tainted by clear and determinative error. The trial judge made clear findings that from virtually the moment that the police arrived at the appellant's residence, they believed that she was a suspect; he concluded that the police *knew* that the person they were meeting was susceptible to being involved in the death of Mr. Hogue. I also note that the trial judge made a clear finding that the officers were not exercising their investigative powers arising from the 9-1-1 call when they came to Ms. Côté's house. Rather, he found that their purpose was to conduct a criminal investigation by speaking with an obvious suspect. The trial judge made these clear findings of fact based on his first-hand assessment of the officers' credibility by observing their testimony in court. There is no basis disclosed for interfering with the trial judge's numerous conclusions with respect to the police conduct and I thus decline to interfere with his findings.

(2) Seriousness of the Offence

[53] The Court of Appeal also emphasized that the offence in question was serious in grounding its conclusion that the trial judge was wrong to exclude the physical evidence obtained from the appellant's residence. This relates to the third branch of the *Grant* analysis that deals with society's interest in an adjudication on the merits. Under this branch, relevant, reliable evidence that is crucial to the prosecution's case will often point towards admission, though these considerations will have to be balanced against other relevant factors. The seriousness of the offence, however, has the potential to "cut both ways" and will not always weigh in favour of admission (*Grant*, at para. 84). While society has a greater interest in seeing a serious offence prosecuted, it has an equivalent interest in ensuring that the judicial system is above reproach, particularly when the stakes are high for the accused person.

[54] The Court of Appeal thus erred in reweighing the impact of the seriousness of the offence. This consideration was fully addressed by the trial judge who was painfully aware of the seriousness of the offence and of the consequences of excluding the evidence. At para. 339 of his reasons, the trial judge acknowledged the seriousness of the offence, and at para. 340, he noted that the

more serious the offence, the greater the likelihood that the administration of justice would be brought into disrepute by its exclusion, especially where the evidence was essential to a conviction. It is clear that the trial judge took this factor into account in his s. 24(2) determination and the Court of Appeal was therefore unjustified in simply assigning it greater importance.

[55] The respondent submits that the trial judge erred in failing to consider the reliability of the evidence and that this affected his weighing under the third factor of the s. 24(2) analysis. While I acknowledge that the trial judge did not expressly state that the evidence was reliable, he was of course fully aware of the nature of the evidence that was the subject of his order of exclusion. The evidence was reliable in the sense that it was objective and material and this would certainly have been obvious to the trial judge, who described all of the evidence at length in his reasons. The respondent's argument also overlooks the fact that the trial judge's decision predates this Court's judgment in *Grant* and thus may have been couched in different terms. I do not accept the respondent's submission that the trial judge failed to consider the reliability of the evidence and that this affected his s. 24(2) determination.

[56] To conclude, the Court of Appeal erred in interfering with the trial judge's s. 24(2) determination on the basis that the police did not deliberately act abusively; they did, as the trial judge found. It should also not have interfered with the trial judge's s. 24(2) determination by assigning greater importance to the seriousness of the offence when the trial judge was fully aware of and properly weighed this factor. The Court of Appeal should not have simply substituted its weighing of these factors for that of the trial judge given that he clearly considered them according to correct legal principles.

D.   *Second Issue*

[57] I now turn to the second of the two issues raised on appeal: Did the Court of Appeal err in intervening on the basis that the evidence was "discoverable"?

(1)   The Court of Appeal's Reliance on Discoverability

[58] As noted, the Court of Appeal was also convinced that the physical evidence (all of which it described as [TRANSLATION] "derivative evidence") should not have been excluded because it could have been obtained legally by warrant, without the appellant's participation (para. 33). Indeed, as I read the court's reasons, this was the principal basis for its appellate intervention. The Court of Appeal's emphasis on the discoverability of the evidence affected its weighing of the s. 24(2) factors, in particular the second one concerning the impact of the violation on the accused's rights. The court was of the view that the impact of the violations was attenuated because the evidence could have been lawfully obtained and, accordingly, its admission would not affect trial fairness nor bring the administration of justice into disrepute.

[59] The trial judge was alive to this issue. He commented at para. 347 of his reasons that it was possible, even probable, that the police could have pursued their investigation effectively and in a constitutional manner had they respected simple and elementary principles governing their actions.

[60] Analysis of the Court of Appeal's treatment of discoverability requires that the following questions be answered:

(a) Did the development of the law in *Grant* and its companion cases justify appellate intervention?

(b) What is the principle of discoverability and how does it affect the s. 24(2) analysis under *Grant* and its companion cases?

(c) Did the Court of Appeal err in its treatment of discoverability in the s. 24(2) analysis in this case?

[61] I will address these questions in turn.

(a) *Did the Development of the Law in Grant and Its Companion Cases Justify Appellate Intervention?*

[62] The Court of Appeal was of the view that *Grant* and its companion cases, decided after the trial judge's ruling, had changed the law with respect to the admission of reliable derivative evidence. By "derivative evidence", the Court of Appeal meant physical evidence discovered as a result of an unlawfully obtained statement. In its broader sense, evidence is "derivative" when it is discovered as a result of other unconstitutionally obtained evidence. Under the trial fairness rationale in *R. v. Collins*, 1987 CanLII 84 (SCC), [1987] 1 S.C.R. 265, derivative evidence obtained as a result of unconstitutional conscription, that is, compelled self-incrimination at the behest of the state of the accused against him or herself, was generally excluded — because of its presumed impact on trial fairness — unless it would have been independently discovered. The Court of Appeal noted that now, as a result of *Grant* and its companion cases, the admissibility of such evidence is to be assessed on the same basis as all other evidence by asking whether its admission would bring the administration of justice into disrepute. The Court of Appeal seemed to suggest that because derivative evidence of a conscriptive nature was more likely to have been excluded under the pre-*Grant* framework, it was necessary to redo the s. 24(2) analysis using the revised *Grant* approach.

[63] The fundamental difficulty with the court's reasoning, in my respectful view, is this: the trial judge did not refer to the fact that this was conscriptive evidence, nor did he suggest that the case for exclusion was stronger because of that. It is therefore difficult for me to see how the trial judge showed any concern that the evidence ought to be excluded because it was conscriptive. Thus, the trial judge

did not place any weight on the conscriptive character of the evidence and it did not appear to affect his analysis in any way. In any event, the Court of Appeal erred by characterizing all of the evidence as being derivative of an unlawfully obtained statement when in fact very little of it was. Only the two guns potentially constitute "derivative" evidence in the narrow sense described by the Court of Appeal, as the appellant had informed Constables Tremblay and Mathieu of their presence in the house. Although she only showed police the gun located in the bedroom, she nevertheless told them that a second gun existed. More importantly, I am of the view that the Court of Appeal erred in its analysis of the doctrine of discoverability as it applies in this case.

(b) *What Is the Principle of Discoverability and How Does It Affect the Section 24(2) Analysis Under Grant and Its Companion Cases?*

[64] The principle of discoverability was developed under the *Collins/Stillman* framework of analysis and has traditionally been applied to derivative evidence obtained as a result of the breach of an accused's right against self-incrimination: see *Collins*, and *R. v. Stillman*, 1997 CanLII 384 (SCC), [1997] 1 S.C.R. 607. According to the *Collins* trial fairness rationale, admitting evidence derived from unconstitutional self-incrimination not only further undermined the accused's right not to be conscripted against him or herself, but it also could be seen as undermining the fairness of the accused's trial at which, of course, he or she is presumed innocent and is not a compellable witness. The fact that the evidence could have been discovered without the accused's participation — in other words that it was discoverable — was considered relevant and often determinative to the s. 24(2) analysis because that fact attenuated the impact of the unconstitutional actions on the accused's right against self-incrimination and his or her fair trial rights. The state would have been able to collect the evidence without the accused's participation, and the fact that the evidence would have been discovered without infringing the accused's right against self-incrimination weakens the causal link between the *Charter* breach and obtaining the evidence.

[65] In *Grant*, this Court established a more flexible, multi-factored approach to the exclusion of evidence under s. 24(2). The earlier *Collins/Stillman* framework had been criticized for being too categorical; exclusion seemed to be virtually automatic if the evidence was found to be conscriptive and not otherwise discoverable. However, *Grant* affirmed that discoverability remains relevant to the s. 24(2) analysis, explaining as follows:

Discoverability retains a useful role, however, in assessing the actual impact of the breach on the protected interests of the accused. It allows the court to assess the strength of the causal connection between the *Charter*-infringing self-incrimination and the resultant evidence. The more likely it is that the evidence would have been obtained even without the statement, the lesser the impact of the breach on the accused's underlying interest against self-incrimination. The converse, of course, is also true. On the other hand, in cases where it cannot be determined with any confidence whether evidence would have been discovered in absence of the statement, discoverability will have no impact on the s. 24(2) inquiry. [para. 122]

[66] The concept of discoverability has been used in relation to derivative evidence to indicate that the police could have obtained the same evidence without unconstitutionally conscripting the accused or that the evidence would have inevitably been discovered without reference to that conscription: *Stillman*, at para. 107; *R. v. Colarusso*, 1994 CanLII 134 (SCC), [1994] 1 S.C.R. 20, at p. 77. However, I will use the term "discoverability" to refer to situations where unconstitutionally obtained evidence of any nature could have been obtained by lawful means had the police chosen to adopt them. Viewed in this fashion, discoverability has, in appropriate circumstances, a useful role to play in the s. 24(2) analysis where the interest at stake is one other than self-incrimination.

[67] In the pre-*Grant* case law, the fact that unconstitutionally obtained evidence, even though not conscriptive, could have been obtained by constitutional means was considered in the s. 24(2) analysis. Discoverability had two main effects on the analysis: first, the fact that the evidence could have been obtained properly in some circumstances tended to make the *Charter* breach more serious, particularly, for example, in cases in which the police simply ignored the requirement of prior authorization for a search. On the other hand, in some circumstances, the fact that the police actually had reasonable and probable grounds to search, although they did not obtain a warrant, tended to lessen the seriousness of the breach.

[68] *R. v. Buhay*, 2003 SCC 30 (CanLII), 2003 SCC 30, [2003] 1 S.C.R. 631, is a good example of how discoverability can, in simple language, cut both ways. There, the police searched a locker. One officer said that the idea of getting a warrant did not even cross his mind, while another said he did not consider obtaining a warrant because he thought he lacked sufficient grounds. The Court endorsed the conclusion of the trial judge that the officer who failed even to consider getting a warrant had demonstrated a "casual attitude" towards the appellant's *Charter* rights and that the other officer's decision to proceed with the search because he thought he did not have sufficient grounds to obtain a warrant suggested a blatant disregard for the appellant's rights which was fatal to a claim of good faith: paras. 60-61. On the other hand, this Court acknowledged that the officer probably did in fact have sufficient grounds to obtain a warrant and that the existence in fact of reasonable and probable grounds to conduct the search has on many occasions been considered as lessening the seriousness of the violation. In the end, the Court accepted that the trial judge had reasonably concluded that the breach was serious and that his assessment should not have been interfered with on appeal: see generally paras. 52-56.

[69] Discoverability remains a relevant factor under the current s. 24(2) analysis. *R. v. Nolet*, 2010 SCC 24 (CanLII), 2010 SCC 24, [2010] 1 S.C.R. 851, is an example. Binnie J., writing for the Court, found that the fact that non-bodily physical evidence obtained in breach of an accused's s. 8 right would otherwise have been discovered was one of the points favouring the admissibility rather than the exclusion of the evidence.

[70] While discoverability may still play a useful role in the s. 24(2) analysis, it is not determinative. A finding of discoverability should not be seen as necessarily leading to admission of evidence. Nor should courts engage in speculation. As stated in *Grant*, where it cannot be determined with any confidence whether evidence would have been discovered in the absence of the *Charter* breach, discoverability will have no impact on the s. 24(2) inquiry. I will describe how, in appropriate cases, discoverability may be relevant to the first two branches of the *Grant* analysis.

[71] I turn to the first branch of the *Grant* test which is concerned with the seriousness of the *Charter*-infringing state conduct. If the police officers could have conducted the search legally but failed to turn their minds to obtaining a warrant or proceeded under the view that they could not have demonstrated to a judicial officer that they had reasonable and probable grounds, the seriousness of the state conduct is heightened. As in *Buhay*, a casual attitude towards, or a deliberate flouting of, *Charter* rights will generally aggravate the seriousness of the *Charter*-infringing state conduct. On the other hand, the facts that the police exhibited good faith and/or had a legitimate reason for not seeking prior judicial authorization of the search will likely lessen the seriousness of the *Charter*-infringing state conduct.

[72] We come now to the effect of discoverability on the second branch of the *Grant* test — the impact on the *Charter*-protected interests of the accused. Section 8 of the *Charter* protects an individual's reasonable expectation of privacy. That reasonable expectation of privacy must take account of the fact that searches may occur when a judicial officer is satisfied that there are reasonable and probable grounds and authorizes the search before it is carried out. If the search could not have occurred legally, it is considerably more intrusive of the individual's reasonable expectation of privacy. On the other hand, the fact that the police could have demonstrated to a judicial officer that they had reasonable and probable grounds to believe that an offence had been committed and that there was evidence to be found at the place of the search will tend to lessen the impact of the illegal search on the accused's privacy and dignity interests protected by the *Charter*.

[73] This is not to say, however, that in such circumstances there is no infringement of an accused's privacy interests. A reasonable expectation of privacy protected under s. 8 of the *Charter* includes not only that proper grounds

exist but also the requirement of prior judicial authorization. Thus the absence of a warrant when one was legally required constitutes an infringement of an accused's privacy. The intrusiveness of such an unauthorized search will be assessed according to the level of privacy that could have reasonably been expected in the given set of circumstances. The greater the expectation of privacy, the more intrusive the unauthorized search will have been. The seriousness of the impact on the accused's *Charter*-protected interests will not always mirror the seriousness of the breach, i.e. the *Charter*-infringing state conduct. For instance, where the police acted in good faith in obtaining a warrant that was found on review not to disclose reasonable and probable grounds to believe that a crime had been committed and that there was evidence to be found at the place of the search, the seriousness of the *Charter*-infringing state conduct is reduced but the impact of the search on the accused's *Charter*-protected interests is greater because the search could not have occurred legally.

[74] The lawful discoverability of evidence may thus be a relevant consideration when a court must determine whether to exclude evidence pursuant to s. 24(2) of the *Charter*. When relevant, courts should assess the effect of the discoverability of the evidence under the first and second *Grant* lines of inquiry in light of all of the circumstances.

(c)   *Did the Court of Appeal Err in Its Treatment of Discoverability in the Section 24(2) Analysis in This Case?*

[75] The Court of Appeal found that all of the physical evidence gathered on the premises, such as the observations of the perforations in the mosquito screen and solarium window, the gunpowder residue on the solarium window and the gun registered in the name of the victim, would have been discovered without the appellant's help. Duval Hesler J.A. held that the 9-1-1 call and the gunshot projectiles lodged in the back of the victim's head would have been sufficient to obtain a valid search warrant even before the first of the warrantless peripheral searches. Relying on *Grant*, she stated that if the derivative evidence could have been discovered independently, the effect of the violation on the accused would be lessened and this would affect the second element of the s. 24(2) inquiry. She then relied, in part, on the discoverability of the evidence to ground her conclusion that the exclusion of the evidence in this case would bring the administration of justice into disrepute.

[76] The finding of discoverability in this case rests on the Court of Appeal's conclusion that the police could have obtained a warrant to search the premises very early in the investigation based on finding Mr. Hogue at the residence with what was likely a bullet in the back of his head and the 9-1-1 call from the residence. While I agree with this conclusion, I part company with the Court of Appeal about the significance of this factor for the s. 24(2) analysis in this case.

[77] Before turning to the issue of discoverability in this case, I should briefly comment on what role, if any, the validity or invalidity of the telewarrants obtained by the police played in the trial judge's s. 24(2) analysis. In my view, whether or not those warrants were valid had little or no impact on the analysis here.

[78] The trial judge found that the warrants which the police ultimately obtained were unlawful. In his view, when the unconstitutionally obtained material was excised from the ITO, what remained was insufficient. The Court of Appeal did not address this conclusion directly, noting simply that the grounds to obtain a warrant existed much earlier, which would have permitted the police to obtain all of the observations and physical evidence legally. In this Court, the Crown argued that the trial judge's ruling about the validity of the warrants was in error. However, even if the warrants were valid, this could have little if any effect on the trial judge's decision to exclude the physical evidence. The trial judge relied on the fact that the totality of the search process was tainted by the unconstitutional searches that preceded the issuance of the warrants.

[79] This finding is consistent with well-established case law. *Grant 1993* provides a good example of how illegal warrantless searches can taint a subsequent search that is otherwise lawful. In that case, the information obtained through the warrantless perimeter search was used to support the police's application for search warrants. This Court held that once the illegally obtained information was excised from the affidavits presented to the issuing justice, the information that remained was sufficient to issue the warrants. While this Court held that the warrants were valid, it found that the illegal searches "were nevertheless an integral component in a series of investigative tactics which led to the unearthing of the evidence in question". It was thus "unrealistic to view the perimeter searches as severable from the total investigatory process which culminated in discovery of the impugned evidence" (p. 255). Similarly, in the case at bar, given the trial judge's findings of fact that the police misconduct was continual and systematic from the outset of the investigation, the question of exclusion must not be approached in a compartmentalized fashion.

[80] I now turn to the impact of discoverability on the exclusion of evidence in this case.

[81] With respect to the first branch of the analysis, it is clear that the trial judge considered the officers' misconduct to be very serious. Like in *Grant 1993*, the collection of the evidence in this case was simply an extension of the earlier warrantless searches conducted by Constables Tremblay, Mathieu and Fortier; there was clearly a connection between the earlier breaches and the evidence obtained pursuant to the warrants. Moreover, by the time the warrants were obtained in this case, there had been multiple, serious and deliberate breaches of the appellant's rights. As mentioned earlier, the trial judge found it

shocking that the police had not sought a search warrant earlier that evening or obtained the appellant's free and informed consent to enter her home. He was also troubled by the fact that the police had constantly minimized, to the appellant, her true legal situation and found this disregard for her *Charter* rights to be part of a systematic attitude evident throughout their dealings with Ms. Côté. He also found that obtaining the evidence pursuant to the warranted searches was part of a larger pattern of disregard for Ms. Côté's *Charter*-protected rights. Given that this evidence was tainted by the earlier *Charter* breaches that involved serious police misconduct, it is obvious that nothing turned on the trial judge's conclusion with respect to the validity of the warrants.

[82] The fact that the police could have demonstrated to a judicial officer that they had reasonable and probable grounds to believe that an offence had been committed and that there was evidence to be found at the place of the search but did not do so, in the circumstances of this case, significantly aggravated the seriousness of their misconduct. The trial judge found that no police officer seemed preoccupied with the absence of a search warrant (a warrant was not even prepared until over five hours after the initial police intervention) or the inherent limits recognized by courts for proceeding without a warrant. The trial judge was particularly troubled by the fact that the search occurred during the night, at a very late hour, and in a dwelling house, typically a place where individuals have the greatest expectation of privacy.

[83] The police misconduct in obtaining the warrants further aggravated the seriousness of the *Charter*-infringing state conduct. The trial judge concluded that the warrants were actually sought as an ill-conceived scheme to attempt to remedy the unconstitutionality of the prior searches and that the police had misled the issuing judicial officer by failing to make full and frank disclosure of their earlier, unconstitutional conduct.

[84] The fact that the police could have demonstrated to a judicial officer that they had reasonable and probable grounds to believe that an offence had been committed and that there was evidence to be found at the place of the search is also relevant to the impact of the breach on the *Charter*-protected interests of the accused. If a search warrant could have been validly issued at the time the search was conducted (putting aside issues about whether the search was conducted reasonably), the intrusiveness of the illegal search arises from the fact that it was not authorized in advance by a judicial officer. This, on its own, tends to reduce the impact of this breach on the appellant's *Charter*-protected reasonable expectation of privacy. However, the absence of prior judicial authorization still constitutes a significant infringement of privacy. Indeed, it must not be forgotten that the purpose of the *Charter*'s protection against unreasonable searches is to prevent them before they occur, not to sort them out from reasonable intrusions on an *ex post facto* analysis: *R. v. Feeney*, 1997 CanLII 342 (SCC), [1997] 2 S.C.R. 13, at para. 45. Thus, prior authorization

is directly related to, and forms part of, an individual's reasonable expectation of privacy.

[85] Having regard to all of the circumstances, the impact of the police misconduct on the appellant's right to privacy was serious: the unauthorized search occurred in her home, a place where citizens have a very high expectation of privacy, and the search was not brief (*Grant*, at para. 113). The officers arrived at the appellant's home at 12:13 a.m. and the appellant only departed for the police station at 2:34 a.m. The appellant, dressed in her pyjamas, accompanied the police as they illegally searched the interior and exterior of her house in the middle of the night for not an insignificant amount of time during which she was detained without interruption. The breach was thus not "transient or trivial in its impact" and implicated her liberty, her dignity as well as her privacy interests (*Harrison*, at para. 28; *Grant*, at para. 113). The appellant certainly had a reasonable expectation of not being subjected to such an intrusive search, without lawful authorization in the middle of the night, and several hours after her spouse had been transported to the hospital. Thus, the absence of prior authorization for a search of this nature was a serious affront to her reasonable expectation of privacy.

[86] In my respectful view, the Court of Appeal was wrong to conclude that the trial judge erred in his appreciation of the seriousness of the impact on the *Charter*-protected interests of the accused. Even though the searches could have been conducted lawfully, this fact would not have changed the conclusion that the second branch of the *Grant* analysis militated in favour of exclusion, in light of the numerous other factors highlighting the serious impact on the appellant's privacy and dignity interests.

[87] In the result, the Court of Appeal erred in attaching great weight to the fact that the evidence was discoverable because it could have been obtained lawfully. In my view, the trial judge's assessment was not tainted by any error of law that is relevant to his ultimate conclusion or by any unreasonable finding of fact. There was therefore no basis to interfere on appeal with the trial judge's weighing of the various factors.

[88] The trial judge analysed the admissibility of Ms. Côté's statements and the material evidence separately. With respect to both, he found that the violations of the appellant's rights were systematic and deliberate and that the police were less than candid even under oath in court in order to minimize the extent of their misconduct. While the misleading character of in-court police testimony does not form part of the *Charter* breach itself, it is a relevant factor under the first branch of the s. 24(2) analysis as a court must dissociate itself from such behaviour: *Harrison*, at para. 26. The trial judge was fully aware that proper investigative methods could have produced the same evidence, that the evidence was reliable and that the alleged offence was extremely serious. He also weighed

the important societal interest in having the appellant's guilt or innocence determined on the merits. He emphasized that the violations of the appellant's rights were the result of "a larger pattern of disregard for the appellant's *Charter* rights" (para. 346, citing *R. v. Greffe*, 1990 CanLII 143 (SCC), [1990] 1 S.C.R. 755, at p. 796) and this sort of disregard by the police for a suspect's rights was carried through to their misleading evidence to obtain the warrants and by their conduct as witnesses before the court.

IV. Conclusion

[89]   To sum up, the trial judge's decision to exclude the observations made by police at the appellant's home and the physical evidence collected pursuant to the warrants was owed deference. With respect, the Court of Appeal misconceived of its appellate role when it substituted its view of the police conduct for the trial judge's and when it placed undue emphasis on the seriousness of the offence. The Court of Appeal's holding that the police had not deliberately acted in an abusive manner was contrary to the trial judge's numerous findings of deliberate and systematic police misconduct. Its emphasis on the seriousness of the offence was also misplaced given that the trial judge had acknowledged that the offence was serious and that the seriousness of the offence had been held not to be a determinative factor. The Court of Appeal also erred in placing undue weight on the "discoverability" of the evidence in its s. 24(2) analysis. While I agree with the Court of Appeal that the police could have demonstrated to a judicial officer that they had reasonable and probable grounds to believe that an offence had been committed and that there was evidence to be found at the place of the search, this fact would not have affected the s. 24(2) analysis in all of the circumstances of this case. Both the police misconduct and its impact on the accused's *Charter*-protected interests were very serious, even taking discoverability into account. The trial judge was obviously and justly concerned about the continuous, deliberate and flagrant breaches of the appellant's *Charter* rights and this consideration played an important role in his balancing of the factors under s. 24(2). He also properly took into account the strong societal interest in having a serious criminal charge determined on its merits. His conclusion was not tainted by any error of law relevant to the ultimate conclusion and, accordingly, it should not have been set aside on appeal.

V.   Disposition

[90]   I would allow the appeal and restore the acquittal entered at trial.

English version of the reasons delivered by

[91]   DESCHAMPS J. (dissenting) — I have read Cromwell J.'s reasons. He would restore the Superior Court's judgment 2008 QCCS 3749 (CanLII), (2008 QCCS 3749 (CanLII)), which in his view contains no error that would

justify the Court of Appeal's decision to intervene. On the basis of the test from *R. v. Grant*, 2009 SCC 32 (CanLII), 2009 SCC 32, [2009] 2 S.C.R. 353, I agree with the Court of Appeal 2010 QCCA 303 (CanLII), (2010 QCCA 303 (CanLII)) that the evidence obtained without the appellant's participation — which I will call "the physical evidence" — should not have been excluded. I would therefore dismiss the appeal.

[92] There is only one point on which my colleague Cromwell J. expressly agrees with the Court of Appeal: the police could have obtained a search warrant very early in their investigation. However, he attaches no significance to this fact because, in his view, the trial judge's conclusions on the exclusion of the evidence were not based on the invalidity of the warrants. With respect, I believe that there are two separate issues here: first, the consequences of the trial judge's failure to consider the possibility that a warrant could have been issued at the very beginning of the investigation; and, second, the consequences of the invalidity of the warrants issued later in the investigation. At no point in his analysis did the trial judge consider whether the physical evidence could have been discovered if a warrant had been obtained very early in the investigation. In my opinion, it is this finding by the Court of Appeal that is relevant.

[93] The trial judge rendered judgment before the decision in *Grant*, in which this Court revised the test from *R. v. Collins*, 1987 CanLII 84 (SCC), [1987] 1 S.C.R. 265, and *R. v. Stillman*, 1997 CanLII 384 (SCC), [1997] 1 S.C.R. 607. Although this fact would not, considered in isolation, justify reviewing a decision to exclude evidence, it is nonetheless appropriate to ask whether the judge considered all the factors on which such a decision must be based. In the case at bar, it is clear that he failed to do so.

I.   Relevant Facts With Respect to the Issuance of a Warrant Very Early in the Investigation

[94] At 11:38 p.m. on July 22, 2006, Constable Jean-François Fortier received a telephone call from Sergeant François Monetta, who told him that a man with injuries to the back of his head had been taken to hospital by ambulance and that an X-ray had revealed that there was a bullet in the man's head. Sergeant Monetta gave Constable Fortier the injured man's name and the address of the residence from which he had been taken by ambulance after his spouse had found him injured there.

[95] On receiving that information, Constable Fortier, as the head of the team of four police officers on duty that night for the area in which the residence in question was located, asked Constables Tremblay and Mathieu to go to the scene to investigate.

[96] The officers arrived there at 12:13 a.m. They began by observing the house. It was not lit and there were no signs of activity. They parked at a certain

distance from the house and walked up to it. They rang the doorbell and a woman opened the door. It was Ms. Côté. The officers explained that they were from the Sûreté du Québec and that they were there to find out what had happened that evening and to make sure that the premises were safe.

[97] After inspecting the interior of the residence and determining that no one other than Ms. Côté was there, Constable Tremblay went outside. He entered the gazebo, where he saw blood, or what looked like blood. Constable Mathieu and Ms. Côté joined him there. Constable Mathieu then went back inside the residence, where he noticed a hole in the glass of one of the solarium's windows. Constable Tremblay then went to the patrol car and relayed these observations to Constable Fortier. It was 12:27 a.m.

[98] I do not question the trial judge's decision to reject the prosecution's argument that the officers' purpose in searching the house was to make sure the occupants were safe. My review of the facts is based strictly on the trial judge's findings of fact and is intended to highlight the information the officers had before they arrived at Ms. Côté's residence and when they discovered the key pieces of physical evidence.

[99] It seems to me that the Court of Appeal's conclusion that a warrant could have been issued very early in the investigation is inescapable. The police were informed that a person had sustained a serious injury to the back of the head and that the injury had probably been caused by a firearm. It could not have resulted from illness, nor could it have been self-inflicted given the bullet's point of entry into the skull. In addition, the police knew the address of the residence from which the injured person had been taken by ambulance. In light of these facts, they had to discharge their duty to investigate and gather evidence related to the incident. It was therefore possible for the police to have reasonable and probable grounds to believe that evidence of an offence could be found at the place from which the victim had been taken by ambulance. Furthermore, the nature of the injury and the fact that the victim had been found on the ground could have given them reasonable and probable grounds to believe that the warrant had to be executed by night, since residue, prints and fresh tracks could have been eliminated or altered if the start of the investigation had been delayed (s. 488 of the *Criminal Code*, R.S.C. 1985, c. C-46). The Court of Appeal analysed the situation as follows (at para. 44):

[TRANSLATION] In a case such as this one, all the [physical] evidence gathered on the premises — including the holes in the gazebo window screen, the hole in the solarium window, the gunshot residue on the inside of the solarium window, the firearm registered in the victim's name and found in his home — would have been discovered without any contribution from the accused. To obtain a valid warrant to search the premises where the incident occurred, it would have been sufficient to refer to the 9-1-1 call and the bullet fragments that penetrated the victim's head from the back, eliminating the possibility of suicide and militating in favour of a serious indictable offence. It is difficult to imagine that a justice of the peace would have refused to issue a warrant in light of such assertions, if only for the purpose of obtaining an appropriate expert assessment of the scene and to perform checks that were obviously relevant, regardless of any suspicion against the accused. Consequently, in this case, the flaws detected by the trial judge in the affidavit used to obtain the general search . . . warrant are not decisive factors.

[100]   To determine how to deal with the physical evidence, the Court of Appeal could not simply rely on the trial judge's overall assessment. It had no choice but to conduct the review the trial judge had failed to conduct. In my opinion, the Court of Appeal was right to conclude that the physical evidence should not have been excluded, although the way I apply *Grant* differs some-what from the way the Court of Appeal applied it.

II.   Application of the *Grant* Test

[101]   In *Grant*, the Court established a three-stage test for determining whether evidence is admissible under s. 24(2) of the *Canadian Charter of Rights and Freedoms*. At the first stage, a court must consider the seriousness of the *Char-ter*-infringing state conduct and "assess whether the admission of the evidence would bring the administration of justice into disrepute by sending a message to the public that the courts, as institutions responsible for the administration of justice, effectively condone state deviation from the rule of law by failing to dissociate themselves from the fruits of that unlawful conduct" (para. 72).

[102]   At the second stage, the inquiry "focusses on the seriousness of the impact of the *Charter* breach on the *Charter*-protected interests of the accused. It calls for an evaluation of the extent to which the breach actually undermined the interests protected by the right infringed" (para. 76). It is important to determine the extent of the violation's impact on the interests protected by the infringed right.

[103]   At the third stage, having regard to the fact that "[s]ociety generally ex-pects that a criminal allegation will be adjudicated on its merits", the court must "[ask] whether the truth-seeking function of the criminal trial process would be better served by admission of the evidence, or by its exclusion" (para. 79). The reliability of the evidence and its importance to the prosecution's case are factors to be considered, and all relevant circumstances must be taken into account.

[104]   In determining whether the maintenance of confidence in the administra-tion of justice would be better served by admitting the physical evidence or by excluding it, the court must balance the implications that are identified at the different stages.

[105]   At the first stage of the analysis, I accept the trial judge's conclusion that the police officers' conduct revealed a serious disregard for Ms. Côté's

constitutional rights. The judge noted that the officers did not concern themselves with obtaining either a warrant or Ms. Côté's informed consent before conducting their initial search. The judge seems to have believed that Ms. Côté's rights would not have been violated had experienced officers been assigned to the investigation. In some cases, the fact that an agent of the state is inexperienced may be a sign that rights have not been intentionally violated, which means that the infringement resulting from the officers' conduct would be less serious. In the instant case, however, the officers' inexperience cannot serve as an excuse, since, according to the judge, they should have known the applicable rules. Also relevant is the judge's observation that the officers' conduct was aggravated by their attempt to conceal the constitutional violations of Ms. Côté's rights by raising arguments he held to be unfounded. The police conduct in this case was such that the courts must dissociate themselves from it.

[106] At the second stage, it is clear that the trial judge did not evaluate the actual impact of the breach. The main interest affected by the unlawful police search was Ms. Côté's expectation of privacy. What must be determined is the impact on it of the failure to obtain prior authorization. To do this, the situation here must be compared with the one that would have prevailed had the search been authorized in advance. It is therefore not enough to find that the search resulted in an invasion of privacy. While that is of course relevant, it is more specifically the difference in seriousness between the intrusion that actually occurred and the one that would have occurred had a warrant been issued that reveals the "extent to which the breach actually undermined the interests protected" (*Grant*, at para. 76). This is the corollary of the previous findings that a warrant could have been obtained at the very beginning of the investigation and that this would have led the police to discover the physical evidence.

[107] However limited the warrant may have been, it would at the very least have authorized an examination of the gazebo and the area surrounding it. The warrant would therefore have authorized a search of both the outside and part of the inside of the house. As a result, if it is accepted that the warrant could have been issued at the start of the investigation, it must also be accepted that the resulting invasion of Ms. Côté's privacy would, in practice, have been identical to the one that resulted from the warrantless search.

[108] I therefore agree with Cromwell J. that the impact of the infringement of the right to privacy is limited to the fact that the search was not authorized by a judicial officer (para. 84). However, it seems to me that his assessment of that impact contradicts the conceptual approach that follows from this premise. To determine the seriousness of the impact of the breach, my colleague considers facts that would have existed even if the search had been authorized. That does not reveal the extent to which the expectation of privacy was actually undermined by the failure to obtain prior authorization for the search.

[109]   All persons are entitled to expect the state to respect their rights, and a court cannot do anything that suggests that their rights have no value. Even where a breach has no practical consequences, the court must play a declaratory role in vindicating constitutional rights. It is this role that must be borne in mind where a duly authorized search would have had the same practical consequences (see, in the analogous context of s. 24(1) of the *Charter, Vancouver (City) v. Ward*, 2010 SCC 27 (CanLII), 2010 SCC 27, [2010] 2 S.C.R. 28). In the instant case, the protected right is the legitimate expectation of any person not to be subjected to a warrantless search. The standpoint from which a court assesses the impact of a breach of protected rights is therefore very different where the intrusion would have been identical had the search been authorized by a warrant. The interest that remains to be protected is what the Court in *Ward* referred to as "[v]indication, in the sense of affirming constitutional values" (para. 28).

[110]   Protection of a person's expectation of privacy is a fundamental requirement in the Canadian constitutional system. For this reason — and to reflect the actual scope of this expectation — it is particularly appropriate to take a nuanced approach when assessing it. The higher the expectation of privacy, the more clearly the constitutional right that protects it must be affirmed. Conversely, the lower the expectation of privacy, the lower the need for affirmation.

[111]   In the case at bar, Ms. Côté was the person who called 9-1-1 and provided her address. She was the person who contacted the doctor and told him that she had found her spouse in the gazebo. She was the first and only person to whom the police officers could speak to find out what had happened in the moments before her spouse was taken away by ambulance. Therefore, the visit from the police could hardly be said to have been unexpected. In short, not only would the intrusion have been the same with or without a warrant, but Ms. Côté did not have the highest expectation of privacy. As a result, the relevant factors at the second stage of the analysis do not weigh in favour of excluding the physical evidence.

[112]   At the stage of the analysis that involves determining whether the search for truth would be better served by admitting the evidence or by excluding it, I must point out that the evidence in question was reliable physical evidence. It was found shortly after the injured person was taken away by ambulance, and it was gathered near the alleged scene of the crime. Although my colleague acknowledges that the trial judge did not speak to the reliability of the physical evidence, he assumes that the judge attached the necessary weight to this factor (para. 55). With respect, I have difficulty seeing how such a conclusion can be drawn.

[113]   It is possible that the trial judge's failure to discuss the reliability of the evidence is due to the fact that he was applying the law as it stood before *Grant*. According to the test from *Collins* and *Stillman*, the discoverability of physical evidence was linked to the protection against self-incrimination and the

assessment of trial fairness (*Grant*, at para. 121). Exclusion was almost automatic (*Grant*, at para. 64). In that context, the reliability of the evidence was of little consequence. However, one of the changes effected in *Grant* was in fact to move away from automatic exclusion toward an analysis in which all the circumstances would be considered. On this point, I agree with my colleague Cromwell J. that the discoverability of physical evidence may be relevant to the decision whether to exclude evidence (para. 74). The relevance of discoverability is no longer limited to the protection against self-incrimination, and it is essential to consider the reliability of the evidence.

[114]   Because the trial judge did not discuss the reliability of the physical evidence, I cannot find that he considered all the relevant factors in determining whether physical evidence should be excluded. In my view, this was a serious flaw.

[115]   As regards the importance of the physical evidence to the conduct of the trial, it is sufficient to note that this evidence was circumstantial. Because the statements made to the police by Ms. Côté had been excluded, it was the only remaining evidence. Its admission was therefore likely to be of crucial importance to the truth-seeking function and to the conduct of the trial.

[116]   At the stage of assessing society's interest in the conduct of the trial, having regard to all the relevant facts, I see nothing that would weigh in favour of excluding the physical evidence. Although the evidence as a whole was limited by the exclusion of the statements made to the police by Ms. Côté, some reliable evidence remained that the prosecution could still have considered sufficient to conduct the trial.

[117]   After completing all three stages of the analysis, the court must balance the factors that weigh in favour of and against excluding the evidence. This is a qualitative exercise and not a quantitative one (*R. v. Harrison*, 2009 SCC 34 (CanLII), 2009 SCC 34, [2009] 2 S.C.R. 494, at para. 36).

[118]   In the instant case, the police misconduct, considered as a whole, is serious and the courts must dissociate themselves from it. However, it is possible to do so in respect of the constitutional violations in this case without excluding *all* the evidence. There are cases of impacts on expectations of privacy that are much more serious. Moreover, where reliable and important evidence exists, society's interest in the search for truth stands out. On the whole, I can only conclude that, in this case, it is the exclusion of the physical evidence that would bring the administration of justice into disrepute.

[119]   For these reasons, I would dismiss the appeal.

Appeal allowed, DESCHAMPS J. *dissenting.*

Solicitor *for the appellant: Centre communautaire juridique de la Rive-Sud, Longueuil.*

Solicitor *for the respondent: Directeur des poursuites criminelles et pénales du Québec, Longueuil.*

Solicitors *for the intervener: Sack Goldblatt Mitchell, Toronto.*

Appendix 4

Glossary of Terms

actus reus — an illegal action or omission

administrative law — category of law that involves boards, tribunals and government officers who make decisions

admissibility — the issue of whether or not evidence can be used during a trial – judge decides

admission — oral or written statement or conduct that links the defendant to a material fact that tends to show legal responsibility or guilt

adversarial system — our trial system – involves a contest between the parties, with a judge acting as an independent arbitrator

advocate — a legal representative for one of the parties – could be a lawyer, paralegal or agent

affidavit — a sworn statement used to provide evidence in written form

agent of the state — government-employed or directed investigators – actions are controlled by the *Canadian Charter of Rights and Freedoms*

balance of probabilities — the standard of proof in the civil justice system

beyond a reasonable doubt — the standard of proof in the criminal justice system

binding — a precedent that a judge must follow

bound — when a judge is legally obligated to follow a precedent

capacity — ability to perceive, remember and communicate information about an event

circumstantial	the type of evidence that requires the judge or jury to make inferences about the significance of the evidence in relation to a material issue
civil law	the category of our legal system that enables individuals who have been harmed by the behaviour of others to sue for financial compensation
commissioner of oaths	person licensed by a province or territory to witness the signature and undertaking of someone who is signing a document with legal significance
common law	a system under which judges are expected to resolve common legal disputes in a common or consistent way – each judge's decision has precedent value
compellable	being able to force someone to come to court to provide evidence
competent	a determination that someone has the capacity to perceive, remember and communicate an event – allowing that person to testify in court
confession	an admission of guilt or legal responsibility
conscriptive	evidence that an accused person supplies that could be used against that person
contempt	defying an order of a judge – can result in incarceration until the person complies
corroborative	evidence that supports other evidence
credibility	believability
criminal law	government, on behalf of society, labels behaviour as unacceptable and establishes a process to punish offenders
cross-examine	asking questions to challenge the witness and the quality of the evidence presented

damages	financial compensation ordered at the conclusion of a lawsuit
defence	a legal excuse for behaviour, or a justification for reduced punishment
demonstrative evidence	charts, diagrams, photos, video or computer models that assist a witness in communicating
derivative evidence	evidence that is discovered because of other evidence
direct evidence	evidence that could directly resolve a material issue without the need for inferences
disclosure	provide the opposition with a preview of the evidence you have gathered or control prior to the hearing or trial
dissenting opinion	an appeal court judge's explanation of why he or she disagrees with the majority of the judges
evidence	items or information a judge, jury or administrative tribunal will take into consideration when resolving a court case or administrative matter
exculpatory	a statement in which a defendant denies involvement in an incident
exhibit	real items or documents admitted for use as evidence – labelled with an identifier
exigency	a pressing, or emergency situation
expert	witness with specialized knowledge or training
fact	the accepted version of a state of affairs or an occurrence
hearsay	statement, writing or communicative conduct by someone outside the courtroom or hearing that would be described inside the court or hearing by someone else
hierarchy	a pyramid of levels of importance, with higher levels being assigned greater significance

hybrid offence	a federal charge that could be dealt with as either a summary conviction or an indictable offence – prosecutor chooses
inadmissibility	judge excludes an item or information from consideration by the trier of fact
inculpatory	an admission that indicates the person was involved in a material way with the incident that is the subject of the trial or hearing
indictable	a serious criminal offence
inference	using one piece of information to make a conclusion about a related issue
influenced	when judges take careful consideration of a precedent but are not bound to follow it
inquisitorial system	a system of justice used in other countries, whereby the judge takes an active part in directing the investigation, the gathering and presentation of evidence
judicial authorization	a judge ordering that an action can be taken
jurisdiction	legal responsibility based on geography or division of powers over a subject matter
lay witness	a non-expert witness
leading	questioning structured to suggest a particular answer
liability	legal responsibility
majority	the larger number of judges in agreement on a court ruling
material	important
mens rea	the mental element that may have to be proven to secure the conviction of someone accused of committing a criminal offence

modus operandi	consistent method of doing something
non-conscriptive	evidence that exists independently of any assistance from the defendant
non-leading	questions that do not suggest an answer
notary public	a person licensed by the province to witness signatures on important documents and to explain the seriousness of the undertaking to the person required to sign
oath	swearing to tell the truth on a Bible or other religious document
objection	asking a judge to rule that a particular piece of evidence not be admitted for consideration in the trial or hearing.
officer of the court	special ethical responsibilities expected of lawyers representing clients in court
opinion	the type of evidence an expert can provide – going beyond a factual account to assist the judge or jury in understanding how or why something occurred
parties	the key players in a trial – the plaintiff and defendant in a civil case, society and the defendant in a criminal case
person in authority	someone engaged in the arrest, detention, examination or prosecution of an accused
precedent	previous court decisions that may be binding or influential on a judge dealing with a similar issue
prejudice	being harmed or disadvantaged
preliminary inquiry	a process during which the prosecutor is required to produce enough evidence to convince a provincial court judge that an indictable offence is worth sending on to a superior court for trial
presumption	a judge will assume a particular state of affairs unless he or she receives contrary evidence

privilege	a special legal right to be exempted from having to share information with the court
probative value	useful in tending to prove something
prosecutor	society's legal representative in a criminal case
real evidence	items and documents a court will consider as evidence if a witness can explain relevance
relevant	having probative value with respect to a material issue
reliability	dependability
res gestae	part of the event
ruling	a judge's decision on an issue that must be resolved
search	a government agent's investigative activity that invades someone's reasonable expectation of privacy
seizure	the non-consensual taking of a thing from a person by a public authority
similar fact	prior behaviour showing a consistent pattern with current behaviour
solemn affirmation	an undertaking by a witness to tell the truth following the wording in section 14 of the *Canada Evidence Act*
standard of proof	the degree to which something must be proven
stare decisis	the common law system of relying on precedents that considers court decisions from a higher level of court binding and decisions from the same level, or from another jurisdiction, influential
statute	government-created written law
subpoena	an order requiring a witness to attend court or a hearing and to bring any relevant evidence in his or her possession or control

summary offence	all provincial, territorial and municipal charges and less serious federal charges
support person	an individual allowed to attend court with a witness
suspicion	an inkling, less than the reasonable probability required for most invasive investigations
telewarrant	a warrant issued over the phone
torts	non-contractual justifications for suing someone
transcript	a written record of all the questions, answers, oral submissions and rulings that occur during a trial
trier of fact	the judge or jury required to make a decision about what happened and whether or not it fits the elements of a crime or civil cause of action
trier of law	the judge who makes legal rulings on procedural matters, including the admissibility of evidence and explains applicable law to the jury
voir dire	a mini-hearing to hear evidence, consider legal arguments before a judge makes a ruling on a procedural matter like the admissibility of evidence
voluntariness	determining whether or not an admission by an accused was made without fear of prejudice or hope of advantage held out by a person in authority
warrant	an order by a judge or justice of the peace authorizing a search, seizure or arrest
weight	the importance that will be assigned to a particular piece of evidence by the trier of fact

INDEX

A

ABUSE OF PROCESS, 165

ACCOMPLICES, 44, 47–48

ACCUSED
co-accused, 44–45, 47–48
compellability, 47–48, 128
competence of, 44–45
good character evidence, 86
rights of. *See* **CANADIAN CHARTER OF RIGHTS AND FREEDOMS**
spouse of accused, 47

ACTUS REUS, 9, 130

ADMINISTRATIVE TRIBUNALS, 15 **OR BOARDS**, 3

ADMISSIBILITY OF EVIDENCE
expert evidence, 62–64
judicial decisions about, 8
jury trials, 32

ADMISSIONS. *See also* **CONFESSIONS**
exculpatory admissions, 111
general, 94, 105, 111
inculpatory admissions, 111
persons in authority, 112–115
right to counsel, 118–123
right to silence, 118–123
voir dire, 117–118
voluntariness, 115–117

ADVERSARIAL SYSTEM
civil trial, 7
general, 4
judge, role of, 7–8

ADVERSE WITNESS, 104

ADVOCATES, 4, 8, 184

AFFIDAVITS, 176–177

AGENTS OF THE STATE, 17, 119, 140–142

AIRPORTS, 137

ALTERNATIVES TO LIVE WITNESSES, 176–177

APPEAL
appeal courts, 26–27, 30
general, 26–27
leave to appeal, 27

APPEAL COURT CASES, 35–37

ARBITRARY DETENTION, 162–164

ARREST
arrest powers, 146
search "incident to an arrest," 146–149

ATTENDANCE OF WITNESSES, 46, 179–180

B

BATTERED WOMAN SYNDROME, 87

"BEST EVIDENCE" APPROACH, 177–178

BINDING PRECEDENTS, 27

BLOOD SAMPLES, 19–20, 73

BOARDS, 3, 15

BODILY SUBSTANCES. *See also* **BLOOD SAMPLES; BREATH SAMPLES**
certificate of breath or blood sample analysis, 19–20
warrant, 20, 73

BREATH SAMPLES, 19–20, 72–73

BREATHALYZER, 162

BUSINESS RECORDS, 96–97, 178

C

CANADA EVIDENCE ACT
business records, 97, 178
compellability, 47–48, 128
competence to testify, 43, 44–45
expert witnesses, number of, 68–69
general, 15–16
government documents, 178
minors, 46
oath, 45–46
previous convictions, 77
prior inconsistent statements, 104
vs. provincial and territorial
    evidence acts, 17
self-incrimination, 48
solemn affirmation, 45–46
spouse
    compellability of, 48–49
    privilege, 48–49

CANADIAN CHARTER OF RIGHTS AND FREEDOMS
agents of the state, 17, 119, 140–142
application of, 18
arbitrary detention, 162–164
compellability, 128
conscriptive *vs.* non-conscriptive
    evidence, 169–171
exclusion of evidence, 8–9,
    17, 33, 168
general, 17–18
Grant case, 169–171
interpreter, 44
investigators, actions of, 171–172
legal rights, 17–18
make full answer and defence, 7,
    51, 56–57, 161–162
previous convictions, 78
protection of, 3
reason for arrest, 118
remedies
    under ss. 24(1), 164–168
    under ss. 24(2), 8–9, 17, 33–34, 168
right to counsel
    Charter right, 94, 116, 118–123
    effect of violations, 123
    narrowing the protections of,
        124–128
right to silence
    Charter right, 94, 118–123
    and compellability of accused,
        47–48
    narrowing the protections of,
        124–128
self-incrimination, 48,
    128–130, 167
unreasonable search and seizure,
    33, 142, 143–145, 155
    See also **SEARCH AND
    SEIZURE**

CANADIAN JUSTICE SYSTEM
adversarial system, 4
balancing privacy expectations and
    criminal control, 133–134
three categories in, 3

CASE-BY-CASE PRIVILEGE, 51–52

CASE LAW
binding precedents, 27
finding case reports, 28–29
influential but not binding, 27
influential common law
    precedent, 28
other common law jurisdictions,
    37–38
provincial and territorial
    appeal and trial court cases,
    35–37
reading case reports, 29–32
stare decisis, 25–28
Supreme Court of Canada cases,
    32–34

CASE REPORTS
case report collections, 29
"facts" of cases, 34
finding case reports, 28–29
reading case reports, 29–32
specialty case reports, 29
trial level case reports, 31–32

CELLPHONES, 136, 146–147

CERTIFICATE EVIDENCE, 176

CERTIFICATE OF BREATH OR BLOOD SAMPLE ANALYSIS, 19–20, 176

CHANGE BLINDNESS, 70–71

CHARACTER EVIDENCE
accused's good character evidence, 86
civil trials, 87–88
denial of commission of offence, 86
exceptions to general rule, 76
general, 75
and previous convictions, 75–78
victim, attacking character of, 86–87

CHARGE, 72

CHARTER OF RIGHTS AND FREEDOMS. *See* **CANADIAN CHARTER OF RIGHTS AND FREEDOMS**

CHILD PORNOGRAPHY, 20

CHILDREN
competency, 46
principled approach to hearsay, 99–100
as witnesses, 55–56

CIRCUMSTANTIAL EVIDENCE, 11–12, 12

CITATION, 29

CIVIL JUSTICE SYSTEM
adversarial system, 7
general, 3
provincial and territorial evidence acts, 16

CIVIL TRIAL
character evidence, 87–88
credibility, 10
damages, 10
defamation, 88
defences, 10
disclosure, 7
liability, 9–10
parties, 4
privilege, 52

settlement, 7
standards of proof, 3

CO-ACCUSED, 44–45, 47–48

COLLUSION, 82–83

COMMISSIONER, 102

COMMISSIONER OF OATHS, 177

COMMON LAW. *See also* **HEARSAY**
exceptions to hearsay rule, 92
See also EXCEPTIONS TO HEARSAY RULE
other common law jurisdictions, 37–38
principles, 28, 33

COMPARATIVE RELIABILITY, 105

COMPELLABILITY, 46–48, 128

COMPENSATION FOR LOSS, 10

COMPETENCE TO TESTIFY, 43–45

COMPETENCY OF ADVOCATES, 8

COMPUTER-GENERATED RE-ENACTMENTS AND RE-CREATIONS, 35–36

CONFESSIONS. *See also* **ADMISSIONS**
general, 94, 111
Mr. Big confessions, 114–115
persons in authority, 112–115
right to counsel, 118–123
right to silence, 118–123
U.S. *Miranda* rights, 126–127

CONFIDENTIAL INFORMATION, 48–52

CONSCRIPTIVE EVIDENCE, 169–171

CONSENT, 149

CONSTITUTION ACT, 1867, 15, 16

CONTEMPT OF COURT, 46

CONTROLLED DRUGS AND SUBSTANCES ACT, 21, 72, 155, 176

CONVICTIONS, PREVIOUS, 10–11, 75–78

CORBETT APPLICATION, 77–78

CORPORATIONS, 128

CORROBORATION, 19

COUNSEL. *See* RIGHT TO COUNSEL

COURT CASES. *See* CASE LAW

COURTS
appeal courts, 26–27
court hierarchies, 25–28
going to court, 188
officers of the court, 184
Supreme Court of Canada, 27, 30

CREDIBILITY, 10, 43, 77, 104

CRIMINAL CODE
actus reus, 9
arrest powers, 146
attendance of witnesses, 179–180
blood sample, 73
breath sample, 72–73
certificate of breath or blood sample analysis, 19–20, 176
character evidence, 76
children, testimony of, 55–56, 56
complainant credibility, 86
criminal organization, 85
drug impairment, and marijuana, 67
expert evidence, 62
gathering evidence for expert analysis, 72–73
general, 18–20
indictable offences, 72
interception of private communications, 150–151

mens rea, 9
perjury, 19
plain view, 146
possession of property obtained by crime, 78
preservation of evidence in event of death, 101–102
primary purpose, 18
prior court hearings, testimony from, 97
seizure, 20
sexual assault, 19
sexual assault complainants, 19, 54–55, 86
torture, 20
videotaped evidence, 19
warrantless search, 20
warrants, 20
warrants to conduct search, 155–157
wiretaps, 150–151

CRIMINAL CONTROL, 133–134

CRIMINAL JUSTICE SYSTEM
general, 3
skewed contests, 4–7

CRIMINAL ORGANIZATION, 85

CRIMINAL TRIAL
credibility, 10
disclosure, 7
false admissions and confessions, 94
homicide trials, 94–96
parties, 4
proof beyond a reasonable doubt, 4–6, 10–11
standards of proof, 3

CROSS-EXAMINATION, 42–43, 91, 103–104, 104

D

DAMAGES, 10

DEFAMATION, 88

DEFENCE, 10

DEMONSTRATIVE
EVIDENCE, 12, 179

DERIVATIVE CONSCRIPTIVE
EVIDENCE, 170

DETENTION, 162–164

DIRECT EVIDENCE, 11

DISCLOSURE
civil trial, 7
criminal cases, 7
duty of disclosure, 161
full answer and defence, 7
right to disclosure, 161–162

DISSENTING OPINION, 30

DNA EVIDENCE, 67

DOCUMENTS, 177–178

DOGS, 152–155

DOORWAY SNIFF TEST, 172

DRUG DETECTION DOGS,
152–155

E

ELECTRONIC
SURVEILLANCE, 150–151

EQUITY, 10

EVIDENCE
admissibility, 8
"best evidence" approach,
177–178
certificate evidence, 176
circumstantial evidence, 11–12, 12
conscriptive evidence, 169–171
corrobative evidence, and hearsay,
102–103
demonstrative evidence, 12, 179
derivative conscriptive
evidence, 170
direct evidence, 11
exhibit, 177
gathering and organizing evidence
affidavits, 176–177
alternatives to live witnesses,
176–177
attendance of witnesses,
179–180
certificates, 176–177
demonstrative evidence, 179
documents and other real
evidence, 177–178
for expert analysis, 72–73
investigators, role of, 183–184
judicial notice, 175–176
photos, 178–179, 183
videotape, 178–179, 183
in inquisitorial system, 7–8
legislation. *See* **EVIDENCE
STATUTES**
non-conscriptive evidence,
169–171
objection to, 8
physical objects, 12
probative value, 9
real evidence, 12, 169–170,
177–178
relevance, 9–10
rules of evidence, 4, 8–9
statutes. *See* **EVIDENCE
STATUTES**
types of evidence, 11–12
weight, 8

EVIDENCE STATUTES.
See also **CANADA
EVIDENCE ACT;
CANADIAN CHARTER
OF RIGHTS AND
FREEDOMS; CRIMINAL
CODE; PROVINCIAL
AND TERRITORIAL
EVIDENCE ACTS**
Canada Evidence Act, 15–16
*Controlled Drugs and Substances
Act,* 21, 72, 155, 176
court hierarchies, 25–28
Criminal Code, 18–20
hearsay evidence, 104
Identification of Criminals Act,
21, 72
other provincial and territorial
statutes, 22
provincial and territorial evidence
acts, 16–17

EXCEPTIONS TO HEARSAY RULE
business records, 96–97
common law exceptions, 92
dying declarations, 94–96
general, 92
original declarant unavailable, 94–104
primary exception, 92
principled approach, 99–104
prior consistent statements, 106–108
prior inconsistent statements, 104–106
purpose exception, 92–93
res gestae statements, 98
statements against interest, 98–99
statements by a party, 94
statements of mental state, 96
statutory exceptions, 92
testimony from prior hearing, 97–98

EXCLUSION OF EVIDENCE
under the *Charter,* 8–9, 17, 33–34, 168
judge's discretion to exclude relevant evidence, 10–11
prejudicial effect, 10–11

EXCULPATORY ADMISSIONS, 111

EXHIBIT, 177

EXPERT EVIDENCE
accused's good character evidence, 86
admission of expert evidence, 62–64
advance notice, 62
anecdotal evidence, 63–64
drug recognition experts, 67
and eyewitness testimony, 70–72
gathering evidence for expert analysis, 72–73
general, 61–62
impartiality, 70
irrelevant evidence, 63–64
limits on use of expert witnesses, 68–70
new areas of expertise, 64–67
novel scientific theory, 65–66
qualification of witness, 62, 64–65
reliability, 65
rule against oath-helping, 68
specialized knowledge, skill or experience, 62–63
subject of the opinion, 63
weight of evidence, 68

EYEWITNESS TESTIMONY, 70–72

F

FACT
"facts" of cases, 34
vs. opinion, 59–60
trier of fact, 8, 61

FAIRNESS, 10

FALSE ADMISSIONS AND CONFESSIONS, 94

FINANCIAL INTEREST, 44–45

FINDING CASE REPORTS, 28–29

FORCE, USE OF, 157–159

FOREIGN COMMON LAW JURISDICTIONS, 37–38

FOREIGN POLICE OFFICERS, 142

FULL ANSWER AND DEFENCE. *See* **MAKE FULL ANSWER AND DEFENCE**

G

GANG INVOLVEMENT, 83–85

GATHERING AND ORGANIZING EVIDENCE
alternatives to live witnesses, 176–177
attendance of witnesses, 179–180

GATHERING AND ORGANIZING EVIDENCE — *cont'd*
demonstrative evidence, 179
documents and other real evidence, 177–178
for expert analysis, 72–73
judicial notice, 175–176
photos, 178–179, 183
videotape, 178–179, 183

GOING TO COURT, 188

GOOD CHARACTER EVIDENCE, 86

GOOD FAITH, 171

GOVERNMENT DOCUMENTS, 178

GRANT CASE, 169–171

H

HEARSAY
basic hearsay rule, 91
case law on, 29
corrobative evidence, 102–103
exceptions to basic rule
  business records, 96–97
  common law exceptions, 92
  dying declarations, 94–96
  general, 92
  original declarant unavailable, 94–104
  primary exception, 92
  principled approach, 99–104
  prior consistent statements, 106–108
  prior inconsistent statements, 104–106
  purpose exception, 92–93
  res gestae statements, 98
  statements against interest, 98–99
  by a party, 94
  statements of mental state, 96
  statutory exceptions, 92
  testimony from prior hearing, 97–98
rationale behind exclusion of hearsay, 91–92

HIERARCHY OF COURTS, 25–28

HOME, 135–136, 143–144

HOMICIDE TRIALS, 94–96

HYBRID OFFENCE, 72

I

IDENTIFICATION OF CRIMINALS ACT, 21, 72

ILLEGAL GAMBLING, 20

IMPLIED LICENCE, 172

INCULPATORY ADMISSIONS, 111

INDICTABLE OFFENCE, 21, 72

INFERENCES, 11

INFORMANTS
competency, 44
privilege re identity, 50–51

INFORMER PRIVILEGE, 50–51

INQUISITORIAL SYSTEM, 7–8

INTENTIONAL ACT, 9

INTERCEPTION OF PRIVATE COMMUNICATIONS, 150–151

INTERNATIONAL BORDER CROSSING, 137

INTERPRETER, 44

INVESTIGATORS, 183–184. *See also* **POLICE**

J

JUDGE
adversarial system, role in, 7–8
discretion to exclude relevant evidence, 10–11
dissenting opinion, 30
judicial notice, 175–176
majority ruling, 30

JUDGE — *cont'd*
role of, 4
ruling, 30
trier of fact, 8, 61
trier of law, 8, 176

JUDICIAL NOTICE, 175–176

JURISDICTION
other common law jurisdictions, 37–38
provincial or territorial, 27

JURY
admissibility of evidence, 32
collusion, evidence of, 83
legal concepts, explanation of, 61
and trial level case reports, 31–32
trier of fact, 8
weight of evidence, 68

JUSTICE SYSTEM. *See*
CANADIAN JUSTICE SYSTEM

L

LAWYERS, 4

LAY WITNESS, 60–61

LEADING QUESTIONS, 42, 43

LEAVE TO APPEAL, 27

LEGAL RIGHTS, 17–18

LEGISLATION. *See*
EVIDENCE STATUTES

LIABILITY, 9–10

M

MAJORITY RULING, 30

MAKE FULL ANSWER AND DEFENCE, 7, 51, 56–57, 161–162

MATERIAL ISSUE, 9, 42

MEMORY, REFRESHING, 186–187

MENS REA, 9

MENTAL STATE, 96

MINORS. *See* **CHILDREN**

MODUS OPERANDI, 80

N

NECESSITY, 99, 105

NEW AREAS OF EXPERTISE, 64–67

NIQAB, 37, 56–57

NON-CONSCRIPTIVE EVIDENCE, 169–171. *See also* **REAL EVIDENCE**

NON-EXPERT WITNESS, 59–61

NOTARY PUBLIC, 177

NOTES, 185–187

NOVEL SCIENTIFIC THEORY, 65–66

O

OATH-HELPING, 68

OATHS, 45–46

OBJECTION, 8, 42, 43

OBSCENE MATERIALS, 20

OFFICERS OF THE COURT, 184

OPINION EVIDENCE
expert evidence. *See* **EXPERT EVIDENCE**
vs. fact, 59–60
non-expert witness, 59–61

ORGANIZING EVIDENCE. *See* **GATHERING AND ORGANIZING EVIDENCE**

ORIGINAL DECLARANT NOT AVAILABLE. *See* **UNAVAILABILITY OF ORIGINAL DECLARANT**

OUT-OF-COURT STATEMENTS, 94, 98. *See also* **ADMISSIONS**

P

PARALEGALS, 4

PARTIES
gathering evidence, 7–8
general, 4
out-of-court statements, 94

PATTERN OF BEHAVIOUR.
See **SIMILAR FACT EVIDENCE**

PERJURY, 19, 130

PERSONAL ELECTRONIC DEVICES, 136, 146–147

PERSONS IN AUTHORITY, 112–115

PHOTOS, 178–179, 183

PHYSICAL OBJECTS, 12

PLAIN VIEW, 136–137, 146

POLICE
actions of, and *Charter* violations, 171–172
arrest powers, and warrantless entry into home, 146
consultation with lawyer before preparation of notes, 187
doorway sniff test, 172
foreign police officers, 142
good faith, 171
implied licence, 172
investigators, tips for, 183–184
Mr. Big confessions, 114–115
persons in authority, 112–115
plain view, 136–137, 146
public duty, 187

PRECEDENT, 25–28, 30, 32

PREJUDICIAL EFFECT, 10–11, 75, 80, 84–85

PRELIMINARY INQUIRY, 98, 101

PRESUMPTION OF COMPETENCE, 43

PREVIOUS CONVICTIONS, 10–11, 75–78

PRINCIPLED APPROACH TO HEARSAY, 99–104

PRIOR CONSISTENT STATEMENTS, 106–108

PRIOR CONVICTIONS. *See* **PREVIOUS CONVICTIONS**

PRIOR COURT HEARINGS, 97–98

PRIOR SEXUAL CONDUCT, 86

PRIVACY
airports, 137
balancing privacy expectations with criminal control, 133–134
context of claim for expectation of privacy, 135–137
home or residence, 135–136, 143–144
international border crossing, 137
invasion of privacy, 54
personal electronic devices, 136
public settings, 137, 151
reasonable expectation of privacy, 134–137
schools, 137
vehicles, 136–137
and warrantless search, 148

PRIVATE SECURITY OFFICERS, 140–141

PRIVILEGE, 48–52

PROBATIVE VALUE, 9, 10–11, 75, 80, 83

PROOF BEYOND A REASONABLE DOUBT, 4–6, 10–11

PROSECUTORS, 4

PROVINCIAL AND TERRITORIAL APPEAL AND TRIAL COURT CASES, 35–37

PROVINCIAL AND TERRITORIAL EVIDENCE ACTS
affidavits, 176–177
business records, 97, 178
vs. Canada Evidence Act, 17
general, 16
government documents, 178
online access, 16
provincial and territorial
offences, 22

PROVINCIAL AND TERRITORIAL RULES OF PROCEDURE
affidavits, 176–177
attendance of witnesses, 179–180
expert evidence, 69
prior court hearing, testimony
from, 97

PROVINCIAL JURISDICTION, 27

PUBLIC SETTINGS, 137

Q

QUALIFICATION OF EXPERT WITNESS, 62–63

QUESTIONING. *See also* **WITNESSES**
basic rules of questioning, 42–43
cross-examination, 42–43, 91, 103–104, 105
leading questions, 42, 43

R

RE-CREATIONS, 35–36

RE-ENACTMENTS, 35–36

READING CASE REPORTS, 29–32

REAL EVIDENCE, 12, 169–170, 177–178

REASON FOR ARREST, 118

REASONABLE DOUBT. *See* **PROOF BEYOND A REASONABLE DOUBT**

REASONABLE SUSPICION, 152–155

REFRESHING MEMORY, 186–187

RELEVANCE, 9–10

RELIABILITY
comparative reliability, 105
expert evidence, 65
eyewitness identification
evidence, 71–72
hearsay evidence, 99
prior inconsistent statements, 105

RELIANCE ON NOTES WHILE TESTIFYING, 185–187

RELIGIOUS FACIAL COVERINGS, 37, 56–57

REMEDIES
under ss. 24(1) of the *Charter,* 164–168
under ss. 24(2) of the *Charter,* 168
stay, 162, 165–166

REMOTE TESTIMONY, 36–37

REPUTATION EVIDENCE. *See* **CHARACTER EVIDENCE**

RES GESTAE STATEMENTS, 98

RESIDENCE, 135–136

RIGHT TO COUNSEL
Charter right, 94, 116, 118–123
effect of violations, 123
narrowing the protections of, 124–128

RIGHT TO MAKE FULL ANSWER AND DEFENCE. *See* **MAKE FULL ANSWER AND DEFENCE**

RIGHT TO SILENCE
Charter right, 94, 118–123
and compellability of accused, 47
narrowing the protections of, 124–128

RULE AGAINST OATH-HELPING, 68

RULES OF EVIDENCE, 4, 8–9. *See also* **EVIDENCE STATUTES**

RULES OF PROCEDURE. *See* **PROVINCIAL AND TERRITORIAL RULES OF PROCEDURE**

RULING, 30

S

SCHOOLS, 137

SEARCH AND SEIZURE
agents of the state, 140–142
Charter right, 33
Criminal Code provisions, 20
foreign police officers, 142
private security officers, 140–141
reasonable expectation of privacy, 134–137
search, meaning of, 138–139
seizure, meaning of, 139–140
sniffer dogs, and reasonable suspicion, 152–155
technology, use of, 150–151
unreasonable search and seizure, 33, 142, 143–144, 155
use of force, 157–159
warrantless search
  and the *Charter,* 18
  consent, 149
  Criminal Code provisions, 20
  general, 142–146
  low expectations of privacy, 149
  other justifications for, 149–150
  search "incident to an arrest," 146–149
warrants to conduct search, 155–157
wiretaps, 150–151

SEIZURE. *See* **SEARCH AND SEIZURE**

SELF-DEFENCE, 86–87

SELF-INCRIMINATION, 48, 128–130, 167

SETTLEMENT, 7

SEXUAL ASSAULT
complainants, 54–55, 86
Criminal Code provisions, 19

SILENCE. *See* **RIGHT TO SILENCE**

SIMILAR FACT EVIDENCE
collusion, 82–83
foreign decisions, influence of, 37–38
gang involvement, evidence of, 83–85
general, 79–83
prejudicial effect *vs.* probative value, 80

SNIFFER DOGS, 152–155

SOLEMN AFFIRMATIONS, 45–46

SOLICITOR-CLIENT PRIVILEGE, 49–50

SPECIALTY BOARDS, 3

SPOUSE
compellability, 47
privilege, 48–49

STANDARDS OF PROOF, 3

STARE DECISIS, 25–28. *See also* **PRECEDENT**

STATEMENTS
admissions. *See* **ADMISSIONS**
confessions. *See* **CONFESSIONS**
against interest, 98–99
of mental state, 96
out-of-court statements, 94, 96
prior consistent statements, 106–108
prior inconsistent statements, 104–106
res gestae statements, 98

STATUTORY RULES, 8

STAY, 162, 165–166

SUBPOENA, 46, 128, 179–180

SUPREME COURT OF
CANADA, 27, 30

SUPREME COURT OF
CANADA CASES, 32–34

T

TECHNOLOGY
computer-generated re-enactments
and re-creations, 35–36
interception of private
communications, 150–151
remote testimony, 36–37
to search, 150–151
videotaped re-enactments, 35

TELEWARRANT, 20

TERRITORIAL EVIDENCE
ACTS. *See* PROVINCIAL
AND TERRITORIAL
EVIDENCE ACTS

TERRITORIAL
JURISDICTION, 27

TORTURE, 20

TRANSCRIPT, 26, 29

TRIAL COURT CASES, 35–37

TRIAL LEVEL CASE
REPORTS, 31–32

TRIBUNALS, 3, 15

TRIER OF FACT, 8, 61

TRIER OF LAW, 8, 176

U

UNAVAILABILITY OF
ORIGINAL DECLARANT
business records, 96–97
dying declarations, 94–96
general, 94
principled approach, 99–104
res gestae statements, 98
statements against interest, 98–99

statements of mental state, 96
testimony from prior hearing,
97–98

UNCONSCIOUS
TRANSFERENCE, 70–71

UNFAIR DISTORTIONS, 12

UNITED STATES
Miranda rights, 126–127
self-incrimination, 48

UNREASONABLE SEARCH
AND SEIZURE, 33, 142, 143–
144, 155. *See also* SEARCH
AND SEIZURE

USE OF FORCE, 157–159

V

VEHICLES, 136–137

VETROVIC CAUTION, 52–54

VICTIM
attacking the character of, 86–87
sexual assault complainants,
54–55, 86

VIDEOTAPE
child's evidence, 56
evidence, 19, 56, 178–179, 183
re-enactments, 35

VOIR DIRE, 112, 117–118

VOLUNTARINESS, 115–117

W

WARRANT
and the *Charter,* 18
to conduct search, 155–157
Criminal Code provisions, 20
failure of witness to come to
court, 46
to obtain bodily substances,
20, 73
telewarrant, 20
use of force, 157–159

WARRANTLESS SEARCH
and the *Charter,* 18
consent, 149
Criminal Code provisions, 20
general, 142–146
low expectations of privacy, 149
other justifications for, 149–150
search "incident to an arrest,"
  146–149

WEIGHT OF EVIDENCE, 8, 68

WIGMORE RULES, 52

WIRETAPS, 150–151

WITNESSES
adverse witness, 104
alternatives to live witnesses,
  176–177
attendance of witnesses, 46,
  179–180
basic rules of questioning, 42–43
children, 55–56
compellability, 46–48
competence to testify, 43–45
confidential information, 48–52
credibility, 43, 77, 104
cross-examination, 42–43
expert witnesses. *See* **EXPERT
  EVIDENCE**
eyewitness testimony, 70–72
key component of any case, 41
lay witness, 60–61
non-expert witness, 59–61
oaths, 45–46
privilege, 48–52
refreshing memory, 186–187
reliance on notes while testifying,
  185–187
religious facial coverings,
  37, 56–57
sexual assault complainants, 54–55
solemn affirmations, 45–46
tips for, 184–185
untrustworthy "*Vetrovic*"
  witness, 52–54

Y

YOUNG PERSONS, 121–122.
See also **CHILDREN**